ISBN 978-1-331-38246-1
PIBN 10182328

English
Français
Deutsche
Italiano
Español
Português

www.forgottenbooks.com

Mythology Photography **Fiction**
Fishing Christianity **Art** Cooking
Essays Buddhism Freemasonry
Medicine **Biology** Music **Ancient**
Egypt Evolution Carpentry Physics
Dance Geology **Mathematics** Fitness
Shakespeare **Folklore** Yoga Marketing
Confidence Immortality Biographies
Poetry **Psychology** Witchcraft
Electronics Chemistry History **Law**
Accounting **Philosophy** Anthropology
Alchemy Drama Quantum Mechanics
Atheism Sexual Health **Ancient History**
Entrepreneurship Languages Sport
Paleontology Needlework Islam
Metaphysics Investment Archaeology
Parenting Statistics Criminology
Motivational

MEMOIR OF THE LIFE

OF

ELIZABETH FRY,

WITH

EXTRACTS FROM HER LETTERS AND JOURNAL.

EDITED BY TWO OF HER DAUGHTERS.

IN TWO VOLUMES.

VOL. II.

LONDON:

CHARLES GILPIN, 5, BISHOPSGATE STREET WITHOUT.
JOHN HATCHARD AND SON, 187, PICCADILLY.

1847.

CHAPTER XVII.

CHAPTER XVIII.

CHAPTER XIX.

CHAPTER XX.

CHAPTER XXI.

CHAPTER XXII.

CHAPTER XXIII.

CHAPTER XXIV.

CHAPTER XXV.

MEMOIR

LIFE OF ELIZABETH FRY.

CHAPTER XIV.

THE storm that had prevailed in the money world, during the latter part of 1825, subsided as 1826 advanced; but it did not pass away without leaving fearful traces of its course. Many mercantile houses were entirely overthrown; amongst them, some, involving much-valued friends of Mrs. Fry; whilst others were so shaken, as never to recover the shock. These things made it a very anxious time to her, and called forth much of her sympathy towards the sufferers.

First Month 28*th*, 1826.—The principle of justice cannot be too deeply impressed upon the youthful mind, also, the greatest uprightness in all money transactions. How do I desire for myself that, however, it may be my duty to be occupied about temporal things, my treasure be not in them; but that my heart and soul may be raised above them. This morning, I think I have had a glimpse of those possessions that cannot be shaken by the ups and downs of life. I see temporally also, that there are innumerable blessings in the outward works of creation, open to all, whether rich or poor. The same glorious sun to enlighten, and other bright and beautiful things made in common for every one.

Thinking over these subjects, those words in Ecclesiasticus struck me much, chap. xi. 21, 22 :—" Marvel not, at the works of sinners ; but trust in the Lord, and abide in thy labour : for it is an easy thing in the sight of the Lord on the sudden to make a poor man rich. The blessing of the Lord is in the reward of the godly, and suddenly he maketh his blessing to flourish." I may say the Lord doth provide, the Lord hath provided, and my humble trust is that the Lord will provide.

Second Month 16*th.*—I mourn over myself for being so much engrossed by the cares of this life ; I fear that my heart may be overcharged by them. Be pleased, O Lord ! to grant a little help in this respect, and let not Thy servant, who loveth Thee, who has sought to serve Thee, and trust in Thee, now in her latter days, have Thy work marred in her, by her heart being overcharged with the cares of this life. Amen and Amen.

Third Month 29*th.*—Yesterday, I attended the Quarterly Meeting, where I think there was to be felt something of celestial showers on thirsty land, partly through the ministry of others, partly from what I trust was an immediate ministration from the Great Minister of ministers. A dear relation, a clergyman, was at meeting, I felt sweetly united to him. After all, however, we may differ as to the means of grace, our end in view is the same, and we feel at times that we have but one Lord, one faith, and one baptism. I increasingly find, that whoever love the Lord Jesus, are without distinction, as brothers, sisters, fathers, and mothers to me ; although I know that I am a very unworthy partaker of this foretaste of that, for which we may look in the heavenly inheritance.

In reply to a slight request, at that time addressed by Elizabeth Fry to Hannah More, she received this gratifying reply :—

My dear Friend,

Any request of yours, if within my very limited power, cannot fail to be immediately complied with. In your kind note, I wish you had mentioned something of your own health, and that of your family.

I look back with no small pleasure to the too short visit with which you once indulged me, a repetition of it would be no little gratification to me. Whether Divine Providence may grant it or not, I trust through Him who loved us, and gave himself for us, that we may hereafter meet in that blessed country, where there is neither sin, sorrow, nor separation.

Believe me, my dear friend, with true esteem and warm affection, to remain yours sincerely,

H. More.

Barley Wood, *15th of April,* 1826.

Mrs. Fry entertained the highest appreciation of this lady's character, and of the benefits she had conferred upon her country, especially upon her country-women.

She always referred with great pleasure to her visit to Barley Wood, and the impression made upon her by the mingled sweetness and dignity of Mrs. More's countenance and manner. In the year 1818, Mrs. More had presented her with a copy of her Practical Piety, with this inscription on the first page :—

TO MRS. FRY,
Presented by HANNAH MORE,
As a token of veneration
Of her heroic zeal,
Christian charity,
And persevering kindness,
To the most forlorn
Of human beings.
They were naked and she
Clothed them ;
In prison and she visited them ;
Ignorant and she taught them,
For *His* sake,
In *His* name, and by *His* word,
Who went about doing good.

Barley Wood, June 16th, 1818.

Fourth Month 20th.—I look forward with some anxiety to the British Ladies' Society Meeting, to-morrow ; I desire preservation for myself in it, that what I do, may be done unto the Lord, and not unto man, with true Christian courtesy. There is a respect due to those, who are placed by a kind Providence in high stations as to this life ; but I also feel that there is a bold Christian character to maintain, as we are all one in Christ, and children of one heavenly Parent. May none of us engaged in the work, suffer loss ; but may the cause in which we are interested be really promoted, and the whole be done to the glory of God our Saviour, and His doctrine be adorned by it.

22nd.—The meeting was a very interesting one ; much good appears to be doing by those who visit prisons. Many places of refuge are also formed. I had a good deal to say at different times in the meeting, and concluded with a little general advice to a very numerous assembly of ladies. At first, I was very peaceful, and really believed that the best of causes had been promoted in that meeting ; but during the night and this morning, I was nervous and low, deeply impressed with the extreme difficulty of acting right in conspicuous places, and the danger on every hand that attends being brought into them, as I at times am. I may say, that I have earnestly sought the Lord for help and preservation. I fully unite in the Christian duty of true simplicity in dress ; I think it rather too much dwelt upon by us, as a Society, but much too little by many in the religious world.

Plashet, 24th.—My mind has not yet recovered the effect of the meeting of the British Ladies' Society ; although it appears to have given general satisfaction, and to have excited much interest. I hardly know what it is in me that makes me so acutely feel public exposure, unless it be pride, and too lively a sense of the opinion of my fellow-mortals. I have desired (whatever infirmity may be the cause of it,) to seek the Best Help to overcome it, and to come to Him, who, from experience, I have found can take our burdens from us, and give us full relief. At times, this has been remarkably the case ; a thing would worry, and greatly oppress my spirit, and yet my mind has become entirely relieved, even when the cause of uneasiness has remained the same. It is a great favour in ever so small a degree, to know Christ to be our helper.

Fifth Month 27th.—We are in the midst of the Yearly Meeting; to me a very important time, as I am greatly interested in the welfare of the Society. I do most fully unite in most of its practices and principles; but still I may say, I have somewhat against it, I see that we may improve as we go on, if that which first led us to be a peculiar people, be kept to by us. I think in our Meetings for Discipline, too much stress is laid on minor parts of our testimonies, such as "plainness of speech, behaviour, and apparel," rather than on the greater and weightier matters of the law; these (lesser things) are well, and I believe should be attended to; but they should not occupy an undue place. I do not like the habit of that mysterious, ambiguous mode of expression, in which Friends at times clothe their observations, and their ministry. I like the truth in simplicity, it needs no mysterious garment. I also can hardly bear to hear Friends make us out to be a chosen people, above others.

I have very much kept silence amongst them, being generally quite clear of any thing to do; but as a spectator, I have rejoiced in the love, the sweetness, and the power of good amongst us, and the evidence that our great High Priest is owning us for good.

Sixth Month 3rd. — Our Yearly Meeting concluded yesterday. I can hardly express the sweetness of the remembrance of the time. We have at seasons, I may truly say, rejoiced together in the Lord, and partaken of that, which as evidently comforts and delights the soul, as outward refreshment does the body, when hungry, thirsty, and faint. I have been really refreshed in spirit.

Dagenham, Seventh Month 20th.—I am once more come to this quiet abode, and cannot but enjoy its refreshing influence, more particularly, as my soul has of late been too much disquieted within me; a good deal, I think, from the perplexed state of the business world. Also, I have been, perhaps, too anxious respecting the well-being of my children, and too prone to fret myself in spirit about them. I have been frequently tried by many fears respecting myself, whether I might not have done, and might not do, more for my children. I do not think I am naturally gifted with the talent of education, as some of my

sisters are.   I have also had some doubts whether our peculiar
views, in many little things, much in the cross to young people,
do not in measure turn them from religion itself ; on the other
hand, I see in others how imperceptibly the standard lowers,
when these minor scruples are given up.   I am persuaded, in the
education of youth, there are two sides to the question.   I have
no doubt whatever of the utility of these things, when adopted
from conviction ; my doubts are, how far they should be pressed
upon young persons, through education.   However, I see no other
way for myself, and believe, that I must bring my children up,
as, I have seen, with such indubitable clearness, to be right for
myself, which has been so wonderfully blessed to my own soul.
That happy day may arrive, when, on their own ground, I may
see some of my beloved children walking in the same way ; if
this would too much gratify me naturally and spiritually, then I
am indeed ready to say, by any means, or in any way, so they
but come to the knowledge of Christ their Saviour, and be saved
through Him, I should be satisfied.   It is certainly very sweet,
for those who are united by natural ties, also to choose the same
path in spiritual things : but experience has proved, in the case
of my beloved brothers and sisters, that much of the unity of the
spirit and the bond of peace may be experienced, when we may
not see eye to eye.

24th.—Yesterday was so very wet and windy, that we spent
a quiet First-day here.   Serious as it is, not to attend our places
of worship, yet, it is not without its advantage, to find, that
the same worship can be performed in private, as in the public
assembly ; and that it is not the place, or the people, but (if in
a right spirit) an acceptable worship may be offered every where.
All our family assembled twice in the day, I think to real edification : so that it proved neither dull nor unpleasant, though we
were all shut up for a long day in this little house.

Plashet, *Eighth Month 3rd.*

We have had our dearest brother D——, and sister H——,
here the last few days ; I have felt nearly united to them, and,
desire to return thanks, that such sweet unity exists amongst us.
He is a dear and most kind brother to me, and I see the hand of

a merciful Providence in his heart being so open towards us: he warmly and steadily does all he can to help us. To my other dear brothers, also, I feel deeply grateful, and still more so, I trust, to Him who hitherto has helped us, and inclines their hearts towards us.

TO HER SISTER RACHEL GURNEY.

Dagenham, *Eighth Month* 12*th*, 1826.

MY DEAREST RACHEL,

It appears rather too long since we have had any communication. I am now very desirous of hearing again of you, and how thou art.——We are comfortably settled here, for which I already feel better, and am revived by the fresh air and beautiful views, for the river and the Kentish hills are to my taste delightful. The longer I live, the more I enjoy quiet and real retirement; I think my inclination would dictate withdrawing very much from the world,—I desire to be thankful that I am enabled to partake of this enjoyment, although, I believe, the time is not yet come for me really to withdraw from the bustle of life.—— We have begun to read my brother Joseph's Essays together, in the morning; and hope to read them through, whilst we are here. We think of getting Pepys' Memoirs, to read in the afternoon. The close contact that we are brought in with each other, and so often having my beloved husband join us, is really valuable; he means to read the Essays with us.

I have time here to think of my friends, as well as to love them.

I am, indeed and in truth, thine and Catherine's nearly attached sister,

E. F.

Dagenham, 29*th*.—I returned from Rochester, yesterday. We went to Gravesend in the steam-packet, which was refreshing; a beautiful calm evening, the river and its banks in great beauty, and nothing in the people on board, to hurt my mind. I distributed a few tracts, but in other respects I fear I did no good. We proceeded to Rochester, where we met with a most kind and cordial reception. I feel watchfulness very necessary with those, who, from our outward situation in life, are prone to estimate us above our desert, and in doing things that may appear humble, the danger of pride taking advantage and being gratified. On the other hand, I felt a little encouraged that my earnest desire to do justice to my servants, and to watch over them for good, had not been in vain: for Sarah T——, whose wedding I went to attend, and who, with her family, was so delighted to have me and some of my children there, lived with me nine years as upper nurse, and in that time, I never remember having the least real difference with her. I am a great friend to doing full justice to servants, and bearing as much as we can with their infirmities, remembering the many disadvantages that they labour under. To proceed with my narrative: we went with the company to the wedding, and had a satisfactory meeting. As soon as the meeting was over, a gentleman came to beg me to attend a Bible Meeting about to be held, which I afterwards understood was a Naval and Military one. On which account, some dear Friends doubted the propriety of our going; but my heart was full of zeal, I felt clear, that of all people, as promoters of peace, we should show ourselves willing and glad to aid them in such an object, as the most likely means of advancing that day, when they "shall beat their swords into plough-shares and their spears into pruning-hooks." Lord Bexley, who came to attend the meeting, called upon me twice at the T——'s, to beg me to go. I made up my mind to do so, and was delighted to see so many naval officers, particularly young men coming forward to espouse so great and good a cause. I feared for myself being in any degree exhilarated in spirit by the kindness and marked attention shown me, and by the honour conferred on me; wholly unworthy as I am of being instrumental in encouraging others in works of righteousness.

We returned home by the steam-packet. I believed it right to enter a little into conversation with most of the passengers, and to give them tracts; also, as the way opened for it, to throw a little weight into the right scale. We then had a boat to meet us, and visited the two female-convict ships now in the river. Their order, cleanliness, and general appearance, delighted me;

I was struck with the wonderful change, since we first undertook them. Elizabeth Pryor has been greatly blessed in her
labours, and it is a true consolation to see what has been
accomplished. My son Joseph, Richenda, and Louisa, returned
with me here safely by boat, just in time to dine with my
husband, and the rest of my children. I have thus minutely
entered into the particulars of this expedition, as, some day
when my head is laid low, it may interest my children, and
children's children, to know how it fared with me at such times.
This morning, my soul was so deeply prostrated in prayer, that I
had to pour it forth after reading. I feel, more particularly after
being engaged in service, like a vessel that wants fresh washing;
and to whom can I go but to Him, who ever remains the fountain
open for the uncircumcised and the unclean. I found, I believe,
access to the throne of grace. Oh! what need is there of the
washing of regeneration, and the renewings of the Holy Ghost.
It is as necessary to the soul, as daily washing and food are to
the body; and if by this means any of us are fitted for any good
word or work, to us, truly belongs nothing but humiliation and
confusion of face; but to our Lord and our God, glory, honour,
power, thanksgiving, and praise.

30th.—Since I last wrote, a good deal has passed, and I
have been reminded of a saying of Cecil, "We are to follow
and not force Providence." Last week, I expected much quiet,
except a visit to the convict-ships, instead of which, all my
plans for myself were altered by circumstances. At Hampstead, we met a gentleman, Cæsar Malan, from Geneva, who
appeared in deep concern for our souls; he seemed to feel
our meeting remarkably in the ordering of Providence. His
belief is, that we are, as believers, not sufficiently sure of
salvation, and that we admit too many doubts, and fears, upon
the subject; as the promises of God are sure, and that, in not
feeling confident, and expressing ourselves to be so, we do harm
to the cause. What he said, savoured too much of "once in
grace, always in grace;" still, I hope I received a good lesson,
which may make me less fearful, and more hopeful. Very likely,
I look too much to my own infirmity, and to the power of
temptation to separate me from the love of God in Christ Jesus;

and too little up to Him, through whom we are called to become more than conquerors.

Dear William Wilberforce, his wife, and children, dined with us. I think I may say, he is one whom I love in the Lord; and highly "esteem for his work's sake."

This day, though not great in its events, was instructive to me; teaching me, where things do not go on in my way, to be quiet, and trust in small things as in great; that "our steppings are ordered of the Lord," though unworthy of such a favour. I returned to Stamford Hill, through a storm, and with some difficulty, because I thought it right to persevere, in case my sick brother and his family should want me. The next morning, I had a time in thanksgiving and prayer with them; also, I visited another family, and endeavoured to encourage them in the way of the Lord. The young man, the master of the house, told me that I had been made, in days past, a remarkable instrument of good to him, in a religious visit paid to him when visiting families, with William Forster, in Gracechurch Street. I returned home to my beloved family after this expedition, in peace.

I find much advantage and pleasure in rising early in this place. I am dressed about seven; read, meditate, &c., till half-past; then breakfast, and attend to my husband and sons before their going to London. After this, our family reading; it being here more convenient after breakfast than before. Then a devotional reading with the children, and, in the course of the day, I read them one of my dearest brother J. J. Gurney's Essays on Christianity. When quietly here, I often write on the prison cause; also letters of business and friendship, and very much enjoy the rest, and the sweet refreshing beauties of the river and country, so that I find the sort of life we lead useful and pleasant. I have been favoured, at times, with feelings of almost inexpressible peace and love, in the enjoyment of natural and spiritual things.

The return of the season had brought with it, the interest of the annual transportation of female convicts. This year, five ships had been taken up for that purpose. There had been two every year from 1823. In 1827, five ships, as well as in 1826. Four, five, six, were the numbers employed the three following years. Of course, this endeavour on the part of Government to increase the female population in New South Wales, occasioned great expense to the British Ladies' Society, with much additional trouble and fatigue.

Though kind friends and assistants undertook the laborious task of minute preparations for the voyage, Mrs. Fry encouraged them by her presence and example, as far as was compatible with her numerous avocations at home and abroad. She met with much kindness from Admiral (then Captain) Young, Principal Resident Agent of Transports on the River Thames, and his family. Their recollections are vivid, of many scenes and transactions, and go far to supply the place of that valuable information which Admiral Young, had he been living, could have himself furnished.

Mrs. Young has often recurred to a farewell visit to a female convict-ship, on the point of sailing, in which she accompanied Mrs. Fry; saying, that she could " scarcely look upon her as any other than an angel of mercy; calmly passing from one to another of the poor wretched beings around her, with the word of counsel, comfort, or reproof, that seemed suited to each individual case, as it presented itself to her notice. With several kind assistants, she was arranging work for them during the voyage; in itself no trifling matter. But many a point of deeper interest and anxiety brought to her ready ear, met with such response as could only be looked for from a devoted follower of Him, who ' went about doing good.' "

On the mind of Miss Young the circumstance was strongly impressed, of accompanying her father (Captain Young) to the female-convict ships, lying off Woolwich, to meet Mr. Wilberforce and Mrs. Fry. " On board one of them, between two and three hundred women were assembled, in order to listen to the exhortation and prayers of, perhaps, the two brightest personifications of Christian philanthropy that the age could boast. Scarcely could two voices, even so distinguished for beauty and power be imagined, united in a more touching engagement: as indeed was testified by the breathless attention, the tears and the suppressed sobs, of the gathered listeners. All of man's word, however there heard, heart-stirring as it was at the time, has faded from my memory; but no lapse of time can ever efface the impression of the 107th Psalm, as read by Mrs. Fry, with such extraordinary emphasis and intonation, that it seemed to make the simple reading a commentary; and, as she passed on from passage to passage, struck my youthful mind, as if the whole series of allusions might have been written by the pen of inspiration, in view of such a scene as was then before us. At an interval of twenty years, it is recalled to me as often as that Psalm is brought to my notice.

" Never, in this world, can it be known to how many hearts its solemn appeals were that day carried home, by that potent voice."

Dagenham, Ninth Month 4th.—I paid a very interesting visit to two female convict-ships, with my dear sister Elizabeth Fry, and cousin Sarah, last Third-day. We there met William Wilberforce, Sophia Vansittart, and many others. The exercise of my mind was deep, and the trial of body considerable, from the inconvenient situation in which I had to read below deck, surrounded by the poor prisoners and the company. What I feel on such occasions is difficult to describe; that it should all be done unto the Lord—that it should be a time of edification—that none may in any way be hurt by it—that my natural great fear of man, and of his judgment, should in no way influence me; and, lastly, that self may neither glory, if helped, nor be unduly mortified if a cause for humiliation arise. It was a uniting time, I trust; many of the poor prisoners seemed to feel it so; several of them wept. It was an interesting, important service: may it not be neglected, after our heads are laid low.

My children going on well ; and some, I think, really advancing.

Since I last wrote, I have attended the Quarterly Meeting, at Leighton Buzzard, with my dear brother Samuel Gurney, and my sister Elizabeth Fry. I also paid a visit to the prison at St. Albans. I can hardly say how sweet were some of the moments I passed in this little journey. It appeared as if I were to go partly for my own sake to be refreshed, and so it proved. The religious services I was called into hardly were a cross, I found my Master's yoke so very easy, even pleasant. I could say, " I delight to do thy will, oh God." I can hardly express the unity of spirit, and the bond of peace, that I felt amongst those who were nearly strangers to me. Oh ! what blessings, and what privileges, do the meanest servants of our dear Lord and Master partake of. There is no joy, and no peace, to be compared to the peace and joy attendant upon doing the will of God : it is meat and drink indeed !

To one of her daughters, who had consulted her on the establishment of a Visiting Society.

Plashet, *Tenth Month* 13*th*.

My dearest R——,

I hope thou didst not think me inattentive to thy wishes in not writing to thee respecting the District Society, but I was very busy at the time, and I hoped that the papers I forwarded would answer the same purpose. I think much advantage will result from its establishment : I only fear it will rest too much upon thee, and in time become a burden with thy other duties, cares, and delicate health. I think thou art like me, in having rather a calling to the care of the poor, and I rejoice in the belief that thou mayst be a blessing to many of them ; but the more thou canst privately be the mover in these good works, the better. I know the pain and difficulty attached to filling foremost places in public works, and DUTY only sustains under it ; I also know how apt persons are to push those forward, who are able and willing, even beyond what is desirable for them.

Now for a very particular message to our dear friend, Edward

Edwards; I have not written to him, for I know that I am but a poor scribe, but I have remembered him and his dear family in their affliction and great privation. I have been glad to hear of the support granted them in the time of trial ; I feel for them in the nature of dear Anne Edwards' illness, but I remembered what Job Scott said on this subject; it is our finite view that makes it painful to us, when disease, as in the case of fever, clouds the mind and affects mental power ; it certainly adds to the pain of parting with those we love ; but how great the consolation to believe, as in this case, that she, whose loss they mourn, had nothing to do but to die ; I trust they will all find the best help near to them. As for dear Edward Edwards, I believe the same goodness and mercy that has hitherto followed him will follow him to the end, until he enters the house of his Lord for ever, to join those who have gone before him, who have washed their garments and made them white in the blood of the Lamb. As for his children, how encouraging it is to observe what a Providential care we see extended to the fatherless and motherless. I think he may indeed trust for his family ; they also know where to look for protection, direction and blessing.

My very dear love to thy uncle, and dear Lady Harriet. What a sweet impression their visit has left on our minds, excepting the sorrow about their baby's illness. I am, my beloved child, your tenderly attached mother.

E. F.

P.S.—Though not mentioned, thy darling boys are near my heart, and often thought of by me.

Plashet, Tenth Month.—I have had to attend much to the sorrowful in our congregation at Plaistow. One Friend had her husband die away from her, amongst strangers on the continent ; other dear friends of mine had their eldest son drowned in a very distressing manner. I have truly sympathized with them, indeed the last case gave me real pain, and brought me into much conflict of mind. I have deeply felt the weight of being the instrument to minister to them, and for them, in these awful dispensations, that I might not hinder, but promote the intention of Infinite Wisdom and Mercy in permitting them. The poor boy was buried yesterday, the other mourners were present part of the time. My sister Elizabeth Fry, and Cornelius Hanbury were there to aid in the ministry. The anointing for religious service appeared freely poured forth.

Eleventh Month 13th.—I am now enjoying a little quiet before breakfast, and a beautiful morning. What a delightful relish does religion give to the beauties of creation, and to the blessings granted us of every kind. Indeed, the longer I live, the more ardent is my desire for all, particularly those nearest to me, to partake of this unspeakable gift. The sting and misery of sin in all its forms, with my observation and experience in life, is increasingly evident to me, so that at times my heart is sore pained within me, because so many forget His law ; but the text I desire to attend to is this, "I will hope continually and yet praise thee more and more."

18th.—I have for some weeks past believed that I must accompany my beloved brother Joseph to Ireland, in the spring, to visit Friends, and also the prisons. It is weighty indeed, and my most earnest desire is to be rightly directed in it ; that if I ought to go, my way may be made manifest step by step, and that if I ought to stay, it may altogether be obstructed. What am I at home or abroad, unless my Lord be with me to bless my labours ? therefore, I can only seek to be altogether passive before Him, praying that He would in His mercy make known His will concerning me, and carry on His own work in me to His own praise. I am very unworthy of being engaged in His service, and always look upon it as an honour that is not my due.

In a letter from Lynn to one of her sisters, Mrs. Fry expresses her anxious desire for right guidance and direction.

Twelfth Month 15th.

My mind is very weightily impressed with the prospect before me, of which my dearest brother and sister can tell thee ; I have thought right to speak of it to D——, and F——, and R—— ; they feel much for me in it, and I think are not able really to discourage me from it. I do not feel in high spirits, although I trust that I am sensible of my many causes for thankfulness.   My first desire for myself and those I love is, that whatever our circumstances may be, we may be conformed to the Divine Will, and fully experience the salvation which comes by Christ.   I hope you will all three, (and dear Francis also if with you), remember me for good just now, and desire my safe direction in all things.

I am nearly and devotedly yours all,

ELIZABETH FRY.

Mrs. Fry was cheered soon after her return home, by an encouraging letter from her sister, Rachel Gurney, who, whilst she saw not with her in all things, nor believed herself called into a similar course, was yet capable of the closest appreciation of her motives of action, and sympathy with her, in the pains and efforts involved.

MY DEAREST BETSY,

Thy letter has interested us much to-day ; with such a prospect as lies before thee, there must be ups and downs, and close straits to go through, and these will bring thee into some low feelings ; but I cannot doubt that the way will in due time be made straight and plain.   I am sure thy concerns will be most nearly interesting to us, and I trust we may be enabled to bear them in mind, so as to be good for ourselves, as well as some comfort and help to thee !   Aunt Jane invited me to stay at the meeting, whilst our dear brother Joseph laid his concern to accompany thee before it.   This was done with much feeling and humility on his own part, and a strong expression of unity from those present.   It was a pain to me that he went off to Ipswich, to attend a funeral there, without my seeing him afterwards; but I think the meeting would be altogether encouraging to him.   By this we lose him for nearly a week, which has come in as a real blank, from having been unexpected, and having taken him off just as Francis Cunningham and our dear friends the Hankinsons were here.   It is a real loss ; but we need more willing spirits in the cause of truth and righteousness !   This will I trust find thee safely at home again, with our dearest sister Chenda by thy side ;

I hope thou wilt not be too much overdone to enjoy her company. It is no small thing to have met as we have done !

Thus adds her sister Catherine Gurney :—

" MY DEAREST BETSY,

" I must add a line of sympathy under these weighty concerns, and, as far as I understand the case ; of encouragement. I am for thy going, notwithstanding the importance of thy calls at home. I cannot but think the expedition will be made the instrument of great good, probably to yourselves and others. Francis entered warmly into it ; he seemed to have no other feeling. This, I think, will give thee satisfaction."

Twelfth Month 27th.—Last Third-day week, I believed it my duty to lay my concern to visit Ireland, before my Monthly Meeting ; at the close of the meeting for worship. We told our dear friends what we had in view, and, feeling the great weight of leaving my family, made me doubt a little, whether Friends could unite in my going ; but for all these things, I think I hardly ever felt a more solemn covering over a meeting, both before and after we spoke ; and a very unusual number expressed their sympathy, unity, and desire to encourage us ; not only the elders and ministers, but the very babes in Christ. There was testimony upon testimony. I felt uncommon peace and relief afterwards, as if the thing was right ; many expressed a belief that the Lord would be with us, and preserve us ; that He would be our shield and exceeding great reward ; that He would go before us, and be our rear-guard.

Dear W. Allen believed " that those who stayed by the stuff would partake of the spoil." I never remember feeling the blessing of Christian love, and unity of spirit, more than at this time ; and how truly the members of the Christian Church bear one another's burdens, and so fulfil the law of Christ.

Yesterday, we laid it before our Quarterly Meeting. The certificate having been signed on First-day, to my rejoicing, by all those who I thought might possibly have been somewhat against it, as well as those who I knew heartily united with us. I had, in both the Men and Women's Meeting, to express something, particularly to the youth, that for all the humiliations and deep baptisms attending it, I considered it an honour and favour that I was unworthy of, to be thus made use of in my Master's service ; for I could in deed and in truth testify, that there are no ways like His ways, no service like His service, and no joys to be compared to the joys of His salvation.   I also addressed the wives and mothers amongst us ; on parting from our women Friends, asking not only their sympathy, but their prayers ; as " the prayer of the righteous availeth much ;" and not only for me, but in a particular manner for those who stayed behind. To-day, my mind feels lightened and peaceful, and I have a confirming hope that this calling is of the Lord, utterly unworthy as I know I am, to do the least thing for such a Master ; as for the outward sacrifices attending this step, I count them as nothing, if I may but humbly trust that my most gracious Lord and Master will, through His own power, and His own mercy, keep those who stay, as well as those who go, near to Himself. The pain of leaving my most tenderly beloved family, my comfortable and commodious home, with my delicate bodily frame, is a sacrifice most willingly made by me, if those left do not suffer harm by it.   I believe I must go in faith, nothing doubting ; trusting all to Him, who knows the deep, earnest petitions of my heart, for them and for us, and who can work with or without instrumentality.   The certificate granted us, by our Quarterly and Monthly Meeting, was this :—

" To Friends of the Nation of Ireland.

" Dear Friends,—Our beloved Friend, Elizabeth Joseph Fry, has, in a weighty manner, informed this Meeting, that her mind has been for many years impressed with a belief, that it would be required of her to offer to pay a religious visit to the Meetings of Friends in Ireland, pretty generally ; and, also, to stand resigned to further religious service, both amongst Friends, and those not of the Society, as truth might open the way, and that she apprehended the time was nearly come for her to enter thereon.   Our beloved Friend Elizabeth Fry, also informed the Meeting, that she believed it right to offer to accompany her sister in the said visit, as her mind had been somewhat similarly impressed for many years past. The said proposals, having had our deliberate and solid consideration, and much unity and sympathy having been felt and expressed with our dear friends, we think it right to set them at liberty to perform the same: informing you that they are ministers of the gospel, in unity and good esteem with us. We commend them to the affectionate care of those amongst whom their lot may be cast. We desire their preservation in a humble dependence on the great Head of the Church, for daily supplies of wisdom and strength, that they may thereby be enabled to perform the work assigned them; to the promotion of the cause of truth and righteousness, and to the peace of their own minds. We remain, in love, your friends. Signed in Ratcliff and Barking Monthly Meeting, held at Plaistow, by adjoinment, the 24th of Twelfth Month, 1826.

    " Signed by forty men, and thirty women."

At a Quarterly Meeting, for London and Middlesex, held the 26th of Twelfth Month, 1826—

" Our beloved friends, E. J. Fry, and E. Fry, have attended this Meeting, and in a feeling manner opened before it the concern described in the foregoing certificate. This Meeting, after a time of solid consideration, and under a feeling of much unity and sympathy with them, in reference to the arduous prospect before them, unites in setting them at liberty; desiring, that they may experience the preservation and guidance of the Shepherd of Israel, and be permitted, when the service allotted to them is performed, to return with the reward of peace.

    " Signed in, and on behalf of, the Meeting, by
            " PETER BEDFORD, *Clerk.*
    " Signed in, and on behalf of, the Women's Meeting,
            " HANNAH MESSER, *Clerk.*"

This important point obtained, and the unity of her friends officially expressed; Elizabeth Fry prepared, with her companions, for their departure, after making various arrangements to ensure the comfort of her family during her absence.

To her Sisters, Catherine and Rachel Gurney.

Plashet, *First Month 3rd*, 1827.

My dearest Catherine and Rachel,

It appears too long since I wrote to you, and since I received your welcome letters. I was rejoiced at our brother Joseph's good account of you. I got through the Quarterly Meeting most satisfactorily. I hardly ever remember such a current of love and unity poured forth on such an occasion; which was particularly comforting, under my peculiar home circumstances. We have had Dr. Pinkerton, his wife, and three of his children, here since Second-day: I have valued their company. We had, last evening, a large party of young people to meet them, and a very cheerful time they had; but, I think, a very innocent one. I like to see young persons happy and merry; it reminded me of some of our days, that are not only passed, but appear now quite in the distance. I felt a little doubtful whether to have it, but I yielded the point to the children, and am glad to say, I see no cause to repent it. I suppose I shall have many farewell visits; indeed, we are full of engagements. I have been deeply interested about the poor woman who was hanged yesterday, in Newgate. Her end, I trust, was happy. I have had much to feel about her; it is such awful work, thus prematurely to have a fellow-creature launched into eternity!

On Second-day, we had a very long British Society committee; that cause, I think, yet prospers much. It was a solemn time, and an encouraging one to us to go forward. My curious book, I hope, will be useful, and promote the cause.* The children are now generally well and comfortable. My dearest husband talks of going to Dublin with us, or else meeting us on our return.

I write this flat letter in haste: it is hardly worth your having; but, as I have so little time for writing, I should like it forwarded to my dearest R. C., at Lynn. I am sorry to hear of dear Sarah B.'s trying accident; express my dear love and

---

* Observations on the Visiting, Superintending, and Government of Female Prisoners. By Elizabeth Fry. 1827.

sympathy to her. Our brother Joseph appeared well and comfortable ; he dined, and spent a valuable evening with us here, on First-day.

In abundance of love to you, and at Lynn, I am your nearly attached

E. F.

To her Daughter, Mrs. F—— C——.

Plashet, Second Month 1st.

My dearest R.,

As the time for my departure for Ireland is now drawing near, I feel bound, in this way, in the most tender manner, to bid thee FAREWELL, in every sense of the word.   May the Almighty be with, and bless thee and thine, my much-loved child ; and, above all things, increasingly manifest Himself, in His own power, to your souls ; to your edification and consolation, your help and strength.   I feel as if my family must increasingly show themselves on the Lord's side, simply, humbly, and faithfully, holding up His standard of truth, and of righteousness ; in which belief I include thee and thy husband.   The time is short ; we can none, therefore, too soon give ourselves up wholly to the Lord, for our own sakes, and the sake of others.

I feel peaceful in my prospect of departure, though deeply unworthy, and naturally unfit for such a service ; but my hope is in this, that " help is laid upon One that is mighty," who alone can enable me to do all things to His praise.

I have abundance to do ; therefore, in near love, once more, I say to thee, and the boys, farewell in the Lord.

Thy loving, tender mother,
E. F.

On the 4th of February, Elizabeth Fry, with her brother Joseph John Gurney, commenced their journey towards Ireland. They were joined on the road by her sister-in-law. Acutely did she feel leaving her family, and most painful was it to them to part with her ; nor was the trial lessened by some of her children, as they advanced in life, not being altogether satisfied as to these engagements, or able to comprehend how a career so peculiar, could be consistent with their mother's domestic duties.

It required the wonderful results of her exertions, and the practical effects of these journeys, to convince them, that it was by the great Head of the Church, that she was "put forth" for such services.

Her last sabbath at home she thus describes:—

The First-day preceding my leaving home, was most interesting. In the first place, I had all the servants collected at the morning reading, and expressed very fully my desires for them, and their preservation in the right way, which they appeared to feel a good deal, and it was a heart-tendering time. My beloved J—— and his R—— were staying with us, and their sweet babe. Before meeting, I had the children a little while alone, and the meeting was in no common degree solemn. The afternoon meeting, if any thing, was still more so ; the ministry very lively and refreshing. My dearest sister, Louisa Hoare was with us to my real comfort ; my brother, William Fry and his children were at both meetings. In the evening, we had a large number to tea, and at our evening reading. It was very interesting taking leave of my most dearly beloved family. The presence of the Most High appeared to overshadow us ; prayer was offered again and again, and testimony upon testimony was given. One Friend expressed his full belief that we should return in peace and safety, and that no harm would come nigh my dwelling ; a general feeling of the rectitude of our going was no small comfort. The next morning, I bid my darling children farewell in their beds. I left home about six o'clock, accompanied by my sons William and Joseph. My natural pain in parting with those most tenderly beloved, was mitigated by a portion of that peace the world cannot give, in making what I trust was a sacrifice well pleasing to the best of Masters.

Extracts from her own letters, furnish not merely the history of her journey, but an account of her natural fears, and her spiritual consolations—the difficulties that appeared before her, and the power by which she was enabled to surmount them. Written in haste, and often when greatly wearied, these letters have nothing to recommend them but their truth, simplicity and earnestness of feeling ; but those who wish to follow her through the journey of life, not alone in what she did, but what she thought and felt in doing, will prefer them, such as they are, to a more laboured history related by others.

Melksham, *Second Month 6th.*

MY MUCH-LOVED HUSBAND, CHILDREN, BROTHERS AND SISTERS.

I now commence the journal of my journey, which I desire regularly to keep until I may be favoured to return home. This, it is my expectation that I shall do ; but if in the ordering of Infinite Wisdom, this should not be the case, may all concerned, be enabled to bow to the dispensations of the Most High ; for in all He doeth, He doeth well.

On leaving my sweet dwelling, and my much-loved family, I felt very quiet, as if after all the deep feeling of the day before, I had only to rest, and could almost have thought myself insensible to what I was doing. After a refreshing breakfast at Mildred's Court, we set off, leaving William and Joseph ; I felt, dear fellows, as if I had not in parting nearly enough expressed my abounding love, and my sense of their kindness in accompanying us there. We had a pleasant journey ; the company of my beloved husband and brother delightful. We were received here with great kindness and hospitality. I have just been refreshing myself by a walk in a farm-yard, with an old farmer, and have bought a nice cheese for Plashet, which I hope you will like ; it should be kept several months before it is eaten. The most important feature of this day, so far, has been parting with my dearest husband. I was enabled to commend him unto Him, who can alone bless and preserve us, whether together or separate. How very, very near you feel to my heart, and how sweet it is, as time advances, to find that our spiritual, as well as our natural bonds increase in strength, which I may thankfully acknowledge I believe to be our case.

Fourth-day evening, Worcester.—My brother Joseph and myself left Melksham after breakfast, this morning. I passed a comfortable night, more so than I could have expected ; but there is a power that makes up our losses, particularly when in the way of our duty ; surely bearing our cross in small and great things, for what we believe to be, the sake of the cause of righteousness, brings peace with it. We travelled through a beautiful country : the Vale of Rodborough affectingly reminded me of days that are passed ; we saw, at Malmsbury, some most beautiful Saxon or ancient gothic architecture. Our distribution of tracts on the road has been really entertaining, it was pleasant to see how gratefully received. We are now in excellent quarters, so farewell for to-night.

We left H. Newman's, after a most hospitable reception, before eight this morning, and have been travelling all day, except stopping at Colebrook Dale to dinner, where I was reminded of very interesting and important days of my youth ; some very sweet ones that were passed in this black-faced country. We met a pleasant party of the Darby family to dinner, many of them I think you know, and a very interesting party of the youth, both boys and girls, young men and maidens : whilst my dear companions gave them a little good advice, I went up stairs, and had some rest. Several little things have given me pleasure on the journey ; the good appearance of the poor, and I should hope their general prosperity ; the animals also,—beautiful deer, sheep, and lambs, and many delightful prospects ; but the thoughts of my beloved family often come in—your kindness on my departure and before it—you each come before me with so much love and unity. I often think of dearest sister Rachel, and hope her cough is better, and my children at Lynn. I feel grateful for your aunt Hoare's kindness to me, and to you ; let her know about me, and let me know how her dear little R—— goes on. I feel rather odd to be here, away from you all, but the duty which brings me here makes it easy, otherwise I should feel sadly out of my place ; but I am bountifully provided for, much more so than I desire. Your uncle's kindness and attention almost unbounded, and your aunt also very kind. Farewell for to-night, my much-loved husband, children, &c., &c.

Sixth-day evening, Holy Head.—We arrived here about eight o'clock, after a beautiful journey : at least the greater portion of it.   I never saw such scenery,—the rocky mountains with long icicles hanging from them, and sheets of ice over parts of them— the mountain torrents full and strong—and the sun just enlightening the tops of some of the mountains, whilst others were in deep shadow.   You can hardly conceive the grandeur and beauty of the scene.   As a work of art, the Menai Bridge exceeds any thing I ever saw, its principle being so simple, yet so wonderful.

Dublin, *Second Month* 14*th*.

MY DEAREST CHILDREN,

I told my tale up to First-day evening.   On Second-day morning we visited the Asylum for the Deaf and Dumb, kept by Joseph Humphreys ; a very interesting institution, well situated within sight of the Dublin Bay ; his collection of Irish shells is beautiful, he means to procure me some of them, with their names, and some minerals.   We made calls on the aged and sorrowful, came home, rested, and dressed ; then went to dine and spend the evening at Robert Fayle's, where we met about seventy Friends ; it was the place my dearest sister Priscilla stayed at, when she was here ; it is very striking to me to observe, there, and amongst many Friends, the effect of her labours.   We had an interesting evening with this large party of fine comely young persons ; your uncle and myself told them anecdotes that we thought useful and desirable.   The Irish are a very interesting people.   Religion has done much amongst Friends and others ; and will I believe do yet more, and so regulate and further polish them, as to bring forth their bright, and overcome their darker qualities.   I like the people, and always did ; they are very kind to us.   Engagements are thickening upon us: one Roman Catholic lady has called, a charming woman, and through her means we are likely to visit the Nuns on Sixth-day.   This evening, we propose having a meeting for the youth : on Sixth-day, for older Friends in the evening, and for the public in the morning ; next week we look to the prisons and public institutions.   Farewell for to-day, in dearest love.

E. F.

Fifth-day, one o'clock.—We breakfasted at the Castle, at Major Sirr's, where we met a number of interesting people; he is in office, one of the heads of the police. In the cross, yet in the power, we had a religious time with them. Afterwards we saw a most curious and beautiful collection of antiquities found in the bogs, and other places in this country; also minerals and shells, one a most rare specimen. Since I came home, many have called. Very striking is the work going on in this land, it appears the time for those who love the truth, to labour for it.

Dublin, *Second Month* 17th.

MY DEAREST HUSBAND,

* * * * *

After I sent off my letter on Fifth-day, we went to the castle to call on the gentleman, who, in the absence of the Secretary of State, is acting as such. He treated us with great kindness, and appeared really pleased at our visiting Ireland: he has invited us to dine with him next Second-day. We then went to A. Maginn's office; he was also truly kind, and says he will forward any letters for us. We dined with a valuable Friend, Sarah Phelps, and met several Friends. My dear sister, E. Fry, all this time was completely poorly, and confined mostly in bed, at the house of our kind friends, Jonathan and Eliza Pim, where we are so hospitably entertained; when to my sorrow, my brother Joseph was taken in the same way; in the evening, he felt himself really ill, so that what with our many guests, and my two patients, you may fancy me (more particularly as Joseph is in the next house, and Elizabeth up high flights of stairs), rather overpressed; each had a medical attendant: however, the next morning, my brother was able to go to Meeting, it was a public one, he preached there as he generally does, much in the demonstration of the Spirit, and of power.

I had the comfort in the morning, to have both my patients better, and I hope it was not a want of resignation, anxiously to desire their recovery; it reminded me of Paul, how much he wished for his companion's revival, lest he should have sorrow upon sorrow. We received afterwards many persons, not Friends, Lady Lorton and others; Joseph and I went to wait on the

Lord Lieutenant, (Lord Wellesley) by his desire, we had a very gratifying and satisfactory interview. His views and ours appeared perfectly to correspond on many things of importance, particularly the subject of punishment. Lady Wellesley was ill, or, he said, she wished to see me. I forgot to tell thee, that I paid a very nice visit to the nunnery of the Sisters of Charity, and heard many particulars of their institution and of their plans ; we also had some interesting conversation of a religious nature, with them. You all know how deeply I have felt being away from my beloved husband and children ; but I think I never remember being any where, with such an opening for service in every way, religiously, morally, and in benevolent objects. Our being esteemed, as in truth we are, quiet and conciliatory in our views, and our being of no party in religion or politics, appears just now important. But if we are the least useful, we must remember that all our powers are gifts. Yesterday, we had crowded meetings, and we had all three in no common degree, to press the point of looking less to the ministers, and more to the Minister of ministers. More of Christian charity, and being all one in Christ, appears the thing wanted here ; there is certainly a great portion of light, and many individuals who seem to be very serious and spiritual.

The people are powerful, and warm-hearted, but not, I think, possessing more feeling, or sensitiveness, than the English. They appear to me formed, bodily and mentally, in a more hardy mould. This city is very fine, its houses and buildings above the mode of living, or the state of the inhabitants.

I feel (notwithstanding the illness of my dear companions) that we are rightly together, for with such a weight of various services, a treble cord was wanted for strength.

Dublin, Second Month.

My dearest Children,

To go on with our journal : on Fourth-day, after I sent my letter off, we visited four prisons—some of them in a most deplorable state, particularly those for debt—almost the deepest distress I ever witnessed. We hope that some remedy may be

found. Should this prove the case, it will be a strong confirmation of our being in our right place; as I find, that those, who
can help in these things, are willing to listen to us.

We dined at the house of the temporary Secretary of State.
We met there, the Archbishop of Tuam, and many connected
with him; Lady Ann Gregory is his sister. Highly valuable
and agreeable people, indeed. I think I never, any where, saw
so many serious people: surely, the true leaven, more or less, is
affecting the whole lump.

Yesterday was the week-day meeting; crowds attended, and
very solemn it was. I forgot to say, that when visiting the
prisoners the day before, the judges were sitting in the court, and
sent for us to go to them there. Picture your uncle, myself, and
some other Friends, in a crowded court, sitting beside the judges.
I could but be reminded of the difference of our situation, to that
of Friends formerly, taken into the courts in time of persecution,
and so cruelly treated; but my belief is, that their standing their
ground as they did, prepared the way for even these services.
" They laboured, and we have entered into their labours." May
the same power preserve us, in what may appear heights, as it
did them in depths.

After writing so far, we went to breakfast at a lady's named
Hoare, some relation to your uncle Hoare, very interesting, good
people; many met us there. After a religious time with them,
we went to the Bridewell, to meet a large number of ladies, to
form and arrange their prison committees. This was a very
arduous, but a very important business; and, I trust, things are
now put in good training, that if we do nothing else, it appears
almost worth while to have come here for this day's work.

Almost as soon as we returned from the prison, we had to go
to the park, for me to see Lady Wellesley; I paid her a very
interesting visit; she is a sweet woman, and, I think, serious.
She is a Roman Catholic. We next went to call on the Roman
Catholic Archbishop; and, as the Protestant one is now, I
believe here, I must stop.

MY DEAREST HUSBAND,

I feel that my journal was cut too short at Dublin, from a press upon me, which appeared unavoidable. I left off, I think, before we visited the House of Industry, almost the most interesting institution I ever saw; but, being accompanied by (I should think) nearly a hundred persons, added to the fatigue, and lessened the pleasure. Afterwards, we had quite an entertainment from the governor, as luncheon. Seeing the lunatics, gave me real pleasure; their order, comfort, and industry, appeared to be great. We then visited the Richmond Lunatic Asylum, and part of the great Government Prison. After one of the most crowded meetings I ever attended, and I think, one of the most solemn, we paid another visit to the Government Prison, and then took our departure from our most kind friends, and the highly interesting city of Dublin; with, I believe I may say, thankful and peaceful hearts, under a deep feeling that " hitherto the Lord had helped us," and out of " weakness we had been made strong." We had a dark evening drive of many hours, to James Forbes', at Christianstown, near Rathangan, where we found every comfort. We had two meetings the next day, at Edenderry: nothing but turf-fires, and the aspect of things very different to England. The next evening we travelled again, and were not fully expected; but fires soon burnt up, and after a while, a nice supper refreshed us.

Armagh, *Second Month 28th.*

MY DEAREST CHILDREN,

We are here comfortably settled by a nice fire-side, in a good inn, and in what appears to be, as far as we can judge, rather a fine city. We left Lord Bective's yesterday, about twelve o'clock, and then went with Lady Bective, and others, to see her charities, and a sad little prison. After this, we set forward for Coote-Hill, two stages, each about twelve Irish miles, which, I can assure you, was a fatiguing day's journey; we dared not stop to dine, and were about six hours on the road, or more, which was done with difficulty, with four horses, the roads were so very bad. The boggy country has a peculiar and desolate look; the generally miserable cabins, and appearance of the poor (though most of the women have cloaks, and the men great-coats), give a very different appearance to England. There is also a general want of order in the manner of cultivating the ground: the hedges half down, and badly kept, excepting near gentlemen's places, where things bear a different aspect. ·We observed a number of goats; I suppose they use their milk. Pigs abound; I think they have rather a more elegant appearance than ours, their hair often rather curled: perhaps naturalists may attribute this to their intimate association with their betters! The turf-fires, mostly used in the neighbourhood of the bogs, are pleasant. We yesterday, met a true Irish funeral; it was a curious sight, and really surprising to see how neat and clean the people turned out of their dirty cabins: some were really good-looking. The howl (if it was the howl) was like a dirge—melancholy, but rather pleasing. We have not lately had so much begging, as nearer Dublin, or the appearance of so much distress. We had a curious meeting this morning, of Friends, respectable persons, labourers, and the very poor people, many, I believe, Roman Catholics.

We have travelled again to-day, twenty-four miles: more fatiguing, I can assure you, than to travel fifty miles in England; but we have not been on the best roads. We visited a large prison at Monaghan, and to-morrow we hope to visit one here, and a Lunatic Asylum; also, to form a committee at Lady Lifford's, to attend a meeting some miles off, and then to go forward to sleep at Thomas Greer's. Our life is a busy one, certainly. So now, my much-loved family, I bid you farewell for this evening.

Thomas Greer's, Rhone Hill, Sixth-day morning.—Yesterday, we began our morning with some Friends to breakfast at the inn, and after reading, we set off to the prison. It was a fine day, and we had a pleasant walk to it. Several were waiting for us, both gentlemen and ladies. We had, for the first time, a religious opportunity with the prisoners; first, Elizabeth and myself, with the women; then all of us, with the men. The Roman Catholics appear very hard to reach; but with the poor men, I think, the power of truth reigned over all, and their spirits appeared brought down. We then went to the Lunatic Asylum,

which was in delightful order ; then to Lady Lifford's, where we
found an excellent committee. We had a religious time with
this charming lady, and then went forward to a meeting at Rich
Hill, a curious place, and as curious a congregation ; but we had
a good meeting. Afterwards, by some accident, I went into a
private house, thinking it was the inn, and gave orders as if at
an inn : I ordered tea immediately, and begged to be shown to a
bed-room, for my sister to lie down, as she was but poorly ; at
last I discovered my droll, and at first, disagreeable mistake ;
but such was Irish hospitality, that the lady of the house made
us stay, gave us some tea, comforted us up, and sent us off, not
knowing whom she had received, nor do we now know her name.
We then had an easy drive here, horses good, roads better ; but
both my dear companions far from well. I feel we have much
cause for thankfulness ; we are daily provided for ; and may,
through unmerited mercy, say with the disciples formerly, to the
query, " Lackest thou any thing?" " Nothing, Lord"—except
to be better ourselves, and more fit for such a service.

Lisburn, Third Month 4th.

MY DEAREST HUSBAND,

I yesterday had the real comfort of receiving letters, in the
evening, from home. I was made quite cheerful by it, and
weighty as it is to begin upon a new field of service in these
parts, yet I went light-hearted on my way, and, I trust I may
say, thankful.

I am sorry to hear of our poor friend William Morley's state,
and particularly wish to be affectionately remembered to him,
and to have him told how much I desire that, as his flesh and
his heart fail, he may know the Lord truly to be the strength of
his heart, and eventually, through his unmerited mercy in Christ
Jesus, to become his portion for ever ; he must cast himself, just
such as he is, on Christ his Saviour, the propitiatory sacrifice for
our sins, whose mercies are unbounded.

Now for my journal :—after I last wrote, we attended a large
meeting of Friends at Grange, where unbelief formerly, had made
much devastation ; we were enabled to preach Christ, I trust
in power ; and it appeared a very solemn time. We find the

meeting we had at Coote Hill made a great impression in the place, particularly amongst the Roman Catholics; numbers have been since to the Friend's house where we slept, for tracts; he had given three hundred away. We arrived here, and had a most hearty reception from Jonathan Richardson and his brother; their kindness is very great to us poor travellers. Yesterday, we had Friends very much alone in the morning, and a very crowded meeting for others in the evening, painfully so to me; I was so much afraid the house was not safe, and I believe one of the higher galleries creaked; it was however, well got through. What a day this is in Ireland! something of a shaking in religion, only there is such a field of service open, that it seems as if we hurried a little from the different places; but we desire to do our best. We have met with a delightful old minister here, John Conran, a most able gospel preacher, eighty-eight years old, he has stood through every storm in the time of heresy here; he was desired to quit the gallery, and no longer to preach, but he kept steady to his gift, and his sun is indeed setting in brightness; he is a man of good family, who came into our Society by convincement. I think such an instance of a lively spirit in old age, is a powerful evidence of the truth of religion; and that there is a principle above the natural part in man, which lives and flourishes when the other part declines. I must now go to breakfast, looking to the Quarterly Meeting to-day. May best help be with us, and grace, mercy, and peace with you. Amen.

Third-day Morning.—We had a very satisfactory Quarterly Meeting. We are now returned from a concluding meeting of worship, one of the most solemn, and striking, I ever attended; the good power and anointing, distilled as the dew amongst us, to the great refreshment, I believe, of all present. The ministry of the old Friend was wonderful—his experience of the power of light, life, and salvation striking; he overflowed with love, and the doctrine he preached, a strong proof of the reality of that power which remains after all the rest is shaken. When the reality of these truths are brought home to us, how earnest becomes the desire for all whom we love, to be made partakers of such a benefit. May husband, children, brothers, sisters, and all near and dear to me, partake of this joyous, glorious, full salvation!

We have here delightful quarters at John Bell's. We dined and rested, then called on some of the sick and sorrowful ; after which, we proceeded to our Public Meeting, to be held in a large school-room at the top of a high building. Feel for us—upon our arrival, the crowd was so great and the press such, that when we endeavoured to ascend the stair-case, I thought we must give up the attempt ; however, after great pressing, we were driven into such an assembly, that my poor heart almost sank ; I so extremely feared accident, whether the building or the flooring would not give way under the weight, however, in tender mercy, after a little while quietness reigned ; I had a few words to say, which appeared to tranquillize the assembly, and then your uncle was enabled beautifully and powerfully to preach the glad tidings of the gospel of Christ. I did afterwards say something, but in weakness, as my voice nearly failed me. Your aunt spoke powerfully, and I had power given me to offer the sacrifice of thanksgiving and prayer at the end. All dispersed without injury, I trust peaceful and edified ; but your dear uncle and myself had had such a shake, that we both passed a very poor night. I felt a little like Peter on the waters, as if fears got too. much hold of me, and made me ready to sink ; your aunt was sadly crushed. We set off after breakfast to the Bridewell, numbers with us ; but we hope that good resulted, and we are to form a committee to visit it. We proceeded to Carrickfergus, a very interesting place, and a most beautiful drive to it ; we passed a fine old castle by the sea. We visited a sad prison, and formed a Ladies' Committee ; also committees for visiting different charities, and had a large meeting of ladies.

TO HER SON WILLIAM STORRS FRY.

Londonderry, Third Month 18th.

MY DEAREST WILLIAM,

I have now matter for a very interesting letter, if I can get time to write it. After my last communication, we went to a second Public Meeting, which was very large and satisfactory. We dined at our dear hospitable friend's, and in the evening, thy uncle went to have a Public Meeting, at Carrickfergus ; and

we had a meeting with the benevolent ladies, to form committees
to visit their different institutions, which had in Belfast answered
well.

We met a cheerful party in the evening, when our labours
were concluded, and set off the next morning: a pleasant company, and the weather bright. We had with us, Thomas Wake-
field, John Christy, and William Bell, all superior Friends, and
highly esteemed. Our drive was beautiful, by the lake called
Lough Neagh, one of the finest pieces of water, looking like the
sea, without a boundary to the eye, in parts. Lord O'Neal's
place is situated on its banks; we passed through its beautiful
scenery. We slept at a Moravian settlement, where we were
pleased and interested, and met a gentleman and lady, who said
they knew thee, and had seen thee at Herrnhut, with Dr.
Pinkerton. We had no religious time with them, but were
interested by the whole thing, though I wanted them to do more
good to the community generally, instead of confining their
exertions so exclusively to their own body. We then set off to a
curious little country meeting, dined at a public-house, in a small
town, where we were almost mobbed for tracts; the energy for
knowledge is great, very different to what we expected: great
eagerness evident in the public mind for more religious light.
Some think there is the beginning of a reformation here, but I
believe this work will be very gradual; much is, however, going
on, of a highly interesting nature. We had a meeting, in the
evening, in an out of the way farm-house, and slept there.
Kindness and cleanliness made all pleasant. We went forward
to Coleraine, and, as we had a leisure morning, and were only
ten miles from the Giant's Causeway, we thought that we ought
to visit it; a fine expedition we had, and an adventurous one:
two horses tumbling down, pouring rain, and so forth. However,
we persevered, and first visited a very fine ruined castle, built on
a rock projecting into the sea, called Dunluce Castle. There is
a little bridge from one rock to another, without defence of any
kind. It was a very fine scene—beautiful black rocks, forming a
sort of amphitheatre on each side of it. We went on, in pouring
rain and violent wind, to the Causeway, and found, as usual,
that we were quite deceived in the distance. After walking over

rocks, and at the edge of cliffs, nearly overwhelmed with wet, we opened upon this wonderful work of nature ; like an unfinished building, formed of stones fitted into each other, being concave and convex, and so rising in pillars of different heights : some with three sides, some as many as nine, of various colours. I am very glad we saw it, as a fresh proof of the wonderful and various works of God.

I hardly knew how I should be able to get back, from the painful effect, walking up hill in the wind, has on me ; however, by the help of some poor working men, I at last effected it. Thy aunt was able to manage better than I did, being light; they carried her over all difficult parts. Curiosities abounded, stones, spa, &c., &c. ; but my excessive fatigue prevented my having wit to get what I ought ; however, I did obtain some. In a place like this, abounding with beauties, both grand and minute, I could delight myself for days with my beloved family.

I have almost ruined my cloak and bonnet, being nearly wet through. We arrived in time at Coleraine, for a large Public Meeting in the town. The next morning we set off for this place, passing by the beautiful Lough Foyle, partly a gulf from the sea. This is one of the most beautiful towns, as to situation, I ever saw ; strongly fortified by a wall, so wide that there is a walk upon it ; a fine river flows before it.

We found, on our arrival, that all our letters had miscarried ; but we had not been long here, before the Bishop, his wife, the Mayor, Magistrates, and Prison Inspector, came to visit us, trying to help us in every way. We dined at the palace ; but, for all this kindness from man, I felt low, and sunk under an awful feeling of service in the place. To-day, we have had one meeting attended by all descriptions of persons.

Evening.—We are just come in after a very large meeting, held in the Presbyterian Meeting-house. Since that, we have been reading to the prisoners, and forming a committee to visit the women.

Omagh, *Third Month* 19*th.*

MY DEAREST CHILDREN,

My letter of yesterday, was so far from giving a full account of some of our interesting proceedings, that, as we are stopped here from the want of horses (being assize time), I shall begin another letter. I think you will be amused to hear, that upon our arrival at Londonderry, we were saluted by a peal of bells : some of the party thought they were for us, which proved true, as we found afterwards, by a very curious letter from the ringers.

The manners of the people in the north of Ireland, and their dress, much resemble the Scotch ; most of them, even the poor, are neat, though without shoes and stockings. I am sorry to say, the great numbers that we find in the prisons, prove an unsettled state in the country ; but, I think, there is a good deal to excite their bad feelings, and, in some parts, they are almost starving, though this is not by any means generally the case in the north. We never go many miles without passing much bog, which is valuable, as it affords such good fireing ; and we see continually cabins made of little else than turf, with a hole at the top, for the chimney, much like those in Scotland. We have this morning visited the Prison, the Lunatic Asylum, and Infirmary at Lifford ; and the Prison, and Infirmary here. We think that in their institutions, there is a great spirit of improvement ; though some of them remain in a deplorable state. The Infirmary we visited to-day, was so ; I found there a poor patient without any linen, laid between blankets, and in an exceedingly dirty state ; but this is not common, some are in beautiful order.

Boyle, *Third Month* 22*nd.*

MY DEAREST HUSBAND,

Since I last wrote, we have passed a very interesting time. We got up about four o'clock. On our way to Enniskillen, stopped at a curious public-house for breakfast ; where we saw a good deal of the people, who flocked after us for tracts. I wish I could picture to you the scene, in a mud-floored parlour, with a turf fire. I took my seat some time in the curious kitchen, to talk to the family. After a time, they sent out to buy us a little bread, and some eggs. We fared well, and had a cheerful meal in our humble abode. The roads bad, and horses bad; we got on very slowly, going twenty miles in about six hours. The roads, too, are often dangerous; many of them being raised very high, without wall or hedge of any kind. In several places, a precipice on each side. Much of it through bog; indeed, I think, we have not passed a stage since we left Dublin, without part of it being through black bog. We reached Enniskillen in time to visit the Infirmary and Prison, and to form a Ladies' Committee. We are shocked to find so many bad cases of murder and cruelty, in the prisons; it shows an awful state of things, proving extreme moral degradation in this part of Ireland. We saw six men, who had through enmity knocked a man's head to pieces, and then put his body down a cave, where it was found. Another instance of burning, nearly to death, a woman, with whom they were angry.

With these impressions, as to the state of this part of the country, we all felt a little alive to our own safety, but were obliged to set off for our journey to Sligo, because we could not otherwise accomplish all we had in view. We could have no other horses, than those from Omagh. We went forward by the side of a fine lake, and beautiful rocks and mountains, till we got to a half-way house, from the place of our destination. We had been nearly five hours going about fourteen miles, and had eight or nine more to go; the question was, whether to pass the night in this solitary public-house, or go on with the same horses. Our dear Irish friends were evidently unwilling that we should remain; therefore, though close by the place of the sad murder that had just happened, we took courage, and set off again.

A curious dark drive we had; but our friends accompanying us, and the belief that we were in our right place, took away fear, on my part at least. We expected to arrive at a nice inn to sleep; but, to our great disappointment, after our fagging day, we arrived between ten and eleven o'clock at night, at a miserable dirty public-house; and we did not get even eggs or bacon, nor ourselves settled, some in one house, and some in another, till one o'clock in the morning. You will not wonder when I tell you we passed rather a nervous night. The next morning, we went to

Sligo, a highly interesting place. We found in that prison again cases of murder; but much as there is of fearful evil, there is great good also stirring, many Roman Catholics turning to Protestantism, several of whom we met this morning; they appear highly interesting, and to be a spiritual people. We spent the evening at the Rector's; met a very large party, and formed a fresh committee, though two ladies have already done wonders here in the prison. The High Sheriff and the Clergy were most kind to us. The inn was so full, we had a private lodging; and were treated by the mistress of the house, with no common attention. We had, this morning, a large Public Meeting, which appeared to give much satisfaction to our numerous new friends. We parted in real love from the people of the place, and then set off here, paying visits to two cabins by the way. We have had no further adventure. Imagine us in the cabin, round a turf fire, on a mud floor, a hole in the top for a chimney, a little dirty straw on the floor for them to sleep, as the woman said, " up and down in the room." Some heath and turf for firing, no windows, and two little dirty benches to sit on; the husband, wife, and children, round the potatoes boiling; they offered us " a prater and an egg;" though so poor, so hospitable!

Moate.—We slept at a tolerable inn, at Boyle, and went on to Roscommon, where, in the prison (as usual in these parts) were murderers; and, at the county town of West Meath, fifteen men, all to suffer death, I believe, for murder. We had a little meeting, fully attended, at Ballymurray. It is curious to observe the efforts made to attend these meetings, by persons generally. After meeting, it was late, and report said that stones were laid on the road to stop our progress, from some evil design, on our way to the farm-house, where we were to sleep; but, happily, this proved false. No fire in our room; still, I did well, and we had much to enjoy, and be thankful for. We are struck by the true kindness of the Friends, and with the effects of true religion, in changing the nature of this people; making them clean, courteous, and gentle.

We got up soon after five o'clock, and set off for Moate; in passing through a large town, we found an eager desire for tracts, before we were through the town, persons running after the carriage for them ; when, out came a man from one of the houses, a sort of lay priest (we suppose), stopped those who were near us with an austere countenance, and made the people tear them in our presence. A priest did the same with one of Joseph's tracts ; they delight in receiving them, generally, when out of sight of their rulers. A want of horses made us late here, and in passing through another large town, we were requested to have a Public Meeting ; room and all ready for us : which we did not accept. To-day, we begin the Quarterly Meeting, which is a weighty prospect.

Our dear friends, who are so kindly yet accompanying us ; had a trial last night, in hearing that sixteen armed men had broken into a house very near theirs, where they have left their wives and children. A Friend, who would keep arms in his house, and did not keep to our peaceable principle, was murdered near where we were yesterday ; and I hear that the woman Friend, who was murdered, was a strange person. The Sheriff of Roscommon said, " the sword of the Spirit was the best defence in this land."

Third Month 30th. Galway, First-day morning.—Here we are, in the midst of what appears gross darkness ; hardly any Protestants, and the Roman Catholics in a highly irritable state, so much so, that the Mayor has just called to say, he thinks a guard ought to attend us at our meetings. This of course we cannot accept. We look forward with some anxiety to our day ; but not without hope. I had meant to send this letter this morning, but shall now wait till we see how the day is accomplished.——Our meeting is well over. In the first place, we had about three hundred persons in the Assembly Room, at this inn, it was very much like being surrounded by those whom we should suppose knew little or nothing of religion ; as for Friends, and women's preaching, it was a marvel indeed to them ; I never was in a place apparently so dark. The Sabbath hardly at all kept, except in going to their places of worship ; but to tell you of the meeting—there was one continued bustle until I knelt in prayer ; then your uncle spoke at considerable length, and there was some thing like quiet; he enlarged beautifully on Christian love and charity, which appears so extremely wanted here, (there is so much contention)

After he sat down, I rose, and said, that when the women brought word that our Saviour was risen, the disciples believed that they were " idle tales," partly, probably, because the instruments were weak who conveyed the tidings, and so it might then be, but I hoped they would lay aside prejudice and not consider what we said, as "idle tales," because, we who spoke them were also weak intruments. The people were very attentive, and a solemn time we had, though so curious a one ; this afternoon, we had another meeting of about a thousand persons, different to any thing I ever witnessed. We had close exercise of spirit, and to our blessed Lord alone could we look for help. Such an assembly of Roman Catholics, for any such purpose, was never known to have met before ; some were heard to say, that if we held them, they would attend them every evening in the week, for all their priests. The Stream gradually rose in the meeting, until it overflowed its banks ; but how do you think it ended ? those in the lower part of the room, showed their satisfaction by knocking with their feet and clapping their hands. We were followed by crowds to our inn, who looked upon us as quite a spectacle ! However we are encouraged to believe such a visit was wanted, and is likely to be of use, in drawing Christians together ; as well as leading them from outward profession, to the real inward work of grace. We enjoyed peace after this awful meeting, and parted in much love, for we have been treated with kindness by Roman Catholics and Protestants. The Irish are a fine powerful people; I have been thus particular in relating the history of to-day, because it has been so important a one to us.

The preceding letter, was almost the last which Elizabeth Fry addressed to her family, during her journey in Ireland ; she was becoming worn and overfatigued, and every day added to the difficulty with which she accomplished the work allotted to it. Happily, they reached the hospitable dwelling of John Strangman, at Waterford, before her powers completely failed her. It was on Friday, the 12th of April, that she arrived there, and for more than a week she needed all the care, and close nursing which she experienced : then she gradually began to rally, and they pursued their onerous work. Her own journal written upon their return home, gives a sketch of the latter part of their journey ; and more is not required, as the publication of her brother, Joseph John Gurney, gives so full an account of the state of prisons and public institutions in Ireland.

Plashet, Sixth Month 2nd.—We continued our journey until the 11th of the Fifth Month ; we went on much the same as I before described, with the exception of visiting some important towns, where no Friends resided ; Londonderry, Sligo, and Galway, particularly the latter, where we held important public meetings, and saw many persons ; we also visited some institutions—amidst serious difficulties, particularly from the Roman Catholics : our way was marvellously made. The great numbers that followed us, almost wherever we went, was one of those things that I believe was too much for me, no one can tell but those who have been brought into similar circumstances, what it is to feel as I did at such times ; often weak and fagged in body, exhausted in mind, having things of importance to direct my attention to, and not less than a multitude around me, each expecting a word or some mark of attention. For instance, on one occasion a General on one side, a Bishop on the other, and perhaps sixty other persons, all expecting something from me. Visiting Prisons, Lunatic Asylums, and Infirmaries, each institution exciting feeling and requiring judgment. I endeavoured to seek for help from above, and for a quiet mind ; and my desire was, that such times should not be lost upon those persons ; they ended frequently in religious opportunities, and many came in consequence to our Public Meetings ; these things proved too much for me, and tired me more than any part of our service.

There were some, I believe, who feared my exaltation, and if they judged from outward appearances, I do not wonder at it ; but a deep conviction of my own unworthiness and infirmity was so living with me, that these things appeared more likely to cast me into the dust, than raise me up on high. We went on thus, from place to place, until we reached Waterford ; we had visited Limerick, Cork, and other places. I felt completely sinking hardly able to hold up my head, and by degrees became seriously ill.   Fever came on, and ran very high, and I found myself in one of my distressing, faint states, indeed a few hours were most conflicting, I never remember to have known a more painful time ; tried without, distressed within, feeling such fears lest it should try the faith of others, my being thus stopped by illness, and lest my own faith should fail.   My pain too in being from home was great.   We were obliged to stop all the meetings that we had appointed for days to come, however, much as I suffered for a short time, I had most sweet peace afterwards, my blessed Saviour arose with " healing in his wings" delivered me from my fears, poured balm into my wounds, and granted me such a sense of having obtained full reconciliation with my God, as I can hardly describe.   All was peace ; I no longer hankered after home, but was able to commit myself and those nearest, to this unslumbering, all merciful, and all powerful Shepherd.   By degrees I was sufficiently raised up to attend meetings, visit some prisons, and see many persons, and we concluded our general visit to Ireland, to my relief, peace, and satisfaction.   The Yearly Meeting crowned all, as to our ministerial services in our own Society. We left Waterford on the 11th of Fifth Month, after visiting Wicklow, and Wexford, at that time remaining at Waterford a few hours only.   We entered the steam-packet, slept on board, and left the harbour about three o'clock in the morning.   I suffered a little, but not from sea sickness, and enjoyed part of the voyage which was most favourable, wind fair, sea calm, and many dear friends on board, who were most kind to us.   We arrived at Milford about one o'clock, but I felt a want of due thankfulness, at being once again on this side the channel : we had an exceedingly kind reception from the Starbuck family, and a meeting with them, and other friends in the evening.

The next day, we went to Swansea, where we slept ; we had a meeting there, and also at Neath.

On Fourth-day, I met my beloved husband at Maidenhead, with a good account from home ; I arrived there in the evening, and although far from well, yet able to enjoy the sight of my beloved family and sweet home.   I find things going on to my comfort and satisfaction, for this I desire to be humbly thankful.

The week following was much occupied by the interests of our own Yearly Meeting, and this week by a deeply anxious dispensation in the serious and sudden illness of my beloved brother Fowell Buxton, the shock was great and our feeling for him and his dearest wife, deep indeed. We have now the inexpressible comfort of his being much better, and likely to recover; we rejoice not only for our own sakes, but for the world generally, that it has pleased a kind Providence to raise up again such a dearly beloved and useful member of our family, and of the community at large.

Sixth Month.—In reviewing our late journey, I may say of my brother Joseph, that he is one who delights my heart,——I think such true Christian conduct is not often manifested; he so remarkably combines the gifts and graces of the Spirit, his constant kindness and humility were striking, and exemplary. We are certainly united in a remarkable manner, not only by close natural bonds but in spiritual unity.

CHAPTER XV.

MRS. FRY's return from Ireland was clouded by the illness of
her sister, Rachel Gurney, who was then at Brighton for change
of air.   Thither she soon followed her, and remained for a few
days with her and one of her own daughters, who was staying at
Brighton to be near her aunt.   Threatening as had been the
symptoms attending the illness of this most beloved sister; it was
on this occasion, that the sorrowful conviction was first driven
home to her heart, that the case was becoming so alarming, that
but one termination could be expected.   From childhood, from
the   happy   days   of   Bramerton,   and   Earlham,   when   " one
cabinet, one little set of tea-things, one small light closet," had
been shared between them ; their love had flowed on, deepening
and strengthening with life, and its vicissitudes.   The depth
and fidelity of Rachel Gurney's attachment to her sister had in
truth been " wonderful."   Self-sacrificing, considerate, and protecting—most sensitively alive to her interests, her cares and her
joys ; but there were distresses approaching, from which this
devoted friend and sister could not have shielded her ; and the
mercy was apparent, when little more than a year had passed by,
of her having been taken hence, without seeing one, so tenderly
beloved, borne down by many sorrows.

Plashet, Sixth Month 24th.—(First-day morning.) The commencement of this day always feels weighty to me ; another week begun, the awful and responsible situation of a minister of the gospel in the services of the day, at home, and at meeting ; all weighs upon me.   Grant Oh Lord ! I pray Thee, a little help, that whatever Thy unworthy servant does, in word or in deed, may be done, as in the name, so through the power of Christ her Saviour.   Bless this day, I pray thee, Oh Lord ! not only to our house and family, and to our religious body, but to thousands and tens of thousands, that however outwardly separated, thy servants may unite in magnifying Thy name, and that their spirits may rejoice in Christ their Saviour.   Amen.

Worse accounts from Brighton induced Mrs. Fry again to go to her sister there ; after a few days sedulous nursing, she was able to move the invalid as far as Plashet, on her return into Norfolk.

Brighton, Seventh Month 20th.—When I arrived here, I found my beloved sister Rachel exceedingly ill, with a fresh attack of illness, and no sister with her ; so that I was greatly needed, and much as I had feared, that seeing this beloved one in a low and suffering state, would be almost more than I could support, I have been wonderfully shielded, and I trust enabled to be a real help and comfort to her, in a time of deep trouble. This I feel cause for humble and renewed thankfulness, to be able, however feebly, to return the unbounded kindness of one, who has been so much to me.   May I continue strengthened in this most interesting engagement, and minister to the spiritual and temporal wants of this tenderly beloved sister.

Plashet, Eighth Month 2nd.—At Brighton, I had a meeting with the members of the District Society, which was humbling to me, as such exposures always are, more or less, and a real effort of duty ; but I desired only to do it as such, and was very much helped to keep to my point, and go steadily on with the business, to my satisfaction, and I trust to the benefit of the institution ; which appears to have done much good to the poor of the place. Nothing of the kind appears to me to effect so much, as forming

and helping these public charities; because so many are assisted
by them. I understood that this Society last year induced the
poor to lay by amongst them, about £1000. Numbers of the
distressed had been relieved, and visiting the poor appears to
have been blessed, both to the visitors and the visited. I also
called at one of the Blockade Service stations, and found that the
libraries I had sent to the Coast Guard stations, after my illness,
three years ago, continued to be very useful to the men and their
families. Out of deep distress, I formed these institutions, (if I
may so call them) little thinking that an illness that appeared to
myself, as if it would almost take away all my powers, should be
the means of producing good to so many: surely out of weakness
I was made strong. May it be a lesson to myself and others to
bow under the Mighty hand of God, however mysterious His dispensations may be.

I was enabled to attend to my beloved sister, during the remainder of her stay at Brighton, and then brought her home here;
she left us, for Earlham, on Second-day, the 30th.

Very peaceful was Rachel Gurney's return to the home of her
childhood; her "flesh, and her heart," were, indeed, "failing,"
yet God was the "strength of her heart," and to Him she looked
with unfaltering confidence, as about to become her "portion for
ever." She wrote to Mrs. Fry, on her journey:—

"The quiet travelling has only been a luxury; both morning
and evening have been delightful to me, as to weather and scenery.
I have felt soothed and comforted, more than any thing else. I
am most deeply sensible of the blessing, thou hast been made to
me: I think it seems to have put me more in the right way of
taking, bearing, and feeling, my present allotment; above all, I
trust it has strengthened me in my *best desires*, and endeavours,
to walk humbly with my God!

"My kind and grateful love to all my affectionate attendants,
and abundance of love to the dear children.

From Earlham.—" I have never wanted yet, and think I never
shall want, the kindest of helpers. I can look around, this
morning, upon the beautiful order of every thing, with something

like pleasure. Thou wouldest be pleased with the beauty of my luxurious apartment : the window, opened to the south, is a beautiful improvement to it. In short, it is something of a paradise here below, that Joseph brings his bride to take possession of ! How differently we are led, and allotted, in this world. Some seem to be taught by trial and bereavement, and others by having all things ' richly to enjoy.' If the heart be turned the right way, and the eye be kept single towards God, I believe all may equally learn that great and most important lesson, that here we have no continuing city."

The sunshine of her mind, her christian spirit of contentment, coloured all around her ; again she says, in another letter :—

" It is almost beyond my power to describe to you the relief to my feelings, of being put into these two rooms of profound quiet ; and wheeled from one to another, without an effort ; looking from my bed, where I am only for some hours in the day, on the peaceful lawn, and green trees ; surely, ' He maketh me to lie down in green pastures : He leadeth me beside the still waters.' "

Dagenham, Eighth Month 15*th.*—Since my beloved sister's return home to Earlham, my dear William, and two of his sisters, have set off, on an expedition into Normandy. My feelings have been much excited, by the very serious account of my beloved sister Rachel, implying a sensible decline of power and health, which touches me in a most tender place. I may say, in the prospect of losing her, that I shall lose the person that has (taking life through) been more to me, than any other mortal, in constant, faithful love and kindness, and in ministering to all my wants, according to her ability. Oh! gracious Lord, grant her a full reward here, and, above all, hereafter ; but, I desire to return thanks for her prepared state of soul, (as far as we can judge, one of another), and the many alleviations granted her. If she be taken,—my companion, my friend, near my own age,— I think it will, in no common degree, bring death home to my view ; and may it lead me to have my heart really more placed on things above, less on things below.

22*nd.*—It is hard, very hard, a most difficult matter, to

know how to help those, whose welfare and salvation are past expression, near to us. We can only go to Him, who is willing and able, not only to hear our prayers on our own account, but on account of those most tenderly beloved; and who does, in His tender mercy, so bear our griefs and carry our sorrows, that our souls can rest on Him. Oh! may I ever have the encouragement of seeing those nearest to me, walking closely with God; not doing their own pleasure, or walking in their own ways, but doing His pleasure, and walking in His ways. I believe it would bring unspeakable joy, refreshment, and consolation, to my soul; and may I never cease to commend them to Him, who can work with, or without, human instrumentality.

I went on Second-day to Lord Lansdowne (Secretary of State) and the Under-Secretary, T. Spring Rice, on prison matters, and was received with the utmost kindness and attention. The prison cause appears prosperous. On Third-day, I attended the Monthly Meeting, and much in the cross with great fear, weakness, and nervousness, I was enabled to minister consolation to others. Peace and refreshment followed to myself, and although trials have since attended me, I felt the sweet balm remain,——that balm which heals the wounded heart.

25th.—The evening before last, an account arrived from Normandy, from my beloved children there, to say that ——— had been very seriously ill. But I desired to be thankful that she was better, and that she had fallen amongst such truly kind persons, (though total strangers to us) who had treated our children like their own; assisted in nursing her with the utmost care, and paid her every attention.

I am at times reminded of these words in Job, chapter xxxiv., 29th verse—" When he giveth quietness, who then can make trouble? and when he hideth his face, who then can behold him? whether it be done against a nation, or against a man only."

How striking a proof of the truth of the Scriptures, and that of which they testify, is the way in which they speak to our individual experience. Oh, may I dwell nearer to the source of all good, and live in a more devoted, quiet, humble, watchful, dependent, and resigned spirit.

Earlham, 30th.—On Seventh-day, the 20th, my son J———

came with an express from town, to say that the accounts from
Earlham were so much worse, that it was thought desirable that
I should go as quickly as possible to Upton, to fix whether to set
off that day or not; this agitated me and brought me very low;
but on our reading the different letters, and seeking for a quiet
mind, I believed that there was no such hurry, and concluded to
wait until after Meeting, on First-day, and an early dinner with
my family, before setting off. I find it very important in such
cases as these, not to act upon what I should call impetuous
feelings, but upon quiet and sober consideration; hurried movements rarely answer to ourselves or others.

We set off, and were favoured with a quiet journey, and a
hopeful one, as I could not believe that we should find any very
great change had taken place, and so it proved. Our much-loved
invalid was certainly sunk, since we were last together, and in
many things gone some steps lower; but there appeared to me so
strong a vital-principle remaining, that I think weeks, rather than
days, are likely to be her portion here below. Her mind is in
a most favoured state, she appears to feel it wonderful how easy
her circumstances are made to her; all fear of death seems to
be removed from her, she talks of it with ease, almost pleasure.
Last night she said, that, she wished not to be in other circumstances than she was, the way in which she had found the
fulness of the power was quite beyond her expectation, and even
her trials only appeared now to fit her for greater joys. At times
her sinkings are great and also her sufferings; but in these states,
though naturally low, faith always appears more than sufficient
to sustain her, and she receives them only as a part of the present
work of preparation. She said, they led her to desire to depart;
but her wish was, to say from her heart, " Not my will, but
Thine be done."

Surely, this is a fresh proof of the wonderful work and power
of grace, and Christian redemption: what consolation it brings!
and how much we see, even in these times of deep trial, the mercy
of a kind Providence, in granting so many mitigations and alleviations. Surely, His tender mercies are over all His works.

I think, I never am brought into contact with many of my
beloved brothers and sisters, without a very humbling feeling of

my own infirmity, and short-comings ; I find them such examples
to me, and am ready to say within my heart,—though I have come
so publicly forward,—though I have preached righteousness in the
great congregation ; What will become of me, and of my house ?
and where is there amongst us the same fruits of the Spirit ?

My merciful Father has helped me, cared for me, sustained and
provided for me, and in many ways blessed me ; but I still see
many hidden evils in my heart, and as for my family, fears often
get hold of me ; and for myself also, lest I should not walk worthy
of my high and holy calling. I can only intercede for us all, that
for the sake of Him who came to seek and to save that which was
lost, our gracious God would have mercy on us. Oh, dearest
Lord ! Thou hast granted the petition of Thine handmaid, for
her brothers and sisters ; she now sees in them, in a great measure,
the travail of her soul, and is satisfied. Reject not her prayers
for her husband and children ; bring them by any ways, or by any
paths, that Thou mayst see meet ; but let them also come to
the knowledge of the ever-blessed truth, as it is in Jesus, that
they may be saved with an everlasting salvation. And oh, gracious
Lord be with Thy poor servant to the end ; and through the continued extension of Thy grace, Thy help, and Thy mercy, let
nothing ever be permitted to separate her soul from Thy love in
Christ Jesus, her beloved Lord and all-sufficient Saviour.

" By any ways, or by any paths, that Thou mayst see meet ;
but let them come to the knowledge of the ever-blessed truth, as
it is in Jesus."

Such had become the language of her heart.

More than twenty-five years had passed, of deepening experience and growing dedication, since the ministry of William
Savery had been the means of producing so marvellous a change
in her. Religion, for the first time presented to her view,
through the medium, and under the aspect of Quakerism, was,
for a length of time, associated in her mind too exclusively with
the peculiar form in which she then had known it, and which
had been so eminently blessed to herself. She appears now

to have attained to the conviction, that the peculiar forms and scruples of sects, may be mistaken and substituted for the cross of Christ; and that there may be faithful and devoted Cross-Bearers, who adopt none of these peculiarities; thus, having learned to recognize the vast distinction, between the diversities of forms in religious worship and the mighty mystery of religion itself; even the "being renewed in the spirit of the mind, and born again from the death of sin, to the life of righteousness."

Among her brothers and sisters, she saw much of the fruits of the Spirit, in dedication of heart, and labours of Christian love; but it was not at first easy to her to believe, that the path that some of them had chosen, was for them as entirely right, as the one she had taken was for herself and others of the family.

To a mind so honestly seeking truth, and desiring to receive it in simplicity, conviction could not fail in its effect, and she became at last reconciled to these "diversities of administration." Her acquaintance with the excellent of the earth, beyond the sphere of her own family, tended to enlarge her boundaries; still, she clave to the peculiar form of Christianity which she had adopted for herself; and for her children, it was long the craving of her heart, her intense desire, that they might become "Friends" from conviction: but, even this strong desire of her heart was to be, in great measure, disappointed. We now find her, fully and unreservedly, petitioning Him who had eminently proved to her a "prayer-hearing, answering God," "by any ways, or by any paths, that He might see meet," but that they might "come to the knowledge of the ever-blessed truth, as it is in Jesus."

Here is no reserve, no holding back; the surrender of will entire, and the spirit of submission complete. Very blessed it is to those of her children, who have been unable to see as she saw, and to receive the views which she entertained, to know, that it was given her by degrees, without any wavering in her own opinions, without any diminution of her entire love for the true principles of Friends, " to recognise no distinction," provided " the narrow path was chosen, and the cross of Christ borne."

Earlham, Ninth Month 2nd, First-day.—My sisters Catherine, Rachel and Richenda, and I have had a very remarkable morning. I thought it better to stay at home from Meeting, to be with my beloved suffering sister. I had a desire for some religious time with her. After she was dressed and removed into the dressing-room on her couch, we read in the Bible; but so overcome was she, from weakness and sleepiness, that she could not keep awake; however, we went on, till I knelt down in prayer and thanksgiving for her and for us: this, appeared more than to revive her, she prayed beautifully and powerfully for us then present, for all her sisters, for my children, and for me and my dearest husband. Afterwards, she sent a particular message to some of the absent: her " dear love, and that they should be told, what a rich blessing she had found there was in seeking, *first*, the kingdom of God and His righteousness." The consoling effect of this time lasted for many hours, so that our beloved invalid remained in a delightful state all day.

First-day, 9th.—I was sent for express this morning from Lynn, where I had gone for a day or two, to see my beloved daughter. This visit proved highly satisfactory. I had it in my power to make all arrangements for her, as to medical attendance; and what was more, in no common degree, I found the spirit of prayer poured forth on her account; so that, I believe, it was well to be there. But my dearest sister passed through so deep a conflict last evening, that I was sent for. The letters from Plashet conveyed the happy news, that my children were returned from abroad, and my C—— better, though far from well.

10th.—My beloved sister appeared much sunk last evening, but awoke early, greatly refreshed, quite clear, and even very bright in her mind, and relieved from suffering. In the night I went to her, and seemed unable to endure witnessing her conflicts of body; but to my help and consolation, I found her thus relieved this morning. So it is, things too hard for us are not permitted; and my humble trust is that as trials come, so strength will be given to endure them. My strong confidence for my beloved sister is, that for her, way will in tender mercy be made through the valley of the shadow of death, and support granted to us also; though from the weakness of the flesh, fears at times overwhelm me on this subject. On seeing her so comfortable, I said to her, "brooks are granted us by the way:" she replied, "yes, and more of them the nearer we approach the journey's end."

11th.—Yesterday, our beloved patient passed through nearly constant conflict, from spasms on her breath, which was deeply affecting to us. We besought for her present relief; some mitigation was granted, and by degrees, during the night, she became more easy: she told me, this morning, it was "as though, the Ruler and Head of the people had been very near to her all night;" and mentioned what a conflicted day yesterday was; but she added, "I leant on the beloved." Her apparent patience and quiet spirit were striking to witness.

13th.—A wonderful revival; she appears better than she has done for many days. This is extraordinary, after watching what has been thought her dying bed for some time past;—last evening, almost all the symptoms of the near approach of death were apparent. I so deeply have felt it, that being in the room has been often almost more than I could bear; indeed, it is a time of much self humiliation to me, my unworthiness is very present with me. I feel as if I did not fulfil my duties towards my loved sister, because I do not sit up at night, and remain constantly with her; I am afraid of being upset by it; my tender inexpressible sympathy is so great for her in her sufferings, though I cannot but thankfully rejoice for her blessed state of spirit. As for myself, these words seem applicable: "Oh Lord! Thou knowest my foolishness and my sins are not hid from Thee."

15th.—Sitting opposite to my most beloved sister in the blue-room:—She appears to be gradually sinking into death, and may we not humbly trust and confidently believe, into the arms of her God and her Saviour. Grant Lord, I pray Thee, if consistent with Thy holy and blessed will, that she may fall asleep in Thee, and that no painful struggles may attend her change; that quietly and imperceptibly, she may cast off this mortal tabernacle, having already testified to us her faith and her hope, and be landed on the other side of Jordan, awaking to joy and glory unspeakable.   And do Thou, Oh Lord ! sustain us also, in this time of trial, and enable us in our low estate to rejoice in Thee, our God and our Saviour, who yet giveth the victory over death, hell, and the grave.

I have been alone and quiet a little while, and I find in this awful time, that "help is laid on One who is mighty;" for that, which ever since I came to an age of understanding has appeared almost impossible to bear, even the loss of *this* sister, who has been like "flesh of my flesh and bone of my bone," now I am enabled to receive, and bow under the dispensation with peace.   I believe that she has done her work, and that we have nearly finished our work for her; but, is there not an all-sufficient Helper near, who is holding up her head above the waves of Jordan, that they overwhelm her not !

17*th*.—About three o'clock this morning, our most tenderly-beloved sister departed this life.   Late in the evening she fell asleep, from which sleep she never appeared to awake.   They came to let me know, about twelve o'clock, how she was going on ; but, at first, I felt unequal to going to her, and she did not want me ; but, gradually, I found my tribulated, tossed spirit, calmed, animated, and strengthened, so that I joined the company round her bed, where I remained until the solemn close. We sat some time in deep silence ; then I knelt down, and asked that mourning and lamentation might not be the garment of our spirits, but thanksgiving, inasmuch as the warfare was accomplished, the conflict over, and through the unmerited mercy of God in Christ Jesus, an entrance was granted through the gates of the City, whose walls are salvation and whose gates are praise. Then I prayed for ourselves, that the loss of such a sister, who had in so remarkable a manner ministered to some of our necessities, might be made up to us by an increased portion of spiritual blessings ; and that her various labours of love to us and to our children, might receive such a blessing, as to produce an increase to our lasting good.   After returning to bed, natural weakness much overcame me ; the death of the body, and its terrors, got hold of me; and the heavenly Inheritance appeared hidden from my view, for a time.   To-day, I feel able to partake of the repose now granted us, in no longer having to travel through "the valley of the shadow of death," with one so beloved; and, in measure, to partake of her rest, as I believe I did, in no common manner, of her sufferings, as if one with her in them.

19th.—Blue-room—with my beloved sister's remains.   All quietness, rest in comparison—over my own mind a solemn feeling of peace, and this truth impressed upon me, "There is a rest for the people of God."   Several important lessons, I think, I have learnt by attending this most beloved sister.   1st, That persons are apt to dwell more on the means of grace, about which they differ, than its simple pure operation leading out of evil into good.   This I have long believed; but, seeing one who united as she did with the good in all, and could hardly be said to be of any sect or body of Christians, so grounded in the Christian life and practice, proves experimentally; that being united fully to any set of people is not essential, and all minor points of difference of comparatively little value.   2ndly, I learn to trust more, and be less afraid.   She like myself was liable to many fears, particularly in her nervous sinking states—how little cause had she for these fears, and how were the things that she most dreaded remarkably averted; also, That the last part of a death-illness gradually appears to diminish rather than increase in conflict, as with natural life and power, sensibility to suffering lessens.   In short, the lesson taught us is, to seek to serve and follow our Lord, and he will be with us and make a way for us, even unto the end.   3rdly, That in passing through life, patience should have its perfect work, that we should seek for a more willing mind to suffer, as well as to do the will of God, looking for daily help in this respect; that we should endeavour in all things for an upright, circumspect walk before the Lord, speaking the truth in love; above all, that we should seek after full understanding of, and reliance on, the work of salvation through Christ; and obtain (if possible) more knowledge of the Scriptures, and a better acquaintance with religious books.

Of my very many outward blessings, the brothers and sisters that I yet have are amongst the greatest.   C—— with her

simple, powerful, noble, yet humble and devoted mind. R——
with her diligence, excellence, cheerfulness, vivacity, willingness and power to serve many. H—— with her chastened,
refined, tender, humble, and powerful character. . Louisa with
her uncommon ability, talent, expansive generosity, and true
sympathy and kindness. S—— my rock ; always my friend
and my companion ; more or less my guide, my counsellor,
and my comforter. His stable mind, his living faith, his
Christian practice, rejoice me often. Joseph, the fruitful vine
whose branches hang over the wall, my prophet, priest, and
sympathiser, and often the upholder of my soul. D——, his
uprightness, integrity, power and sympathy, and son-like as well
as brother-like attentions to me, invaluable ; he has sweetened
many of my bitter cups.

The various places, taken in our beloved sister's sick-room by
the different sisters were very beautiful to see, how conscientiously
they filled their different allotments. I have been struck in this,
as in other instances, how much real principle is needed, to enable
us to nurse and do full justice to the sick, particularly, in very
long illnesses, and how much patience and watchfulness are required even with the most favoured patients. I should like to
give a little account here of this most beloved sister. We began
life very much together, she was a year and a half the elder.
We were partners, as children, of almost all that we possessed, we were educated a good deal together, and mostly slept in
the same room. She was also very strongly united in early life
to Catherine. She was when young, beautiful, lively and warm-
hearted ; she was very attractive, so as even to excite in some of
us who were much less so, feelings of jealousy. She formed a
strong attachment when quite young, under very painful circumstances, being contrary to our father's wishes. It eventually was
broken off, although our father withdrew his opposition, when
she reached twenty-one years of age. This produced a wonderful change in her, destroyed her naturally fine spirits ; brought
her into deep distress, but I believe also led her to seek better
consolation, and that love which could satisfy and would remain.
She was a most constant, faithful, devoted friend to her own
family, most particularly to myself, a companion and helper in

illness and distress, such as is rarely met with or heard of ; both
before and after my marriage. Of her it might in no common
degree be said, " self was of no reputation," she was able to
give up her own will, her own way, and her own pleasure to others,
in an extraordinary manner.

My becoming a Friend, was, in the outset a trial to her, she
would weep over it, and endeavour to show me the folly of it, as
at that period her own mind was only opening to receive religious
truth ; but on perceiving that my peace was concerned in it, and
that my desire was simply to obey that which I believed to be the
manifestation of duty, she soon became one of the foremost to
make my way easy, in any sacrifice or cross that this led me into ;
and so far from remaining a hindrance, she became a faithful
constant, steady, helper to me.   Even to the last, she would in
the spirit of love and truth, warn me or any of us, of such rocks
as she thought our peculiar views would endanger our stumbling
against ; and I may truly say, I have for one, often found them
watchwords in season—words, that I trust have taken deep root
in my heart, and been blessed to me. In religion, her ground was
expansive.   As it respected worship, I think she united much
with Friends, in some other matters with the Established Church,
she had peculiarly the power not only to see, but to unite with
the good of all persuasions ; and according to the ability granted
her, to help all on their way.   She was cheerful, hopeful, but
very sensitive ; yet so remarkably grounded on the everlasting
Rock, as not to be greatly moved by, though deeply sensible of,
the various trials and fluctuations of this life.   She owed much
also to her well-regulated and self-possessed mind.   Her heart
was in no common degree affectionate, even so as at times to
prove a trial to her, but deep and strong as was her affection for
her own family and friends, her dependence was on higher
ground ; and He who gave himself a ransom for her, and was her
Lord and Master, had her first love.

Her sound mind, good understanding, and clear judgment were
very conspicuous ; her patience and long-suffering, united with
natural cheerfulness, very marked, particularly in her last illness ;
amongst her minor virtues, her order, regularity, and punctuality were great.   She had peculiar power over children, and

possessed, in no common degree, the gift of training and educating them ; she was strict, though most kind to them ; she particularly cultivated habits of industry, and having whatever was done, well done ; she also early proved a teacher to bring them to Christ, and was able, not only to instruct them in the Scriptures, but general religious truth, and many bear testimony to her invaluable labours with them, on these most important subjects. She not only sympathised particularly with the afflicted in her own family, but was a frequent and faithful nurse to many others in sickness, and a comforter to them when sorrowful. In short, she was greatly gifted by nature and grace, and what is far above all, she "gave diligence to make her calling and election sure !"

The funeral of Rachel Gurney took place on the 23rd. An occasion of very deep feeling, and one that wakened many sorrowful recollections and associations.

On the 24th, Mrs. Fry went to Lynn, and the following evening wrote to announce the birth of a little grandson, thus rapidly passing from the last, to the first scene in " man's eventful history." She had been anxious to come to her child, and yet could scarcely leave Earlham sooner. To her family at home she says, " I cannot but thank a kind Providence for bringing me here in the needful time, and thus guiding my steps aright." One day later she was sent for to Runcton, in consequence of the birth of a nephew ; whose life, which hung upon a most slender thread, was apparently saved through her unremitting exertions. She set an unusual value upon infant life ; she was almost displeased at the death of little children being lightly considered ; " You none know how good or how great they may live to be." Nor was it only in reference to this world that she felt thus, for " Are there not 'many mansions?' different degrees of glory, in the heavenly inheritance." This estimate of life, and the use to be made of it, was perfectly consistent with absolute submission to the will of God, whenever it was His

good pleasure to take it.   There were four lines of Sir William
Jones, which she greatly delighted in ; often and often has she
recited them, with some little one in her arms, whose soft skin,
and meaningless expression, bespoke how lately it had become
an inhabitant of this world —

> " On parent knees, a naked new-born child,
> Weeping thou sat'st—while all around thee smiled,
> So live, that sinking to thy long last sleep,
> *Safe* thou may'st smile—whilst all around thee weep."

A press of engagements awaited her return to Plashet.   Business and correspondence, public and private, at home and abroad.
Communications addressed to her had become increasingly
numerous, especially from the continent.   Dr. Julius of Hamburgh, became a frequent correspondent.   This gentleman had
long devoted himself to the subject of Prison Discipline.
During this year, he had lectured at Berlin, for two months,
upon the subject, the course being attended by above a hundred
gentlemen of rank and fortune.   From M. Ducpetiaux, at
Brussels, a zealous advocate for Prison Reform, she had received
communications.   A long letter, of great interest, had reached
her from Madame Potemkin née Galitzin, at St. Petersburg ;
also, through John Venning, Esq., she received details of Prisons
and Lunatic Asylums, by desire of the Empress Dowager of
Russia.   From another quarter, she had details sent to her, of
the Grand Duke of Baden, having in his dominions, instituted
inquiries as to the best method of constructing prisons.   Again,
from Paris she received communications of the state of prisons
in France, with, among other matters, an account entitled,
" Fragmens d' un compte rendu sur les Prisons de Lyons, 1827,"
&c. &c. ; presenté à Monsiegneur le Dauphin, par M. le Baron
De Girando.

The era of advance was come ; and those who wished well to
their fellow-creatures, marked the progress of good with intense

satisfaction. Few and scattered as were the efforts made, the great principle was gaining ground, that preventing crime was of sounder policy than punishing it ; and the reformation of the culprit, the end to be sought in penal legislation.

Plashet, First Month 3rd, 1828.—This year commenced with many interests. On the morning of the new year, we assembled almost all our large household, and many guests, principally young people. Before we began reading, I mentioned some of the striking marks of Providential care and mercy, shown to us during the last year. We then read, and afterwards had a solemn time, in which I returned thanks " for mercies past, and humbly craved for more." My dearest brother Joseph joined us, and under a serious, yet cheerful influence, our large party sat down to breakfast. This is often to me a most agreeable time of the day, after the repose of the night, and often some spiritual refreshment in our readings. I can hardly say how much I enjoy my family circle, and thankfully receive the blessings conferred on us.

31st.—During this month, my beloved family, husband and children, have occupied most of my time and attention, and in many respects I have had much comfort ; but at their present age, when there is so much to excite the susceptible mind of youth, my anxieties are many on their account, and I feel that I have to watch with at times fearful care over them and their associates, and perhaps when they do not know it, sympathise with them in their passing troubles arising from such circumstances. I sometimes pour forth my prayer for them, that if they are to be united to others in life, their affections may settle on the right objects. How deeply, how tenderly, to be felt for, and watchfully to be cared for, are young people at this period of life ; and how difficult for us, who apprehend ourselves, as Friends, to be bound by unusual restrictions in marriage connexions, exactly to know the right line to pursue. I have been, as usual, much occupied by public objects, and have met with both encouragement and disappointment. Encouragement, because the government has greatly aided us in the female convict ships ; and disappointment, from not succeeding in more generally obtaining permission for ladies to visit prisons. In our own Society, I have had one important call to Birmingham, to attend a funeral; a very serious and weighty occasion it proved; numbers of the children and grandchildren of the deceased, of various descriptions were present. There was a crowded meeting, and few ministers, so that the weight of the service appeared to devolve on me, there, and at the house. The help granted me was marvellous in my eyes; and I was enabled, at these different times, to preach the glad tidings, the liberty and the peace of the gospel of Christ. So it is, out of weakness, we are, when dependent on our Lord alone, made strong, and fear is removed in the most remarkable manner—my dearest brother Samuel accompanied me—who has such brothers as I have, to help in the needful time? I think, as it respects the ministry, I am never so much helped as when without other ministers to look to, my dependence being then singly on my Lord, and on His anointing. I yesterday went to see one of my sons at school, and attended Epping Meeting, which I thought a satisfactory time. I tried to make my visit pleasant to all the boys, by taking them a walk, and giving them oranges; I like that the instruments, who communicate religious instruction to the young, should be pleasant to them. I have had interesting, and encouraging communications from Ireland, as if, in some parts particularly, our labours there had not been in vain. I have once or twice been to see my sister Hoare, and have felt the value of the near union between us; my dearest sister Rachel is often present with me; the way in which I have been enabled to support this inexpressible loss, is surprising to myself; surely it is only the tender mercy of my God that has thus healed my wounds, and upheld me under it. Indeed, at the close of this month, I may raise up a fresh Ebenezer, and say—the Lord be magnified for His loving-kindness to me, His poor unworthy, yet dependent one. Oh! may He see meet to keep me in the way that I should go, and preserve me from right hand and from left hand errors.

Second Month 2nd. — Yesterday, was a full day, and one humbling in its effect. In the first place, I earnestly desired preservation, that I might keep my eye single to God, and not bow to man in spirit. I then went to town, and to Newgate, under a feeling of rather deep concern, where I unexpectedly found numbers of persons, a magistrate, foreigners, a Jew, a clergyman, many ladies; some Friends, and my brother Samuel. Before I began to read, I in secret asked for preservation, at least it was my earnest desire to have my eye kept single to my God. But either the fear of man got too much hold of me, or the "unction" was not with me, for I did not feel the power of Truth over us, as it very often has been at such times. I am ready to believe, that if I had not looked at man, but dwelt yet deeper in spirit, I should have openly called upon the Lord, and should have found help and power in so doing. I went away humbled. My sister Elizabeth said something; but of late there has been so much felt and said about our doing too much in these things with the prisoners, and going out of our province, that it makes me fearful, and consider, that as far as the Spirit is rightly subject to the prophets, so far, at this critical time, we ought to curtail in these things. I then went with my beloved brother Samuel to the Bishop of London, to talk to him about religious services with prisoners, to inform him of our situation respecting it in Newgate, and the extreme care necessary in the appointment of chaplains for gaols; also to speak to him of the state of our parish. I spoke, I trust, to the point, and that good and not harm will result from the visit; but I always fear, after such times, lest I should have said too much. We then made a call; there I pretty boldly spoke my opinions of theatres and public places; and in reply to the question, "How I went on, in reforming the world?" I replied, that my zeal was strong in my declining years to do what little I could towards reforming things. Afterwards, I feared that I might have said too much. We went to the Secretary of State's office, and saw the Under-Secretary; there, again, I had to speak my mind fully on many things, prisons especially.

Now, during this day, my services were numerous: some of an important nature, and such as might by some persons be supposed exalting, to be admitted, although a woman to represent things of consequence to persons of influence and power; and to be received as I am by them;—but He who searcheth the heart, only knows my humiliation, and how, in these services, fears for myself get hold of me, lest I should bow to man and not to God ; lest any thing but the simple object of promoting "the thing that is good," should influence me. This I certainly know, that such engagements often bring me into deep exercise of spirit before the Lord, that I may be kept as a clean instrument ready for His service, and not become contaminated by the spirit of self nor the spirit of the world. Truly, my desire is, to walk humbly, faithfully, circumspectly, before my God in the first place, and, secondly, before my fellow-mortals ; but ever and in all things, to seek to serve my Lord, doing His will and His pleasure, before serving myself or others, or doing my own will or the will of man. Lord, continue to be my help, my strength, my glory and the lifter up of my head ; and if consistent with Thy holy will, bless my labours and the labours of others, in these works of charity, and keep us, the unworthy instruments employed in them, so, as to be fitted to perform them, or any other service Thou mayst see fit to call us into. Amen.

25th.—At times, I have felt distressingly overdone in body and mind ; but in the midst of fatigue and bustle, I have sought the Lord for help and endeavoured to wait upon Him, that a quiet spirit might be granted me, which, in tender mercy, has frequently been the case, so that the storm has become a calm. Generally speaking, I do not think that I work too hard, for I am deeply sensible that we do not serve a hard Master, and that He will never require more of us, than we have strength to perform. I think our health, strength, and life, are valuable gifts, that we have no right to play with, but should take all reasonable care to preserve ; although, I am also of opinion, that active employment for body and mind is preferable and conduces to the health of both, whilst many suffer great loss for want of it ; sitting, as it were, in their "ceiled houses," taking undue care of themselves. I also believe, that a portion of rest, quiet and recreation, is not only allowable but right, and in the ordering of a kind Providence for us all. Surely, in a spiritual, as well as an outward sense, I may fully and heartily testify, that in unmerited mercy the "brook by the way" is often partaken of, sometimes in a large and overflowing manner, so that I may say, "my cup runneth over." I am at times ready to exclaim, "Oh

Lord! our Lord, how excellent is Thy name in all the earth!"
The works of the outward creation give me delight; and I am
enabled to perceive the beauty and the excellency of the spiritual
dispensation, as revealed to us, through the unspeakable blessing
of the gospel of Christ.

Third Month 5th.—May I not say to Him, who seeth in
secret, Thou hast known my soul in adversity! but amidst these
dispensations, is not the "Lord known by the judgment which he
executeth?" What peace, what blessing, what fulness of help
and consolation, have I also experienced. How have gospel
truths opened gradually on my view, the heighth, the depth,
length and breadth of the love of God in Christ Jesus, to
my unspeakable help and consolation: principally, I believe,
through the dispensations of Almighty wisdom; partly from the
soundness of faith of some near to me. My brother Joseph,
my sisters Priscilla, Catherine, and Rachel, as well as many others
of different religious persuasions. I think that my general religious association, has delightfully extended my spiritual borders.
I can, from my heart say, all one in Christ; all dearly beloved,
as brethren and sisters, who love His name, and seek to follow
Him. Although, I remain a decided Friend in principle, and
believe for myself and for many others, that it is our calling: for
I consider ours to be a highly spiritual dispensation, and that
not only we ourselves, but others would suffer much loss by our
not keeping to it.

Seeing, that I can not only sing a song of praise, but testify
that I have found, (however He may hide His face for a season),
that, blessed be His name, help is laid upon one who is Mighty,
who remains an all-sufficient Saviour; may no humiliating thing,
no love of the world, nor undue devotion to my natural claims
and lawful callings, in any degree prevent my cleaving very closely
in spirit to my God, or preferring Him and His service, to my
chief joy. May I never mistake my natural ease and liberty
of mind, for the perfect freedom of the service of Christ;
for, in nothing am I, more changed than in this, I feel such
liberty, (though not for anything wrong, I trust,) to enjoy
the things even of this life, and am less anxiously scrupulous
about some smaller matters. May I make no ill use of this

liberty, but seek to watch and pray, that I may use, without abusing it.

27th.—On Second-day, I attended the Select Quarterly Meeting, and was appointed representative to the Yearly Meeting. The next day the meetings were satisfactory. How striking to me, and how humbling: here am I, that used to be one of the last, least, and lowest in this Quarterly Meeting, now obliged to be one of its foremost members in the Meetings of Discipline; partly, from so many vacant places being now left amongst us, partly, from my long experience of its ways, and many years in its service; and last of all, truly, deeply unworthy as I am, because it has pleased a kind Providence to grant me the unity of my beloved friends, and thus to raise me up. My spirit, notwithstanding my outward cheerfulness, was much bowed down within me, in earnest cravings to be washed, renewed, and more fitted for my Master's service.

In April, Mrs. Fry accompanied her husband on a short journey. To visit some meetings of Friends, and several Prisons, formed her chief inducement; but she also was glad to avail herself of the change of scene and travelling for some of her family. "To follow, and not force Providence," was a favourite sentiment with her; she had taken it from "Cecil's Remains," a book in which she delighted. "To avail ourselves of the openings," was another expression to be frequently heard from her lips. Extracts from two of her letters, pourtray something of her various objects and interests.

Matlock, Fourth Month 19th, 1828.

My dearest Children,

The beauties of this delightful place, even amidst pouring rain, are such, as to make me long to have you all around us, to admire them. I am sitting in a bower window; a sweet little garden, cut out of the side of a high hill, on one side, a deep valley on the other, the river Dove at the bottom, full with the late rains, flowing over rocks; and very high rocky hills, covered

with trees, beyond.   We are in a quiet, comfortable hotel, kept
by a widow, where we feel quite at home, and only want all of
you, and a little fine weather, to complete the pleasure of our circumstances.   We feel the comfort of quiet and rest the more,
because we have had such a very full time, almost as much so as
in Ireland.   At Leicester, Nottingham, and Derby—Meetings,
Prisons, Friends, other people, forming Prison Associations, and
various engagements.   I have hardly had time for rest or meals.
We unexpectedly met my dear brother Joseph at Leicester, on
First-day ; and the next day he greatly helped me, as usual, in
the prisons and in endeavouring to form committees.   He and I
went forward to attend the Quarterly Meeting at Nottingham,
which we were favoured to get well through.   On Fourth-day, I
was very busy receiving visitors and taking care of your dear uncle
(who was very unwell), until he left us.   We then proceeded to
visit three Prisons and a Lunatic Asylum ; and in the evening
there came about thirty ladies to form themselves into an Association, and to revise the Prison Committee now existing.   We
arrived at Derby on Fifth-day, in time for Meeting ; afterwards I
set off with our dear friend Henrietta Newton and others, to visit
the different prisons.   The town one is vile, and the country one as
beautiful ; there I think six, at least, of the principal magistrates
met me, as well as other persons.   I was sadly tired, and only returned to Leylands in time to dress for dinner with our charming
host and hostess, and their dear children.   The next morning
there was a party to breakfast with us ; after a solemn reading.
About eleven o'clock, many ladies, Friends and others joined us,
to form associations for the Asylum and Prisons.   This done, I
had to write to the magistrates, go and visit the Asylum and
Infirmary, then dine at a kind friend's, where we met several
persons ; and set off for this place about six o'clock.

Now, in the nearest love to you all, farewell.

Your mother,

E. F.

Uttoxeter, Fourth Month 21st.

My dearest William,

We are just arrived here after a pleasant visit to Matlock,
although it rained nearly the whole time we were there.

Yesterday was very interesting. We went eleven miles to sit Meeting with some persons of the lower class, in a stocking-weaver's room ; a very striking scene it was, and very pleasant afterwards to see these poor people. But, my dear children, you know enough of mama's eye for the ludicrous, not to wonder that my fancy was tickled to see the mistress get up during our Meeting, to attend to dressing the dinner : two Friends also sitting on the stocking-loom for want of chairs ; and we believed that those chairs we had, were lent by the neighbours to help the party out. It is a very remarkable case : a poor man, a wheelwright, in a little out of the way place called Cowhouse Lane, about ten miles from Matlock became convinced of the principles of Friends at a public meeting, and it has spread to several of his neighbours, who sit down in silence together on First-days. We were all much pleased and interested by them. We returned to Matlock about four o'clock, and spent a quiet pleasant evening, until a smell of fire excited anxiety in some of our party. We were sitting in our little parlour, at the end of a long passage, three stories high. I asked Foster R—— to go into my room, as there was a fire there, and see if anything was burning. What should he find all in a flame, but my cloak hanging up, a large packing-cloth, towels, towel-horse and side of the fire-place. Some how or other, from the window being open, part of the towel must have blown into the fire, and all the other things caught. We think that, as it was very near to the bed, and that the flames were up to the ceiling, or nearly so, had we delayed only a few minutes longer, the whole large inn would have been burnt ; and what is more, we could not have passed the door, which it was necessary for us to do to go down stairs. Thus we have had a most providential escape. Foster gave no alarm, but began to put it out before we got to him ; then, with thy father's aid, throwing water on the flames extinguished the whole. We happened not to have begun reading, therefore, our attention not being occupied, we were particularly alive to what passed ; we were just going to read something very interesting. It made us think of thy escape at Bristol. What a mercy to be preserved from such awful dangers.

Thy nearly attached mother,

E. F.

Plashet, Fifth Month 7th.—I am once more settled at home, after a journey to Lynn, and into the midland counties, with my husband, my daughter Richenda, and Foster R——. In the course of it, I visited thirteen prisons, also some Meetings; often to my wonder that so unworthy an instrument should be so honourably made use of as to minister to the spiritual state of others, and to visit and be the means of assisting so many in prison and in bonds. It is perfectly curious to me to observe how my way is made when I go to a place, hardly knowing a person in it; how soon I am favoured to be surrounded by the serious and the good of different descriptions; to partake of sweet unity of spirit with them, to encourage them in their good works, and often induce them to visit the prisons. Surely the hand of Providence is in some of these things, small and great? It was strikingly manifested in many instances on this journey: I was enabled to form three new Committees for visiting prisons, and to re-organise others, in a way that I hope will prove useful. Where my lot was cast amongst Friends, I also found the best help to be near. I attended the Derby and Nottingham Quarterly Meeting, as well as several other Meetings, and met my dearest brother Joseph at Leicester, where I was enabled to assist him in the needful time; it appeared almost providential. I walked into the Meeting where he was at Leicester; he did not expect me, neither did I know he was in that town. He appeared greatly in need of help, being fatigued and very unwell. Since my return home, the British Society Meeting has much occupied my attention. It was on the last day of last month; it was a very numerous assemblage of ladies, many of them of high rank. I had much to do in it from time to time: when the different reports were read, I explained a little, and at other times poured forth much of my mind on the subject. However, I went away low and humbled at the conspicuous part I had to take, not doubting that it would bring me into evil report as well as good report; and fearing lest the Secretaries and other valuable members of the Society might feel my doing so much, and their doing comparatively little; and yet my heart was so full of interest upon the subject, and my head so full of matter, that I did not nearly express all I had to say. The general impression I hear was satisfactory, and I trust good was done : but I may set my seal to this—that public services are fearful services, and none but those engaged in them, know how much those are spared who do good privately. Still, if the Master calls us into public duties, it is not only well, but honourable ; and in them much more good is accomplished, because so many are concerned : still I would have no one seek for them, but if rightly brought into them, preservation will I believe be granted. A watchful, humble spirit is called for ; one that is not exalted by the undue approbation of fellow-mortals, nor too much cast down by disapprobation or evil reports. There must also be a willingness to commit all these works to Him, who can prosper them or not, according to His own good pleasure.

For this meeting of the British Society, Mrs. Fry had prepared rough notes, or memoranda, which exist. They contain allusions to some facts but not the facts themselves, as illustrations of her opinions as to the proper treatment of female prisoners. They were much the same, as those contained in the little work published by Mrs. Fry in 1827. The same ideas are to be found in her evidence before the Police Committee of the House of Commons, and in letters to official persons. They include observations on the good effect of ladies visiting prisons, workhouses, hospitals, lunatic asylums and other public institutions; the necessity of ·classification, female officers, regular occupation ; enforced plainness of appearance, separation, and where that cannot be enforced, absolute silence after retiring for the night; with many details that must present themselves to every one who has entertained the subject of Prison Discipline ; but above all, the infinite importance of religious instruction. She enlarged on the state of female convict-ships, the need of better clothing for the women, the wretched condition of their little nurslings, and various topics connected with the peculiarities of a sea voyage. She finished by a heart-stirring appeal to the many present, gifted with influence and talent, wealth and position, on

the subject of the increase of crime in this country, the responsibilities of all, the sphere of usefulness open to every individual,
even to the tender and delicate woman, who might be said scarcely
"to have the air of Heaven visit her face too roughly," as a wife
to influence, as a mother to educate and train, as the mistress of
a family to guide, control, reprove, encourage.   She touched
upon district societies, libraries for the lower classes, general education,—and concluded by urging upon her hearers in nothing
to be discouraged ; but in humble confidence to go on, remembering that the work is not ours—therefore, we may look to
Him Who is mighty, upon Whom help is laid ; to be "stedfast,
immoveable, always abounding in the work of the Lord, foras-
much as their labour would not be in vain in the Lord."

Plashet.—Last Sixth-day, we had a very interesting visit to
Newgate. Numbers were there ; clergy, some of the nobility, the
Sheriff, many ladies, gentlemen, and Friends. It was a solemn
time ; the fear of man much taken away. After the reading I had
to speak to them, and pray for them. I have of late been surrounded by my family, and deep cravings of spirit have been my
portion for them. Through all, I have at times almost panted for
a surer and a better resting-place, more particularly where there
will be no more sin or responsibility. I see much to enjoy here ;
but the temptations that are in this world, at times make me
feel, if not weary of it, at least longing for a Heavenly inheritance; although the fear of the passage to it always makes me
flinch from this great change, as well as the knowledge of my
own unutterable unworthiness.

   Since I last wrote my journal, death has been brought closely
home to me.   I was unexpectedly called to attend my dear
aunt C——, in a violent illness, which ended in her death.
I went to her on Seventh-day, and for some hours every
day afterwards, and one night ; till she died. I fully believe
her state was a blessed one, and that in her trial she knew
the Rock to be her stay. Still, as far as I can judge from
observation, death is even to the righteous an awful conflict,

generally attended with distress of body, reduction of spirits, some obscurity of mind, and great difficulty in communicating to others, either the wants or the feelings. My aunt seemed in her distress to depend much upon me; I appeared to be a comfort to her, and was enabled, in measure, to minister to her bodily and spiritual wants. The day after all was over, and after having had a very solemn time with the family, I became ill myself; much as I had been at Waterford, hardly able to hold up my head, or go on my way. On Sixth-day I was worse. It was a sudden, unexpected loss of strength, being brought down as to the ground, when I was anticipating with no common degree of pleasure the Yearly Meeting, and after it my child's wedding; looking for rather prosperous days. As usual in my illnesses, I was greatly cast down at times; and wonderfully reduced in a short time. In the midst of my conflict and distress, I still thought I could see the hand of God in it to keep me low; may it be at His *ifootstool*. I abounded also with outward comforts and mitigations. My husband, my sister Buxton, my children, my sister Elizabeth Fry devoted to me, I wanted no outward thing; but was plunged under a deep feeling of my infirmity and great unworthiness before God. I am now much relieved, very thankful, full of love, may I not say to all; sweetly in unity with my beloved Friends at the Yearly Meeting; in degree overflowing towards them all, still abundantly sensible of my unworthiness before the Lord. Oh! may He see meet further to fit me, to suffer as well as to do His will.

20th.—I think I am better, but am remarkably reduced for so short an illness. If during such times of trial, or in the end,—I am supported, the whole glory must be given to God; for I think it impossible for any one to be more naturally distressed or overset by bodily illness. Even if my sun sets under a cloud, all must be laid to my great natural infirmity in this respect. With God all things are possible, but if He should see meet at that awful hour to hide Himself from me, may none be discouraged; but all look upon it as a dispensation permitted in some way for good. In times of health, also at times in sickness, I have had to rejoice in His salvation, and frequently when most favoured with clearness of judgment, have perceived the wisdom and mercy of all his dispensations, particularly some of these afflictive ones. Why He saw meet to permit sin to come into the world is not for us poor frail finite mortals to comprehend ; but that we have an enemy to buffet us, I cannot doubt.   May we look to that blessed day, when God shall be all in all and shall put all enemies under His feet, even Death itself.   Dearest Lord, increase my faith more firmly, more fixedly establish me upon the Rock of Ages, that however the winds blow, the rains descend, or the floods beat against me, I may not be greatly moved ; and let not any of the hindering or polluting things of this world lessen my love to Thee and to Thy cause ; or prevent me from going steadily forward in heights and in depths, in riches and in poverty, in strength and in weakness, in sickness and in health ; or prevent my following hard after Thee in spirit, with a humble, faithful, watchful, circumspect, and devoted heart.   Amen.

21st.—The day before yesterday the wedding was accomplished. The Meeting was solemn and satisfactory.   Our bride and bridegroom spoke well, and with feeling.   My dearest brother Joseph prayed for them and ministered to them, as did others ; I prayed at the close of the Meeting most earnestly for them, for the other young people, and ourselves further advanced in life.   After a short solemn silence the certificate was read and signed.   In the morning we had a satisfactory reading with our children.

Thanks be to our Heavenly Father, there was, I think, throughout the day a great mixture of real solemnity with true cheerfulness.   It was certainly no common day.   William Foster Reynolds and his wife, my husband and myself, with nineteen of our own children in the two families, besides children-in-law and some grandchildren, and nine of my brothers and sisters.   Through everything, order, quietness and cheerfulness were remarkably maintained.   After dinner I returned thanks for our many blessings, and could with a few present feel how many outward deliverances we had experienced ; that we had had our heads kept above the waters, spiritually and temporally, and were able to have such a day of rejoicing.   Our dear bride and bridegroom left us in the afternoon.   The evening was fine, and our lawn looked really beautiful, covered with the large and interesting party.   In the evening we assembled together, and had a solemn religious time ;

giving, I trust, the praise that was due alone to Him from whom all good and blessings flow.

This marriage was hailed by Elizabeth Fry with sincere pleasure : not only was the connexion highly acceptable to her, and one that she believed likely to promote the happiness of her child, but it also possessed what was, in her estimation, the peculiar advantage, of being with a member of the Society of Friends. Whilst her hospitable and affectionate nature was gratified with the prospect of receiving the bridal party at Plashet, she craved spiritual blessings for the two most interested, and that the occasion, like the marriage at Cana in Galilee, might be owned by the presence of the Lord. It was a beautiful summer day,—the sun shone brilliantly,—Plashet was arrayed in all its verdure, gay with bright flowers, and sprinkled with groups of happy young people. After the bride was gone, one of the sisters crossed the lawn to speak to her mother, she said something of the scene before them, and the outward prosperity which seemed to surround that beloved parent. The reply was remarkable; for, after expressing a strong feeling of gratification and enjoyment, she added, in words which have rivetted themselves upon the memory of her, to whom they were addressed ; " But I have remarked, that when great outward prosperity is granted, it is often permitted to precede great trials." There is an old rhyme which says,

> " When joy seemeth highest
> Then sorrow is nighest !"

Surely this was verified, in the contrast between that day and the scenes, which so shortly followed in that long-loved home.

Shortly after the wedding, the family removed to Dagenham for their summer retreat ; and in the autumn Mrs. Fry accompanied her husband into the North of England, where he went on account of some business transactions. In this journey, her daughter Hannah was with her. She received at that time, as she had

frequently done before, very great kindness from her valued friends
of the Benson family.   Nor was theirs the friendship which
existed only in the day of sunshine ; for when so soon afterwards
the storm arose, and adversity prevailed, they were among those
whose efficient kindness was singularly manifested.

Plashet, Eleventh Month 4th.—I have been favoured to
partake of very sweet feelings of peace, and refreshment of soul,
since my return home ; that which I am ready to believe, in the
most unmerited mercy, is something of the " Well of water
springing up unto eternal life." But I find outwardly and about
me there are storms,˜ not at present so much in my very own
borders, as close to them.

15th.—The storm has now entered my own borders—once more
we are brought into perplexity and trial ; but I have this consolation, " He will regard the prayer of the destitute, and not despise
their prayer." To whom can I go in this time of emergency,
but to Him who hitherto has helped me, and provided for me
and mine in a marvellous manner—made darkness light before
me and crooked things straight.   Lord ! Thou who remainest
to be the God of my life, above all things, in this our sorrow
and perplexity cast us not out of thy presence, and take not
Thy Holy Spirit from us; keep us from evil and from the
appearance of it ; that through the help of Thy Spirit our conduct may be kept upright, circumspect and clean in Thy sight,
and amongst men ! that in all things, at all times, and under
all circumstances, we may show forth Thy praise. Keep us in
love and unity with those with whom we have to act, even if they
do contrary to our wishes and judgment. But, oh, dearest Lord,
if it be Thy holy will, make a way of escape for us, from the
calamity we so much dread, and continue in Thy unmerited mercy
to provide for Thy unworthy servant, her family and all concerned
in this trial, that we may not want what is good and needful for
us, and that others may be kept from suffering through us. If
it be possible remove this bitter cup from us ; yet if it be Thy
will that we drink it, enable us through the grace and spirit of
Him who suffered for us, to drink it without repining,—yet
trusting in Thy love, Thy mercy and Thy judgment.

But it was not at this time, the will of God to remove the bitter cup from His servant, but rather to grant strength and grace to drink of it, as coming from His Holy hand.

It is a marvellous thing to the natural mind of man, and wholly beyond the unassisted scope of his reasoning powers, why, eminent Christians are often so intensely afflicted. Faith's estimate is different, and holy writ solves the problem, by showing us that it is by this process they are fitted for the heavenly inheritance, the most fine gold purified, the diamond of the first water polished for the Master's use.

The failure of one of the houses of business in which her husband was a partner, though not that which he personally conducted, involved Elizabeth Fry and her family in a train of sorrows and perplexities which tinged the remaining years of her life. Nature staggered beneath the blow ; but the staff on which she leaned could not fail her, and she fell not.

Eleventh Month 25th.—I have been brought at times, into little short of anguish of spirit ; not I think so much for what we must suffer ourselves, as for what others may suffer. The whole thing appears fraught with distress. When I look at this mysterious dispensation permitted by Almighty wisdom, I am ready to say, How is it Lord, Thou dealest thus with Thy servant, who loves Thee, trusts in Thee, and fears Thy name—and then I say this is my infirmity, thus to query. Need I not chastisement ? do I not deserve it ? may it not be a mysterious dispensation of deep and sore affliction, laid not only upon us, but upon others, to draw us all more from the things of time, and to set us more on the enduring riches of Eternity. I cannot reason upon it, I must bow, and only bow and say in my heart, which I believe I do, " Not as I will, but as Thou wilt." Well, if it be of the Lord, let Him do as seemeth Him good. Lord let Thy grace be found sufficient for us in this most awful time, and grant that we faint not when Thou rebukest us !

The following Sunday the question was much debated, as to

whether she, and her family generally, should attend their Meeting for worship or not ; but she felt it right to go, and of course was accompanied by her husband and children. She took her usual seat, bowed down and overwhelmed, with the bitter tears rolling down her cheeks—no common thing with her.

After a very solemn pause she rose with these words, her voice trembling with emotion : " Though He slay me yet will I trust in Him ;" and testified, in a short and beautiful discourse, that her faith and love were as strong in the hour of adversity, as they had been in the time of prosperity. Her friends were deeply affected, marking by their manner their sympathy and love.

To her only absent child she wrote.

Plashet, *Eleventh Month 27th*, 1828.

My dearest R——

I have at last taken up my pen to write to thee ; but to one so near, and so much one with myself, it is difficult. I do not like to pour out my sorrows too heavily upon thee, nor do I like to keep thee in the dark as to our real state. This is, I consider, one of the deepest trials to which we are liable ; its perplexities are so great and numerous, its mortifications and humiliations so abounding, and its sorrows so deep. None can tell but those who have passed through it, the anguish of heart at times felt ; but thanks be to our God, this extreme state of distress has not been very frequent, nor its continuance very long. I frequently find my mind in degree sheathed to the deep sorrows, and am enabled not to look so much at them ; but there are also times, when secondary things arise—parting with servants, the poor around us, schools, and our dear Place. These things overwhelm me ; indeed I think naturally I have a very acute sense of the sorrow. Then the bright side of the picture rises : I have found much help and strength in prayer to God ; and highly mysterious as in some points of view this dispensation may be, yet I think I have frequently, if not generally, come to be able to say, " Not as I will, but as Thou wilt," and to bow under it. All our children, and children-in-law, my brothers and sisters, our many friends and servants, have been a strong

consolation to me ; and, above all, a little refreshment to my
tribulated spirit has been granted me at times, from what I trust
are the well springs from on High.

To her Sister, Mrs. Buxton.

Plashet, *Twelfth Month 2nd.*

MY DEAREST HANNAH,

I have received your valuable and excellent letters ; and the
advice, as well as consolation in them, I trust will do us all good.
My desire is, that we may entirely and altogether bow under our
circumstances and the various pains attached to them. I feel
with thee, and have felt all along, that a still greater pain and
trial might in many ways have been permitted us ; but one of its
deepest stings is from the peculiar and perplexing nature of it.
It abounds with temptation, as my dear friend, Mary S——, so
deeply felt under similar circumstances ; but there is a power that
can preserve amidst them all, and in this power I trust. I see
that I have many blessings left, and do earnestly desire to estimate
them as I ought. Your very kind offer for Hannah, I do not at
present think it right to accept ; I think it better for her to drink
the cup with us for a time, but I may be glad before long gratefully to accept it. I feel all your kindness, and trust I shall never
be a burden to any of you. I expect our way will open ; we must
commit it in faith.

The tide of sympathy flowed in marvellously from all quarters.
The mass of letters that exist, attest by how many, and how well,
she was loved ; how highly she was valued, and upon how many
hearts, she and her sorrows were borne.

Amongst such numerous communications, it is difficult to
select ; but a few of them ought to be known, to give some idea
of the feeling excited towards her amongst persons of different
classes and denominations.

From William Wilberforce, Esq.

"*Farnham Castle, 29th November,* 1828.

" My dear friend,

" Though my eyes are just now weaker than usual, I must claim a short exercise of their powers, for the purpose of expressing to you the warm sympathy which Mrs. Wilberforce, and, indeed, all of my family that have the pleasure of knowing you, as well as myself, are feeling on your account. Yet you, I doubt not, will be enabled to *ifeel* as well as to *know,* that even this event will be one of those which in your instance are working for good. You have been enabled to exhibit a bright specimen of Christian excellence in *doing* the will of God, and, I doubt not, you will manifest a similar specimen in the harder and more difficult exercise of *suffering* it. I have often thought, that we are sometimes apt to forget that key, for unlocking what we deem a very mysterious dispensation of Providence, in the misfortunes and afflictions of eminent servants of God, that is afforded by a passage in St. Paul's Epistle to his beloved Philippians ' Unto you it is given not only to believe on Him, but also to suffer for His sake.' It is the strong only that will be selected for exhibiting those graces which require peculiar strength. May you, my dear friend, (indeed, I doubt not you will) be enabled to bear the whole will of God, with cheerful confidence in His unerring wisdom, and unfailing goodness. May every loss of this world's wealth, be more than compensated by a larger measure of the unsearchable riches of Christ. You will not forget that the time is short ; but there will be no end to that eternity of happiness and glory which, I doubt not, will in your instance follow it. Meanwhile, you are richly provided with relatives and friends, whom you love so well as to relish receiving kindnesses from them, as well as the far easier office of doing them. That you may be blessed with a long continuance of usefulness and comfort in this world, to be followed by a still better portion in a better, is the cordial wish, and shall be the prayer also, of (begging from you a frequent performance of the last-named office of friendship for myself and mine).

" My dear Mrs. Fry,

" Your sincere and affectionate Friend,

" W. Wilberforce."

Mrs. Backhouse addressed Mrs. Fry's sister, Mrs. Samuel Hoare, finding it less difficult to express to her the earnest breathings of her heart for one united to her, not alone by ties of consanguinity, but by a close agreement in religious opinions and spiritual experience.

"26th of Eleventh Month, 1828.

" I have felt far too much for her (Elizabeth Fry), and for many of her family, not to acknowledge a little of the near and dear sympathy I feel for her and for them. I hardly know how to express it to herself immediately ; through thee I can do it more easily. I think if ever I have known what sympathy is, it has been with her, and especially at times during the course of the last year or two, it has sometimes nearly melted all within me to come near her. Well, I can make no doubt she is graven on His hands, who chooses his servants in the furnace of affliction, and that in due time she will come out of this yet more pure. Deep searchings of heart may be her portion, yet I trust the enemy will not be suffered to prevail, so as to call her good evil, either in her own estimation, or in the estimation of those among whom she has stood so high. I think I never loved her half so much before."

From the Rev. John W. Cunningham.

" Harrow, November 26th, 1828.

" My very dear friend,

" I need not tell you, with what sorrow, I have received the most unexpected intelligence which reached me yesterday. It is but a short time, since I was called to sympathize with a near relative in similar circumstances, and now again I am called to mourn as for a brother and a friend. My experience in the former case, has enabled me to take a more hopeful and cheerful view of your heavy trial. Perhaps, dear friend, this event may be made a blessing to every member of your family ; and we must not complain of a little rough handling when the jewels are to be polished for the treasury of God. All that drives us home to Him, and to the power of His spirit, for grace, and strength, and joy, is beyond all price to the soul.   Is it not a comfort to you, dear friend, at this moment, that you have spent so much of your time and property for God and for His creatures.   Is not money given to the poor lent to the Lord, and to be returned again in some form or other, "with usury!"   I beg my very kind remembrances to Mr. Fry, and your dear children.   I have already been led to pray for them more than once, that this affliction may be sanctified to them ; and that they may more and more seek the durable riches of the kingdom of Christ.

" My wife unites with me in very kind regards, and I am very affectionately yours.

" J. W. CUNNINGHAM."

FROM HER BROTHER-IN-LAW, T. F. BUXTON, ESQ.
(AFTERWARDS SIR T. FOWELL BUXTON).

"Northrepps, December 1st, 1828.

" MY DEAREST SISTER,

" I have hitherto, I confess, shrunk from writing to you. Not surely, however, from any want of feeling for you, and with you ; but from so deep a sense of your calamity, as to make all attempts at comfort appear almost idle. A very quiet day yesterday, and a long time spent over the 69th Psalm, from the 13th to the 17th verse, with peculiar reference to you, have given me more encouragement. I am more able to feel, that we may confidently commit you and yours to that most merciful Lord, from whom the dispensation has come ; and I have been comforted by the reflection, strange comfort as it may seem, that you and all of us have not long to live ; that in truth it signifies little how we fare here for a few years, provided we are safe in that long and endless journey upon which we shall soon enter. I think, however, I have in some degree followed you in the little mortifications, as well as the great ones, of this trial. I am not sure that the great and lasting disaster is so galling to my mind at the moment, as some of the little provoking and humbling attendants on it. But since the time I spent in heart with you yesterday, I have been able in some measure to get rid of these intruders, and to look upon you under the aspect of one beloved of God, honoured of men, and more than ever loved, cherished, and delighted in, by a large brotherhood. I never felt so keenly as now, the privilege of belonging to you, or so conscious of the honour and the benefit of such a sister ; and I feel no distrust about your future lot. I cannot doubt that years of contentment and happiness await you. I expect that your light will shine forth more brightly than ever. You have ever been a teacher to the whole family, and now, I am confidently persuaded, you will instruct us with what humility, with what submission, and with what faith, we ought to bear the deepest trials. What comes from above cannot be bad for us ; and under the sense of this, I adopt David's words, ' Why art thou cast down, Oh my soul ! and why art thou disquieted within me ; hope thou in God, for thou shalt yet praise him.'

" Ever, my dearest Betsey,

" Your most affectionate brother,

" T. F. BUXTON."

The following extract is from a letter addressed by the Marquis of Cholmondely to Mrs. Opie, inquiring after Mrs. Fry. He had been acquainted with her for many years, and his friendship was highly valued by her ; he had supported many of her benevolent objects, and had strenuously exerted himself in behalf of more than one wretched object, at the time when executions for forgery were so rife at the Old Bailey.

" It is a consolation to hear that that exemplary woman, Mrs. Fry, is enabled to look to her God in this hour of trial, and I do hope that she may be yet made an instrument of much good ; even if her own ability should unfortunately be lessened, she has the comfort of knowing that she began the good work of Prison Reform. I have seen it suggested, in the " Record" newspaper, that it would be grateful to Mrs. Fry's feelings, if additional subscriptions were now made to one or two societies which have lost so much, owing to the stop which has been put to her benevolent exertions. I should be much obliged to you to let me know if there is any truth in this suggestion."

FROM MRS. OFIE.

"Twelfth Month 17th (First-day morning), 1828.

" Though I have not hitherto felt free in mind to write to thee, my very dear friend, under thy present most severe trial, thou hast been continually, I may say, in my thoughts, brought feelingly and solemnly before me, both day and night. But I am now desired by thy sister Catherine to tell thee, that she will be with thee to-morrow evening. I must also tell thee, to please myself, that two nights ago I had a pleasing cheering dream of thee !—

" I saw thee looking thy best, drest with peculiar care and neatness, and smiling so brightly that I could not help stroking thy cheek, and saying, ' dear friend ! it is quite delightful to me to see thee looking thus again, so like the Betsey Fry of former days ;' and then I woke. But this sweet image of thee lives with me still, and I trust, that when this dark cloud has passed away from you (as it has passed away from so many, many others), I shall not only see thee in a dream, but in reality, as those who love thee, desire to see thee always.

" Since your trials were known, I have rarely, if ever, opened a page of scripture, without finding some promise, applicable to thee and thine. I do not believe that I was looking for them, but they presented themselves unsought, and gave me comfort and confidence. Do not suppose, dear friend, that I am not fully aware of the peculiar bitterness and suffering which attends this trial in thy situation to thy own individual feelings ; but then, how precious and how cheering to thee must be the evidence it has called forth, of the love and respect of those who are near and dear to thee, and of the public at large ! Adversity is indeed the time to try the hearts of our friends, and it. must be now, or will be in future, a cordial to thee, to remember that thou hast proved how truly and generally thou art beloved and reverenced."

The committee of the Ladies British Society evinced their deep sympathy, in a letter from one of their members, Miss Neave.

"Albemarle Street, *Tuesday Night.*

" I was deputed by our friends of the British Society Committee to address our dear absent leader, which under these circumstances will not be considered an intrusion. No answer is claimed. Your note was read, and its contents received with strong emotion ; and ere it was read, prayer had been made orally and silently, I need not add fervently, for you and yours.

" The conduct of the Navy Board, and the account of the Penitentiary being completed for the convicts on their arrival, were cheering circumstances. How pleasant to find that text verified, ' They that wait upon the Lord shall renew their strength.' May you, my dear friend, under your present afflicting trial, find every part of this text verified in your experience. May you mount up as with eagle's wings above every earthly cloud, and be enabled to fix your eye solely on the Sun of Righteousness, who has arisen for you, with healing on his wings, who has received gifts, and laid them up for you. You may have need of patience, but may the Spirit, the Comforter, make you now to feel what He has indited—that afflictions are light, and the glory that awaits the Christian a weight ; you have received the earnest, having been sealed with that Holy Spirit of promise, and the purchased possession is yours : all things are yours, and all things must work together for your good, for thus saith the Lord. We have His oath and His promise, and nothing can separate us from His love.

" My dear friend, you cannot now trace God, but you can trust Him ; if you can no longer equally relieve the temporal wants of others, you may still minister to their spiritual necessities ; and your inability may open other sources, and teach those who before were inactive, to labour : be that as it may, the poor are God's creatures, not ours, and His will must be done in this also. I have continued still to place my Asylum women most advantageously ; there are now thirty-two, of whom we entertain no doubt, who have been many of them from one to four years in respectable service.

" And now, my dear friend, commending you, and all that are near and dear to you, to the care of the good Shepherd of the

sheep : his own sheep, whom He knows by name, and with
whom in all their affliction He is afflicted.

" I remain,

" Yours, with much esteem and affliction,

" C. H. NEAVE."

A severe accident to her eldest grandson, for a few days detained his mother in Norfolk. She had last seen Plashet really
and figuratively basking in sunshine. All the family had been
assembled then, all were again together; there was the same
pleasant dwelling, the same expanse of verdure, the same beloved
ones to receive her; but all was changed. The countenance and
effect of her mother at that time, were emphatically her own—
an expression of such intense suffering, and yet such immoveable
peace. Her soft full-toned voice, saddened, yet sweet as ever;
her chastened smile, whilst she could point to better days, and
hopes to be fulfilled, even in this life; and then the wonderful
judgment—clear, discerning, and practical—with which she would
enter into details so little suited for women, and without minutely
following their different points, from her ready quickness, arrive
at true and just conclusions.

She had a quality difficult to describe, but marked to those
who knew her well: the power of rapidly, and by a process of
thought that she could herself hardly have explained, arriving at
the truth, striking the balance, and finding the just weight of a
doubtful question; nothing could be more valuable than this
quality, under such circumstances.

Mr. and Mrs. Fry resolved upon at once leaving Plashet, and
seeking a temporary home in St. Mildred's Court, then the residence of their eldest son. One immense mitigation attended this
calamity: that the mercantile business formerly their grandfather's,
and conducted by their father, remained to the young men of the
family; who were thus enabled, with the important aid of their
mother's brothers, to re-establish their parents in comfort. With

leaving Plashet came much that was sad—uprooting habits, long-formed tastes and local associations ; parting with servants, and leaving many old pensioners and dependants.

The surrounding poor found a kind and judicious friend in the Vicar of East Ham (of which parish Plashet is a hamlet), to whom the living had very recently been presented. He had come to reside in his parish, a circumstance which had not occurred in that place for a series of years. To him, the schools hitherto supported by Mr. and Mrs. Fry, conjointly with William Morley, Esq., of Green-street House, were transferred, and in his hands and under his care, they have since remained and flourished.

It was no easy thing to arrange for a very large family party, accustomed to country habits, and the liberty of space, when confined to a city dwelling ; and that under circumstances of such peculiar pain. Mrs. Fry had for many years displayed singular wisdom and economy in her household arrangements, as well as in her charities and benevolent objects ; varying according to the various circumstances in which she had been placed. To " be just before generous," was a maxim often expressed to those around her. On this occasion, these powers were called into full action. As the winter advanced, her health greatly failed. Circumstances occurred to weaken her husband and children's attachment to the Society of Friends : truly the sorrows of her heart were enlarged. She exclaims in her journal (which was very irregularly kept), that her " soul was bowed down within her, and her eyes were red with weeping." Yet was she enabled to adopt the language, " I will hope continually, and yet praise Thee more and more ;" and also to acknowledge that she was much sustained inwardly, and that at times her heart was kept almost in perfect peace. But in addition to domestic trials, her tender feelings were at times grievously and unnecessarily wounded ; from without, there was much of bitterness infused into her daily cup, which can only be appreciated by those, who have had to bear the brunt of a similar calamity.

Plashet, Twelfth Month 16*th.*—I have had some quiet peaceful hours, but I continue in the low valley, and naturally feel too much, leaving this sweet home; but not being well makes my spirits more weak than usual. I desire not only to be resigned, but cheerfully willing to give up whatever is required of me, and in all things patiently to submit to the will of God, and to estimate my many remaining blessings. I am sorry to find how much I cleave to some earthly things—health, ease, places, possessions. Lord, Thou alone canst enable me to estimate them justly, and to keep them in their right places. In thine own way, dearest Lord, accomplish Thine own work in me, to Thine own praise! grant that out of weakness I may yet be made strong, and through Thy power wax valiant in fight; and may I yet, if consistent with Thy holy will, see the travail of my soul and be satisfied, as it respects myself and my most tenderly beloved family. Amen!

Mildred's Court, First Month 19*th,* 1829.—My first journal in this year! What an eventful one was the last! prosperity and adversity were peculiarly our portion. It has been in no common degree a picture of life comprised in a small compass. However, through all, in prosperity and in adversity, however bright or cloudy my present position or my prospects may be, my desire for myself, and all whom I love is this : so strongly expressed by the Psalmist, " I will hope continually, and yet praise Thee more and more ! " So be it, saith my soul, and if it be the Lord's will, may light rise in our present obscurity, and our darkness become as the noonday, both as to temporal and spiritual prospects !

The deep discouragement passed through by Mrs. Fry at this period, is evinced by the following letter from her kind and faithful friend, Mr. Wilberforce, to whom it would appear, by the reply, that she had expressed some doubts of the propriety of resuming her labours in the prisons.

"Highwood Hill, Middlesex, 30*th* *January*, 1829.

" MY DEAR FRIEND,

" Though my eyes are just now so indifferent that I must be extremely sparing in the use of my pen, yet I cannot forbear or delay assuring you, that I do not see how it is possible for any reasonable being to doubt the propriety (that is a very inadequate way of speaking—let me rather say, absolute duty), of your renewing your prison visitations. A gracious Providence has blessed you with success in your endeavours to impress a set of miserables, whose character and circumstances might almost have extinguished hope; and you will return to them, if with diminished pecuniary powers, yet we may trust, through the mercy and goodness of our Heavenly Father, with powers of a far higher order unimpaired, and with the augmented respect and regard of every sound judgment, not merely of every Christian mind, for having borne with becoming dispositions, a far harder trial (for such it is) certainly than any stroke which proceeds immediately from the hand of God. May you continue, my dear madam, to be the honoured instrument of great and rare benefits to almost the most pitiable of your fellow-creatures.

" Mrs. Wilberforce desires to join with me in saying, that we hope we shall again have the pleasure of seeing you, by and by, at this place. Meanwhile, with every kind regard and friendly remembrances to Mr. Fry, and your family circle,

" I remain, with cordial esteem and regard,

" My dear friend, very sincerely yours,

" W. WILBERFORCE."

Mildred's Court, Third Month.—It appears late to begin the journal of a year; but the constant press of engagements, and the numerous interruptions to which I am liable in this place, prevent my having time for much writing. We are remaining here with our son and daughter, and their children, until there is some opening for having a settled home. However, my desire is, that we may in faith and in humility entirely bow. I have of late not visited the prisons, and been much occupied at home; but

I trust that I may be permitted to enter this interesting work again, clothed, as with fresh armour, both to defend me, and qualify me for fresh service, that my hands may be taught to war, and my fingers to fight; and that if consistent with the will of my God, I may, through the help of the Captain of my salvation, yet do valiantly.

During that mournful winter in London, there were periods of peculiar suffering and anxiety. Mrs. Fry's own health being so shaken by her severe mental distresses, as nearly to confine her to her room with a bad cough. Her beloved and valued son William was on the bed of sickness from oppression of the brain, the result of an overstrained and exhausted mind. Shortly afterwards, her daughter-in-law was in the same house in an alarming state of illness, and a lady, who came to assist in nursing, was taken ill with the measles. The measles in a grown-up family becomes a serious disease. They were driven from London in consequence, though too late to escape infection, and took shelter in the vacant house at Plashet, which, for many weeks, became a scene of anxious nursing.

Thence they removed, early in June, to a small but commodious dwelling in Upton Lane, immediately adjoining the Ham House grounds, the residence of her beloved brother, Samuel Gurney, Esq.

Upton, 10*th.*—We are now nearly settled in this, our new abode; and I may say, although the house and garden are small, yet it is pleasant and convenient, and I am fully satisfied, and I hope thankful, for such a home. I have at times been favoured to feel great peace, and I may say joy, in the Lord—a sort of seal to the important step taken; though, at others, the extreme disorder into which our things have been brought by all these changes—the pain of leaving Plashet—the difficulty of making new arrangements, has harassed and tried me. But I trust it will please a kind Providence to bless my endeavour, to have and keep my house in order. Place is a matter of small importance, if that peace which the world cannot give, be our portion; even at times, as a brook by the way, to the refreshment of our weary and heavy laden souls. Although a large garden is not now my allotment, I feel pleasure in having even a small one; and my acute relish for the beautiful in nature and art is on a clear day almost constantly gratified by a delightful view of Greenwich Hospital and Park, and other parts of Kent, the shipping on the river, as well as the cattle feeding in the meadows. So that in small things and great, spiritual and temporal, I have yet reason to raise up my Ebenezers, and praise, bless, and magnify the name of my Lord.

Sixth Month 23*rd.*—I little expected to attend the Yearly Meeting, having of late appeared to be so much taken out of such things and such services; but, contrary to my expectation, way opened for me to attend every sitting, and to take rather an active part in it, to my real consolation, refreshment, and help. The unity of Friends was remarkable. I certainly felt very low at its commencement. After having for so many years received dear friends at my house, and that with such heartfelt pleasure, it tried, not to say puzzled me, why such a change was permitted me. But I rest in the weighty import of the words, " That which I do, thou knowest not now, but thou shalt know hereafter."

CHAPTER XVI.

1829, 1830.   Foreign Correspondence—Dr. Julius, Madam de Pastoret,
Madam de Barol—Letter to a daughter—Summons to the sick-bed
of a niece—Poor men by the road-side—Prepares her Text-Book—
Anecdote—Letter—Attends Suffolk Quarterly Meeting—Visits Pake-
field and Earlham—Letter to her children at home—Foreign prisons
—Death of a connexion—Illness of a nephew—Visit to Brighton—
Death of her uncle Robert Barclay, Esquire—Of a little grandchild—
Of a nephew—Of her uncle, Joseph Gurney, Esquire—Attends his
funeral at Norwich—Letter to her family from Earlham—Interest in
prisons unabated—Capital punishment—Prison reform.

AMIDST her own personal sorrows and perplexities, Elizabeth
Fry was cheered from time to time, by finding that the subject
so near her heart continued to prosper.   At Berlin, a Committee
of Ladies had been formed to visit prisons.   Dr. Julius had
informed her, a few months before, of the publication of his
" Lectures on the improvement of Prison-discipline, and on the

moral amendment of Prisoners." Prefixed to them, was a long and laborious introduction on the causes, number, and different kinds of crime, in most of the countries of Europe and in America, with remarks on the most likely means of prevention.

The result of Dr. Julius' observations amounted to this:— that in those countries where the education of the people is decidedly on a moral and religious basis, crime diminishes ; but where instruction aims only at the increase of the means of wealth, and imparting human knowledge, there, crime increases.

From Madam la Marquise de Pastoret, she received interesting accounts of the efforts making in France, amongst pious and benevolent individuals, to benefit the unfortunate. In a letter addressed to Miss Fry, that lady mentions some of the existing associations, and still further enlarges on the subject in another communication to Mrs. Fry of rather later date.

Differing essentially, as do the Protestant churches from that of Rome, they may yet learn from her, in the performance of practical duties towards their fellow-creatures ; for amongst pious Roman Catholics, there is to be found eminent devotedness of purpose, in the fulfilment of these self-imposed offices of mercy. Knowledge and system, it is true, are wanting; for combined endeavour is incompatible with the power of the priest, and cannot exist whilst his will controls, directs, stimulates or arrests exertion. In countries where the laity have no human interposition between God and their own consciences, where education freely flows forth to all, where the Bible is to be found up and down in the lanes and streets of our cities, what might not be effected, if the spirit of self-sacrifice and self-devotion that is to be met with in the prisons and hospitals of Roman Catholic countries, existed and prevailed ?

What is there in our Protestant institutions to prevent sisters of mercy—devoted ones of the female sex—being wholly given to such works ; or amongst the more busy part of mankind, hours

and periods taken from the needful occupations of life, and devoted to good deeds? In the patient teacher of the ragged school,
in the laborious district visitor, who threads his way through the
endless mazes and foul air of the worst parts of our metropolis,
we recognize the dawn of a better day; nor is this hope diminished by the fact, that it is not alone in the middle classes, but
amongst the sons of our nobles and our statesmen, and amongst
those nobles themselves, that may be found the most resolute and
persevering in these labours of love. An immense stimulus is
given to acts of charity, amongst the members of the Church of
Rome, by their favourite dogma, that " good works" can be performed to the exceeding benefit of the individual, and the covering
of many sins; but he who simply takes the Bible as the rule of
life, and receives the words of scripture in their direct and literal
meaning, there learns, that from the moment he has received the
Lord Christ into his heart, his time, and talents, and powers, are
consecrated to His service: not to the exclusion of any relative
or domestic duty, nor to the neglect of his outward calling, but
to the serious consideration of what may be required of him
individually for the service of God, and the good of his fellow-
men. Were this spirit more devoutly entertained, and more
practically exercised in England—civilized, educated, reflecting as
she is—how new an aspect would her children wear: misery and
crime would stalk no longer unchidden through the land; tenderness and sympathy would be offered to the afflicted, counsel
and wise reproof to the offender. The best regulated and well-
planned institution is but a body without a soul, whilst rules and
regulations are enforced, unaccompanied by personal influence or
individual communication. The prisoner, the lunatic, the hospital
patient, require these to touch the heart, to reach the mental
malady, or give confidence under suffering and painful treatment.

Very frequently did Elizabeth Fry urge upon others the importance of these acts of benevolence. She believed that not

merely were they blessed to the receiver ; but to the giver " twice blessed." Earnest were her desires, and strong her hopes, that English men, and English women, would increasingly awake to their responsibilities, that they would not rest content with subscribing of their abundance, or even of their penury, to refuges, to hospitals, and schools, but that they would give of that which is more precious—of time, sympathy, communion between man and man, and mind with mind. For how admirable would be the results, could the well-planned Protestant institutions of Great Britain be visited, and cared for, and watched over, by spontaneous benevolence and unpaid services, with something of the love, and of the zeal, which can illumine even the dark regions of Popery. A greater proof of this devotion, can hardly be found than is pourtrayed in the following letter, describing the Refuge established at Turin, by Madame la Marquise de Barol, neè Colbert, for penitent females.

"Turin, *ce 1er Avril*, 1829.

" C'est avec beaucoup de regret que j'ai appris, Madame, la cause de votre silence ; le mien a aussi été l'effet d'une longue maladie, dont je ne suis pas encore guérie. Elle m'a empêchée, Madame, de vous remercier de votre aimable lettre et des intéressants rapports que vous avez eu la bonté de m'envoyer. Vous désirez que je vous rende compte des soins donnés aux prisonnières, et moi je désire vivement pouvoir faire quelque chose qui vous soit agréable.

" Nous continuons à suivre la même marche pour l'amélioration des prisonnières. Nous sommes le même nombre de personnes, nous employons les mêmes moyens. Quelques heureux résultats nous soutiennent dans une entreprise qui, comme vous le savez mieux que personne, a souvent des moments pénibles. J'espère que cette marche que nous suivons avec uniformité et exactitude, a quelque chose de bon, car elle amène le repentir. J'ai pendant quelque temps, ainsi que je crois vous l'avoir mandé, placé dans différentes maisons des femmes repentantes et sorties de prison. Je croyais qu'il valait mieux les disséminer que de les réunir dans une maison de refuge ; mais l'expérience m'a prouvé combien j'avais tort.   J'ai donc sollicité et obtenu de la bonté du Roi une maison dans un des faux-bourgs de la ville : cette maison peut contenir de 50 à 60 personnes ; elle est dans un bon air ; il y a un grand jardin, une chapelle.   Elle a déjà vingt-sept femmes repenties· Quatre sœurs de St. Joseph (ou de la Charité) sont à la tête de cet établissement.   Il y a un Confesseur, mais point de Directeur. Nous n'avons point de revenus : jusqu'à présent la charité fournit aux besoins de ces pauvres filles.   J'espère avec le tems obtenir de la bonté du Roi un revenu fixe.   Je tâche en attendant de réunir les fonds nécessaires.   Je les remets à la superieure qui ne rend qu'à moi compte de son administration.   Je crois qu'il vaut mieux ici ne pas mettre d'hommes à la tête d'un. établissement de ce genre.   Et j'ai pensé à la manière de me faire remplacer quand la mort viendra interrompre mes soins.   Le travail peut être compté pour quelque chose pour le soutien de l'établissement ; mais comme cette maison est un lieu d'éducation et non une manufacture, le travail ne peut suffire au payement de la nourriture et des vêtemens.   Les femmes apprennent à faire de la toile et des étoffes en coton.   Elles font des robes, des jupons de toute sorte d'ouvrage en tricot.   L'administration du Bureau de la guerre leur donne à coudre des chemises de soldats.   Plusieurs travaillent à faire des gants.   La Supérieure de la maison sait bien blanchir et raccommoder les dentelles.   Elles n'apprennent pas toutes tous ces différents ouvrages ; mais cependant chacune est instruite de manière à avoir plus d'une ressource au moment où elle sort de la maison.   Elles apprennent toutes le Catéchisme, l'Evangile, et à lire ; les plus intelligentes, celles qui le désirent, apprennent aussi à écrire et à compter.

Rien n'est fixé pour le temps de la sortie.   Il faut que l'on sache suffisamment travailler pour pouvoir gagner son pain, et que la conduite soit assez bonne pour que nous puissions espérer que ces pauvres femmes, se trouvant dans les mêmes occasions, n'y commettent plus les mêmes fautes.   J'en ai déjà placé plusieurs qui jusqu'à présent se conduisent fort bien ; dans ce nombre il y en a eu de rendues à leurs parens ; une s'est mariée ; d'autres placées comme servantes ; deux, dont la santé n'était pas trop bonne et qui savaient bien travailler, se sont réunies dans une chambre · elles vivent du produit de leur ouvrage. Le repentir seul donne accès dans cette maison ; et lorqsu'on est renvoyé pour cause de mauvaise conduite, on n'y est jamais plus admis. Il y en a qui quelque fois ont voulu sortir dans un mouvement de colère ou d'inquiétude ; lorsque celles-là sont bien repentantes, on peut encore les recevoir : mais comme il est certain que dans la maison on fait pour leur amandement tout cc que la charité peut inspirer, et qu'on les renvoie parcequ'elles sont incorrigibles, il est nécessaire qu'elles sachent bien qu'une fois chassée de cet asile, il leur est fermé à jamais.

Les filles de la maison de refuge peuvent sortir quelque fois pour des choses nécessaires ; mais toujours accompagnées. Quand elles sortent, elles quittent leur costume. Ce costume, fort simple, est de toile blanche et bleue. Dans les premiers mois elles adoptèrent avec peine ce genre de vêtement, et deux d'entr' elles se sont sauvées de la maison pour ne pas le porter. Maintenant être habillé aux frais de la maison, est une récompense que l'on n'obtient que lorsque l'on sait faire un alphabet en points de marque. Ce travail qui les applique beaucoup et qui est un peu minutieux, a été choisi exprès pour les obliger à l'application, et profiter du premier moment de ferveur qui les amène. Les pénitences sont toutes fort légères. La plus grande est de manger à genoux au milieu du réfectoire, de ne manger que du pain et boire de l'eau, et de garder le silence pendant l'heure de ses récréations. La manière d'infliger les pénitences était cc qui m'embarrassait le plus, car, toutes ces femmes étant à peu près d'un âge où l'on doit être raisonnable, il était très-embarrassant de les traiter comme des enfans. D'ailleurs elles sont non seulement volontairement dans cette maison, mais y être admises est une récompense. Aussi ai-je pris le parti d'établir que cc soient elles-mêmes qui demandent la punition. Jc leur ai expliqué qu'elles étaient ainsi plus utiles, plus méritoires, et cette méthode a apporté beaucoup de calme et de paix dans l'intérieur. Quand une fille a fait quelque faute, elle demande elle-même sa pénitence, et le plus souvent la Supérieure à qui elle s'adresse, est moins sévère que la coupable ne l'est pour elle-même, et retranche une partie dc la pénitence demandée.

" Dans les premiers tems j'avais promis aux repenties de leur donner, au moment de leurs sortie, le tiers de l'ouvrage qu'elles auraient fait dans la maison ; mais j'ai trouvé à cet arrangement un inconvénient. Elles calculaient l'argent qu'elles pouvaient avoir, faisaient des projets, des plans qui nuisaient à la subordination. Maintenant elles se fient à moi, comme elles le feraient à une mère occupée de leur bien. Comme je l'ai dit au commencement, il n'y a point de Directeur ou d'administrateur dans cet établissement. Jc vois dans la prison des jeunes filles qui annoncent les meilleures dispositions. Je les fais mettre dans une chambre séparée sous la tutelle d'une prisonnière, dont la conduite est bonne et les sentimens religieux ; et après un peu de temps d'épreuves, quand le terme de la condamnation est arrivé, ou bien si je puis obtenir grâce, ce qui m'arrive quelque fois, je conduis (le plus souvent moi-même) les repenties de la prison à la maison du refuge. Quand l'une d'elles arrive, elle se met aux genoux de la supérieure à qui on donne le titre de mère. Elle lui demande de la recevoir par charité au nombre de ses enfants. Elle lui promet obéissance : l'obéissance, le silence et la prière sont les bases du régime moral de cette maison. Une grande douceur est aussi indispensable ; c'est par elle que l'on ramène au bon Pasteur ses brebis égarées. Quant au régime physique, il est simple et entremêlé de mouvement et de travail. On se lève á cinq heures, et on se couche à neuf. Il y a, outre le temps des repas, deux heures de recréation par jour, pendant les quelles on court dans le jardin. On joue à des jeux propres à leur faire faire de l'exercice. Leur nourriture est grossière, mais saine et abondante. Elles ont du pain blanc à discrétion, deux soupes par jour, et à l'heure du diner des légumes et de la viande. Elles boivent du vin mêlé avec beaucoup d'eau, excepté celles qui travaillent à faire la toile et à qui l'on donne un verre de vin pur. La chaleur et l'humidité de ce climat obligent à ne point refuser cette boisson fortifiante.

Il me semble, madame, que je vous donne des détails trop minutieux ; mais votre amour du bien vous fera, j'ose l'espérer, prendre de l'intérêt à tout cc qui est essayé pour l'obtenir. Permettez moi encore avant de finir cette lettre, de vous faire part d'une bonne action d'une de mes prisonnières : elle était avec quatre de ses compagnes et une surveillante dans une chambre séparée où elles attendent leur sortie de prison pour venir au refuge.   Mais comme il ne serait pas prudent d'en faire entrer un grand nombre à la fois, je les avais prévenues que je les prendrais l'une après l'autre, choisissant toujours celles qui se conduiraient le mieux.   Elles se piquérent d'honneur ; et vraiment sans injustice, je ne pouvais faire un choix.   Je fis tirer au sort leurs noms qui avaient été écrits sur des morceaux de papier.   Le nom de Thérése Borat sortit le premier ; toutes les autre se mirent à pleurer, en disant : " au moins si ce n'était pas celle-là ! elle sait un peu lire et nous apprend, afin que nous ne soyons pas si ignorantes en arrivant au refuge." Je fis sortir Thérése un instant de la chambre, et je lui dis : Tu vois le chagrin de tes compagnes ; il ne vient point de jalousie ; mais elles regrettent de perdre en toi un moyen de s'instruire. Dans ta vie, mon enfant, tu as nui à ton prochain ; tu l'as aidé à mal faire ; tu lui as donné de mauvais exemples : veux-tu réparer cela, et céder ta place à une autre pour continuer à instruire celles qui restent ? "Elle me répondit : " Oh ! oui, Madame, je veux faire tout ce que vous croirez bien, tout pour réparer mes fautes." Elle rentra, et dit à ses compagnes : "je ne sortirai que la dernière." Ce qui ajoute à sa bonne action, c'est que nous étions au milieu de l'hiver, et qu'elle était fort mal couverte par une vieille robe de toile.   Je lui ai, comme vous pensez, donné tout de suite des vêtemens chauds ; mais elle est restée la dernière, et, depuis son entrée dans la maison du refuge, elle continue à se bien conduire. Ces pauvres filles ont un grand esprit de prosélytisme : elles m'avertissent que, dans tel lieu, je trouverai un être faible, coupable, qu'un peu de secours aiderait à sortir du vice ; et, quand je puis suivre leurs conseils et amener, parmi les repenties, celles que leurs vœux ont appelées, c'est une grande joie ; mais ces événemens sont rares.   En général toutes les habitantes du refuge ont été habitantes de la prison.

"Il faut cependant finir cette lettre : je voudrais, Madame, vous offrir encore l'assurance de tout le prix que j'attache à votre souvenir, à votre amitié.   Veuillez me les conserver et croire à ma reconnaissance.

"LA MARQUISE DE BAROL NÉE COLBERT."

Eighth Month 29th.—Our wedding-day! twenty-nine years since we married! My texts for the morning are applicable:— " Our light affliction which is but for a moment, worketh for us a far more exceeding and eternal weight of glory."—" We walk by faith, not by sight." As far as we can judge from external appearances, mine has not been a common life. He who seeth in secret, only knows the unutterable depths and sorrows, I have had to pass through, as well as at other times, I may almost say, joys inexpressible and full of glory. I have now had so many disappointments in life, that my hopes, which have so long lived strong, that I should see much brighter days in it, begin a little to subside, and my desire is, more entirely to look beyond the world, for that which can alone fully satisfy me ; and not to have my heart so much set upon the things of this life ; or even those persons nearest to me, but more set upon the life to come ; and upon Him who is faithful, and will be all in all to His dependent ones. At the same I desire faithfully to perform all my relative duties ; and may my heart be kept in tender love to all near to me.

Upton, Tenth Month 21st.—Something has occurred which has brought me into conflict of mind ; how far to restrain young persons in their pleasures, and how far to leave them at liberty. The longer I live, the more difficult do I see education to be ; more particularly, as it respects the religious restraints that we put upon our children ; to do enough, and not too much, is a most delicate and important point. I begin seriously to doubt, whether as it respects the peculiar scruples of Friends, it is not better, quite to leave sober-minded young persons to judge for themselves. Then the question arises—When does this age arrive? I have such a fear that in so much mixing religion, with those things which are not delectable, we may turn them from the thing itself. I see, feel, and know, that where these scruples are adopted from principle, they bring a blessing with them ; but where they are only adopted out of conformity to the views of others, I have very serious doubts whether they are not a stumbling-block

On First-day, we were rather suddenly summoned to Plashet House, to attend Anna Golder (aunt to my faithful Chrissy)

who had charge of the house.   She was one of the lowly, retired,
humble walkers before the Lord ; she was suddenly taken very
ill, and died in half-an-hour after her niece got there.   It was
apparently a departure without sting, to mind or body ; as far
therefore as it respected her, all was peace.   But to myself it was
different.   I arrived there after dark, drove once more into the
dear old place—no one to meet me but the poor man who lived
in the house, no dog to bark, nor any life, nor sound, as used
to be.   Death seemed over the place.   Such was the silence, until
I found myself up stairs in the large, and once cheerful and full
house ; when I entered the bed-room, there lay the corpse, in
her gown, she having died in her chair, only our washerwoman
and the woman who lived in the house in the room besides.
Circumstances combined to touch some very tender feelings,
and the inclination of my heart was to bow down upon my
knees before the Lord ; thankful, surely, for the release of the
valued departed ; but deeply and affectingly impressed with such
a change ! that once lively, sweet, cheerful home left desolate—
the abode of death—and two or three watchers.   It brought, as
my visits to Plashet often have done, the hymn to my mind,—

> " Lord, why is this ? I trembling, cried."

Then again I find I can do nothing, but bow, trust, and depend
upon that Power, that has, I believe, thus seen meet to visit us
in judgment as well as in mercy !

31st.—Since I last wrote I have been called to another death-
bed scene : our old and valued Roman Catholic friends, the P——s,
have lost their eldest son, a sweet good boy.   I felt drawn in love,
I trust I may say, Christian love, to be much with them during
their trial ; I felt it right to leave my family, and spend First-day
evening with them, when all hope of the child's life was given up.
I had not only to sympathise with them in their deep sorrow,
but to pour forth my prayer on their behalf.   The next day, I
was with the poor child when he died, and was nearly the whole
day devoted to them.   We had a deeply interesting time after
his death—my dear friends themselves, all their children, their
mother, sister, and old nurse.   My mouth was remarkably

opened in prayer and praises, indeed, all day at their house something of a holy influence appeared to be over us.   A fresh living
proof that what God had cleansed we are not to call, or to feel
common nor unclean.   It surely matters not by what name we
call ourselves, or what outward *means* we may think right to
use, if our hearts are but influenced by the love of Christ, and
cleansed by His baptism, and strengthened by His Spirit, to
prove our faith by love and good works.   With ceremonies, or
without ceremonies, if there be but an establishment upon the
Rock of Ages, all will be well. Although I am of opinion, the more
our religion is pure, simple, and devoid of these outward forms,
the better and the safer for us ; at the same time, I do earnestly
desire a more full union amongst all Christians ; less judging one
another, and a general acknowledgment, in heart, judgment, and
word, of the universality of the love of God in Christ Jesus
our Lord.

To her youngest Daughter, who was spending the
autumn at Earlham—

My dearest Louisa,

It is rather too long since I wrote thee a full letter.   Having
J—— H—— here is quite a pleasure to us, he is better, but I
am doubtful whether he will be fit for school next week ; we
moderately employ him, and I think the real quiet he has here
will be very useful to him.   It appears to me, and tell thy uncle
and aunt so, that his mind has been rather overworked, a little
above his years.   I see great advantage in children being well
employed and industrious ; but their minds, particularly at an
early age, require a good deal of rest and recreation, which gives
power in future to receive and retain knowledge.   Dr. Babington
told me, he thought children in the present day suffered materially
in body by over-study, particularly boys ; and that Latin and
Greek were too much pressed upon them.   But at thy age, my
dearest girl, which is so much more mature, I think it the time to
work, and that very diligently.   When the soil is prepared before,
and a good foundation laid, which I hope in some degree is thy

case, *real* accomplishment is easily received and retained from fifteen to eighteen years of age.   It is a time when good habits should be formed, and good seed thrown in, that will tell in a future day.

Farewell my darling girl.   Be sober, and watch unto prayer; and may the God of peace be with thee.

Thy loving, tender mother,

ELIZABETH FRY.

Upton, Eleventh Month 18*th.*—The last few days have brought with them trials of faith, and humiliations.   I have for a little time past, looked to joining my dear brother Joseph at Chelmsford, to attend the Meetings there with him, on First-day.   On Seventh-day, I found my dear son's baby so very ill, that it was a great effort to leave it and its mother; but duty rather pointed the way to go, therefore I went, and certainly felt much peace in being there.   I believe that I was really helped to minister in the power, that is not my own, in the Morning Meeting; but before the evening, so sad an account of the dear child came, that I was brought into real conflict, to know whether to stay the Evening Meeting, or to return to London: however, outwardly and inwardly, the way opened most clearly to stay, although for some time, I felt unduly tried and tossed by it; but in tender mercy, after a while my spirit was quieted, and I again was enabled to minister, I trust, in the name of the Lord.   When I arrived in town, the poor babe was still alive, and has since revived.   In looking back to my distress for a time at Chelmsford, these words might have been applied, "Oh thou of little faith, wherefore didst thou doubt?"

After the recovery of her little grandchild, she was called into Norfolk to attend the sick-bed of her most beloved niece, Priscilla B——, who was dangerously ill; to her she administered spiritual help, and the most judicious nursing.   Referring to this illness especially, Priscilla B——, describes her aunt's skill in a sickroom as "peculiar indeed; her very presence and aspect as perfectly calming: possessing an authority mixed with soothing tenderness, which gave her a most helpful power, quieting both body and mind by her judicious and always indulgent advice, and by her unfailing power of hoping, perhaps too well; yet under feelings of need and discouragement, what an instrument for good !" She speaks of her " as condescending to the humblest services;" recalls " her soft hand, her exquisite reading, and delicious company;" concluding, " Oh that we could hear her, feel her, see her once more !"

She slept at Earlham, on her road to North Repps, and there found her daughter L——, looking so ill that she could not make up her mind again to part from her, but took her with her.

On the road, they saw a man lying apparently at the point of death. Mrs. Fry immediately went to him, desiring her daughter to open her dressing-case and bring a vial of brandy, which, from her frequent attendance in sickness, she had learned always to have in readiness.

She knelt down by the poor man, whose head she found dreadfully torn, she carefully replaced the scalp which was lying back, tied it down with her pocket-handkerchief; then gave him brandy, and he began to revive. After a time a cart came by, into which she had him lifted, and carefully conveyed to the next village. He had been driving a powerful team of horses—they ran away, and the waggon-wheel went over his head. He died in Norwich Hospital, after lingering some weeks and apparently ready for that solemn change. Mrs. Fry returned by Lynn to visit her daughter and her family; and was accompanied by her, from Norfolk to her " comfortable little home."

Her return thither, was however clouded, from finding that her beloved son William, who had been under every circumstance a firm support and great comfort to her, now thought it best for himself, to lay aside the peculiarities of the Society of Friends in dress and manners; he having come to the conclusion, that unless conformity to them arose from personal conviction of their importance, however becoming in a very young person under the immediate direction of his parents, their practice was inconsistent with truth in one of more mature years.

Writing on this subject, she says :—

Upton, Twelfth Month 24*th.*—I truly desire not to be unreasonable upon the subject, or to require of my dearest William, at his age, that which his own judgment does not dictate. Beyond a certain point, I have believed it right not to press it, and oh, if I thus take from him my yoke and my bonds, may the Lord take him up and put His yoke upon him. Oh! most merciful Lord God, hearken to the earnest prayer of Thy servant for this dear child ; make him Thine own, prepare him in Thine own way for Thine own service, grant that through Thy help and Thy power he may wax valiant in the Christian warfare, until all his enemies be wholly subdued before him ; and if consistent with Thy holy will, make him in his own family an instrument to draw others nearer to Thee and Thy kingdom. Lord God make no tarrying, but visit and revisit my family, lead them more from the vanities of time, to the enduring riches of eternity ; keep also Thy very unworthy servant alive unto Thyself ; even yet make her joyful in Thy house of prayer, and more faithful in the field of offering ; let Thy grace continually rest upon us. Amen !

Early in 1830, we find this entry in Mrs. Fry's journal, "my time has lately been much occupied in writing my text book." She had long felt the difficulty of young people generally, and older ones in active life, possessing themselves of any scriptural instructions, before commencing the employments of the day. The experience of life, had infinitely confirmed her value of the written word. She deplored the feeling, wherever she met with it, that the Bible was to be approached as a sort of sacred mystery, to be applied to, only occasionally, and with something, almost amounting to awe.

At the period of Mrs. Fry's early life, this was too much the

case amongst Friends ; nor was a circumscribed use of the holy
scriptures, by any means confined to that body. How much
more general now, than fifty years ago, is the habit of reading the
word of God in families ; how much more universal its close and
individual study. But Mrs. Fry considered, that there was something more wanted, to enable those, who have but a short period
for a hasty toilette before an early breakfast, still to taste of the
spiritual manna provided, and to have a portion of holy writ,
however short, impressed upon their minds.

Amidst her numerous avocations, she found time to select a
passage of scripture for every day in the year. She endeavoured
to combine in it, that, which is " profitable for doctrine, for
reproof, for correction, for instruction in righteousness ; and in a
little preface, she urged the importance of endeavouring to appropriate the truths contained in it, with a heart uplifted, that the
blessed Spirit might apply the word ; and concludes, " The rapid
and ceaseless passing away of the days and weeks, as well as the
months of the year, as numbered at the head of each day's text,
it is hoped may prove a memento of the speed with which time
is hastening on, and remind the reader of the importance of
passing it as a preparation for eternity, in the service of God and
for the benefit of mankind." As soon as her little work was
finished, she began its distribution, thousands and thousands did
she give away, besides multitudes that were otherwise circulated.
Where have not these little text books penetrated, from the
monarch's gilded hall, to the felon's dungeon ?

Many instances of their usefulness came to light, but one only
shall be mentioned here. Two or three years after their publication, a text book, bound in red leather, which she had given to a
little grandson, fell out of his pocket at the Lynn Mart, where
he had gone to visit the lions. He was a very little boy, and
much disconcerted at the loss of his book, for his name was in it,
and that it was the gift of his grandmother, written by herself.

The transaction was almost forgotten, when nearly a year afterwards, the clergyman of a parish, about eight miles from Lynn, gave the following history of the lost book. He had been sent for to the wife of a man, living on a wild common at the outskirts of his parish a notorious character between poacher and rat-catcher. The wife no better than himself. The message was brought to the clergyman, by the medical man who attended her, and who after describing her as being most strangely altered, added " you will find the lion become a lamb" and so it proved ; she, who had been wild and rough, whose language had been violent, and her conduct untamed, lay on a bed of exceeding suffering, humble, patient and resigned.

Her child had picked up the text book, and carried it home as lawful spoil. Curiosity, or some feeling put into her heart, by Him without Whose leave a sparrow falleth not to the ground, had induced her to read it, the word had been blessed to her, and her understanding opened to receive the gospel of truth. She could not describe the process, but the results were there. Sin had in her sight become hateful ; blasphemy was no longer heard from her lips. She drew from under her pillow, " her precious book," her " dear little book," which had " taken away the fear of death." She died soon afterwards, filled with joy and hope in believing ; having in these detached portions of scripture, found a Saviour, all-sufficient to bear her heavy burden of guilt, and present her, clad in his own spotless righteousness before the throne of God.

Perhaps of the thousands of Text-books given by Mrs. Fry, no two were ever offered with the same words. Her adaptation to all states, ages, and conditions, in her intercourse with her fellow-creatures, was one of her means of power ; always courteous, invariably self-possessed, but ever displaying an exquisite tact, and most acute perception of position, circumstance, character, and the best method of approach. That her skill in dealing

with others was partly intuitive, no one can doubt; that her
compassionate feelings were unusually strong is equally obvious ;
but her highest power was unquestionably derived from the knowledge she had obtained of the heart of man, greatly, if not
chiefly from the close study of her own, its feelings, and ten-
dencies. After an evening with Mr. Buxton, and her sister, in
London, about this time, where she had met a large and congenial party, she reviews herself, and her own doings, in a note
written the following morning.

"I passed a very low night, because I felt last evening I was
made too much of; it gave me *real pain* my being put more
forward than ———. I also feared I had put myself forward,
and it led me to say in my heart, ' I abhor myself, as in dust and
ashes,' or to that effect. I have hardly yet recovered the effect
of it, though I partly attribute it to a nervous state from fatigue,
that I saw things through too strong a medium, yet it afresh
brought me to feel,—what should we do,—were not a fountain
open for the uncircumcised and the unclean ? I think I hardly
can go to such parties. I am almost sure to be low after them,
under the deep feeling of short-coming." In February, Elizabeth Fry believed it her duty to lay before her Monthly Meeting,
a concern, which had for some time rested upon her mind, to pay
a religious visit to parts of Suffolk and Norfolk, and attend the
Quarterly Meeting at Ipswich. Doing this, involved many pains
and much effort ; she considered herself called to go by her Great
Master, but she had cause to believe, that there were individuals
in that neighbourhood, to whom her visit would be scarcely
acceptable. It was with fear and trembling, that she set forth on
this errand of Christian love. Accompanied by her sister-in-law,
Elizabeth Fry, and their valued friend Joseph Foster, they left
home one Saturday, spent the Sunday at Bury ; on Monday went
to Needham, where "the kindest sympathy and hospitality was
extended" to her by Thomas and Lucy Maw ; that evening

moved to the house of Dykes Alexander ; and the following days attended the Quarterly Meeting at Ipswich. There Christian love and unity rose higher and higher, till "all obstacles were removed," and she permitted to partake of something like "joy in the Lord," and unalloyed communion with her friends.

She wrote, whilst on this little journey, to her children at home, upon their being invited to attend the consecration of a Church, and to be present at a party afterwards.

Earlham, *Third Month* 23rd, 1830.

MY MOST BELOVED CHILDREN,

The information received to-day, that you should any of you have admitted a serious thought of attending our kind friend's party on the 31st, surprises and pains me ; not but that I am also fully sensible of your willingness fully to be guided by my judgment in it. With respect to those over whom I have authority, I feel it impossible to leave them in any degree at liberty about it ; it is a thing that must not be. I look upon it not only as perfectly inconsistent with our views as Friends, but perfectly so for all religious professors, because if I did approve of *consecrating* a church for the worship of the Almighty, I could not possibly conceive it an occasion for amusement or gaiety, but one of real seriousness. I see the thing to be altogether inconsistent with religious truth, both as to the thing itself, and this commemoration of it, and I trust that none of you will be present. I am sure it was, in the first instance, your own view of the case ; do not, my dearest children, be shaken in your judgments about it ; I believe it will be a cross that you will never repent taking up, but on the contrary, be glad you have done so ; for, now and then, sacrifices must be made to duty. Can you approve sacred things and the world's pleasures, being thus mixed together ? Can you think the consecration of churches, as it is too frequently conducted, consistent with the purity and simplicity of the gospel of our blessed Lord ?

Upton, Fourth Month 26th.—My Suffolk and Norfolk journey

proved an interesting, instructive, and I think very satisfactory one. My way appeared to be remarkably made in Suffolk, where I almost feared to go. At Ipswich, when the Quarterly Meeting was over, I think for a time I partook of perfect peace ; my re-joicing was, I may say, in the Lord. It was well worth suffering, only to taste of such a brook by the way. At Pakefield, we had a highly valuable and edifying visit to my much-loved brother and sister Cunningham ; although their religious path is certainly in many respects, very different to my dear sister Elizabeth Fry's and mine ; yet it appeared, as if it pleased the great Head of the Church, in no common degree to bless our intercourse, Christian love breaking down all partition-walls ; we were sweetly refreshed together. We indeed, have but one Lord, one faith, one baptism, and one God over all, above all and in us all. I have for many years felt much liberality towards those who differ from myself ; but I may say, with increased years and experience I know hardly any distinction, all one in Christ. Those in my own family, who have gone to the Church, are so very near to me spiritually. After our visit to Pakefield, we went to Earlham and met with a cordial reception ; but I think that we were all in a low place. My arrival at home was clouded by a party, to which my children were invited and rather wished to go. We had some pains about it ;—my path is a very peculiar one, and as to bring-ing my family up consistent Friends, a most difficult one. My husband not going hand in hand with me in some of these things, my children, in no common degree, disliking the cross of the minor testimonies of Friends, and from deeply sorrowful circum-stances, often having had their faith in them tried, also their being exposed unavoidably, to much association with those, who do not see these things needful, renders it out of my power to press my own opinions beyond a certain point. I believe it best and most expedient for them in small things and great, to be Friends ; it has to me been a blessed path, and my belief is that it would be so to them, if conscientiously walked in ; but it is not I, who can give them grace to do it, and if their not walking more consistently brings reproach upon me, even amongst those nearest to me—I must bear it. I cannot deny that much as I love the principle—earnestly, as I desire to uphold it, bitter experience has proved to me, that Friends do rest too much on externals ; and that valuable, indeed jewels of the first water, as are many amongst them, yet there are also serious evils in our Society and amongst its members.   Evils which often make my heart mourn, and have led me earnestly to desire, that we might dwell less on externals, and more on the spiritual work ; then I believe that we should be as a people less in bonds, and partake more of the glorious liberty of the children of God.   My desire is, only to do what is for the real good of my children, and for the good of the cause I love, and leave myself altogether out of the question, whether it bring me into evil report or good report. I have often been brought by these things, especially of late, into deep conflict of spirit ; and out of the very depths can only cry, Lord, help and guide me ! and give us not over to the will of our spiritual enemies.

Sixth Month 7th.—I had a difficult path to tread during the Yearly Meeting.   I did not of course receive Friends, but went as I was kindly asked, to various houses.   I could not but at times naturally feel it, after having for so many years delighted to entertain my friends, and those whom I believe to be disciples of Christ, and now in considerable degree to be deprived of it.   But after relating my sorrows, I must say, that through the tender mercy of my God, I have many blessings ; and what is more, at times such a sweet feeling of peace, that I am enabled to hope and trust, that through the unbounded and unmerited mercy of God in Christ Jesus, my husband, my children, and myself, will eventually be made partakers of that salvation that comes by Christ.   The state of our Society, as it appeared in the Yearly Meeting was very satisfactory, and really very comforting to me ; so much less stress laid upon little things, more upon matters of greater importance, so much unity, good-will, and what I felt, Christian liberty amongst us ; love appeared truly to abound, to my real refreshment.   I am certainly a thorough Friend, and have inexpressible unity with the principle, but I also see room for real improvement amongst us ; may it take place ; I want less love of money, less judging others, less tattling, less dependence upon external appearance.   I want to see more fruit of the Spirit in all things, more devotion of heart, more spirit of prayer, more

real cultivation of mind, more enlargement of heart towards all ;
more tenderness towards delinquents, and above all, more of the
rest, peace, and liberty of the children of God ! I lately paid an
interesting visit to the Duchess of Gloucester.   Our British
Society Meeting has been well got through.   There is much yet
doing in this cause ; Oh ! for a right and diligent, and persevering spirit in it, and may the grace of our Lord Jesus Christ
be with all those who are engaged in it.

The accounts received at this Meeting from various Committees for visiting female prisoners in Great Britain, were very
encouraging.

" Liverpool, Sixth Month 5th, 1830.

" The Ladies' Committee who visit the House of Correction at
Kirkdale, near Liverpool, beg Elizabeth Fry's acceptance of a
counterpane worked by the female prisoners, and trimmed with a
fringe of their making.   This memorial of a class of her unhappy
fellow-creatures, so eminently benefited and tenderly felt for
by Elizabeth Fry, will, the Committee believe, be peculiarly
grateful to her, as well as bring a proof of their own affectionate
regard.

" Signed, on behalf of the Committee, by
" REBECCA CHORLEY, Secretary."

A   counterpane, elaborately embroidered, accompanied this
letter.

From Hamburgh, Elizabeth Fry received an application that a
copy of her likeness might be engraved for an Almanac published
by Beyerink, entitled, " For that which is Beautiful and Good."

With this was sent to her a translation of some lines inserted
in the " Almanac for the Beautiful and Good."

" 1830.—Though faithful to her duty, as a wife and mother,
into the night of the prison Elizabeth Fry brings the radiance of
love—brings comfort to the sufferer, dries the tears of repentance,
and causes a ray of hope to descend into the heart of the sinner.
She teaches her that has strayed, again to find the path of

virtue, comes as an angel of God into the abode of crime, and preserves for Jesu's kingdom that which appeared to be lost. Is not this, indeed, what may be called, loving our neighbour more than one's self?"

" Leenwaarden, *September*, 1829."

From Berlin, Elizabeth Fry had received letters from the Countess Von der Grœben, giving encouraging details of the results of Ladies visiting Prisons ; and there, and at Potsdam also, of the establishment of places of refuge for such liberated prisoners, as seemed anxious for amendment.

The effect of kindness and patient instruction even on the most abandoned characters, is beautifully exemplified in a letter from Madam Potemkin née Galitzin, addressed to Mrs. Fry, from St. Petersburg.

" Gastiletta près de Petersbourg, 12 *Juin*, 1830.

" En entrant dans la société des Prisons, Madame, mon cœur avait regardé comme un de ses devoirs les plus doux d'entrer en relation avec un être, qui a été d'une si heureuse influence dans son pays et à notre société des prisons, et qui est depuis tant d'années, l'ange consolateur des malheureux confiés à ses soins.

" Aujourd'hui, Madame, que trois années viennent de s'écouler depuis le jour où j'ai été associée au sort des malheureux, je viens, avec le même sentiment de confiance et d'affection chrétiennes, vous exposer l'état des choses telles que je les laisse en ce moment, où des circonstances de famille me forcent à quitter Petersbourg pour m'établir à la campagne.

" Nos prisons, établies à l'instar des vôtres, Madame, offrent l'aspect le plus satisfaisant quant à l'ordre et au bien-être qui y règnent. Tout ce qui peut légitimement s'accorder avec l'état de la recluse et l'adoucir, y est employé. Les mesures sévères et les chambres obscures n'ont pas été employées deux fois cette année, à notre grande satisfaction. Le nombre des prisonnières a diminué de beaucoup à partir des années précédentes. Nous n'y avons plus vu les mêmes individus qui souvent, dans le

courant de l'annéc, se retrouvaient en prison. D'après ces résultats, j'en augure une amélioration bien sensible dans l'état
moral de nos prisonnières. Leur attachement pour la Surveillante, nommée par le comité, la soumission, et l'esprit d'ordre et
de docilité qui se maintient parmi elles, nous encouragent à per-
sévérer dans un but où le Seigneur est notre seule espérance.

" Les prisonnières qui savent lire, en profitent pour faire la
lecture aux autres ; et c'est dans un séjour de réclusion qu'on
peut surtout apprécier le bonheur d'avoir reçu l'éducation pre-
mière, et de pouvoir venir avec un bon livre au secours de sa
misère et de sa solitude. Mon expérience m'a démontré ce
bienfait plus encore en prison que partout ailleurs : car, les mauvais livres étant prohibés, et le choix des lectures se bornant
uniquement à la parole de Dieu, celles qui s'en occupent, Madame,
y puisent des consolations nouvelles, et un goût pour la lecture
sérieuse qui naguères leur était tout-à-fait étrangère. J'ai eu la
consolation de voir une prisonnière, dont le départ pour la Sibérie
était retardé par une maladie, se nourrir avec avidité de la parole
de Dieu, lire avec une foi véritable et un cœur contrit les souf-
frances de notre Seigneur Jésus-Christ, et puiser dans ces souf-
frances la force de supporter ses maux, et la douce résignation que
donne l'espérance d'une vie future. Sa résignation contrastait
fort avec le sort d'une de ses compagnes, qui, plus ignorante
qu'elle, ne pouvait se soumettre à son avenir, et qui se tordait
les mains de désespoir.

" Voici, Madame, en peu de mots l'état présent de notre Prison
de ville. Espérons que le Seigneur daignera de plus en plus
bénir le zèle et les charitables soins des Dames qui composent
notre petit comité. Toutes, Madame, sont dévouées de cœur
à l'œuvre du Seigneur, et la regardent comme le plus cher et le
plus sacré devoir de leur vie. Je me suis séparée de mes chères
compagnes avec tous les regrets qu'inspire leur charité ; mais je
m'en sépare avec confiance et emportant la conviction, qu'il n'y
en a pas une qui ne remplisse mieux ma tâche, et avec plus de
zèle que je ne l'ai fait. Car, je vous parlerai en chrétienne,
Madame : je n'étais pas digne de présider une Société, dont la
charité était l'unique bien ; mais mon cœur était à leur suite, et
désirait faire comme elles.

" Adieu, Madame ; jè n'ai pas le bonheur de vous connaître et pourtant je vous aime, parceque je sais que vous aimez Celui, que nous devons seul aimer, et qui réclame notre cœur tout entier.

"TATIANA POTEMKIN."

Woodford, Eighth Month 14th.—Last evening, a Bible Meeting was held here, my brother Samuel in the Chair ; seeing my beloved sister and her lovely family all there, swimming in the current of full apparent prosperity, spiritually and temporally, brought feelingly home to my mind days that are past, when I used to delight to take my family upon similar occasions, in some degree, I believe, to manifest my love to the cause of Him whom I most desire to serve.

Not one week had passed over, from the time of this entry being made in the journal, before a heavy blow fell, where prosperity had been so apparent.   The only brother of Mrs. Samuel Gurney being called to endure the bitter affliction of losing his wife.

Dagenham, Eighth Month 2nd.—Last First-day fortnight, I was suddenly sent for to my much loved and highly esteemed friend Lucy S——.   She had been very ill, however she appeared nearly recovered, but was taken with extreme sinkings, and from one of these she did not revive as usual.   My beloved sister Elizabeth Gurney was with her, and being alarmed, sent for me.   I had a deeply affecting scene to witness, no less than the sudden and unexpected death of this dear friend : her husband leaning over her—her poor children—and our dear sister in almost an agony of grief.   I think so affecting a death-bed scene I never witnessed, where there was the inexpressible consolation of believing, that the departed one was really ready.   She was in the very prime of her day, in every sense of the word ; in the meridian of her power and usefulness, a person of good understanding, uncommon disposition, and all sanctified by grace.   I believe that she not only knew, but loved her Lord, and through the assistance of His grace, appeared to me in no common degree to be fulfilling the relative duties as wife, mother, mistress, daughter,

sister and friend, and to the poor particularly.—Indeed, I feel
our loss to be very serious, and very great, and that it should
strongly stimulate us who remain, to seek to be ready, and whilst
we live, to fill our right places, and perform in love, meekness,
gentleness and humility, all our relative duties.   May this affliction be sanctified to all parties! and may the blessing of the
Most High rest upon those most bereaved.

My dear Gurney has been to pay a visit to France with his
tutor, which proved a very interesting one ; he received great
kindness from many French persons, particularly my valued
friends the Delesserts : it brought me into communication with
them, and I have felt much sweet unity of spirit with them.
What matters it to what nation or sect we belong, if we love the
Lord in sincerity, and our neighbours as ourselves ?   Since my
dearest boy left France, there has been a most awful time there,
through the arbitrary and imprudent conduct of King Charles
the 10th.   The people have risen—there has been a dreadful
battle between the opposite parties in the streets of Paris, and
the King has fled.   I felt the mercy of having my boy safely at
home, but I may truly say, afflicted for the French.   War in all
forms is awful and dreadful ; but civil war worse than all, as to
its present effect, and future consequences

*   *   *   *   *   *   *   *   *   *

Eighth Month.—In bringing up our children, it is my solid judgment that a real attachment is not a thing to be lightly esteemed,
and when young persons of a sober mind are come to an age of
discretion, it requires very great care, how any undue restraint is
laid upon them, in these most important matrimonial engagements ; we are all so short sighted about them, that the parties
themselves should after all be principally their own judges in it.
Therefore, unless I see insurmountable objections, I believe duty
dictates leaving our children much at liberty in these matters.
May a gracious and kind Providence direct them aright.

Upton, 11*th.*—I felt it right yesterday, to lay before the
Monthly Meeting, a view that I have had of attending the
Quarterly Meeting of Sussex and some of its particular Meetings.
My sister Elizabeth Fry felt disposed to join me.   It appeared
to meet with rather unusual unity, therefore we are likely to go
forward in it.

Tenth Month 12*th.*—We, (my sister E. F., my brother Samuel Gurney, and myself,) returned home from our journey on Seventh day evening, after being out a week and two days. We were in the first place outwardly cared for by our dear friend Joseph Foster, who is truly a helper, spiritually as well as naturally; he accompanied us to Horsham, where, as usual under such circumstances, I felt ready to query, why I was there, and fears got hold of me. Friends received us with much kindness and apparent openness.

At Brighton, Elizabeth Fry attended the meeting for Friends on the Sunday morning, and in the evening held a Public Meeting; for persons of different persuasions. She had at the Pavilion an interview with the Countess Brownlow, and through her communicated a message of serious import to Queen Adelaide.

My prayer for the King and Queen was, that a blessing might rest upon them; that they might be strengthened by the Spirit of God to do His will, and live to His glory, (or to that purpose); then for the Queen, I felt the great importance of her situation, that she was indeed like a city set upon a hill, amongst women; and my desire for her was, that her light might so shine before men, that they, seeing her good works might glorify our Father who is in heaven. I expressed my desire that, for the good of the community, she might promote the education of the poor, the general distribution of the scriptures, and the keeping the Sabbath seriously, by discouraging parties, &c., &c., on that day, amongst the higher ranks; as I was sure the tendency of them was very injurious to the lower classes, and the community at large; then I touched on the anti-slavery subject, and the abolition of capital punishment, and presented for the Queen, my brother Joseph's Essays; also his Peculiarities of Friends, and my little book on visiting Prisons.

On Fourth-day morning, after several calls and attending a Bible Meeting, we dined with some Friends very agreeably; and in the evening went to our kind friends the Elliots, who invited about seventy persons to meet us on account of the District Society. It was truly encouraging to me, to hear what wonders it had done for that place. We had a delightful meeting, a great variety of Christians present, and so much good-will and unity felt, that it comforted my heart. At its close, our dear and valued friends, Charles Simeon, and Joseph Hughes gave us some sweet religious counsel ; I felt the power such, that I could not help following them, and found that " out of the fulness of the heart the mouth speaketh"—giving glory to the Lord. As far as I can see, how much more marked a blessing has attended my benevolent labours for public good, than any other labours of love that I have been enabled to perform in my own house, or amongst my own people.

On Fifth-day, several of the higher classes were invited to Meeting, and to my own feelings, a remarkable time we surely had ; it appeared as if we were over-shadowed by the love and mercy of God our Saviour. The ministry flowed in beautiful harmony ; I deeply felt the want of vocal prayer being offered, but I did not see it my place upon our Meeting assembling toge- ther ; when, to my inexpressible relief, John Rickman powerfully and beautifully offered up thanksgiving and prayer, which ap- peared to arise as incense and as an acceptable sacrifice. After a time of silence, I rose with this text : " There are diversities of gifts, but the same spirit ; differences of administration, but the same Lord ; diversities of operations, but it is the same God who worketh all in all." In a way that it never did before, the subject opened to my view whilst speaking ; how did I see and en- deavour to express the lively bond of union existing in the Chris- tian Church and that the humbling, tendering influence of the love and power of Christ, must lead us not to condemn our neighbours, but to love and cover all with charity. My sister E. Fry was rather closely and differently led, and I had to end the Meeting by praying for the King, Queen, and all their subjects every where ; for the advancement of that day, when the knowledge of God and His glory would cover the earth as the waters cover the sea ; for those countries in Europe that are in a disturbed state, and that these shakings might eventually be for good : after a most solemn feeling of union the Meeting broke up. We dined at our dear friends', the Elliots, where was Charles Simeon, Henry Elliot, (valuable clergymen) and others. A pleasant, sweet, refreshing time we had; I think I never feel so able to rejoice in the Lord, as when united with real Christians of different denominations. We went that night to Chichester; slept at Maria Hack's, and were much interested by her and her family, some of whom have joined the Church of England, but they appeared to us truly valuable and serious, and we were much pleased with our visit.

I have been thus full in the accounts of this journey, because it is I think well, in this way, to leave some memorial of the tender dealings of my gracious Lord and Master with me, when engaged in His service.

Upton, Eleventh Month, 3rd.—We returned home yesterday from Bury Hill, where my brother Samuel and myself went on Seventh-day, in consequence of the death of my dear uncle Barclay, whose funeral we attended the preceding Sixth-day, when thirteen of his children and children-in-law attended. It was to me very affecting, following the remains of this dear uncle to the grave, who was such a kind generous friend, and helper to me. It is very striking to see one generation so nearly gone; so many of us, now entering the evening of our day, and our children and children's children coming up. after us. Life thus passing away, "as a tale that is told."

Twelfth Month, 7th.—May I be enabled, so to give an account of the various dealings of the Almighty with me and mine, that it may be useful to some; at least to my most beloved children and children's children. I have to begin with rather a melancholy tale:—My beloved children, F—— and R—— R——, lost their sweet baby upon the 4th of last month, after a few days severe illness. Death is awful and affecting, come as it may! and this I truly felt, when seeing the sweet babe in its coffin, still retaining its beautiful colour. I could not but feel the uncertainty of all our possessions; the comfort, that death had only entered our family and taken one for whom we could feel no fear for the future. At her grave, the desire was very strong within me, that we might all become like little children, fit to enter the kingdom of God, being washed and made white in the blood of the Lamb. Since then, my dear nephew Harry B—— has been called hence. His ·end appeared in no common degree peace, if not joy in the Lord;

he was about seventeen years of age. A remarkable instance of
the care and religious instruction of parents being blessed ; he
was greatly protected through life, from any evil influences ; and
most carefully and diligently instructed by his dear mother, particularly in all religious truth. He was a child, who in no common
degree appeared to be kept from evil, and to live in the fear and
love of the Lord ; he was cheerful, industrious, clever, very
agreeable, and of a sweet person—a very deep trial it is to
his dear parents to lose him. Still I feel, as if I could give up
all my sons to be in such a state ; but I may be mistaken
in this, and perhaps my Lord may yet be pleased, to raise them
up to His service here below, which would be even a greater
blessing, than having them taken in the morning of the day.
I think the way in which the children of my sisters turn out,
proves the efficacy of much religious instruction, and not too
much religious restraint. It certainly is a very serious thing,
to put upon young persons any crosses in their religious course,
that Christ does not call them to bear !

First Month 11*th.*—When dressing, last First-day fortnight,
A—— came in to tell me, that my dear and valued uncle Joseph
Gurney had suddenly dropped down dead at his house at the
Grove, near Norwich, my aunt only with him at the time. It
exceedingly affected me, for he was very dear to me, and more like
a father than any one living ; he was one in whom the religious
life was beautifully manifested, more particularly in his humility, in his cheerfulness and in his obedience. He was a lively
minister of the gospel, a valuable and a delightful man, and his
loss is indeed very great to those nearest to him, as well as
to many others. I had a painful struggle to know whether I
ought to go to his funeral or not. However, I decided to go ;
in which I felt peace, and then could leave it all comfortably.
I have seldom of late felt more discouraged from a deep sense
of the evil of my own heart, than when I first arrived at Earlham. There are times, when with my brothers and sisters
particularly, the contrast of my circumstances with theirs pains
me ; the mode of my feeling these things oppressed me. I
walked alone through some beautiful parts of Earlham, and
how did it remind me of days that are past ! The sun shone

brightly, and hardly a tree, a walk, or a view, but brought interesting remembrances before me ; how many gone ! how many changes ! and then how far was I ready for my great change ? It was New Year's Day ; little did I expect to keep it there. I returned home, wrote to my husband and children, and poured out a little of my heart to them. I went to the Grove—felt my much-loved uncle being *really gone*—all changed there. I went to Norwich to call on a few sick, &c. ; the place the same, but again how changed to me ! However, as my dearest family assembled, I became more comfortable.

She wrote to her family from Earlham.

First Month 1st, 1831.

My dearest Husband and Children,

I have withdrawn into my own room for a little quiet and retirement, and my attention has been much turned towards you. I am just returned from a solitary walk about this beautiful place; the sun shining upon it ; so much of it bearing the same aspect as in my childish days, and circumstances so greatly changed ; my feelings were greatly affected. How many gone that used to delight in its beauties, and rejoice together in no common bond of love ! Surely the passing scene of this life could hardly be more feelingly brought home to the heart. Then I was led to look at my family, and oh ! what love, what tender desire, what inexpressible travail of soul was and is excited for you all ; that amidst all changes, (and you have already known many) you may each for yourself have a real substantial hold of that, which can never be changed and will live through every storm, even death itself. On Second-day, I went with my brother Buxton and Priscilla to North Repps, and paid a very interesting visit to my dearest sister. I was truly comforted and edified by my visit to them ; religious principle appeared very present to help and sustain them ; nothing could exceed their kindness to me, it cheered me on the way, and helped me. Indeed, I may say, that the stream so rose on First-day and Second-day, and the healing power was so near, that I experienced a little what it is to have "beauty for ashes, the oil of joy for mourning, and the garment of praise for the spirit of heaviness."

First-day, First Month.—I desire to remember a few of the principal events, and some of the mercies and deliverances of the last year—an important one in the political world,—the French revolution, and its consequence in other countries, and in our own in measure. I think, I unusually see the hand of Providence in some of these things. I never remember my prayers to have been more raised by any public event, than on behalf of the French, during their revolution. Their conduct in it has given me great comfort, because it shows a wonderful advancement, at least in Christian practice, since the last revolution. I feel still deeply interested about the French, and have a hope that a great and good work is going on amongst them. I have a hope also that the general stirring amongst the European nations is for good, and I have the same hope respecting our own country. I see that it is in rather an unsettled state, yet, as I also see that many things want a remedy, and as the process of fermentation must be passed through before a liquor can be purified, so at times with nations—such a process, though painful whilst it lasts, ends in the good of the people. May it prove so with us, and with other nations, and may all these turnings and overturnings advance the coming of that blessed day, when the "earth shall be full of the knowledge of the Lord as the waters cover the sea."

My interest in the cause of prisons remains strong, and my zeal unabated ; though it is curious to observe how much less is felt about it by the public generally. How little it would answer in these important duties, to be much affected by the good or bad opinion of man. Through all, we should endeavour to go steadily forward, looking neither to the right hand nor to the left ; with the eye fixed upon that Power which can alone bless our labours, and enable us to carry on these works of charity to the good of others, our own peace, and His praise.

The excitement occasioned by Mrs. Fry's first visits to Newgate, the strangeness of ladies visiting prisons, the astonishment of the public mind at finding the sin engendered, and the misery permitted, within the prison walls of christian and enlightened England, had indeed passed ; but a steady, resolute spirit of improvement was making its way, and men from all classes and all parties, were coming over and ranking themselves among the labourers, or at least the well-wishers to progressive improvements. Sir Robert Peel had been for years grappling with the difficulties of the criminal code respecting forgery, and had, during the last Sessions, presented to Parliament his acts for consolidating its various sanguinary enactments.

The subject had become one of general interest ; and after many discussions, a majority of the House of Commons voted for the abolition of the punishment of death, in all cases of forgery. These clauses were restored in the Lords, notwithstanding a petition signed by a thousand bankers, supporting the vote of the Commons. The effect, practically, however, of this assertion of public opinion was, that the extreme sentence of the law in cases of forgery, was not again carried into execution.

Thus, the work was advancing ; but much remained to be done. He who set fire to a stack of bean stalks in an outlaying field was still to lose his life, whilst he who burnt a helpless family in their beds, could have no greater punishment awarded him; again, the half-starved peasant, who carried home the sheep he found fallen and bruised in a neighbouring ditch, was to endure the same fate as the man who might waylay the farmer on his return from market, despoil him of his well-earned gains, and then to prevent detection, leave him lifeless—weltering in his blood by the road side.

The Prison Discipline Society continued its exertions. The greater number of County prisons were either rebuilt or re-modelled, and classification and occupation introduced. Amongst female prisoners, officers of their own sex were becoming increasingly general.

Many of the Borough gaols and Scotch prisons continued

however, in their former state of neglect, wretchedness, and pro-
miscuous intercourse amongst the prisoners ; but there were exceptions, as for instance at Derby and Leicester, where the Borough
magistrates purchased the old County prisons, after the removal
of the prisoners to the admirable new County gaols erected there.
At Penzance, a new town prison was built ; at Barnstaple, the
old one had been rebuilt. A new gaol was erected at Norwich.
The Yarmouth prison remained unaltered in cells, and yards, and
hired management ; but under the teaching of Sarah Martin,
and her devoted labours of love, wonderful results were produced,
and an admirable lesson taught to her country-women, of what
may be effected by kindness, perseverance, and discretion.

CHAPTER XVII.

The last day of January, brought Mrs. Fry accounts of the severe illness of one of her daughters, and the following morning saw her, through most inclement weather, setting forth to go to her.

To one of her Daughters.

Ely, *Second Month 1st.*

My dearest Hannah,

Here I am shut up at the Inn at Ely, unable to go on. It was with some difficulty we arrived here, from the snow, and when we reached this place we found that the way to Lynn was quite obstructed, and that no person had come from thence to-day. But now I must tell you a little about our journey: there was one Lynn gentleman, and two young men, no doubt students; at first we were all flat and said little, but after awhile we entered into very interesting, and rather intellectual conversation, upon some important subjects. I found the Lynn gentleman knew me and called me by my name. I tried to make the conversation useful. We talked of the state of the Established Church, and much belonging to it, in England and Ireland; tithes, &c. &c., then we went to prophecy, then to theatres, and so on. At last, I

felt free enough to give the young men each a text book, with
which they appeared to be much pleased.   My dear nephews
met me at the Inn, at Cambridge ; they were most kind.   Upon
my arrival here, the coachman, the outside passengers, and one
of the owners of the horses, came to consult my wishes as to
what to do ; but when a medical man who had been out, told
us that six miles from hence, the roads were impassable and
really dangerous, there appeared to be no doubt for us, but to
remain quietly where we were.   They were all very kind and
attentive to me ; and so are the landlord, landlady, and servants.
I believed it right to ask my fellow-passengers to breakfast ; the
outside passengers proved to be two very interesting clergymen,
related to the Styleman family.   We had a solemn reading together with part of the family here, and all felt (I believe) what a
sweet bond Christians have with each other, and how truly they
are friends to each other.

The coach is now come in from Lynn ; therefore, I hope to
proceed there safely.

Farewell, in much near and dear love,

ELIZABETH FRY.

Upton, Second Month 12*th.*—I returned last evening from
Earlham with my dear brother Joseph, having been suddenly
called into Norfolk, in consequence of my dearest R——'s alarming illness.   I heard of it late on Second-day week, and set off
to her on the Third-day morning: the snow so great, I was
stopped on the road, and slept at Ely.   Upon my arrival at Lynn
the next day, I found dearest R—— going on favourably.   The
pleasure is great of having with my children the double tie, not
only of mother and children, but a friendship formed upon its
own grounds.   I certainly think, that in no common degree my
children feel me their familiar friend.

Third Month 19*th.*—I went on Second-day to attend the
Kent Quarterly Meeting, accompanied by my dear sister Elizabeth Fry and Joseph Foster.   I was much engaged from Meeting to Meeting, laboured to encourage the low, the poor and
the sorrowful ; to lead to real practical religion, and to shake
from all outward dependencies ; and that our principles and testi-

monies of a peculiar nature should not be maintained simply as
a regulation amongst us, but unto the Lord, and in deep humility,
in the true Christian spirit, particularly as to tithes, war, &c.
I felt much peace afterwards ; and in going from house to house,
breaking, I trust, a little bread spiritually, and giving thanks.
It appeared *very* seasonable though long delayed, as I have had
it on my mind many months, but hitherto have been prevented
by various things ; yet this appeared to be the right time, and I
take the lesson home, quietly to wait for the openings of Providence, particularly in all religious services, and not to attempt to
plan them too much myself.

The kindness of Friends was great, and I received much *real*
encouragement from them ; some from the humble ones, that did
my heart good.   Indeed I cannot but acknowledge, in humiliation
of spirit, however any may reason on these things, and however
strange that women should be sent out to preach the gospel, yet
I have in these services partaken of joy and peace, that I think
I have never felt in the same degree in any other.

30th.—Yesterday, I felt delicate in health and flat in spirits ;
however, I attended our large Quarterly Meeting, and kept silence,
perhaps unduly so, in our Women's Meeting.   I felt (as I often
do from numerous calls) driven two ways, whether to go to
Devonshire Street, after my dear brother Buxton, who I apprehended to be under much discouragement in bringing forward his
slavery question that night in the House of Commons, or to
attend the adjournment of the Quarterly Meeting ; however, I
made up my mind to go to Devonshire Street.   I went, greatly
exhausted,—my cough poorly, the wind cold,—and in walking
and going in the stage, in my infirmity I was ready to query,
why I had been permitted to lose my carriage, who so often
wanted it ; whilst others who appeared to have less call, were so
much indulged.

Fourth Month 16*th.*—Since I last wrote, very deep sorrow
has been our portion in the illness of my dear nephew, J——
G—— ; my nights have been truly suffering ; *very deep* has
been the exercise of mind on his account.   Oh, dearest Lord
God ! grant, that before this dear child goes hence, he may be
fitted, through the blood of his Saviour, for a place in glory.

20th.—I have seldom witnessed earthly prosperity more cloudt for a season, than by this illness in the family of my beloved brother and sister. Where the sun appeared to shine so *very* uncommonly—health, riches, houses, lands, in abundance ; children amiable and sweet—indeed, in going to their house, I have been ready to tremble, because it is not in the general ordering of Providence that such a full cup should continue : and what a change—what an inexpressible trial, and what a cloud over the picture ; however, He who can dispel the darkest clouds, and quiet the heaviest storms, saw meet to arise in His own Almighty power, and manifest His mercy and love, by granting us deliverance from our great distress. I was reminded of these words on his account, " I have seen his ways, and will heal him, and restore comforts unto him and his mourners."

Fifth Month 14*th.*—About three weeks ago, I paid a very satisfactory visit to the Duchess of Kent, and her very pleasing daughter, the Princess Victoria. William Allen went with me. We took some books, on the subject of slavery, with the hope of influencing the young princess in that important cause. We were received with much kindness and cordiality, and I felt my way open to express, not only my desire that the best blessing might rest upon them, but that the young princess might follow the example of our blessed Lord, that as she " grew in stature she might grow in favour with God and man." I also ventured to remind her of King Josiah, who began to reign at eight years old, and did that which was right in the sight of the Lord, turning neither to the right hand nor to the left, which seemed to be well received. Since that, I thought it right to send the Duke of Gloucester, my brother Joseph's work on the Sabbath, and rather a serious letter, and had a very valuable answer from him, full of feeling. I have an invitation to visit the Duchess of Gloucester next Fourth-day; may good result to them, and no harm to myself, but I feel these openings rather a weighty responsibility, and desire to be faithful, not forward. I had long felt an inclination to see the young princess, and endeavour to throw a little weight in the right scale, seeing the very important place that she is likely to fill. I was much pleased with her, and think her a sweet, lovely and hopeful child.

The Yearly Meeting begins next week : I am rather low in
the prospect ; having no house to receive my dear friends in
London, continues to be a pain to me. I desire to attend it in all
humility, looking to my Lord, and not unto man ; I desire to be
kept in the unity of those with whom I am in religious communion, for I am one with them in principle ; but we must forbear
with each other in love, and endeavour through every trial of it,
" to keep the unity of the Spirit and the bond of peace." Be
pleased, oh Lord ! to be near to Thy most unworthy servant,
defend her with Thine own armour from the various shafts of the
adversary, keep her safely in thy Thy pavilion from the strife of
tongues. If Thou see meet to call her into Thy service, be a
light unto her feet, and a lamp unto her path.

Sixth Month 3rd.—The Yearly Meeting concluded this day
week. I was highly comforted by the good spirit manifested in it
by numbers. I think I never was so much satisfied by the ground
Friends took ; leading us to maintain what we consider our
testimonies upon a scriptural and Christian ground, rather than
because our forefathers maintained them. My opinion is, that
nothing is so likely to cause our Society to remain a living and
spiritual body, as its being willing *to stand open to improvement ;*
because, it is to be supposed, that as the Church generally, emerges
out of the dark state it was brought into, its light will shine
brighter and brighter, and we, as a part of it, shall partake of
this dispensation. My belief is, that neither individuals nor
collective bodies should *stand still* in grace, but their light should
shine brighter and brighter unto the perfect day. My dearest
brother Joseph had a valuable meeting for the youth, further to
instruct them in Friends' principles, which delighted me ; he
was so clear, so sound, so perfectly scriptural and Christian, and
so truly in the spirit of charity and *sound* liberality, *not laxity.*

25th.—I must give an account of the British Society Meeting.
It was, I trust, well got through, and I feel the way in which its
objects prosper, cause for humble thankfulness. Surely the result
of our labour has hitherto been beyond my most sanguine expectation, as to the improved state of our prisons, female convict-
ships, and the convicts in New South Wales. I desire to feel
this blessing and unmerited mercy towards us, and those poor

creatures, as I ought, in humility and true thankfulness of heart. The day before yesterday, I had a very satisfactory interview with the Queen, and several of the Royal Family, in rather a remarkable manner. There was a sale on account of the Hospital Ship in the River, in which I was interested ; and hearing that the Queen was to be there, whom I wished to see, I went ; but was so much discouraged when I arrived, by the gaiety of the occasion, that I should have turned back, had not my sister Catherine made me persevere. We saw the Queen and her party, and quickly passed through the gay scene. When we got out, we found ourselves with a valuable friend of mine, Captain Young, in a quiet airy place, at the head of the staircase ; we were told by him, that the Queen would go down that way, and we should have an excellent view of her. We therefore waited until some of the royal family came down ; their carriages not being ready, they withdrew into a private room, where Captain Young admitted us ; the Duchess of Gloucester met me with her usual kindness, and presented me to the Duchess of Cumberland. The Princess, sister to the Queen, Prince George of Cumberland, and Prince George of Cambridge, were there with them. The Duchess of Gloucester soon withdrew, and the Queen's sister and I had rather a full conversation, together with the Duchess of Cumberland and Prince George. Then came the Duke of Sussex and the Princess of Hesse Homburg ; the Duke appeared pleased to see me, and we had a good deal of conversation ; the Duke said he would present me to the Queen, who soon came into the room, with the Princess Augusta, whom I knew, he did so in the handsomest manner, and the Queen paid me very kind and marked attention. I had some conversation with the Queen, almost entirely on benevolent objects. I expressed my pleasure in seeing the Royal Family so much interested in these things; my belief that it did much good, and that being engaged in them brought peace and blessing. I was enabled to keep to my simple mode of speech, as I believe right, and yet to show them every respect and polite attention. I did not, enter religious subjects with any of them; though I trust the bearing of my conversation was that way. We spoke with the Princess Elizabeth, of Friends, of the love her father George III. had for them, his visit to our great-grandfather Barclay, and my meeting Queen Charlotte in the city, and many other things.   My dearest sister Catherine's simple boldness, certainly got me into the room, and made me go through the thing ; her company was delightful, helpful and strengthening.   It was a very singular opening, thus to meet those, some of whom I so much wanted to see ; it is curious, but for days I had it on my mind to endeavour to see the Queen, and by night and day seriously had weighed it, lest my motives should not be right ; but when I remembered, that from not having been presented to her, I could never on any point communicate with her in person, I felt that if there should be an opportunity to put myself in her way, I had better do it.   It was striking, how the whole thing was opened for me, I may say providentially ; for already I believe some good has been done by seeing one of the party, and I look upon it as a very important event in my public objects for the good of others.   Afterwards, I felt as I mostly do, after any thing of this kind, rather anxious, and extremely fearful for myself, how far it was safe for me thus to be cast among the great of this world ; how far it was even right to put myself in the way of it, and how far others would judge me for it ; however, the next day, my mind was much quieted, my fears much allayed, and my present sober view is, that it was a remarkable opening, and my desire, that it may please the Most High to bless it, that good may result from it.   I lately have had a deeply interesting visit to a female convict-ship ; surrounded as I am at such times by poor sailors, and convicts, it is impossible not to feel the contrast of the circumstances in which I am placed. The last time I was in the ship Mary, there was such a scene round me—parting from them, probably for ever.   So many tears were shed, so much feeling displayed ;—and almost all present the low and the poor.   Then, within a few days to be in such a scene of gaiety, though the object in view was good ; surrounded by royalty and the great of this earth.   The contrast was striking and instructive.   I ought surely to profit from the uncommon variety that I see, and the wonderful changes that I have experienced in being raised up, and cast down.   Oh ! may it not prove in vain for myself and others.

At our last Monthly Meeting, I proposed to Friends to hold a

Public Meeting at Maldon in Essex, and some among the lower classes around Barking and Dagenham. This is a weighty service ; may the Lord be with me in it, to my own help, and the comfort and real edification of those I am thrown with, and may my beloved family partake of it.

Dagenham, Seventh Month 6th.—I have now before me, some deeply weighty family matters respecting my children. May the Lord, in His tender mercy, be pleased to direct me in my conduct towards them ; keeping me on the one hand from giving them undue liberty, and on the other from using any unnecessary restraint. May I be enabled truly, faithfully, and humbly to do my duty towards them. Oh Lord ! be Thou my helper and their helper, my guide and their guide, my defence and their defence, and whatsoever is right for them bring to pass ; whatsoever wrong, prevent by Thy power and Thy providence ! Amen !

Eighth Month 1st.—Last evening we finished our Public Meetings in barns. I passed a humbling night : even in our acts of obedience and devotion, how evident is the mixture of sin and infirmity (at least so it appears to me) and we need to look to the great offering for sin and for iniquity, to bear even these transgressions for us. I apprehend, that all would not understand me ; but many who are much engaged in what we call works of righteousness, will understand the reason, that in the Jewish dispensation there was an offering made for the iniquity of their Holy Things. Humiliation is my portion, though I may also say peace, in thus having given up to a service much against my inclination, and I hope, thankfulness for the measure of power at times granted in them.

Notwithstanding many family cares, and the weighty objects in which she was engaged, the summer of this year, which was passed at Dagenham, proved a very happy one. The two cottages were fully peopled ; the larger one inhabited by Mr. and Mrs. Fry, and as many of their home party as it could be made to contain ; the further cottage was lent to a married daughter, and received the overflowings from the other house. The first burst of the calamity in 1828 had passed away, the younger members of the family had been transplanted sufficiently early, to take root at Upton Lane; this was never the case with their parents, or the elder children, but Dagenham was not new to them, and though the arrangements were different, yet no charm was lost by that. Pleasant it was, to listen from the larger boat, especially appropriated to their mother (and bearing her name) in the quiet of a summer's evening, to the joyous voices of the younger members of the party, borne from the other boats, as they rose and fell in cadence, singing the burthen of some old song, to the dipping of their oars. The gentlemen generally spent the morning in London, but about the time when the heat of a summer day is beginning to abate, the ladies and the children looked for their return. One of the little watchers would announce that the boat sent to meet them was in sight, and then the expectant party poured out of their cottages. Foremost in the group and conspicuous from her stature, she might be seen, whose smile was ever ready to greet them, her gentle voice to bid them welcome. An unbroken band, they met in love, abounding in hope; with life before most of them, coloured by the prismatic hues of youthful fancy; even she, who had suffered so much, and encountered so many disappointments, would catch their tone, and join with delight in the feelings of the party and the scene around her.

Dagenham, Eighth Month 24th.—Upon my return home to Dagenham this day week, in the pony chair, with little Edmund Gurney, there was a severe thunder storm the greater part of the way; but I felt quite easy to persevere through it. But when I arrived at the Chequers Inn, I thought another storm was coming, and went in. We had been there but a few minutes, when we saw a bright flash of lightning, followed instantaneously by a tremendous clap of thunder: upon being asked whether I was alarmed, I said that I certainly was, and did not doubt that an accident had happened near to us. My dear husband who was in it, arrived safely, but in a few minutes, a young man was carried in dead, struck with the lightning, in a field close by. I felt our escape; yet still more the awful situation of the young man, who was a sad character; he had been at the Meeting at Beacontree Heath. This awful event produced a very serious effect in the neighbourhood, so much so, that we believed it right to invite all the relations of the young man (a bad set) and the other young men of the neighbourhood, to meet us in the little Methodist Meeting House, which ended in one more rather large Public Meeting. The event and circumstances altogether made it very solemn, it appeared to set a seal to what had passed before in our other Meetings. My belief is, they have had a stirring effect in this neighbourhood, but they have been very humbling to me; the whole event of this young man's awful death has much confirmed me in the belief, that our concern was a right one, and tended to prepare the minds of the people to profit by such a lesson. My dear brother and sister Buxton and their Priscilla were with us, at many of our Meetings.

27th.—We are just about leaving this place. I have endeavoured to promote the moral and religious good of the people since the Meetings, by establishing libraries of tracts and books at different places; and my belief is, that my humble labours have not been in vain, nor I trust will they be. I have felt so strikingly the manner in which the kindness and love of the neighbourhood has been shown to me, after thus publicly preaching amongst them; and as a poor frail woman advocating boldly the cause of Christ, I expected rather to be despised, whereas, it is apparently just the reverse. The clergyman and his wife almost loading us with kindness, the farmers and their wives very kind and attentive, the poor the same; I felt how sweet it is to be on good terms with all—one day drinking tea at the parsonage, abounding with plate, elegancies, and luxuries; the next day at the humble Methodist shoemaker's, they having procured a little fresh butter, that I might take tea under their roof; the contrast was great; but I can indeed see the same kind Lord over all; rich to all, and filling the hearts of His servants of very different descriptions, with love to each other.

In the autumn, Mrs. Fry accompanied her husband into some of the South-Western Counties.

Sandbrook Hotel, Tenth Month 9th.—This is the place in the Isle of Wight, where my most beloved sisters Rachel and Priscilla spent a winter. I may truly say, since coming to this beautiful and interesting spot, my heart has been much tendered, in remembering those so inexpressibly dear; feeling deeply, that their places here know them no more; it has revived a very strong feeling respecting the past. Their course finished, mine not yet fully run; and as I am deeply sensible that I cannot keep alive my own soul, oh may He, who remains to be our light and our life, keep me alive unto Himself, until He may fit me, by His own Almighty power and unmerited mercy, to enter a new life with all His saints in glory.

Barnstaple, 23rd.—First-day morning.—My distress is great this morning, owing to the steam-packet, with our dearest son Gurney, not arriving as we expected last evening. I have passed a conflicting night; my husband is gone to Ilfracombe, in hopes of hearing something of the packet, and seeing after our dear boy, if he arrives: I stayed, because I thought that duty pointed out attending the little Meeting here; but I feel nervous, afflicted, and desolate. I believe it well, to be now and then brought to these trials of faith and of patience; may I not say, like the disciples formerly, " help Lord or I perish;" may my experience be this day, that I cried unto the Lord in my trouble, and He delivered me out of my distresses. Oh, gracious Lord! quiet my troubled mind, increase my hope, trust, and full reliance upon Thee, upon Thy wisdom, Thy love, and Thy mercy; both as it respects myself and my most dear children; particularly this beloved boy—give me faith to do Thy will this day; and even to prove a helper to those amongst whom my lot may be cast, and if Thou seest meet, give me help from trouble, for vain is the help of man in these extremities.

Linton, 27th.—I heard before I went to Meeting (at Barnstaple), that the people of Ilfracombe were not much alarmed for the packet. How far my mind was influenced by this I cannot say, but I was favoured with a sweet calm in Meeting, and was enabled, I trust faithfully, to attend to the openings of duty there, to my own relief and peace, and I hope to the comfort and edification of those present. I had hardly entered the Friend's house afterwards, when the glad tidings came of my dearest Gurney's safe arrival. I have not for some time felt so much joy; I might almost say, that my heart rejoiced and leaped for joy; and I was enabled not only in heart, but on sitting down to dinner with my friends, to return thanks to Him, who in His tender mercy, granted me this deliverance.

Shortly after this anxiety, when at Ilfracombe, a woman asked me if I should like to see a poor man, who was wrecked, and had had a very wonderful escape, the night before Gurney was on the sea; of course I assented, and Gurney, the woman and I, set off to see him. When we arrived at his cottage, we found a very fine, rather tall young man, who appeared to have been much bruised, shaken, and wounded; with a nice looking young woman, his wife: the house very clean, and a few books; but one particularly struck our attention—a Bible, with an inscription upon it in gilt letters, to this effect, " In commemoration of the courageous conduct of Samuel Marshall, in saving the lives of two women, (who had been out on a Sunday party, a third was drowned) off the pier at Ilfracombe." It appeared by the short history of this young man, that he had from his great courage, good swimming, and kindness to others, been at different times the means of saving eight lives at least; he had gone out to ships in danger, near Ilfracombe, where, from the rocky nature of the coast, there often are shipwrecks. His own simple story about himself, was as follows:—He was fishing in a small boat with two other men; about twelve o'clock at night, a sudden squall or land wind blew from between the hills; he called out to his companions, " we are lost;" the boat capsized; they, poor fellows, prayed for mercy and sunk. Marshall knowing his great power of swimming, would not give himself up, but caught hold of an oar, which proved to be a good one, nearly new; and although he knew that he was a mile from the shore, and the sea in consequence of this land wind very boisterous, he felt it right at least to make the effort to reach land. He soon found that with all his clothes on, it would be impossible, but how to take them off was the difficulty; his presence of mind appears to have been wonderful, he first got off his jacket, then his trowsers with extreme difficulty, because they became entangled in his feet; but by a violent effort he succeeded ; he then found he could not well get rid of his shirt, nor swim with it on.　He was driven to great extremity, his shirt being a new stout cotton one—he therefore once more made a violent effort, and tore it down in front ; but the hem was so strong, that he there stopped, this he put to his mouth, and bit it through ; he then swam on until he nearly reached the shore, where the breakers ran so high, that he lost his oar, once more, he almost entirely gave up hopes, but resolved on one last effort, and found himself thrown upon a rock, very seriously bruised ; he climbed beyond the reach of the water, and laid himself down, cold, hungry, and exhausted, either to perish or to rest.　He told me that, it being quite dark, he could not tell where he was cast ashore, but he was fully sensible that it must be where the rocky high cliffs could be only here and there climbed by man :—his anxiety was consequently great, till day dawned, when he saw some sheep feeding up the cliff side.　He was sure that wherever sheep could go, he could climb.　As his poor feet were sadly cut, he took his stockings, (which he still had on) and bound them round his feet with his garters ; with this exception, he ascended the rough cliff naked ; his exhaustion and fatigue great indeed.　After walking awhile, he arrived at a farm-house ; the farmer took him for a lunatic, and at first spoke to him sharply, but soon finding his real case, he took him in, and treated him with the utmost hospitality.　The farmer's wife prepared him a bed.　I now stop my narrative to say, that from my conversation with Samuel Marshall, I took him to be a man actuated by religious principles, but not possessing an enlightened understanding on these subjects ; one who endeavoured to do, as far as he knew it, his duty ; which he had so remarkably shown in risking his own life, to save the lives of others, particularly in the instance of the women, who were poor and unable to remunerate him.　I was strongly reminded in hearing of his deliverance, of these words of scripture, " with the merciful Thou wilt show Thyself merciful."　The poor man said, also, that he prayed constantly when the salt water was not in his mouth ; which showed on the one hand, his value for prayer, and on the other, his ignorance in supposing that when he could not speak, he would not be equally heard by Him, who looketh in the most secret desire of the heart. However, as I doubt not his prayers were offered in sincerity, they appear to have been answered and accepted. He was carried home to his sorrowful wife, who had heard of the boat being lost, and did not know that her husband was saved.

The mother of one of the other men, I found in the deepest distress, almost out of her mind. I tried to pour a little balm into her deep wounds, by endeavouring to lead her to look to Him, who can alone heal and help, in our greatest trials

Upton Lane, Eleventh Month 16th.—I felt greatly helped in the quiet performance of my duties yesterday up to a certain time, when, I believe, I gave way a little to natural infirmity about a trifle, and I felt how soon a cloud may be brought over the best principle, and what care and watchfulness is needed; and if there be the least fall, how necessary immediately to have recourse to the justifying principle of faith, that no further separation take place from good. I fully believe, that our spiritual enemy remains the accuser of the brethren, and endeavours, when he sees those, who desire to serve the Lord give way, even in a trifle, to take advantage of it to discourage them, and further to insinuate himself into their hearts. It is I believe one of the most important points in the Christian life, if we find ourselves tripping in thought, word, or deed, immediately to fly to the fountain that is set open for the unclean ; that we may at once be cleansed, and obtain peace with God, through our Lord and Saviour Jesus Christ. Oh ! for a little help this day, to come to the living fountain, that I may be fitted for my Master's service, and enter it with a quiet mind. Lord let it be so.

Twelfth Month 20th.—I am once more favoured, after being far from well, with a renewal of health and power, to enter my usual engagements, public and private. Yesterday, I went to town,— first attended the Newgate Committee, then, the British Society, which was very encouraging to me ; there were many present, of different denominations of Christians, and a sweet feeling of love and unity pervaded the whole. Elizabeth Dudley spoke in a lively manner, and I had to pray. There is still much ground for encouragement in the prison cause; and I believe a seed is sown in it, that *will* grow and flourish, I trust, when some of us are laid low. It is a work that brings with it a peculiar feeling of blessing and peace;

may the Most High continue to prosper it! Afterwards I went to Clapham to visit a poor dying converted Jew, who had sent a letter to beg me to go and see him ; my visit was highly interesting. I often wish for the pen of a ready writer, and the pencil of an artist, to picture some of the scenes that I am brought into. A man of a pleasing countenance, greatly emaciated, lying on a little white bed; all clean and in order, his Bible by his side, and animated almost beyond description at seeing me ; he kissed my hand, the tears came into his eyes, his poor face flushed, and he was ready almost to raise himself out of his bed. I sat down, and tried to quiet him, and by degrees succeeded. We had a very interesting conversation ; he had been in the practice of frequently attending my readings at Newgate, apparently with great attention ; latterly, I had not seen him, and was ready to suppose, that like many others, his zeal was of short duration ; but I lately heard that he had been ill. He is one of those Jews, who have felt perfectly liberated from keeping any part of the Law of Moses, which some other converted Jews, yet consider themselves bound to observe. I found that when he used to come so often to Newgate, he was a man of good moral character, seek- the truth. But to go on with my story—in our conversation, he said, that he felt great peace, no fear of death, and a full reliance upon his Saviour for salvation ; he said that his visits to New- gate had been to him beyond going to any church; indeed, I little knew how much was going on in his heart. He requested me to read a Psalm that I had read one day in Newgate, the 107th. This I did, and he appeared deeply to feel it, particularly as my dear friend M—— W——, and S—— and I made our little remarks in Christian freedom as we went along, truly, I believe (as Friends say) in the life. The poor Jew prayed very strikingly ; I followed him, and returned thanks ; what a solemn, uniting time it was! The poor Jew said, "God is a spirit, and they that worship Him, must worship Him in spirit and in truth," as if he felt the spirituality of the Christian administration. His countenance lightened with apparent joy, when he expressed his undoubted belief that he should soon enter the kingdom, and that I should, before long, follow him ; then he gave me his blessing, and took leave in much tenderness, showing every mark he could of gratitude and love. He did not accept any gift of money, saying, that he wanted no good thing, as he was most kindly provided for by serious persons in the neighbourhood.

I arrived at home, about eight o'clock, peaceful, after my day's work, but humbled, because of the great imperfection even in what may be called our works of righteousness, and the need even in these, of pardon for the evil, that may have crept in, through the sacrifice that atoneth for all sin, even for the iniquity of our Holy Things.*

But a few days remained to the close of the year, filled as it had been, by incessant occupation and much bodily fatigue : but even in that short time, another call was to be made upon her time and feelings.

Mrs. Elizabeth Fry her sister-in-law, had continued to reside at Plashet, in a cottage which she had built on a part of the property many years before. With her lived an elder cousin, Mrs. Sarah Fry. She was one of kindly cheerful nature ; the children, the poor, but especially any one in a scrape or difficulty, or a little in disgrace with the rest of the world, were sure to share her peculiar protection and kindness. Their pleasant pretty residence was a happy retreat to the tired and invalided—in so much peace and quiet did they pursue the even tenor of their way. In peace and calm emphatically, was the journey of one of them now about to terminate.

Last Third-day, I went to Plashet Cottage to see my dear sister Elizabeth Fry, and my cousin Sarah Fry, both of them ill in bed with severe colds. Dear cousin Sarah was full of lively conversation ; I much enjoyed her company, and waiting on them both, and left them tolerably comfortable, but on Fourth-day morning I was sent for in great haste, understanding that dear cousin Sarah was much more ill. When my husband and I arrived at the cottage, we found her lying dead

* After about two or three weeks, I received an account of the peaceful end of this poor Jew.

in bed, by my sister's side. It was a considerable shock, and very affecting, still not without strong consolation on her account; for my belief is, that she was one of the retired, humble, devoted believers in, and followers of the Lamb, that she was indeed one of His redeemed ones, ready to depart and be with Him for ever. It was particularly sweet to observe the work of grace appear to increase with her years, and her light to shine brighter and brighter, as her outward powers declined. This always strikes me as a sure mark of living faith, because it is natural, as infirmities of body increase, for infirmity of mind and temper to increase also, but it was very different with her ; the gentle and sweet, cheerful and lamblike spirit, appeared to abound more and more as her years increased. I could hardly help desiring, if ready, to be favoured with such a translation from time to eternity. My dear sister is still very unwell, but wonderfully supported under this trial ; she says, that she has been shielded as on every side, and though unworthy of it, wonderfully upheld. This was one of those scenes I long to have pictured—the sweet appearance of dear Sarah Fry's remains lying by dear Elizabeth's side, who looked so wonderfully quiet and supported, though so very ill. It really was no common sight, the living and the dead thus together.

First Month 2nd, 1832.—I think I have seldom entered a year with more feeling of weight than this. As the clock was striking twelve, the last year closing and this beginning, I found myself on my knees by my bed-side, looking up to Him who had carried me and mine through the last year, and could only really be our Helper in this. We have had the subject of marriage much before us this last year, it has brought us to some test of our feelings and principles respecting it. That it is highly desirable and important to have young persons settle in marriage, particularly young men, I cannot doubt ; and that it is one of the most likely means of their preservation, religiously, morally and temporally. Moreover, it is highly desirable, to settle with one of the same of religious views, habits and education, as themselves ; more particularly for those, who have been brought up as Friends, because their mode of education is peculiar ; but, if any young persons upon arriving at an age of discretion, do not feel themselves really

attached to our peculiar views and habits, then, I think their
parents have no right to use undue influence with them, as to the
connexions they may incline to form ; provided, they be with
persons of religious lives and conversation.　I am of opinion, that
parents are apt to exercise too much authority upon the subject
of marriage, and that there would be more really happy unions,
if young persons were left more to their own feelings and discretion.　Marriage is too much treated like a business concern, and
love that essential ingredient, too little respected in it.　I disapprove the rule of our Society, that disowns persons for allowing
a child to marry one not a Friend—it is a most undue and unchristian restraint, as far as I can judge of it.

I see and feel the present to be a stirring time in our family,
and in our country also.　The cholera is an anxious thing ; the
stir about the Reform Bill, the general spirit of insubordination
amongst people, and the clashing amongst the highly professing
in the religious world, I consider also to be serious ; but I do not
take the violent alarm that some do, as to the state of the times ;
or as to any very great event being about to take place.　Some
are of opinion, that the second coming of our blessed Lord is just
at hand.　As we are sure at all events, that He will soon come
to us individually, may we above all things seek to be found ready
for that day.

Upton, Second Month 21st.—We have lately been brought
to feel very seriously the approach of the cholera to our own
borders, as it is said to have been as near as Limehouse.　I have
not generally felt any agitating fear, but rather the weight of the
thing, and desirous that it should prove a stimulus to seek more
diligently after eternal things, and to be ready spiritually for
whatever may await us ; and outwardly to use all proper precau-
tions.　I have desired earnestly, that we should do our very
utmost to protect our poor neighbours, by administering to their
many wants.　This led me to make some efforts with some of our
women Friends, also with some other kind and influential people,
and although perhaps thought by some a busybody in it, yet
more has been already accomplished, than I could have looked for.
The poor are likely to be really helped and cared for.　In such
works of charity, I always desire to be preserved from a forward

spirit, or an over active one ; yet on the other hand, when I feel any thing laid upon me, as I did in this instance, I feel much bound to work in it, even through some discouragement and opposition ; I mostly find in such cases, that way has been made for me, as if He, who called me to the work was indeed with me in it. I was too poorly to go to our Monthly Meeting to-day; which I do not much regret, as my dearest son J—— was to send in his resignation of membership ; I so much feel it, that I think perhaps, I am better away. I believe my dear J—— has done what he now thinks best; there I leave it, and though I certainly have much felt his leaving a Society, I so dearly love, the principles of which I so much value; yet no outward names are in reality of much importance in my view, nor do I think very much of membership with any outward sect or body of Christians—my feeling is, that if we are but living members of the Church of Christ, this is the only membership essential to salvation. Belonging to any particular body of Christians has, I see, its disadvantages, as well as advantages ; it often brings into the bondage of man, rather than being purely and simply bound to the law of Christ ; though I am fully sensible of its many comforts, advantages and privileges. Earnestly do I desire for this dear child, that his Lord may make his way clear before him, that he may be truly here a member of the militant Church of Christ, and hereafter of His Church triumphant.

Third Month 21st.—To-day is proclaimed " a fast-day" on account of the cholera : it is one of those occasions, in the observance of which, we must each follow our own consciences. If the government of a country could make a people keep a day really holy unto the Lord, in real fasting, penitence and prayer, much good would result ; but this, no government can do, and I fear that the present will rather be made a day of lightness and recreation. However, those who do keep it seriously, I trust will be blessed in so doing, and their prayers answered, and that this awful disease may be (if right for us) checked in its progress.

I rather feel having to go before the Committee of the House of Commons, on the subject of prisons. May any good to this important cause be done by it, and may I be helped to do my part with simplicity, as unto God, and not unto man !

The object of this Committee, was to ascertain the best mode of Secondary Punishment, so as to be the most effectual in repressing crime. The points Mrs. Fry earnestly insisted upon were these :—

The expediency of having matrons, and only female officers in female prisons, and as much as possible in convict-ships also.

The necessity of employment, and the advantage of its being suited to the sex, at all events with those least hardened, or who show symptoms of amendment.

The importance of separation, especially at night.

The good to be derived from compulsory instruction, where prisoners are unable to read.

That solitude does not prepare women for returning to social and domestic life, or tend so much to real improvement, as carefully arranged intercourse during part of the day with one another, under the closest superintendence and inspection, constant occupation, and solitude at night.

The value of the visits of ladies to prisons, as a check upon the matron and female officers, and an incentive to good conduct among the prisoners ; but on this point her own evidence may be adduced.

Every matron should live upon the spot, and be able to inspect them closely by night and by day ; and when there are sufficient female prisoners to require it, female officers should be appointed, and a male turnkey never permitted to go into the women's apartments ; I am convinced, when a prison is properly managed, it is unnecessary, because, by firm and gentle management, the most refractory may be controlled by their own sex. But here I must put in a word respecting ladies visiting. I find a remarkable difference depending upon whether female officers are superintended by ladies or not. I can tell, almost as soon as I go into the prison, whether they are or not, from the general appearance, both of the women and their officers. One reason is, that many of the latter are not very superior women, not very high, either in principle or habit, and are liable to be contaminated : they soon get familiar with the prisoners, and cease to excite the respect due to their office ; whereas, where ladies go in once or twice, or three times in a week, the effect produced is decided. Their attendance keeps the female officers in their places, makes them attend to their duty, and has a constant influence on the minds of the prisoners themselves ; in short, I may say, after sixteen years' experience, that the result of ladies of principle and respectability superintending the female officers in prisons, and the prisoners themselves, has far exceeded my most sanguine expectations. In no instance have I more clearly seen the beneficial effects of ladies visiting and superintending prisoners, than on board the convict-ships. I have witnessed the alterations since ladies have visited them constantly in the river. I heard formerly of the most dreadful iniquity, confusion, and frequently great distress ; latterly I have seen a very wonderful improvement in their conduct. And on the voyage, I have most valuable certificates, to show the difference of their condition, on their arrival in the colony. I can produce, if necessary, extracts from letters : Samuel Marsden, who has been chaplain there a good many years, says, it is quite a different thing ; that they used to come in the most filthy, abominable state, hardly fit for any thing; now they arrive in good order, in a totally different situation ; and I have heard the same thing from others. General Darling's wife, a very valuable lady, has adopted the same system there ; she has visited the prison at Paramatta, and the same thing respecting the officers is felt there, as it is here. On the continent of Europe, in various parts—Petersburg, Geneva, Turin, Berne and Basle, and some other places—there are corresponding societies, and the result is the same in every part. In Berlin, they are doing wonders ; I hear a most satisfactory account ; and in Petersburg, where, from the barbarous state of the people, it was said it could not be done, the conduct of the prisoners has been perfectly astonishing ; and an entire change has been produced.

Upton Lane, Sixth Month 3rd.—We have just concluded the Yearly Meeting. It has been in some respects a marked one, and I hope an instructive one. We had much advice, particularly from one Friend, upon the subject of Christian faith ; holding up much more decidedly to our view, the doctrine of the Atonement, showing, that our actuating motive in all things must be faith in Him who suffered for us, and love for Him who first loved us.   In this I quite agree, but I felt with her, as well as with some others, that they strain the point of all our minor testimonies being kept to, as a necessary proof of this love.   I fully believe, that many of us are called thus to prove our love ; but I also believe there are some, if not many among us, to whom this does not apply, and that we cannot, therefore, lay down the rule for others.   I had to speak decidedly, twice in the Meetings ; once in the first Meeting, acknowledging the loving-kindness and tender mercy of our God as manifested to us during the year that was passed, and what an inducement it should be to love and faithfulness.   This appeared greatly to relieve and comfort many minds, for they freely spoke to me about it afterwards.   I had particularly to make allusion to the cholera not having made further devastations amongst us.   I had in another Meeting in a similar way to return thanks, and pray for us, as a Society, and for the Universal Church.   I also had from a deep feeling of duty, to express my thankfulness, that the Christian standard had been upheld amongst us ; so much encouragement given to read the scriptures, and attend to their holy precepts ; but I felt a fear, whether the influence of the Holy Spirit, as our guide, had been quite enough dwelt upon, which, as a fundamental part of our principles, I trusted we should ever maintain.   I also expressed my desire, that the fruits of the Spirit should be more manifest amongst us, not only in our peculiar testimonies, but in the subjection of our tempers and wills, which I thought to be much wanted : fearing that some maintained our testimonies, more from expediency than principle, which produced great inconsistency of conduct.   I then added my earnest hope, that individually and collectively, we should stand open to improvement, making this our prayer : " That which I see not, teach Thou me ;" that we should be willing to be taught of God immediately and instrumentally, that our light might shine brighter and brighter to the perfect day.

9th.—I yesterday was favoured to get through the British

Society Meeting. It was to me a very serious occasion ; our different reports were highly satisfactory and encouraging ; but I felt it laid upon me to speak so decidedly on some points, that I could not fully enjoy them. After the British Society report was read, I first endeavoured to show the extreme importance of the work in which we were engaged, and the best means of producing the desired effect,' of reforming the criminal ; but what most deeply impressed me was, considering the awful extent of existing crime, and the suffering and sorrow produced by it—how far the conduct of the higher classes may influence that of the lower, and tend in many ways to the increase of evil, by ladies not setting a religious example to their servants, nor instructing them in the right way ; by not keeping 'the Sabbath strictly,—by very late hours, and attending public places,—by vanity in dress, and by hurrying mantua-makers and milliners, and so causing them to oppress and overwork their young women,—by not paying their bills themselves, or through some confidential person ; but trusting them to young or untried servants, thus leading to dishonesty on their parts, or that of the tradespeople,—by allowing their maid-servants or char-women to begin to wash at unseasonable hours, and consequently to require ardent spirits to support them. Then I represented how much they might do to promote good and discourage evil ; by educating the poor religiously in infant and other schools ; by watching over girls after they leave schools, until placed in service, and by providing for them suitable religious, instructive and entertaining books ; also, by forming libraries in hospitals, and workhouses, and by preventing the introduction of irreligious and light books. I also urged the establishment of district societies. These things I had forcibly and freely to express, showing the blessing of promoting good and the woe of encouraging evil.

Seventh Month 14*th.*—I have just parted from my dearest G——, for a sojourn on the Continent, with three of his young friends, and their tutor. It has been a subject of serious feeling giving him up ; but there has appeared no other opening so suitable for him. This has arisen in a very satisfactory manner, and as far as I can judge from his character, it appears the most likely means for his improvement ; there are remarkable advantages likely to attend them, from my serious friends abroad being interested for them. I have been enabled, in faith, to commit him to the keeping of our Heavenly Father. In His mercy do I hope, above all, that He may keep him from evil, and if consistent with His holy will, bring him back again in peace and safety. Gracious Lord ! grant for Thine own sake that it may be so, and that this beloved child may so grow in grace, that he may be enabled to resist the temptations that are in the world. My prayers have also been raised for the other dear children, particularly ———— whom I have felt much for, and taken much pains in reading with him and G—— in the morning,—may it take deep root in their hearts.

To the gentleman who accompanied her son and his young companions, she presented a written sketch of her wishes and opinions. Some of these hints, are as follow :—

Never allow the boys to be out alone in the evening ; nor to attend any public place of amusement with any person, however pressing they may be. I advise, thy seeing that they never talk when going to bed, but retire quietly after reading a portion of the holy scriptures. In the morning, that they be as quiet as possible, and learn their scripture texts, whilst dressing. I recommend the party accepting all suitable invitations from German families, as an important means of improving their general knowledge, as well as their German. It must be remembered that no study is equal to that of mankind, and nothing so likely to enlarge the mind as society with the good and the cultivated of every nation. I advise their taste for our best poets being encouraged, by occasionally learning some by heart, and reading it aloud. Also, their being led particularly to observe and admire all the productions of nature, and to study geology, &c., &c., as far as their time will admit of it.

Above all things, and far beyond every other consideration, mayst thou be enabled to teach them, that the first and great object of life is, to seek the kingdom of God and to do His will.

Upton Lane, 19th.—I have been brought very low on account of one of my dear children, who has since her return home had a serious cough, united with great prostration of

strength, so as to excite our anxiety as to what it may end in ;
besides this, the very important affair of last year is again
hanging over her.   I deeply feel it, far more than I like to
acknowledge to myself, or others, and am at times brought into
deep conflict of spirit before the Lord.   I must seek to have no
will about her, much as I long naturally for her restoration ; but,
rather most earnestly pray, that, whatever our heavenly Father
may do with her, He may keep her His own, that she may be a
member of His militant church on earth, or of His triumphant
church in heaven ; and oh ! may He be pleased to make the way
clear for her and for all, that will conduce to peace here and
happiness hereafter.   Notwithstanding this weighty cloud, I
believed it right to walk by faith, not by sight, and propose to
my Monthly Meeting, to attend the Half Year's Meeting in
Wales, next month, and ask also liberty for such other services
as Truth might lead into ; but I can hardly say how much it
cost me.

Before leaving home for this journey, during which, she visited
parts of Ireland, Elizabeth Fry, communicated her intention
of visiting some of the county Gaols, to the Under Secretary
of State, S. March Philips, Esq., and her wish to make arrangements by which ladies might be allowed to attend to the female
prisoners confined in them.   She received on this occasion,
a highly gratifying communication, with permission to make
its contents known, dated Home Office, August 10th, 1832,
assuring her, that—" Lord Melbourne was fully sensible of the
good which had been done by herself, and the ladies connected
with her in many of the prisons ; and of the great benefits
derived from their exertions, by the female transports ; and that
his Lordship was anxious, that as far as it could be done, the
Visiting Magistrates should favourably entertain and second her
benevolent intentions."

Ninth Month 18*th*.—We returned home from our journey
last Sixth-day evening, having been absent just five weeks.   We

visited several places in the south of Ireland, a good many in Wales, and some in England. I think I never remember taking a journey in which it was more frequently sealed to my own mind, that we were in our right places ; through much difficulty, our way was opened to go, and to continue out. Though I believe we have scripture authority for it—still further confirmed, by the internal ˙evidence of the power of the Spirit, and its external results,—yet, I am obliged to walk by faith rather than sight, in going about as a woman in the work of the ministry ; it is to my nature a great humiliation, and I often feel it to be " foolishness," particularly in large Public Meetings, before entering upon the service ; but generally, when engaged in the ministry, I find such an unction, and so much opening upon Christian doctrine and practice, that after a Meeting, I mostly say in my heart, " It is the Lord's doing, and marvellous in our eyes." Such was often the case in this journey. I felt, amongst Friends in Ireland, as if my service was to lead them from all external dependence, either on their membership in the Society, their high profession or their peculiar testimonies ; and to show, that these things are only good as they spring from simple Christian faith and practice, and avail nothing, unless the heart be really changed and cleansed from sin, though I believed that these things would follow as the result to those who fill the important place in the church, that in my opinion, Friends are called to occupy. Above everything else, I endeavoured to lead all to the grand foundation of Christian faith and practice. My dear sister was much led in the same line of ministry.

On some occasions, I felt a far greater openness than others ; I believe, in places, there was rather a jealousy over me ; I apprehend that my believing it right, as much as possible, to avoid mysticism in my mode of expression, is not fully understood by all Friends ; I desire to·be sound, simple, and clear, and not to clothe anything in a mysterious garb, even if with individuals it might give it more weight. The unfeigned kindness shown me by several persons can never be forgotten by me.

We visited many Prisons, and had cause for deep humble thankfulness and rejoicing, to see how much has been done in this cause, and the effect of some of our labours when last in Ireland :

it is marvellous to myself, how it has pleased my Lord and Master to bless some of my unworthy labours. Now for the narrative of the journey :—We set off under outward discouragement, more particularly two of my children being very unwell, but my dearest brother Samuel going with me, was a great support, though I also felt the weight of taking him from his family. We set off in his carriage, a very pleasant open one, my sister Elizabeth Fry, my niece Sarah Gurney, Samuel, and myself, the day fine, with all outward comforts and indulgences—the Lord surely doth provide. We visited Cirencester on First-day, Gloucester on Second-day, and so on to Brecon ; taking Meetings, Prisons, &c., forming Committees as we went in our way to Milford. There we had a most interesting time. Crossing to Ireland, we all rather dreaded the weather being stormy, and we much feared being ill ; however, by delaying one day, we had a delightful voyage, and also a very satisfactory Meeting with the poor and the sailors, near Milford. We met with a kind reception in Ireland ; I think I never felt more in my right place ; there appeared an indescribable evidence of it. Now and then, a feeling of almost unmixed peace. Our visit to Cork was highly interesting ; we were frequently in the neighbourhood of cholera, and at times I felt fearful about it, but generally was raised above it ; the weather was mostly fine, and much of the country that we went through, lovely, so that the journey was not without outward refreshment to me. We saw grievous evils remaining in some Prisons, which we trust that our visit may remedy, by bringing them to notice. At Carlow, I had a deeply-interesting, and for a time, afflicting season, hearing that my dearest H—— had broken a blood vessel on the lungs, happily, the account did not arrive till a week after it had happened, and with it came a second account much more favourable. I was, in mercy, favoured with a trustful, hopeful spirit ; happily, too, our steps were turned homewards. The letters became more and more comfortable, so that we were enabled to remain in Dublin the full time, to perform what we believed to be our various calls of duty, in that very important and interesting place. We had a delightful passage from Dublin to Wales, of five hours and a half ; wind and all in our favour, and a very satisfactory journey home.

Mrs. Fry returned, strengthened and refreshed by this journey. Matters of deep import awaited her return, in the approaching marriages of two of her children. Her son William was now, almost for the first time, about to quit their dwelling. His mother subsequently beheld his advance in the Christian life : from year to year she marked his exemplary fulfilment of all the relations of husband, son, father, master, friend, and lived long enough to see "the place that had known him, know him no more." With her whole heart could she then acknowledge, that God had led him, although by paths that she knew not, and by ways that she had not seen.

It is proposed, that my dear son William's marriage should take place in little more than a week. I cannot help feeling deeply giving him up. To have this dear child married, and not be able to be with him, is very affecting to me. With three children likely to marry out of the Society, and the life of one of them very uncertain, I have much, very much to feel ; but respecting her and all of my children, if they do but get to the kingdom, I may be thankful ! and shall I hold them back ?—My desires are unutterable, my prayers frequent and fervent, to be directed amidst all my difficulties, to do that which is right,—first in the sight of God, then in the view of my family, and lastly in that of the Society to which I belong.

Dagenham, Tenth Month 3rd.—Here am I sitting in solitude, keeping silence before the Lord ; on the wedding day of my beloved son William. As I could not conscientiously attend the marriage, I believed it right to withdraw for the day. Words appear very inadequate to express the earnestness—the depth of my supplications for him and for his—that the blessing of the Most High may rest upon them. I was yesterday enabled, when with him and his sisters alone, to pour forth my soul in prayer for him, and read such portions of scripture as I thought would be for his good and comfort ; he was low, and so we were all, but as the day advanced, we brightened, and as dear William himself said, there appeared a spirit of good over us. I stayed with him almost all day, and went in the evening with him to Ham House, where their kindness was almost unbounded. We then went to our dear friends the ———'s, where I had a warm reception; they very sweetly bear with my scruples, for it must appear odd, very odd to them, my not feeling it right to attend the wedding of such a son; but my heart is full of love to them. Though I do not see as they see, I most deeply feel that all who truly love Him are one in Christ, yet the more simple, and spiritual, the administration of religion, the more I believe we are enabled to abide in Him; therefore I feel zealous, perhaps too much so, to have my children thorough Friends; but of this I now see little or no hope, though I expect many of them to be serious in another line, and fully believe, that my striving and labours have been blessed, in leading them to a love of holiness and true righteousness, and beyond all, of their Saviour. We concluded the evening in quietness, and strange to say, I slept well and peacefully. This morning, we almost all assembled before breakfast, with one or two valuable dependants, and W—— C—— S—— with us; I was enabled to exhort earnestly, and to pray fervently, not only for the beloved couple, but all the children, and those who were to be, or were already united to them, and for their children; for ourselves, household, &c.: it was a very solemn time, and I humbly trust that the presence of the Lord was with us. I desired also to return thanks for this dear son in giving him up from my care; that he had been so much preserved from the evil which is in the world, that he had ever displayed such near love to me and to all of us, and had been so good a son to us. There is much to be thankful for respecting him, and though it has been a great disappointment his not marrying a Friend, yet there is also much to value in this connexion. I have a secret hope it may prove in the ordering of a kind Providence for his good. As for myself, I sit solitary in many things; but I thought to-day (from this wedding bringing these things home to me.)—Have I not my Lord as my friend, and my comforter? and is He not as a husband to all the members of His church? and am I not often satisfied and refreshed by His love? I may indeed say I am— so that I am ready to trust, that the great and curious turnings and overturnings that my family have met with, will in the end

work for good, through the love and unmerited mercy of God in
Christ Jesus ; and that we may more and more all become one
in Him !   Amen.

A month afterwards, another child was married.   Mrs. Fry considered that the case of a daughter was different to that of a son,
and the wedding taking place at her own house, that it was for
her to remain at home.

Upton Lane, Eleventh Month 5th.—Last Fourth-day, the 31st
of the Tenth Month, my dearest H—— was married to W— C—
S——.   The morning was bright, the different families collected,
—of course I was not present at the ceremony.   The bride and
bridegroom went to Ham House to take leave of their dear party ;
they then came home, and we soon sat down to breakfast, about
thirty in number.   There appeared a serious and yet cheerful feeling over us.   I felt prayer for them, but saw no opportunity
vocally to express it.   As we arose to leave the table, William
Streatfeild, the vicar of East Ham, returned thanks for the
blessings received ; when, quite unexpectedly to myself, there was
such a solemn silence, as if all were arrested, that I was enabled
vocally to ask a blessing upon them, and to pray that the Most
High would keep them and bless them, cause His face to shine
upon them, and be gracious unto them, lift up the light of His
countenance upon them, and give them peace ; and through His unbounded love, and unlimited mercy in Christ Jesus, that He would
grant them enough of the fatness of the earth, and so cause the
dew of heaven to descend upon them, that they might be fruitful
to His praise, and live to His glory, and be His in time, and His
to all eternity.   After a short further pause, we withdrew, walked
in the garden, or rested, until they left us.   The tears often flowed
from my eyes in parting from this beloved child.

The little band at Upton Lane was now greatly diminished.
Mr. and Mrs. Fry, with the two daughters who remained at
home, sought, after these events, the refreshment of a visit to
their relatives in Norfolk.   They first went to Lowestoft, and

remained some days at the vicarage ; there Mrs. Fry saw the schools just established, united in the cottage-readings, and entered warmly into the various interests of the place. Her sister, Mrs. Cunningham, wrote at the time her own impressions of this visit :—

" November 22nd.—We had the treat and great advantage of a visit from our dearest sister. She was encouraged to come and assist us in the formation of our District Society, which, in this large place, we find to be essential for the right working of the parish. We are most thankful for the assistance of our dear sister ; our brother and two of our nieces accompanied her ; it is almost like having an angel visitor, so full of loveliness and grace is she. On Sunday, my dearest sister being at Pakefield with the Friends, induced my remaining all day there. She drank tea with me, at the Hawtreys. Mr. Hawtrey and she had some animated and delightful conversation, before we went down to the lecture in the school-room ; dearest Betsey accompanied us, and some of the other friends joined us. After the usual singing and prayer, Mr. Hawtrey read very impressively the latter part of the third of Ephesians ; we then had silence, after which she arose, and beautifully addressed the meeting, on the necessity of domestic and private religion, and enlarged a good deal on the duty, spirit,- and manner, in which scripture should be read and studied ; it would not do to hear it only in public service. After the powerful outward means which had been granted to the people of Pakefield, how were they called upon, to examine, and digest for themselves, the written *word* of God. Then, in a full and beautiful prayer, she seemed to bring the blessing of heaven upon us. I hardly know any scriptural treat so great, as uniting with her in *prayer !* it is such a heavenly song —so spiritual—so elevating, enjoying glimpses, as it were, of the eternal world ! Oh ! may we long retain the power and the blessing of it ! Her last short address was very impressive : that we should not come short of our rank in righteousness ; that we should follow our crucified Reedemer, in humility, meekness, and self-denial ; that we should walk worthy of our very high calling, &c. Mr. Hawtrey ended with a very feeling prayer, and after taking an affectionate leave of the people, I drove our beloved sister home. On Monday, we were all in movement, in preparation for our District Society Meeting ; this was held at our house, and well attended. Our dear sister displayed much of her tact and power, and gave us the *greatest* assistance ; how marvellously gifted she is ! Through her influence, all parties were brought together, and the District Society begun under most favourable auspices ; the town was divided, and every arrangement made, according to her advice. Our meeting was highly satisfactory, and promised the most favourable results ; every one seemed willing to yield to her wisdom and eloquence. What a power of communicating good she possesses ! what a faithful steward in that which is committed to her! A very interesting party dined with us, which increased much in the evening. After the reading, our dearest sister prayed most beautifully to our comfort and edification. On Tuesday, we went off to breakfast with the Hawtreys. As usual, we met with a warm reception, and had a cheerful, pleasant talking breakfast with them ; the family service afterwards was peculiarly edifying. Mr. Hawtrey read the fourteenth of John ; our dearest sister's address to the children, and to the parents, and then to Mr. Hawtrey, as a minister, was most touching and edifying. Surely these times do leave a peculiar savour, which is not to be forgotten ; it adds to the precious seasons which are foretastes of heaven. Her mind appears to me in more lively exercise, and more gifted than ever ; rich both in grace and gifts. She is indeed beloved of the Lord, and dwells in safety by Him. After this she paid visits to the Friends, and we did not return till towards the latter end of the morning ; the evening was occupied by the Committee for the District Society. Wednesday was a full day, my sister and I walked about most of the morning, visiting the schools, making calls, &c., &c. Nothing can be more benevolent and beautiful than her spirit, overflowing with love and tenderness. Our dinner-party was not very large, but cheerful and pleasant : the first part of the evening was necessarily devoted to the agreeable ; after which, my little society of women, and several others, assembled in the parlour ; my beloved sister went to them, and gave them a little sketch of her New-gate histories. We afterwards all removed into the drawing-room, and had a beautiful meeting, very suited to the subject we had been upon. My husband took the Prodigal Son as the subject for reading, which my sister applied to herself, and to all of us, as being led as penitents to return to our Father's house, and oh ! the display of mercy, and of goodness, and long-suffering, in the exquisite character of the God of Israel. The prayer at the con-clusion was as usual, like an air from heaven. Our large party then broke up in much love. On Thursday, our beloved sister left us, after again enjoying prayer together, and commending each other affectionately to the care and keeping of the good Shepherd of Israel."

They then went to Earlham, that home of the past ; after-wards to North Repps Hall. The all-absorbing subject of Slavery was occupying Mr. Buxton's mind. It was to her most interesting, to listen to his details of the struggle of the preceding Sessions of Parliament, one replete with importance to this vast question, now approaching the crisis of its fate. All but alone, and nearly single-handed in the House, he had brought forward a measure for emancipation in opposition to the wishes of Govern-ment, at a cost of effort and self-sacrifice little known to lookers on in general.

Her stay at North Repps Cottage delighted her ; she visited the schools, met the hardy fishermen of that boisterous coast, in the school-rooms at Overstrand and Trimmingham, and partook, as no common privilege, of social intercourse with the inmates of that lovely retreat. Their journey concluded with visits to Runcton and Lynn. The different administrations which they had seen were very striking to her, and particularly cheering, under the circumstances of her own family. To a sister she wrote soon after her return home.

I think of your dear party with much interest, and feel the

sweet remembrance of having been with you, I hope that I
received profit, as well as pleasure, from it; indeed, I think our
journey was an instructive one in many ways.   My desire is, as I
go along, to take a leaf out of every one's book; and surely at
Lowestoft, Earlham, North Repps, Lynn, and Runcton, I might
do it.   It is well to see the truth through different mediums ; for
however the colour of the glass that we see it through may vary,
the truth itself remains the same, and beholding it of many hues,
may be the means of throwing fresh light on diverse parts of
it.   How does the knowledge of others often make us think
little of ourselves ! at least I find it so, and am much humbled
in most of your houses.

Upton Lane, First Month 28th, 1833.—It has been a serious
time to the country, the cholera prevailing nearly throughout
England and Ireland.   We were frequently where it was on our
journey, but were favoured to escape unhurt.   A great stir in
the elections for the new Reform Parliament.   Joseph Pease, a
Friend, admitted ; this opens a new door for our Society—to what
it will lead is doubtful.   A war for a short time with Holland.
Much stirring in the world generally, religiously and politically—
great variety of sentiments.   Notwithstanding all these things,
it appears to me, that the kingdom of God is spreading its pure,
blessed, and peaceable influence, and that the partition walls
that have been built up between Christians generally, are breaking down.   The suppression of Slavery—the diminution of
Capital Punishment—the improvement in Prisons, and the state
of the poor prisoners—the spread of the Scriptures, also of the
Gospel to distant lands—the increase of education and knowledge
generally, and many other such things, are truly encouraging.
I do thankfully believe that there is a great and glorious work
going on, promoting the advancement of that day, when the
knowledge of God, and His glory, will cover the earth as the
waters cover the sea.   For Thine own name's sake, gracious
Lord, hasten this day, when all flesh may see and rejoice in Thy
salvation !

Fourth Month 12th.—One of my near relations has died suddenly—my cousin Martha B——.   I can hardly think why it

should have spread such an influence over me, as our spirits were not particularly united here ; but it may be so, for from my own experience I am much inclined to believe in the communion of spirits, both with those here, and those departed. I think it by no means impossible, that those who remain a little longer to maintain the warfare, may sympathise in spirit with those who have entered into their rest, and whose warfare is accomplished. With my dearest and most beloved sister Rachel, I have thought she has been as a ministering spirit to me, and like one formerly, that her mantle has in degree descended upon me ; for. I certainly have, in some respects, ever since that period, been under rather a different influence, and have had different views and feelings. It may be only the effect of her blessed example in life, and at last in death. I desire neither to indulge imagination nor superstition on religious subjects ; but some of these private views can harm no one, and are a comfort to myself, and what is more, I think I have scripture authority for them.

Sixth Month 5th.—Yesterday, we finished the Yearly Meeting, as far as women have to do with it. I think, as it respects the Society, it has been an important time ; there is much stirring amongst Friends, arising from a considerable number taking apparently a much higher evangelical ground, than has generally been taken by the Society, bordering, I apprehend in a few, on Calvinism. This has caused a strong alarm to some, far beyond I believe what is needful, so great, however, as to produce something of two sets amongst us, and at times an uncomfortable feeling. Still harmony has prevailed, and through all, real Gospel Truth appears to me to be spreading amongst us.

Seventh Month 10th.—We have been favoured the last two days, to have all our fifteen children around us, and the day before yesterday, we had all to dine at our table, and our nine grandchildren afterwards at dessert, our dearest sister Catherine Gurney, the only other person present at table—(excepting our sister Elizabeth Fry and Rebecca Sturges, for a short time), it was a deeply interesting, and to me touching, as well as pleasing sight. It is remarkable, their none fully seeing religious truth with me ; yet I cannot repine, if I may but see real marks of the Christian life. Outwardly, through all our difficulties, I could not but feel how all had been provided for, and a liberal table spread before us. The married children all provided for, some abundantly—the grandchildren generally bringing up so well, is a great cause of thankfulness—I could not rejoice or give thanks as I desired, at our many unmerited mercies, but I felt bowed in spirit under a sense of them. We had a cheerful dinner, Rachel C—— the only one really out of health at this time ; but she enjoyed herself. After dinner, we walked a little about, then had tea. After tea, we read the 103rd psalm, and I spoke to my children, earnestly impressing upon them the importance, now most of them were no longer under our restraint, that they might be conformed to the will of God, and be faithful stewards of His manifold gifts ; and that if we went by different ways, we might in the end meet, where there will be no partition walls, no different ways, but all love, joy, peace, and union of view, and of conduct—I blessed them, and most earnestly prayed for all ; we then separated in much near love.

DAGENHAM.

CHAPTER XVIII.

1833, 1834. Sojourn in Jersey—Visits to Guernsey, Sark and Herm—
Objects in these Islands—Recall to England—Death of a nephew—
Nurses one of her daughters in severe illness—Letters to three of
her daughters—Return to Upton Lane—Marriage of a son—Attends
the Meetings in Dorset and Hants—Crosses to the Isle of Wight—
Fresh Water—Coast-Guard Stations there—Visit to a Convict Ship—
A walk in the Plashet grounds—Intercourse with Members of Govern-
ment—Coast-Guard Libraries—Convict Ships—Journey into Scotland
—Prisons there—Brighton District Society.

At this period, in consequence of the marriages which had
taken place, and other circumstances, the press of interests and
engagements had become greater than the family could bear. A
long absence from home appeared the best resource; and after
some deliberation, the Island of Jersey was selected as the place
of retreat. Its lovely scenery and fine air afforded strong induce-

ments ; augmented by the interest attached to the peculiar language, government, and internal regulations of the Channel
Islands, that only remnant of Norman ducal power, still united
with England. Some of the party preceded the rest, to prepare
for their mother's reception, with the second detachment. They
had a long and stormy passage, and their first encounter with the
rocky approach to the island, from a boisterous sea, in the obscurity of twilight, gave an unfavourable impression of the navigation, which their letters conveyed home. Mrs. Fry naturally
dreaded the sea, so that after receiving their accounts, she felt
peculiarly alive to the mercy and indulgence of a tranquil voyage.
She arrived in the morning—the lovely bay of St. Aubin's smooth,
full and blue—the rocks mostly covered by the tide—the verdant
island before her smiling in sunshine. A profusion of flowers
and fruit ornamented the breakfast table that awaited her in
" Caledonia Cottage," which had been engaged and prepared for
their residence, and charmed with the beauties that surrounded
them, they could hardly believe the discomforts that had attended
the arrival of the first party. They were supplied with a few excellent letters of introduction amongst the island families, with
some of whom friendships were formed, which lasted till the close
of her life. The circumstances by which she was surrounded,
were very congenial to her. The beauty of the scenery, the
luxuriance of the productions, the prosperity of the inhabitants, the refinement and intellectual cultivation of the upper
classes, combined with simplicity of habit, and in many instances
with true piety and active benevolence, rendered the period of
her residence in Jersey, one of peculiar refreshment and pleasure. With her husband and children, and a few of her intimate friends, she would often spend the day in the remote
parts of the island, amongst the secluded and romantic bays of
its northern coast. The little party would picnic in the open
air, or, as was then a very common practice, in one of the

empty rooms of the small barracks scattered round the coast; left under the care of some invalided soldier and his family. On these occasions, the tract bag was never forgotten : whilst the rest of the party were sketching or walking, she would visit the cottagers, and making herself as well understood as their antique Norman dialect permitted, would give her little French books, and offer the kind word of sympathy or exhortation. Alive to the beautiful, especially to the picturesque, and with her quick eye for the droll, the peculiarities of the Jersey cottage and its inmates were all observed and enjoyed by her. The fire of Vráck (sea weed) burning on the hearth, with a large kettle suspended over it, in which the soupe à la graisse, or potage, was preparing for the family repast : the knitting of the women from the wool of their own sheep, occasionally with the fleeces of one or two black ones intermingled to produce the desired grey tint ; the dairy, and their far famed cows tethered in picturesque little enclosures ; orchards rich in fruit, and gardens painted and perfumed by the carnation, picotee, hydrangia, and many brilliant flowers that so peculiarly flourish there. Amidst these scenes, the summer passed away, but higher and more important objects were not unheeded. There was in the island, a little band of persons, in very humble life, who professed the principles of Friends, one or two only however being members of the Society. They assembled for worship on the Sunday morning, in the cottage of Jean Renaud, an old patriarch, residing on the sea shore, about a mile from the town of St. Heliers. There was a quaint old-fashioned effect about the low large room in which they assembled : whilst from large bundles of herbs suspended from the beams to dry, a flower or a leaf would occasionally drop on-to those sitting below.

The appearance of the congregation was in keeping with the apartment ; seated on planks, supported by temporary props. An antique four-post bedstead stood in one corner ; when the mistress of the house died, which occurred during their sojourn in Jersey,

she was there laid out, a circumstance which did not prevent
the Meeting assembling as usual, the drawn curtains screening
the corpse from view.   High-backed chairs were prepared for the
seniors of the assembly, the younger members of Mrs. Fry's
family appropriating to themselves the window seat.   The
novelty of the occasion was increased, by the English ministry
having to be interpreted to render it comprehensible to the greater
part of the hearers.

Nor were the Afternoon Meetings much less peculiar.   They
also were held at a private house, situated in the suburbs of the
town ; but the heat in-doors being considerable, the congregation not unfrequently removed to the small walled garden, and
sat beneath the shade of some ever-greens.   This, however, was
found practically so inconvenient, that a room in the town was
engaged for the purpose, and properly fitted up.   There, until
Elizabeth Fry left the island, large congregations assembled,
including many of the gentry and principal inhabitants ; these
meetings were exceedingly solemn and instructive.   In this important service, she was greatly helped by the company of her
sister-in-law, Elizabeth Fry, with her friend and companion,
Rebecca Sturges.   Philanthropic objects also presented themselves to her notice, especially the state of the Hospital, including
Workhouse and Lunatic Asylum, and of the Prison.   Acts of
the British Parliament have no power in the Channel Islands ;
as part of the ancient Duchy of Normandy, they are governed by
their own laws and customs.   To explain these, would involve
an historical and antiquarian discussion, out of place in a work like
the present.   It is sufficient here to bring forward the result that
none of the recent improvements in Prison Discipline had been
effected in Jersey.   After repeatedly visiting the Prison, and
communicating with the authorities—she believed it the best
course to have a letter which she had addressed to them, printed
for circulation.

To the Authorities of the Island of Jersey, who have the Direction and Management of the Prison and Hospital.

Gentlemen,

Having been requested by a number of persons of influence and respectability in this Island, to make known to the competent authorities my views on the subject of your Prison and Hospital : I have decided on the present method of doing so, as the most easy to myself, and the most likely to be accurately understood ; and I trust you will excuse me, if the interest I feel in the unfortunate inhabitants of those, and similar institutions, should induce me to take the liberty of offering some strong and decided observations on their condition and management.

Our protracted residence in this beautiful and interesting Island, has afforded me a full opportunity of observing the manner in which the defective system pursued in the management of the Prison, appears to operate upon its inmates ; and I feel it to be my duty to represent to you the effects, which my experience has taught me, must necessarily result from its operation ; as being nothing less than a gradual but certain demoralization of the lower, and some of the middling classes of society ; and the increase rather than the diminution of crime.

I shall begin by remarking, that the great and leading objects of Prison Discipline are in a very material degree overlooked.

Allow me to state, that the proper purpose which confinement in a prison is intended to accomplish—is not merely safe custody, but a suitable, and (if the imprisonment be just) a decided, but well and legally defined measure of punishment, of a nature tending to deter others from the commission of similar offences, and to produce salutary reform in the prisoners themselves ; of these objects the only one noticeable by an observer in your prison, is (with the single exception of cases of solitary confinement) that of the safe custody of the person.

In order to attain the salutary penal effect of imprisonment, together with the reformation of offenders, and to prevent the contamination of association and example, I beg to observe, that in addition to the restraint and confinement of a prison, the following objects are necessary, viz :—

I. A full sufficiency of employment, proportioned to the age, sex, health, and ability of the offender.

II. As much wholesome privation of those comforts and enjoyments, which they might be able to obtain when at liberty, as is compatible with the preservation of their health and strength.

III. A proper system of classification ; consisting, in the first place, of a total separation of the men from the women, (which latter ought always to be under the superintendence of one of their own sex) and next, a complete separation of debtors from criminals, and of the tried from the untried, (and were your prisoners numerous) of great criminals from misdemeanants ; but in the present case, it might suffice to separate any very bad offenders from the rest, and except at stated times, and under the constant observation of the Gaoler, or Turnkey, no visitors whatever should be admitted to the tried criminals, but in cases of special emergency.

IV. A fixed and suitable dietary for criminals, under the management of a Gaol Committee, who ought to contract regularly for the articles of food ; and in no case should the prisoner be allowed to supply himself, or be farmed out to the Gaoler, or to any other person whatsoever.

V. An absolute and total prohibition of spirits, wine, and all fermented liquors, with a penalty for its infringement, except when specially ordered by the medical attendant, (or a moderate portion of beer or cider might be allowed daily to those who work hard, or are not strong in their bodily health)—also a prohibition of cards, and all other gaming.

VI. A suitable prison-dress, with sufficiently marked distinction, which has been found by experience to have a humbling and beneficial effect on the minds of the prisoners generally.

VII. A complete code of rules and regulations, for the direction and government of the Gaoler and other officers of the prison, of the nature of those contained in an Act of Parliament, lately passed in England for the Government of Gaols, 4th Geo. IV., cap. 64.

VIII. A law or regulation, that should be imperative on Visiting Magistrates, or Gaol Committees, regularly and frequently to visit the prison, and minutely to investigate the details of its management.

IX. And lastly, but of primary importance, the due and stated performance of Divine service, and regular religious and other instruction of the prisoners ; every criminal who stands in need of it, being taught to read and write.

By the system at present pursued, nearly all the above regulations and restraints are wholly omitted.

The criminals, instead of being kept to employment, are constantly idle.

Indulgences of nearly every description, and money may be introduced to those who can procure them.

Prisoners of all descriptions are mixed up together, or at any rate allowed frequent intercourse, male and female, criminal and debtor, the hardened offender with the unpractised youth ; and all of them (with the exception of the cases of solitary confinement alluded to) exposed to communication with the public through the grating.

And in addition to these serious evils, your Gaoler is only remunerated according to the numbers his prison contains, and the quantity of spirits, wine, and other fermented liquors sold to the prisoners ; consequently, however conscientious the individual may be, it necessarily involves his own personal interest to make the prison agreeable to its inmates, that their stay there may be prolonged, and others induced to come in ; and my observation has led me to conclude, that this circumstance powerfully operates in increasing the number of your prisoners, and the duration of their stay.

I wish to add, that after having carefully examined the building and the ground appertaining to it, I am of opinion that these crying evils might be obviated, and the needful improvements introduced, and a House of Correction (which I consider indispensable) superadded to the present Prison, without any very considerable expense, especially with the assistance of a person from the Prison Discipline Society of London : and further, that if the Gaoler and his wife received a moderate salary for their attention to the male and female prisoners, it would not prove more expensive than upon the present plan, more especially if coupled with productive labour on the part of the prisoners, and that it would essentially contribute to its improvement.

I am well aware that your island is not subject to the Acts of the British Legislature ; but as the important improvements in Prison Discipline, which have taken place of latter years in the dominions under its control, are the productions of men of large experience, and have been also substantially introduced into the most enlightened European States, and the United States of America ; I trust you will not object to adopt the progressive wisdom of the age, from whatever quarter suggestions may arise, and I have therefore taken the liberty of appending some abstracts from Acts of Parliament of the 4th George IV., cap. 64, and others, on the subject of Prison Regulations, and which bear upon most of the points to which I have adverted.

I am, &c., &c.,

ELIZABETH FRY.

The funds devoted to the support of the Jersey Prison being wholly insufficient for that purpose, rendered it impossible to carry out any system of classification and instruction. It was a case in which nothing could be done effectually, without a complete renovation of the existing system. It became, with Mrs. Fry, an object of continued interest and exertion : though years elapsed, and she again twice crossed to Jersey, before the desired ends were accomplished.

The Hospital was an institution of mixed character, intended not only for the sick and for accident cases, but it served also as a place of confinement for persons guilty of small offences, or wilfully idle or disorderly.

The building was being at this time enlarged, with a view to classifying its inmates. In this institution she urged the necessity of—

I. An entire separation of men and women, both in house and yard, &c.

II. A subdivision of each sex into classes. First, the sick ; secondly, the aged and infirm ; thirdly, the children ; and fourthly, those who are confined for idleness or small offences ; the latter description to be allowed no intercourse with the other inmates, not to have the same comforts and indulgences, as this class of persons being admitted for vagrancy or crime has a great tendency to degrade the character of the institution, in the eyes of the honest and praiseworthy poor, who are admitted here for causes for which they are in no way blameable, and to render the most deserving objects in necessity, unwilling to avail themselves of the benefits of the charity.

A woman having become pregnant in the prison, was afterwards, on her discharge, sent on this account, as a punishment, to the hospital, and as she tried to escape from this new imprisonment, she was compelled to wear a chain and a heavy log by night and by day for several weeks. No instance can more forcibly prove the absolute necessity of improvement in both establishments.

The Treasurer and Master of the Hospital have endeavoured to improve the state of the lunatic cells ; but they are only suitable for violent, incurable, or outrageous patients. Upon this point, an entirely different arrangement and mode of treatment is indispensable. It is a lamentable fact, that in this enlightened age, there can exist a Christian country, possessing so many advantages, and containing a population of nearly forty thousand persons, in which there is no public provision for the treatment and cure of persons, labouring under that most melancholy and humiliating visitation of Divine providence, mental aberration, whatever their sex or condition, other than cells suited only for the worst of condemned criminals.

Mrs. Fry took great pains in establishing a District Society at St. Heliers. A gentleman of high standing and importance in the island, thus bears testimony to the results of her exertions :—

" I can only affirm, with perfect truth, that your dear mother's visits to Jersey were blessed, as a means of incalculable good. It was through her peculiar talent and persevering exertions, that a District Society was formed in St. Heliers. Mr. John

Hammond and Mr. Charles Le Quesne very ably seconded her views, in connexion with this matter."

The Island of Jersey, Seventh Month 30*th.*—We arrived here last Seventh-day, after a most beautiful and favoured voyage, which I felt an answer to prayer, and a mark of Providential care towards us. I had a very great deal to accomplish before I left home, but was enabled to leave all in peace ; and now I desire as far as it is permitted me to rest in the Lord, at the same time being open to any service I may be rightly called into ; and in faith to do what my hands may find to do. There are a few interesting Jersey Friends, but I find the difficulty of communicating with them on account of the language ; I endeavour to do my best, and look to Him who can bless my feeble labours.

I think the island and country delightful ; I never saw so little poverty, no beggars whatever, which is to me a real relief. Few amongst the inhabitants appear to be in high life ; but as far as I have seen, all appear to be well off. I expect my sister Elizabeth and Rebecca Sturges soon to join us, which I trust may prove right for them, for us, and for the people here. May it please my gracious and merciful Lord God, to bless us in this place, preserving us from doing harm, and enabling us to do that which is right and acceptable in His sight, and what may be for the real good of the people.

Eighth Month 12*th.*—We feel much at home in this lovely island, and in rather a remarkable manner, our way opens in the hearts of those amongst whom we are residing. A very extensive field of service appears before us in many ways. To try and thoroughly attend to the prisoners—to try to correct evils in the hospital—to assist in various ways the Friends and those who attend Meeting—to visit several in Christian love, and try to draw them nearer together—oh ! gracious Lord God, grant Thy poor unworthy servant the help of Thy Spirit, to do Thy will, and let not her labour be in vain in Thee, her Lord and her God ; but through Thy unmerited mercy in Christ Jesus, grant that her way may be made *very* clear before her, and ability given her to walk in it, to Thy praise, her own peace, and the real edification of those among whom her lot may be cast. Amen !

To a daughter and son-in-law preparing to leave
England for Madeira.

Eighth Month 25th, 1833.

My much Loved Children,

I fully expect one more opportunity of writing to you, before
you leave England, but as our communications are now likely to
be very seldom, I mean to take every opportunity to pour out my
heart to you. I am, I hope, thankful to say, though truly and
deeply touching to me, peaceful and satisfied about your proposed
very important step. I remember Cecil's remarks, we are to
follow and not to force Providence ; and as far as we can tell, the
openings of Providence for you appear to be, for you quietly, hopefully, and trustfully to go forward in your proposed plans. I live
much under the feeling that we are poor impotent creatures, that
we cannot save each other spiritually or naturally ; and though
nothing I believe can in feeling exceed a mother's love or lively
desire to serve her children, yet how little can she do ! in short
nothing, but as she is helped from above to do it, and the same
power that can help her, can also work with or without His
instruments ; this I most sensibly feel, therefore to Him, who is
the keeper of His dependant ones, (which I believe you are) I
entirely commit you, body, soul, and spirit. May He " do more
abundantly for you than we can either think or ask !" I desire for
you, amidst the ups and downs, the storms and calms, the joys and
sorrows that may attend your course, that your hearts may be fixed
trusting in God. It is most important to seek for this fixedness
of spirit, which sustains in trouble and sanctifies our enjoyments.
I have suffered from too deeply and acutely feeling things, and
from much undue fearfulness : I wish my children to guard against
these weaknesses, and to live more constantly in the quiet and
trustful spirit. You must expect some little trials and difficulties
in the voyage, but I trust they will not be great. Pray try to be
of use to the crew, have tracts, testaments and psalters, to be got
at for them, it might be of real use to the men, and a nice object
of interest for you.

That grace, mercy and peace may be with you both, is the
earnest desire and prayer of your most loving mother,

ELIZABETH FRY.

Jersey, Ninth Month 10*th.*—I have much enjoyed and valued the pleasant retreat we have here. I desire in deep gratitude to acknowledge the renewed capacity to delight in the wonderful works of God. The scenery, and feeling fully at liberty to spend part of many days in the enjoyment of this beautiful country and weather, with my beloved husband and children, has been very sweet to me! What has not religion been to me! how wonderful in its operation. None but He, who knows the heart, can tell. Surely it has brought me into some deep humiliations ; but how has it raised me up ! healed my at times wounded spirit, given me power to enjoy my blessings in what I believe an unusual degree, and wonderfully sustained me under deep tribulations. To me, it is anything but bondage, since it has brought me into a delightful freedom, although I had narrow places to pass through before my boundaries were thus enlarged ; so that from experience, I wish to be very tender over those still in bonds.

Since this time of rest on first arriving, my way has remarkably opened to a tide of service, of various kinds, as a minister of the gospel, and in philanthropic concerns. The prison, hospital, and the formation of a District Society, take up much of my attention, and visiting religiously the families who attend the Friend's meeting. I have very much felt the weight of these meetings ; and duty alone, and what I believe to be the help of the Spirit, could carry me through such services, for which I am so totally unfit and unworthy. My dear sister and Rebecca Sturges have lately been with me, and I have valued their company.

LETTER TO HER BROTHER JOSEPH JOHN GURNEY, OCCASIONED BY HEARING OF THE DEATH OF RACHEL FOWLER, (HIS MOTHER-IN-LAW.)

Jersey, *Ninth Month 5th*, 1833.

MY DEAREST JOSEPH,

I received thy deeply interesting letter to-day, which has produced in my mind much mixture of feeling ; for death, in its most mitigated form, is awful, and to our natural feelings very touching. But on the other hand, to have the warfare of those we love accomplished, the good fight fought, and a membership in the church militant changed for one in the church triumphant, brings such a feeling of peace and thankfulness, that it heals the wounds. Amidst much engagement, I have dwelt with you to-day in spirit, and not only felt for *you*, but I have also been in measure afflicted at the loss of the poor female convicts in the "Amphitrite," on the French coast—a hundred and twenty women, several of whom we knew in Newgate, besides many children : it has brought death very home to us !

I am glad that dear Rachel Fowler thought of the poor French, for whom I feel much interested, and if attention is paid to her wish, which I doubt not it will be, I think that it would be better than sending the whole Bible, to give something to Captain Bazin for printing certain parts of the Testament, to be distributed as tracts. There is a fine field for service in many ways ; how sweet for us one day to labour together in it, if permitted. I feel myself so very weak, that if any good is ever done, it will be only by Him, who out of weakness can make strong. Our party are generally well and comfortable ; we deeply feel about the absent, dear S—— H——, and our own dear R——, and C—— and H—— ; but we can only commit them to the Everlasting Keeper of His people, whose tender mercies are over all His works. The danger of the sea has been painfully brought home to us here, many vessels having been in distress with these high winds.

I am, with dear love to all, particularly our dearest Mary,

Thy tenderly attached sister,

ELIZABETH FRY.

Captain Bazin, to whom allusion is made in the preceding letter, commanded the "Ariadne" steamer, which crossed from Southampton to Guernsey and Jersey, and during the summer months used to proceed thence to St. Malo's and Granville.

He was a hardy Jersey sailor, an experienced pilot, and a devoted Christian ; he had a missionary spirit, and without abandoning his calling, or changing those circumstances in which he was placed, he strove to occupy with the talent committed to him, and to turn those opportunities to account. He distributed Bibles, Testaments, and tracts, in those French ports which he

visited : nor was he satisfied with this ; he established, both at
St. Malo and Granville, a sort of meeting for religious instruction, reading the Bible, singing and prayer, and when a minister
was present, for preaching also.   These meetings were attended
by numbers at Granville ; the functionaries and soldiers were
often present ; occasionally the superior officers.   The demand
for books was curiously great—multitudes would watch for the
vessel, to go on board and ask for them ; and often, before the
passengers and luggage could be cleared out, the quarter-deck
was crowded with applicants.

These details greatly interested Elizabeth Fry.   Captain Bazin,
in the intervals of his voyages, often came to " Caledonia Cottage"
to confer with her, and exceedingly confirmed the interest she
long had felt in the religious state of France, and her wish to
return home by that route.   She had mentioned it in a letter to
her brother Joseph John Gurney, who was staying at Melksham.
He read it aloud in the sick chamber of Mrs. Fowler, a devotedly
Christian woman, of lovely and enlarged character, and a valuable minister among Friends.   The subject occupied her dying
thoughts.   After her family had been for some time sitting
silently by her bed, supposing that the slumber of death was
upon her, and that she would speak to them no more, she suddenly roused, and seemed as though she had yet something to
communicate.   On going quite close, they could just hear her
twice repeat the name of the vessel " Ariadne ;" one of them
caught her meaning, and said, " Money to buy Bibles."   She
faintly repeated, " Money to buy Bibles," fell back into an apparently unconscious state, and spoke no more.

The thirty pounds which her family sent for the purpose were
of the utmost consequence at that time, in enabling Captain
Bazin to circulate the Holy Bible, in whole, or in parts, where
the demand was so great, and the power of meeting it so small.
After some weeks in Jersey, the party crossed to Guernsey ; they

remained there about a fortnight, received with the hospitality of the " olden time :" Mr. and Mrs. Fry at Miss Le Marchants, their daughters at Castle Carey, and Mrs. Elizabeth Fry and her companion at the house of a Friend, named Edmund Richards. The islands of Guernsey and Jersey have separate and independent legislative assemblies, and differ in some minor points of law. Mrs. Fry's time was divided between social enjoyments, objects of benevolence, and above all devotedly caring and labouring for the good of others. She visited the Prison, and found, that since the death of Sir William Keppel, the last Governor, it had been supported by the Board of Treasury out of the revenue of that island, formerly appropriated to the Governor ; a portion of which was always expended on the maintenance of the prisoners, and the same proportion was still expended for the same object by the Treasury.—The building such, that debtors and criminals easily and freely conversed with each other, and the internal arrangement of the building bad, in almost every respect. Tried and untried prisoners, as well as those convicted of almost every degree of offence, freely associating together, and even when sentenced to solitary confinement, too frequently placed in one small cell for want of room.—The gaoler, having little remuneration, except the profit to be obtained out of ninepence a day, allowed for the support of each prisoner, and upon the sale of wine and spirits to the prisoners ; the latter checked in measure by an order limiting criminals to two wine glasses of spirits a day, besides other liquors.—No employment, nor any chaplain or religious service ; no instruction, except that, occasionally given by any charitable person who might visit the prison. In short, she found the whole system entirely defective, tending continually to promote and increase crime among its inmates, which in a small island, like Guernsey was severely to be felt, counteracting the efforts of the upper classes for the general good of the community. The Hospital she considered in excellent order, though in a few minor points capable of some improvement.

One most important work she accomplished in that island—establishing the St. Peter's Port Provident and District Society. It is spoken of at the present time in Guernsey, as being "a real blessing to the poor of the community, not only in having administered to their temporal wants in sickness or accidents, but also in having greatly improved their domestic comforts and moral character, by the inculcating of frugal and temperate habits."

From Guernsey, Mrs. Fry crossed to Sark. This singular island lays between Guernsey and Jersey, and is seen on the horizon from both ; though rarely communicated with, from the latter island, being distant twenty miles, and extremely difficult of access. The best approach, is by crossing the channel called the Great Russell, from Guernsey, nine miles in breadth. Sark is a rock, precipitous on all sides, about three miles long, by one and a-half wide. It is divided into Great and Little Sark, by a very curious natural bridge of rock, about eighty yards in length, in breadth not exceeding four or five feet ; it is very steep on one side, but on the other absolutely perpendicular. They went in an open sailingboat, but as they approached its rocky shore, perceived no inlet, nor any indication of ascent on-to the lofty table land. A small jetty, from a natural projection, formed a little basin, where they landed, amidst impending rocks ; it was not till they were on the narrow shelf of pebbly beach, that they perceived what appeared to be the mouth of a cavern ; there a cart was waiting, and in it were placed two high-backed chairs ; this was the carriage to convey the ladies. The cavern gradually narrowed and at length the party emerged through a ravine on-to the plain. A lodging had been engaged for them at a farm-house. The island consists of a level plain, intersected with valleys, well cultivated ; there are woods, cottages, small gardens and orchards, fields dotted with cattle, and a village collected around the Manor House. Sark is a dependency of Guernsey, but the legislative power is vested in the Hereditary Lord of Sark, and his forty tenants ; a curious remnant of feudal tenure. They stayed three or four days there ; they also visited Herm, an islet between Guernsey and Sark, nearly four miles in circumference, but the population very small.

Jersey, Tenth Month 12th.—Since I last wrote, I have visited the islands of Guernsey, Sark, and Herm, accompanied by my husband, and part of the time by my sister and Rebecca Sturges ; my children with us when in Guernsey, and my kind and valued servant, C. Golder. It has been a full tide of engagements, with here and there, by the way, a little rest and recreation, although but little. I have deeply and weightily felt two very large Public Meetings in Guernsey, one by invitation, one not. In both of them I think we were much helped to express our concern towards the people ; but holding such Meetings, goes to the *very extent* of what I apprehend women are called to in public service. I view it very differently from ministering in their own assemblies ; and I have often thought it is rather too lightly entered into ; although at times, I believe it is called for. I feel peculiarly bound, when I do hold these great and important meetings, simply to preach the gospel and its practice, more particularly the importance of the unity of all members of the Church of Christ, of every denomination. This I have much to press upon in these islands. In the small island of Sark, with about five hundred inhabitants, they are quite divided religiously, about half of them Methodists, and half members of the Church of England. They will hardly speak to each other. I tried to use influence, and trust it may not be in vain. In the island of Herm, there is neither school nor place of worship : but there appears to be there, a most providential opening for forming a school,—a young lady willing to live on this desolate island, and devote herself to educate the poor. May the Lord be with her, and bless her in this undertaking ! our visit appeared to make way for this opening. In Guernsey,

I think some grievous evils are likely to be remedied in the prison, in time; I have also recommended some alterations in the hospital, which is a very large and important institution. A District Society will be probably established, I trust to the great benefit of the poor.

26th.—On Seventh-day evening, in the midst of a very large party, our letters arrived; some from our dearest H——, of a very touching nature; she had suffered so extremely on her voyage (to Madeira) as to bring on her confinement on board ship. Her child died, and her sufferings appear to have been extreme. The whole account was exceedingly affecting to me. But I desire to look above the agency of man, to Him, without whom not a sparrow falls to the ground, who orders all things in love, as well as in wisdom. My trust must be complete, my reliance entire, my hope continual. Lord, as all my springs are in Thee, I pray Thee daily, hourly, minutely, increase and renew my faith, patience, reliance, and hope, that I never cast away my confidence, but that my soul may follow hard after Thee, even unto the end.

The time had now arrived to break up the pleasant Jersey party. The accounts from England were very anxious. Several of her children required her attention; one of her daughters was dangerously ill, and her beloved sister, Mrs. Hoare, had just closed the eyes of her eldest son. To divide the party, renounce the route through France, and take the long sea-passage, with only her maid and her little boy, was not decided upon without great conflict. The season had been peculiarly stormy, and several vessels had been lost in the Channel; amongst others, the "Amphitrite." Many of the poor creatures in her were personally known to Mrs. Fry, although she had never been on board that ill-fated vessel. The *Times* newspaper contained, however, a statement, said to have been made by one of the sailors named Owen, in a letter addressed to the editor of that journal, dated Boulogne-sur-Mer, October 7th. Dr. Whately, in his letter to Earl Grey on " Transportation," Appendix (No. 4,) speaking of the " Amphitrite," mentions this sailor's statement, and adds,—

" There is one passage, which I hesitated to publish, from the fear that it might wound the most excellent lady mentioned in it ; not for her own sake, for ingratitude can wound her only, as an indication of failure in her benevolent attempts at the culture of virtuous feelings, but for the sake of the unhappy beings whom habitual vice has steeled against such cares as hers."

The passage in the sailor Owen's statement, to which the extract from the letter refers, is as follows ; after giving a shocking account of the depraved habits of the prisoner women, and of the absence of all attempts to restrain or bring them under discipline, on the part of the surgeon-superintendent, this passage occurs :—

" There was no divine service on board. Each woman had a Bible given her at Woolwich by Mrs. Fry and two other Quaker ladies ; most of them could read and write. Those from Newgate had been taught in the school there. Mrs. Fry and the other ladies came on board at Woolwich four or five times, and read prayers."

In reply to inquiries, as to the previous life and habits of the women, the sum of Owen's answers were as follows :

" Forty of the women were from Newgate—most of them were very young."
" Those who had been longest in Newgate were the worst."

It was Owen's place, as boatswain, to sling the chain for Mrs. Fry and the other ladies when they came on board. He " *heard the Newgate girls wish she might ifall overboard and be drowned.*" It is startling to find circumstances such as these, asserted on authority, apparently unquestionable ; to be not only incorrect, but wholly unfounded.

At this time the Jersey post had become quite irregular, from the packets being detained by weather. The feeling of confinement in a small island, to those unaccustomed to it, and on the eve of departure, was so uncomfortable, that, sad as it was to separate, it was almost a relief, when the two parties found themselves fairly embarked in the different directions they had taken.

No date.—Before I left Jersey very serious accounts came of our dearest R——. Of such a nature were they, last First-day, just before an important Public Meeting ; that it became necessary for me to decide to return home direct, and not by France, with my husband and daughters. I felt greatly afflicted, and earnestly prayed that I might be permitted to see my tenderly beloved child again. I was brought into a state of deep conflict, walking about the room, weeping bitterly, and hardly knowing how to go to the Meeting appointed at the Hospital, for the poor there, and the public generally : however, I went, and power was present to calm my troubled spirit, and enable me to preach the Gospel to the poor, the sinners, and the afflicted. It was a very solemn parting with the people of the island ; but, through mercy, I felt so clearly in my right place, and such a blessed calm came over me, in spite of myself, that undue anxiety was taken away. I passed a calm night, and was enabled to commit my dear child and my all, to Him who can do all things for us. The next day I had many little matters to finish off, and to take leave. On Third-day morning, after a short solemn time in prayer, my husband set off for France with my daughters, and I, with my maid and my little boy, for England.

Lynn, Eleventh Month 12th.—As related in my last journal, I left Jersey in the steam-boat for Southampton. Parting, with many beloved friends there, I felt much. It is a place and people in which I have taken great interest ; I also felt the uncertainty of the prospect before me, and in what state I should find my beloved child. I was much cast down ; the wind rather high, and evidently rising. My maid and child quickly became ill, as did even our little dog. The passengers, one after another, almost all, in the same state. The day gloomy, only now and then a ray of sunshine to enliven us. I remained, through mercy, quite well. We stopped at Guernsey, where I found, to my encouragement, some of my objects really prospering, and I was much pleased to hear that the School was established in the island of Herm. We dined whilst in the harbour there. Afterwards the weather became so boisterous, my cold so indifferent, and my poor boy so ill, that I remained in the cabin the whole evening, and a low time it was; fears got hold of me that I should never see R—— again alive; but on the other hand I knew that I had a merciful Lord to deal with, who heard my prayers, knew my weakness, and I believed would not permit so overwhelming an affliction to overtake me. I desired humbly and patiently to trust. I felt the seriousness of our situation in the high wind, but was enabled entirely to leave it to Him, who orders all things well. We arrived at Southampton the next morning; I felt much cast down and overdone, and during the journey to London, I had almost an inexpressible feeling of fatigue. I found rather a better account of R——, to my unspeakable relief.

From the accounts continuing better, Mrs. Fry was, for a day or two, able to remain in the neighbourhood of London. One day she spent at Hampstead, with her sister Mrs. Hoare; entering into the depth of her bereavement, and that of her widowed daughter-in-law,—but cheered by the greatness of their consolation.

Then she pursued her way to Lynn, where her presence was greatly needed; for six weeks she remained devoted to her daughter, and to that devotion, guided by singular skill, was apparently to be attributed her child's gradual restoration to health. From Lynn, she wrote to her youngest daughter, then just entering life, to greet her on her return home.

Lynn, Eleventh Month 9th, 1833.

MY DEAREST ——,

I feel inclined to write thee a few lines of salutation on thy return home. Thy sister and thyself have very important places

to fill, although they may differ ; and as I have told her my mind,
I mean to do the same to thee : remember these words, " be
sober, be vigilant." At thy important age much depends on not
letting the mind *out*, if I may so express myself : it is a period of
life when this is natural—various prospects in life may float before
the view ; but how infinitely important to know the heart to be
staid upon God, and to find it, meat and drink to be doing
His will—how important to attend to *present* duties ; this
is the best preparation for the future, whatever that future may
be.   I see that much devolves on thee ; thou hast not only to
look to thy own soul, but younger ones are looking up to thee,
whom, I believe, thou mayst be the means of winning to Christ.
Thy friendship with the ——— family I trust will be of use
to thee ; but on no account let imagination wander upon it ;
this will do thee harm, and on the contrary, I wish thee to
profit by it.

Farewell dearest ———,

In much tender love,

E. F.

To the daughter she had been so long nursing, she wrote continually, for some time after her return home ; offering the wisest
counsel, as to the conduct both of body and mind. Amongst
other things, she says, in one of her letters :—

The better accounts of thee are certainly very encouraging,
and set me more at rest about thee ; still, my beloved child, I feel
thou needest my sympathy and prayers ; there is much to feel,
even if it pleases Providence quite to raise thee up again ; there
is much to go through.   I have often found, in recovering from
long and severe illness, and entering life again, that our enemies
spiritually are yet lively and strong, and even, we may say, after
the " Beast has had a deadly wound, it still lives ;" I know this
has been my experience. Though thou thinkest I feel with the
Psalmist about long life, yet I am deeply sensible of the conflicts
and temptations it involves ; still, if we are through grace enabled
to live to a great and good purpose, and to promote the welfare
of our fellow-mortals, it is well to have such an opportunity
granted to us, of proving our faith and our love towards our Lord

and Saviour.   Mayst thou, my much-loved child, be raised up
for this blessed purpose.

Her advice, under differing circumstances, was very discriminating.   To another daughter she wrote :—

I feel in the first place, earnestly desirous that thou shouldest
think as little as possible of thy nervous feelings.   I know how
extremely painful they are, but experience has taught me, the less
I think of them the better.   It is most important to look upon
them as much as possible like the toothache—that it must be
endured while it lasts, but is not dangerous in its nature.   As
for the discoloured view, the imagination may at the time give
to things, nothing is more important than to set it down as a
clear and fixed thing in the mind, that whilst this nervousness
lasts it is not sound, and *must not* be believed or taken heed to.
I would not have thee discouraged at this return of it.   I believe
I never had death brought home very closely, without being
brought into a low nervous state, it is after all, so awful ; though
I increasingly see, that this is real weakness, and that those who
are believers in the Lord Jesus, however unworthy, need not fear
it, as through Him, its *plague* and sting will be done away.   But
it is folly in one sense to look ahead, we have enough to do to
seek for help and grace for the present time to do our *present
day's work.*   When the day comes that we have to give up " this
mortal life," we may and ought humbly to trust, that through
the unmerited mercy and love of our Lord, His grace will be
found sufficient for us.   I observe, for my great encouragement,
that what we call nervousness often proves no common blessing,
if made a right use of, and not given way to.   It so wonderfully
humbles, prevents the creature glorying, and makes willing to do
any thing to come to that peace, which quiets every storm.   Thy
uncles and aunts have nearly all been striking instances of this :
and I believe, hard, very hard as it is to bear, it is a baptism to
fit for a fulness of joy and glory rarely partaken of ; but it in no
common degree calls for patience.   I always think both David
and Paul largely partook of this sort of humbling experience.
Therefore my dear ——, if tried this way, possess thy soul in
patience, and look upon it as a suitable, though bitter medicine,

prescribed by the Physician of value to promote thy health and
cure.   L—— is to add ; therefore I must in the most near love
say farewell.

I am thy most tenderly attached mother,

ELIZABETH FRY.

Upton Lane, Twelfth Month 28*th.*—In my own Church, when
at home, I have been rather unusually active, and in the present
stirring and unsettled state of things, had to take the quieting
and hopeful side.   I now feel as if the clouds rather over-
shadowed me ; but I desire to have my heart fixed, trusting in
the Lord, that in due time the Sun of Righteousness will arise with
healing on His wings. My dearest son J—— is likely to be married
on the 1st of next year.   Oh ! may the Lord be with him in it :
it has been a subject that has very greatly occupied my heart and
mind lately.   My dearest brother Joseph has been labouring
amongst us in the Gospel, with wonderful brightness ; this I feel
a deep cause for thankfulness.   Ah ! for a heart, a spirit, and a
power more fully and more abundantly to praise the Lord for his
goodness, and to show forth His marvellous works to the children
of men !

31*st.*—The last day of this year ! I much feel these epochs:
time going so fast.   Peace and quietness are my portion this
morning.   I have cause for thankfulness and a good deal
of encouragement ; I have certainly had many proofs that my
Lord has been near to me and mine during the last year, and
helped us in many ways.

Third Month 2*nd,* 1834.—First-day. I only to-day heard of
my unworthy labours being greatly blessed in the Island of
Guernsey ; and lately the same from Jersey and France.   Not
so much individual instances of reformation, as the various
plans for the religious, moral and temporal good of the poor,
&c., &c., really prospering.   I have also in my home circle, my
dearest son Joseph and his valuable wife living here, to my
great comfort.   Surely, several of my children are drawing near
to good.

21*st.*—I have to record, some highly interesting and important
visits paid to the different branches of our family, by my

brother Joseph, that have greatly tended to my encouragement, and the increase of my hope respecting them.

Fourth Month 1*st.*—I am likely to leave home to-day for religious service in Dorset and Hants. Oh Lord! I pray Thee be with me and anoint me for Thy work, that it may be fully to Thy praise, the edification of those I go amongst, and to my own help and peace; and be pleased to keep my children and family during my absence. Grant this, dearest Lord, for Thine own name sake. Amen.

12*th.*—I returned yesterday from my expedition, which I may thankfully say, proved very satisfactory.

She was accompanied on this journey by her friend William Forster, and her nieces, Priscilla B—— and Priscilla G——. Her aunt's address and manners on that occasion, and the impressions made upon her own mind, are admirably described by one of them; being at the time in very delicate health, she was, perhaps, the more sensitively alive to her aunt's peculiar powers of soothing—

" There was no weakness or trouble of mind or body, which might not safely be unveiled to her. Whatever various or opposite views, feelings or wishes, might be confided to her, all came out again tinged with her own loving, hoping spirit. Bitterness of every kind died; when entrusted to her, it never re-appeared. The most favourable construction possible was always put upon every transaction. No doubt her failing lay this way; but did it not give her and her example a wonderful influence? Was it not the very secret of her power with the wretched and degraded prisoners? She always could see hope for every one; she invariably found or made some point of light. The most abandoned must have felt, she did not despair for them, either for this world or another; and this it was that made her irresistible.

" At Southampton, time and opportunity were rather unexpectedly afforded for an excursion to the Isle of Wight. I think she undertook it chiefly for the sake of pleasing Priscilla G—— and myself; but it had important consequences. We travelled

round by Shanklin, Bonchurch, and the Undercliff. She was
zealous as we, in the enjoyment of the scenery and the wild flowers;
but the next day, on reaching Freshwater, she was fatigued, and
remained to rest, whilst we went to see Alum Bay. On our return,
we were told she had walked out, and we soon received a message
desiring us to join her at the Coast Guard Station. We found
her in her element; pleased and giving pleasure to a large group,
who were assembled around her. She entered with the greatest
sympathy into their somewhat dreary position, inquired into their
resources for education for their children, and religious improvement for themselves,—found them much in want of books : and
from this visit originated that great undertaking, of providing
libraries for all the Coast Guard Stations in Great Britain ; an
undertaking full of difficulties, but in which her perseverance
never relaxed, till it was accomplished.

From the long low inn upon the beach, at Freshwater, when
you look from the beautiful sea, the range of cliffs beyond, and
the two lonely rocks in the foreground ; you see nothing, but a
few fishers' cottages, and the dark gloomy-looking Preventive
Service buildings beyond them, just where the hills which enclose
the little bay begin their ascent. It was very early in the year ;
before the great metropolitan hive had thrown off its endless
swarms of summer travellers. Something of gloominess and
desolation rested on the place ; her companions had left her, and
she sat and pondered the condition of the inmates of the dwellings before her. It was at Brighton, in 1824, that the idea
first suggested itself to her mind, of the great need there was
for supplying this class of men with employment, that would
at once occupy the long intervals of time left to their own dis-
posal, and furnish them with subjects for thought, during the
weary hours of lonely watching, that they must of necessity
pass. She knew idleness to be a fruitful source of ill, and that
the human mind preying upon itself, becomes inert, if not
vicious. Circumstances had precluded her making any general

or systematic exertions to remedy this evil, yet it rested upon her thoughts. She waited long to see her way clearly, and to be convinced that the duty was laid upon her; but no sooner had the conviction arrived, than she set herself vigorously to the work.

'The experience of life had taught her, that He, who rules as a God of Providence, directs as a God of Grace—that with duty comes opportunity, and that with outward circumstances, the inward call is sure to harmonise, where man desires to act only in submission to his Master's will, and to occupy with the talents given him to use.

Upton, Fourth Month 12th.—At Portsmouth, we paid an interesting visit to the Haslar Hospital, the Hulks Hospital Ship, and some prisons; we also paid a delightful little visit to the Isle of Wight. I felt more able to enjoy the great beauties of nature, from having been owned by my Lord and Master, in my religious services. What a relish does true religion give for our temporal as well as spiritual blessings! I have still much to feel respecting the offer of marriage made to my dear L——. It is a very serious thing, my children thus leaving Friends; and I have my great fears, that in so doing, they are leaving that which would be a blessing and preservation to them. At the same time, I see there is no respect of persons with God; nor in reality is there the difference some would make out in the different administrations of religion, if there be but a true, sincere love of our Lord, and endeavour to serve Him. What is above all to me, I have felt peace in it rather peculiarly: still, we at present are exceedingly feeling the weight of the affair; it is also a considerable pain to me to go through the discipline of the Society respecting it—but in bearing it patiently and humbly, I may in that way be enabled to preach Christ. Lord be it so—Help me Thyself through all these rather intricate paths, and make a way for Thy servant in all these things; that she may do right in Thy sight, and not offend even the weakest of her brethren and sisters in religious connexion with herself—Help, Lord, or we perish!

21st.—Yesterday (First-day) I attended Meeting, rather oppressed in body and mind. Ministered to by dear Elizabeth Dudley, but had such heaviness of body as to hinder spiritual revival. In the afternoon I went, accompanied by Elizabeth Dudley, Rebecca Sturges, and some others, to visit the female convict ship ; the sun shone brightly, the day delightful, the poor women rejoiced to see us ; but my spirit was in heaviness, from the difficulty of leaving my family, even for a few hours, on that day. It was a fine sight to see about one hundred and fifty poor female convicts, and some sailors, standing, sitting, and leaning round us, whilst we read the scriptures to them. I spoke to them, and Elizabeth Dudley prayed. Surely to witness the solemn effect, the tears rolling down many cheeks, we must acknowledge it to be the Lord's doing ; still I felt flat, though the others thought it a very satisfactory time ; but in the evening I became more re-vived, and comforted and thankful, that it has pleased the Lord to send me to the poor outcasts, although at times feeling as if I went more as a machine moved by springs, than in the lively state I desire ; but at other times it is different, and there is much sense of light, life, love and power. To-day, I expect to go to the Duchess of Gloucester, and amongst some of the high in this life. May the Lord be with me, that my intercourse with these, may not be in vain in Him. I feel it no light responsibility, having the door so open with the Government of our country, and those filling high places, I am often surprised to find how much so ; and yet the Lord only knows the depth of my humiliations, and how it has been out of the depths, that I have been raised up for these services. At the Admiralty, I have lately had im-portant requests granted ; at the Home Office, they are always ready to attend to what I ask ; and at the Colonial Office, I expect that they will soon make some alterations in the arrange-ments for the female convicts in New South Wales.

Who has thus turned the hearts of those in authority ? surely it is the Lord. May He give me wisdom and sound discretion rightly to use the influence He has given me. Be near to Thy servant this day, gracious Lord, in every place, and so help her by Thy Spirit, that she may do Thy will and not bow to man, but alone to Thee, her God, doing all to Thy glory. We made several

other calls, and dined at my brother Buxton's, where we met
some gentlemen. I felt, as I mostly do after such days, fearful
and anxious, lest I had done any discredit to the vocation wherewith I am called ; or in any degree, in my own heart or conduct
towards God, done amiss. It caused me rather a watchful, fearful
night. I see it much easier, and in many respects safer, in the
religious life, to be quiet, and much at home ; yet I also feel that
in a more general association there are great advantages : enlarging our spiritual borders, and removing our prejudices ; and if we
are really enabled to stand our ground as Christians, in the meekness of wisdom, and so adorn the doctrine of God our Saviour,
it may be the means of promoting the good of others.

24th.—We dined at Lord Bexley's, and met Captain Mangles,
the great traveller, several clergymen and others. I desired to
maintain the watch ; but the company of serious, intellectual and
refined persons, is apt to draw me a good deal forth in conversation and mind, and often leads me to many fears afterwards, lest
there should imperceptibly be any thing of showing off, and being
exalted by man ; but I may truly say, inwardly, I mostly feel
reduced and humbled after such times, and fearful, lest I should
have a cloud over me, so as to hinder my near communion with
my Lord. A few words in the Proverbs rather encouraged me :
"Reproofs of instruction are the way of life,"—(Proverbs 6th
chapter 23rd verse). I see it well to be reproved ; may I profit
by it ! I often fear for myself, lest I am forsaking my first
love, or becoming lax, because I certainly feel far more liberty
than I used to do, in uniting with others in their prayers,
grace, &c., &c., and less in bonds generally ; in short, my
borders are greatly enlarged ; may this arise, not from my love
becoming cold, but from experiencing the service of my Lord
to be already to me, in measure, perfect freedom. Oh dearest
Lord ! make manifest in Thy own light, if this be in me laxity,
that I may be reproved and amend my ways ; if, on the contrary,
it be the liberty wherewith Thou hast made me free, cause me in
Thine own power, firmly and fixedly to stand in it, even if
some of my fellow-mortals, whom I love and esteem, appear to
remain under a different dispensation.

A few days ago, I visited Plashet : it was almost too much for

my natural spirits. When I saw our weedy walks, that once were
made and kept up so neatly—our summer-houses falling down,—
our beautiful wild flowers, that I had cultivated with so much
care, and no one to admire them—the place that had cost us so
much, and been at times so enjoyed by us, the birth-place of so
many of my children, the scene of so many deep and near
interests—the tears trickled down my face, and I felt ready to
enumerate my sorrows, and say, " Why is this ?"" But I felt the
check within, and desired and endeavoured to look on the bright
side of the picture, and acknowledge the tender and unmerited
mercy of my God, in Christ Jesus. Mine has been, I fully
believe, a very unusual course in many particulars ; in some
things known, in some hidden from the eye of man. Oh ! may
all end in good and blessing.

Fifth Month 5th.—Yesterday was the Sabbath. I can hardly
say how deeply I feel these days as they come : first, as it
respects the ministry of the word. Its wholly resting on two or
three women in our rather large assembly, is an exercise of my
faith, and a real trial to my natural feelings ; then to believe, as
I do, that some of our congregation are in an unregenerate
state; how must their silent meetings be passed ? and for the
babes in Christ I have great fears, inasmuch as true, solemn,
silent worship, is a very high administration of spiritual worship.
I frequently fear for such, that more external aid is wanted,
though I see not how it is to be given. I also feel the want
of each one openly uniting in some external act of worship, for
there is much in taking an absolute part in what is doing, to
feel a full interest in it ; but I see not with our views (in which
I unite) how this can be remedied. Then for myself, as a
minister of the Gospel, I desire to be very faithful, and give the
portion of meat in due season to the household ; but even here,
deep humiliation is my portion, in its appearing, that though I
preach to others, I cannot manage my own ; my children, one
after another, leaving a Society and principles that I love, value,
and try to build up. My Lord only knows the exercise of my
spirit on those days. Then for my home hours: not having
space as we had at Plashet, in which my boys can recreate in the
way I consider advisable, during part of this day, now, I have

anxiously to watch where they go, and what they are about, so that I am not often favoured to know the Sabbath a delight, or day of rest; yet through all these things, and my too anxious nature, help is wonderfully granted to me : I find the spring within that helps, keeps, revives, sustains, and heals ; but I feel that I am bound to seek, and to pray not to be so exquisitely anxious.

Sixth Month 10*th.*—Since I last wrote, I have got through the Yearly Meeting, which I attended nearly throughout. There appeared to me much more apparent love and unity than last year, still it is a serious and shaking time, and some of the Leaders of our Tribes think they differ in some points of doctrine ; but I believe it is more in word than reality ; and as they love the Lord Jesus, if they have wandered a little, they will be brought back. I was a good deal engaged, having to take a quiet view, neither on one side nor the other, but seeing the good of both ; but I have a very great fear of ever being too forward, a thing I very much dislike and disapprove. May my Lord preserve me from it.

I was favoured to get well through the British Society Meeting, and could not but return thanks that our Holy Head had so blessed this work. With respect to my dear L——'s engagement of marriage, I have apprehended that the hand of the Lord is in it ; and oh ! saith my soul, may it prove so. The pain of her leaving our Society, and the steps attending it, have begun, to the wounding of my spirit ; for though I do not set much value on outward membership in any visible church, yet it has its pains, at times great pains to me, and I am ready to say, in my heart, How is it ? When I have one after another of my family thus brought before our Meeting, it has its trials and humiliations. It would be to me a pleasanter, and I think a more satisfactory thing, if the discipline of our Society had not so much of the inquisitorial in it, and did not interfere in some things that I believe no religious body has a right to take a part in ; it leads, I think, to undesirable results. Though I approve persons being disowned for marrying out of our Society, I had rather the act of marriage in itself forfeited membership.

Seventh Month 21*st.*—I have been very busy trying to obtain libraries for all the Coast Guard Stations, and have had to see men in authority, who received me in a way that was surprising to myself : at the Custom House by Lord Althorp, as Chancellor of the Exchequer ; also, about the District Society concerns at Brighton, by the Archbishop of Canterbury, the Bishop of Chichester, Lord Chichester, &c. &c. These things might probably exalt, had I not deep inward humiliations. I forgot also to add, that Lord Melbourne, as Home Secretary, and Spring Rice, as Secretary of the Colonies, received me lately in the handsomest manner, respecting our British Society concerns.

Her objects at this time were almost overwhelming, even to her—indefatigable and earnest as she was.

Her desire was, to extend the plan of libraries to all the Coast Guard Stations in the United Kingdom ; but the project was vast, there being about five hundred of these, divided into twenty-four districts, and comprising upwards of 21,000 persons, including the wives and children of the men.

The estimated expense was considerable. Mrs. Fry proposed that £1000. should be raised by private subscription, and £500. would, she hoped, be granted by Government, for the advantage of so numerous and useful a body of its servants. Lord Althorp, then Chancellor of the Exchequer, received her proposal favourably, but considered his continuance in office too uncertain to undertake it, although he promised to recommend it to his successor.

Her communications with Lord Melbourne were upon subjects connected with the Ladies' British Society ; chiefly that of transportation, female convicts on board ship, and their treatment upon arriving in the colony.

Nothing could be more courteous than her reception, or that of her friends, in an after interview with Mr. Young, Lord Melbourne's private secretary. These ladies strongly recommended that there should be a Depôt for female prisoners, where they might be instructed, before being sent abroad, much on the plan

that is now pursued at the Millbank Penitentiary. Mr. Spring
Rice (Lord Monteagle), in the Colonial Office, gave Mrs. Fry
and her companions, the Honourable Mrs. Upcher and Miss
Fraser, a kind and patient hearing.

Lord Melbourne granted another interview, when the subject
of matrons for convict ships was discussed with him. The first
matron who undertook that office, with the joint sanction of
Government and the Ladies' British Society, was Mrs. Saunders,
the wife of a missionary, who went out in the " George Hibbert."
Her passage was paid by Government, but she suffered so much
sickness, that her own exertions were continually impeded. Mr.
Saunders supplied her place, as far as it was possible to do so,
and very satisfactory were the results. They cannot be better
described than by extracts furnished by Miss Fraser, from the
books of the Convict Ship Committee, held September 12th, 1834.

" The ' George Hibbert' convict ship embarked one hundred
and fifty female convicts, and *forty-one* children ; also, nine
free women, and twenty-three of their children. It was visited
four times by members of the Convict Ship Committee, and the
usual articles distributed. The ship was found to be much
crowded, and serious inconveniences were felt, and were to be
apprehended, during the voyage, from this circumstance. It is
however to be noticed, with thankfulness, that both the captain and surgeon-superintendent appeared to be peculiarly well
qualified for the offices to which they were appointed. We have
also to state, that a lady (who, with her husband, a missionary,
had been accustomed to visit Newgate) had a free passage
granted her in this ship, with the understanding, that they
should assist in the superintendence and religious instruction
of the convicts.

" Mr. Saunders writes on the 26th :—' Two services last
Sunday. I have seen great improvement in the women, arising,
I believe, from the ladies' reading, and the remarks of the
surgeon on the use of bad expressions. Our present rule is, to
read the scriptures, and pray with one half of the prisoners one

evening, the other half next evening.   I believe soon, I shall be
able to have morning service and school every day.

" ' December 12th.—The Convict Ship Committee have the
satisfaction of laying before the British Society, some most interesting accounts from the ' George Hibbert,' written by the Rev. J.
Saunders, to his brother :—Sunday : Church service at half-past
ten and two o'clock.—Sermon after each service.   The remainder
of the week : ten to twelve, children's schools.   We have four
school-mistresses, and two give me great pleasure.   Two to three
o'clock, adult schools, twenty-four scholars, the same school-mistresses.   Three to four o'clock writing school, two classes, twelve
scholars each day ; but I have not yet hit upon the right method
for the writing school, the women are eager to learn, but I cannot,
as yet, put them in the right way.   When I have set the schools
at half-past ten o'clock, I meet a Bible class of about twenty ; they
are chiefly Scotch girls, and it gratifies me to see their attention.
At a quarter past eleven o'clock, another Bible class of fourteen ;
this contains better readers, and persons of more intelligence, and
gives me great pleasure.   Monday and Thursday are washing
days, and the Bible classes are intermitted : rainy weather will of
course interfere, as all these services are on deck.   The church and
the schools are on the poop ; the Bible classes on the quarter-
deck ; but in the evening, when the women are mustered, I go
between decks, into each of the two prisons ; separately read the
scriptures, and pray, always concluding with the Lord's Prayer,
because that is familiar to all.' "

How marvellous a change within twenty years !   True, that
much was only external ; for the heart of man is not touched by
outward order and observances. 'True, most sorrowfully true—
that many restrained for a time, by circumstances and regulations,
would return, when at liberty to do so, to their former depravity.
But yet to those who deserved better things, to those of the
female sex, who, although they had fallen, were not utterly cast
down ; who, guilty perhaps of theft or robbing an employer, were
not utterly lost and degraded, there was now offered hope and
encouragement, the decencies of life were preserved, propriety and

industry could be maintained, and even some advance might be made towards restoration. Character might once more be earned, integrity and industry practised, and the opportunity given, to prove that sin was repented of, and amendment of life desired and chosen. Of course much depended upon the Surgeon Superintendent, and upon the Matron, when that appointment became general ; but some good was effected, and much absolute evil was spared. Nor were these advantages confined to the voyage. When arrived at their destination, a ticket of good conduct was given to such of the women, whose behaviour had deserved it, by the Surgeon Superintendent, which almost insured their obtaining a good situation in service ; and for all, there was a shelter ; the horrors described by Mr. Marsden, in 1819, no longer existed. The factory of Paramatta, at least afforded an asylum, overlooked by the Governor, and regularly visited by the venerable Chaplain.

Upton, Ninth Month 25th.—To-morrow I expect to set off on a journey into Scotland. I have taken an affecting leave of my family, praying, that we might again, (if the will of God) be refreshed together, and my way has satisfactorily opened to go.

Her husband, and two daughters preceded her ; and awaited her coming at Birnam Inn, near Dunkeld.

She arrived there on the 5th of August, and after giving her a few days' rest from her journey, the party set off for Loch Tay, taking a most delightful route by the Braes and town of Aberfeldy, so famed in Scottish song ; up Loch Tay to Kenmore, a village at that end of the Loch, where the river Tay, a deep, clear, rapid sweeping current flows out of it. At Kenmore, they enjoyed a quiet Sunday, and tolerable highland accommodation. In the evening, anxious to turn the day to some good account, Mrs. Fry invited the servants of the inn, to attend the reading she intended to have with her own family. Some ladies were polite enough to offer the use of their sitting room, as it was more roomy; a large congregation of barefooted chamber-maids, and blue bonnetted hostlers, assembled. She read part of her brother Joseph John Gurney's letter to a Friend, on the Evidences of Christianity; the people were very attentive, and anxious each to possess a copy, that they might read the remainder of the book to themselves. The next day, some game-keepers who came to the inn requested a similar gift, having heard from the people there, all that had taken place.

By Lock Tay, Eighth Month 9th, First-day—Not having a Meeting to go to, and not believing it right for me to attend any other place of worship; I desire to spend a time in solemn searching of heart before the Lord, and may I be enabled to hold communion with Him in spirit. On the morning of the 1st, the day appointed for the liberation of all the slaves in the British dominions, and on which my dear niece, Priscilla B—— was to be married, I poured forth my soul in deep supplication before my heavenly Father, on behalf of the poor slaves; that a quiet spirit might be granted them—that their spiritual bonds might also be broken—that the liberty prepared for the children of God might be their portion. I also prayed for my beloved niece and her companion in life, that the Lord would be with them, keep them, and bless them. My son Gurney, accompanied me from Newcastle, and we arrived at Dunkeld on the 5th, where we met my husband and daughters. I ought thankfully to remember how my way has been made, where I could hardly see any opening to join them; how difficulties have vanished, and how a kind Providence has been with me, and provided for me, and brought me to these dear ones; may I be edified and refreshed by beholding the wonderful and beautiful works of God; and may I rightly attend to such little services as may open towards others. Lord be with me, and help me by Thy Spirit, to perform all my duties to Thy praise. I pray Thee be very near to us all; protect us by Thy providential care over us, and above all, further visit us by Thy love, power, and Spirit. Oh Lord! turn us, and we shall be turned; help us, and we shall be helped; keep us, and we shall be kept. Amen.

On Monday, the 19th, the weeping climate seemed to forbid their progress, and the mountains were enveloped in clouds ; but departing when the rain ceased, they had a fine drive along the banks of Loch Tay to Killin.   The clouds rose considerably, and the mountains seen to great advantage—heavy masses rolling over them, sometimes resting on them, sometimes leaving them bare, with Ben Lawers towering magnificently over all.   At Killin, the troubles of real highland travelling began.   The inn was small and full, and Mrs. Fry and her party were obliged to take up their abode in a cottage, in some little humble bed-rooms, without a sitting room ; the highland mistress and her family carding and spinning wool in the kitchen.   Notwithstanding the incommodious accommodation, the party remained over the next day to enjoy the romantic scenery of this spot, especially where the river Dockhart, broad, rapid, and roaring along its headlong and resistless course, rushes round two rocky islets, and under a long bridge, to where it falls into the Loch.   Whilst the gentlemen were fishing, Mrs. Fry and her daughters rambled with delight through this wild highland scenery.   From Killin, the party proceeded to Mrs. Stewart's famous inn, near Loch Katrine. The inn was fuller than usual, but accommodation having been secured beforehand, they found comfortable apartments ready ; but they had not them long to themselves : as travellers arrived, weary and hungry, for whom there was no room in the inn, Mrs. Fry could not resist sheltering them for a time.   Just at the close of the day, a party of ladies drove up, extremely fatigued, and dreading the danger of the roads in the darkness of night ; the entreaties for admission were heard from without, they were invited to share their sitting-room, and with their maid passed the night on its floor.   These traits of character may be considered trifles, but trifles in daily life often tell more than greater things.

Edinburgh, Eighth Month 28th.—I left my dearest husband and two daughters in the highlands, to accompany my boy on his way to England, and above all, to attend the Meetings, see the Friends, and visit the prisons here. I came under the belief ' that duty called me to do so. We experienced some danger in our journey, from an accident in a steam-boat; but the Lord protected us. I feel it to be a fearful thing to be here ; there are many ministers besides me. Lord, be near to Thy servant, who is here without one relation or companion, and has left all, for what she apprehends to be the call of duty. Guide, guard, and keep her ; qualify her for Thine own service, of whatever kind it may be, to Thine own glory ; keep her eye very single to Thyself and the direction of Thy Spirit.

Tarbet, by Loch Lomond, Ninth Month 14th.—I have been more than a week returned to my husband and children, and have had; during that time, the real comfort of having Andrew Johnston and my beloved niece Priscilla with us. They returned with me from Glasgow. In Edinburgh, I had much to be thankful for, in the help granted to me in such religious services, as I believe I was called into, in Meetings, families, and institutions. I had a very solemn religious time in the Gaol and large Refuge; also a shorter one in the Bridewell and another Refuge. The hearts of many appeared to be peculiarly opened towards me, and entire strangers wonderfully ministered to my wants, and upheld my hands, particularly the Mackenzie family. Our dear friends who knew me before were abundantly kind to me. May the Lord, in His love and mercy, reward them for all their great kindness to me, His very unworthy servant ; and may He still soften and enlarge their hearts towards me, until the work that He gives me to do amongst them be accomplished. I find a field for much important service for the poor, and to make more arrangements for the ladies who visit the prisons. I desire, and earnestly pray to be preserved from an over-active spirit in these things ; and on the other hand, faithfully, diligently, humbly, and watchfully, to do whatever my Lord gives me to do, that may be to His glory, or the good of my fellow-creatures.

We have passed through very lovely country ; but the sun has not shone much upon us, and the atmosphere of my mind has partaken of the same hue, which is not so pleasant as more lively colouring over the mind, but I am ready to think more profitable, and perhaps more likely to qualify me for the weighty duties before me.

From Loch Katrine the party passed to Balloch, and Luss, and thence to Inverary and Loch Awe ; from which place Mrs. Fry returned (her son with her) to Edinburgh. Whilst on the banks of Loch Awe, the party spent a few days at Inistrinich, under the hospitable roof of K. M. MacAllister, Esq., enjoying the beauties of that fine district, and on their return, they passed a Sunday there. In the evening, Mrs. Fry had a solemn reading with a large party of guests and the assembled household. It was her invariable practice on this journey, even at the inns, to invite the servants to join their evening scripture reading, and many of the visitors frequently joined them.

The party having re-assembled at Oban, with the addition of Mr. and Mrs. Andrew Johnston, remained quietly a few days, and then retraced their steps through Dumbarton and Glasgow to Edinburgh, where Mrs. Fry was again received with the most affectionate kindness by her friends. Her time and energies being devoted to the completion of those objects begun on her former visit.

But whilst many institutions of value directly or indirectly owe their existence to her exertions—and she sowed the seed of many a noble tree—she did not omit the smallest opportunity of benefiting others. Her's was a constant endeavour to leave some savour of good on all with whom she had any communication. The chambermaid and the waiter received the word of kindness and counsel, and a little tract or text book, to impress it upon their memories. The postilion at the carriage window, or the cotter at the road side, met with appropriate notice, and this mingled with the most unaffected enjoyment of the country, and spirit in all the incidents of travelling.

The results of her observations on the state of the Scotch
Prisons, she forwarded to the proper authorities after her return
home.

A Prison Discipline Society, at this period established in Edinburgh, composed of many gentlemen of position and influence,
was carrying on its important work, in spreading information, and
leading to more general interest on the subject. With them Mrs.
Fry held much communication, and letters passed between her
and the indefatigable secretary, Dr. Greville, on different matters
connected with prisons; his enlarged and Christian view of the
subject being very congenial to her.

Mrs. Fry's remarks addressed to the authorities, include many
of the topics so continually urged by her.

The care of women, being intrusted to women.

Employment of some nature for all.

More instruction to be given, and that not only for the sake of
the thing learned, but for the good effect of change of occupation,
both for body and mind.

Proper books to be furnished to those who can read.

A uniform prison dress.

A proper and sufficient dietary—the purchase of food, or receiving it from friends, to be absolutely prohibited.

Water for all purposes, to be thrown up, on every floor. Officers
to sleep close to the prisoners.

Arrangements for worship and instruction on the Sabbath-
day.

She was also becoming anxious on questions then occupying
much attention.—The solitary and silent systems; imported from
America, where in many respects, and under the closest and most
careful inspection they appeared well to answer, but which were
to her feelings both liable to grievous abuses. She was always
slow in forming decided opinions, and even more so in expressing
them; but on these points she became very clear, as to their uses

and their dangers, and at a later period she believed it her duty very strongly to express her fears on the subject.

After her return from Scotland, Mrs. Fry resumed her visits to Newgate. At that time, she went once a week regularly. On a few rare occasions, she did not confine her ministrations to the female prisoners. Her faithful coadjutors and valued friends, Mrs. (now Lady) Pirie, and Miss Fraser, were her frequent companions. The journal of the latter lady, contains many entries of interest, which, most kindly, she has furnished for the present work : among others—

" November 29th, 1834.—I spent an interesting time in Newgate, Mrs. Fry and I were there together for several hours. She went with me to the cells, and read to the men just sentenced to death.

" Amongst them, there were two brothers, convicted, I believe, of housebreaking. The youngest was drawn into the commission of the crime by the elder brother. James, the youngest, could not read ; he was married to a very pleasing looking young woman, and had two children.

" I recollect Mrs. Fry told the poor men who could not read, that if they would try to learn while they were in Newgate, she would give those who succeeded, each a Bible. James took very great pains, and before he left the prison to be transported (which the whole of the men were, five in number) he could read very tolerably. On the 7th of January following, Mrs. Fry again went with me to the cells. James then read the 7th chapter of St. Matthew's gospel, and received his Bible. He became a valuable servant to the gentleman, to whom he was assigned in New South Wales ; and his wife, who had been assisted by Lady Pirie and some friends of her's, in obtaining needle-work, was sent with her children to him. It was a pleasing circumstance, that his master, as a reward for his good conduct, sent an order for a sum of money to defray the expenses of the voyage, in order that the family of this poor young man might join him. The letter with this order arrived after the wife and children were on their way. So remarkably favoured was this poor convict and his family, through the goodness of the all-seeing Father of mankind, that it is most probable his sojourn in Newgate was overruled for the good of himself and family, both spiritually and temporally. It was indeed a remarkable instance of the benefit of prison visiting."

Tenth Month 7th.—I have had a note from the Secretary of the Colonies to say, that all our propositions for improving the arrangements for the convicts are forwarded to the Government in New South Wales. At the Home Office, they are forwarding my recommendations about Scotland.

After recording the birth of another grandchild, the first of a now numerous family, the journal contains the following remark :—

I feel it cause for deep and humble thankfulness to see the happiness of my son and his wife ; I feel it also a fresh proof in the important step of marriage, how well it is for young persons to choose for themselves, provided there is no insurmountable objection. Indeed, I have unusually felt comfort in my beloved children of late—beginning to partake of that enjoyment in them that I have all along hoped would one day be mine. May I be encouraged, with a thankful heart, to persevere in training up my younger ones in the Lord, and to trust for them, when walking in the slippery paths of youth ; not to be too anxious about them ; earnestly seeking for help, strength, and direction in doing my duty towards them, and there commit it. I have been unusually discouraged the last day or two, by —— and —— taking a very decided part in things appertaining to our school at East Ham, and in our Newgate Committee. I have not felt them tender over me or my views, which were rather different to theirs ; I felt a little roughly handled, but as I firmly believe they did not mean it, and as I attribute it much to the warm zeal of dear —— ——, I have truly desired to take all in a humble Christian spirit ; I mean to seek to be doubly and unusually kind to those who have hurt me, and admit no other than kind constructions upon all they have done. —————— cast reflections upon me for my "incorrigible love of the Church," as she told me she considered it.

I find in most things in the religious Society I belong to—in charities—in education—I am so much disposed, from inclination and early habit, to take enlarged liberal ground, that perhaps watchfulness is needed, lest Christian liberty degenerate into laxity; but, oh! the love, the enlargement I feel towards all, at times, inexpressible; the deep unutterable sense I have of the largeness of the foundation, the fulness and real freedom of the Gospel; how it brings glad tidings to all who love the Lord and His righteousness; how it breaks down partition walls; how it unlooses heavy chains, and unlocks prison doors; how it enables us even to bear with the prejudices of our fellow mortals, and yield to them, if in so doing we do not hurt our own consciences. For my poor self, how do I desire, that however slack in the view of my fellow-mortals, I may not be slack in the sight of the Lord. How I fear for myself, lest I should get from under His cross, or in any way forsake my first love. Oh! gracious Lord, be Thou my Judge and my Lawgiver; examine and prove me. Be pleased ever to˙ preserve that freedom which is of Thee—let me be in bondage to no mortal; but, whatever is not of Thee, manifest Thou it, that it may come under the restraint of Thy cross. And if it be Thy will, keep me, I pray Thee, in the unity of those who love Thee, and whom I love; or if, for my humiliation, Thou seest meet they should in some things set me at naught, let me ever rest satisfied in Thee and Thy love. Amen.

Twelfth Month 25th.—I returned from Brighton the day before yesterday, having felt a drawing of love to visit the Friends there, and to attend to the difficulties of the District Society. I went quite alone, and yet not alone, because I believe my Master was with me. I quite hope and trust the valuable District Society will be continued. I had about a hundred guests to meet me. We read the 90th Psalm, and I felt called to pray for them and the Society. Afterwards I strongly pressed the importance of Christians of different denominations working together in unity of spirit; also of diligence in the work, and the care of all the districts. I advised a diminution of the premium on deposits. I also saw some of their leading gentlemen, and I think an ear was opened to hear what I had to say. It is a weighty responsibility, the opening our Heavenly Father has given me with different classes of persons—oh! for grace to make a simple right use of it. I returned home well satisfied ; though, by remaining a little longer, I might have accomplished more.

At the close of this year,—in public matters, I look upon Slavery being abolished, as an unspeakable blessing ; Capital Punishment much lessened, I also think cause for thankfulness ; and that in the Prisons it has pleased my Gracious Master yet to bless our unworthy labours of love. I have also had very satisfactory accounts of the District Society formed in Jersey ; and I trust the Scotch Gentlemen and Ladies' Societies will prove the means of good.   Oh ! for a thankful heart, for being in any degree enabled to be useful to our fellow-creatures.   I have yet many things stirring; and what a favour to have health granted me, thus far to attend to these important duties ; and I am informed, that though quite a new party is now in power, the members of Government are still ready to listen to my requests.

CHAPTER XIX.

The close of the year 1834 was marked by the death of the Duke of Gloucester. He had been highly esteemed by Elizabeth Fry, from the time when quartered at Norwich, in the latter part of the last century, His Royal Highness was amongst the few, who addressed words of friendly caution and sound advice to the young and motherless sisters at Earlham. To the Princess Sophia of Gloucester, she wrote upon the occasion—

Upton Lane, Twelfth Month 13th, 1834.

My dear Friend,

I hope thou wilt not feel it an intrusion, my expressing my sympathy with thee in the death of the Duke of Gloucester. To lose a dear and only brother is no small trial, and for a while makes the world appear very desolate. But I trust, that having thy pleasant pictures marred in this life, may be one means of opening brighter prospects in the life to come, and of having thy treasure increased in the heavenly inheritance.

The Duchess of Gloucester kindly commissioned a lady to write to me, who gave me a very comforting account of the state of the Duke's mind. I feel it cause for much thankfulness that he was so sustained through faith in his Lord and Saviour ; and we may humbly trust, through His merits, saved with an everlasting salvation. It would be very pleasant to me to hear how thy health and spirits are, after so great a shock, and I propose inquiring at Blackheath, where I rather expect to be next week ; or if thou wouldest have the kindness to request one of thy ladies in waiting to write me a few lines, I should be much obliged.

I hope that my dear and valued friend, the Duchess of Gloucester, is as well as we can expect after her deep affliction. With desires for thy present and everlasting welfare,

I remain, thy attached and obliged friend,

ELIZABETH FRY.

Upton Lane, First Month 27th, 1835.—I yesterday went, by appointment, to visit the Duchess of Gloucester, after the death of the Duke. She gave a highly interesting account of his death. He appeared to depart in the full hope of a Christian. This I felt satisfactory and comforting, after having traced him from his youth up, and seen his conduct, and known his principles when a young man. I observe how gently the Lord deals with His people, and how, under the most varied circumstances, He visits all, and how He bears with those that fear Him. It appeared to me that the Duke desired to act up to the light received, and his faith was strong in his Saviour, which proved his stronghold in the day of trouble.

Second Month 8th.—The way appears opening with our present Ministers, to obtain libraries for all the Coast Guard Stations, a matter I have long had at heart. My desire is, to do all these things with a single eye to the glory of God, and the welfare of my fellow-mortals, and if they succeed, to pray that He, who alone can bless and increase, may prosper the work of my unworthy hands, and that I may ever wholly give the glory to Him to whom it is due, even my Lord and my God.

25th.—The affairs of our Society cause me real anxiety and pain, and reconcile me in measure, to so many of my children leaving Friends. Though it is painful and humbling, in my own Meeting, my children's names being on the books only for disownment, yet I deeply feel my Lord is still with me and mine, and my trust is, that He is working in a "mysterious way His wonders to perform" amongst us. I have a very strong sense of His mercy and pity towards us, and the wonderful loving kindness already shown us in heights and in depths, in riches and in poverty, in strength and in weakness.

Third Month 13*th.*—I returned yesterday from my expedition with my dear brother Samuel. I find much satisfaction and true peace, in now and then giving a portion of my time and strength to the service of my own Society; it is useful to myself, and in no service does the presence of my Lord and Master appear to be more evidently round about me. Upon going to the Custom House, on my return, I found Government at last had granted my request, and given £500. for libraries for the Coast Guard Stations; this I think cause for thankfulness, and my desire is, that the measure may be blessed by the Lord.

The beneficial effects of the libraries introduced through her influence into the Naval Hospitals at Haslar and Plymouth, and the testimony borne to their utility by Sir William Burnett, the highest medical authority in the navy, had confirmed her desire to extend this advantage to all the Coast Guard Stations, without further delay. It was brought under the notice of Sir Robert Peel, then first Lord of the Treasury, by means of a letter addressed by Mrs. Fry to his brother Lawrence Peel, Esquire, who had already ably seconded her views in the Brighton District Society. This application met with the approbation of Sir Robert Peel, by whom it was referred to Sir Thomas Freemantle: from him an assurance was received, that there existed a strong disposition on the part of the Board of Treasury to give effect to this object, and that as soon as the proposed plan was matured it should receive all the assistance in his power.

Captain Bowles, R.N., at that time Comptroller of the Coast Guard, gave the project his cordial support. Captain Sir Edward Parry united with Mrs. Fry in this movement, and under such powerful patronage it rapidly advanced. A formal application was made to the Treasury for a sum of money for this purpose, and the result was, the grant of £500. Large private subscriptions had still to be sought, and were obtained, chiefly through Mrs. Fry's influence. The details of the arrangement were almost entirely her own, and curiously adapted to meet the requirings of those she desired to benefit, having made herself mistress of the subject, and of the nature of the service, with surprising rapidity.

Besides subscriptions in money, many liberal donations of books were received from some of the most eminent booksellers, which, with the grants from the Society for Promoting Christian Knowledge, the Religious Tract Society, and other similar institutions, amounted in value to upwards of a thousand pounds.

The selection of the libraries was a work of considerable difficulty, demanding much caution, and examiners were appointed to decide on suitable books for this important purpose. The gentlemen selected were the Rev. John W. Cunningham, Captain Sir W. E. Parry, and Captain Bowles.

The libraries, for the Stations alone, amounted in all to 25,896 volumes. Fifty-two different works were prepared for each Station, whilst a still larger and more important collection was to be attached to every one of the seventy-four districts, in order to afford the needful variety and change. The packages of books, the greater part carriage-free, were dispatched in the course of the summer, from the Custom House, in Government vessels, to their different destinations. But all this was not done without much fatigue and exertion, many wearisome journeys to London, and a great deal of writing; but in the latter she was much helped by Mr. Timpson, a dissenting minister, who undertook the office of Secretary, and proved an efficient and useful agent to herself and those gentlemen who acted with her.

On the 22nd of May, Mrs. Fry was ordered to attend the Select Committee of the House of Lords, appointed to inquire into the present state of the several Gaols and Houses of Correction in England and Wales. She was accompanied by Mrs. Pryor, Mrs. Pirie (Lady Pirie) and Miss Fraser, who were likewise to be examined. Sir T. Powell Buxton was with Mrs. Fry. The ladies were conducted by him to an ante-room, where they found the Duke of Richmond and Lord Suffield ; the Duke of Sutherland came in shortly afterwards. The Duke of Richmond, as Chairman of the Committee, presided ; Mr. Gurney, the shorthand writer, was seated at the corner of the table ; and Mrs. Fry, Mrs. Pryor, Mrs. Pirie, and Miss Fraser, at the right hand of the Duke. There might be from twelve to fifteen noblemen present.

An eye-witness writes :—

" Never, I should think, was the calm dignity of her character more conspicuous. Whatever her inward feelings might have been, nothing like excitement was visible in her manner—nothing hurried in her language. Perfectly self-possessed, her speech flowed melodiously, her ideas were clearly expressed, and if another thought possessed her, besides that of delivering her opinions faithfully and judiciously on the subjects brought before her, it was, that she might speak a word for her Lord and Master in that noble company."

Perhaps the heads of a little strip of paper, prepared by her to assist her memory, will prove the best guide to those subjects she the most earnestly desired to press upon her auditors.

NOTES FOR EXAMINATION BEFORE COMMITTEE OF THE HOUSE OF LORDS.

General state of female prisons.—Want of more instruction. —Ladies visiting in female prisons.—Objections to instruction being given privately and *alone* to women, even by chaplains or ministers of their own persuasion.

The Tread-Mill—injurious for women, under many circumstances of health and constitution—often destructive to the health of men, when too prolonged, upon a meagre diet—unfitting for labour afterwards. Matrons, to be efficient, must be of character and weight. Gaoler's daughter of sixteen, as in one instance in Wales, acting in that capacity. ·

The state of most Borough prisons—instance, a woman alone, for a considerable time in one prison, never seeing any of her sex, in the power and under the care of men.

Equality in labour and in diet, in different prisons, though the kind of diet must depend upon the local habits. Great need of Government Inspectors in English and Scotch prisons, the plan answering so well in Ireland. Chaplains, for general daily instruction, and the services of the Sabbath.

Convict ships—difficulties about choosing matrons—women more competent to judge of the qualifications of their own sex· than men.

But far beyond all other topics, did she urge the vast importance of scriptural instruction for these poor fallen ones. Warmed by her subject, with her voice a little raised, and a look of solemn earnestness, she went on to say, after replying to one of the questions addressed to her—

I believe the effect of religious and other instruction is hardly to be calculated on ; and I may further say, that notwithstanding the high estimation and reverence in which I held the Holy Scriptures before I went to the prisons, as believing them to be written by inspiration of God, and therefore calculated to produce the greatest good ; I have seen (in reading the scriptures to those women) such a power attending them, and such an effect on the minds of the most reprobate, as I could not have conceived. If any one wants a confirmation of the truth of Christianity, let him go and read the scriptures in prisons to poor sinners ; you there see, how the gospel is exactly adapted to the fallen condition of man. It has strongly confirmed my faith, and I feel it to be, the bounden duty of the Government and the country, that those truths should be administered in the manner most likely to conduce to the real reformation of the prisoner ; you then go to the root of the matter ;—for though severe punishment may in a measure deter them and others from crime, it does not amend the character and change the heart, but if you have really altered the principles of the individuals they are not only deterred from crime, because of the fear of punishment, but they go out and set a bright example to others.

The quiet self-possession with which she delivered her opinions, won confidence and consideration ; even, where they failed to convince ; and she had the satisfaction to believe, that some points of importance were forwarded by the information she furnished.

The varying forms of the kaleidescope, change not more rapidly than the scenes in the life of Elizabeth Fry.

On the 22nd of May, she went before the Committee of the House of Lords ; on the 28th, she went into Norfolk, to be with her daughter ; and on the 29th, she announces the birth of a little grandson. She returned home on the 2nd of June ; and on the 10th, in the retirement of her morning room, within sound of the burst of bells that announced the event, we find her before the Lord in prayer, during the celebration of the marriage of her youngest daughter.

Upton, Sixth Month 10th.—Alone in my little room, my whole family gone to Church to the wedding. I feel solitary, but I believe my Lord is with me. Oh gracious Lord ! at this moment be with my child ; pour out Thy Spirit upon her, that she may not only make solemn covenant with her husband, but with her God. Help her to keep these covenants, be with, help, and bless her and her's. Grant enough of this world's goods, but above all, far above all, grant them durable riches and righteousness ; that joy and peace, which the world can neither give or take away. Not that I am worthy, to ask for these blessings, but I ask them for the sake of Him, who is our righteousness ; and through whom, Thou showest Thy tender mercy towards us. Amen, and Amen.

13th.—I can hardly express what the desire and prayer of my heart was on the wedding-day, that it might be rightly spent, and that a blessing might be with us, and all our mercies, remembered and acknowledged. I think this was a good deal the case; they returned from Church, soon after I wrote in my little room: the party appeared cheerful, peaceful and sober-minded; the dear grand-children, many of them with us, looking truly lovely, they had their wedding-meal, a sweet group round a table with some other children. We sat down about fifty; at our table, we had fifteen of our children, my sister Catherine, and my sister Buxton, the P—— family, and a few of our dear and valued friends. I have seldom seen a more lovely party, or apparently in a sweeter spirit; really quite a delightful and beautiful sight. I felt that I could not let the party separate, without some expression of my deep feeling, my pleasure, and satisfaction in our table being so surrounded; my gratification at the interest shown for the bride and bridegroom, and ourselves; and my desire, that this fresh union with our friends and neigh-bours might be blessed indeed to us all; then my prayer for our dear young people, that they might walk with a perfect and upright heart before the Lord; that they might be of good com-fort, be of one mind, live in peace, and that the God of love might be with them, even unto the end. I also expressed, that I had remembered in my prayers, those members of the family that were afar off—that grace, mercy and peace might be with them! We then broke up, and wandered a little about until our dear bride and bridegroom left us. After which, our party dispersed, but an uncommon feeling of love, sweetness, peace and blessing, appeared to me to rest upon us; for which, as a token for good, I desire, very humbly and reverently to return thanks.

Some important affairs requiring her husband's personal atten-tion in the south of England; it was decided for Mrs. Fry and their remaining daughter to accompany him; it appeared a desir-able opportunity for seeing the Commanders of the different Coast Guard districts, through which they would pass, and endeavour-ing to stimulate them, with the officers and men under their com-mand, to a proper application of the books they were about to receive. This proved, however, almost needless, for in nearly every instance, these gentlemen warmly seconded her views, and approved of the plan.   Her suggestions were received by them with the utmost attention and politeness, and greatly did the intercourse with the Coast Guard officers add to the interest of this agreeable journey, along the whole southern coast of England, from the Forelands to the Land's End.

She almost always visited the Stations, and conversed with those she found there ; frequently the officers would follow her to the inn for further communication.   At Portsmouth, she visited Haslar Hospital, speaking kind and pitying words to the sick and deranged.   Admiral Garrett and his family paid her the most hospitable attention ; with Miss Garrett she visited the Penitentiary at Portsea.   While they went over the house, the unfortunate inmates were assembled in the parlour, where they were all standing, when Mrs. Fry, and the party with her, returned to the room.   This lady describes Mrs. Fry as "sitting down, laying her bonnet on the table, and making some inquiries as to the arrangements of the place, and the conduct of the young women there.   Two were pointed out to her as being peculiarly refractory and hardened ; without noticing this, she addressed some words of exhortation and advice to all ; and when she arose to go away, she went up to these two, and extending her hand to each of them, said, in a tone and manner quite indescribable, but so touching :—' I trust I shall hear better things of thee.' The hearts that had been proof against the words of reproach and exhortation, softened at the words of hope and kindness, and both burst into tears."

The travellers made a three days' tour of the Isle of Wight ; but at Cowes Mrs. Fry separated from her husband and daughter, believing it her duty to cross to Jersey, in the hope of effecting something towards remedying the crying evils which still existed in the prison there.   She was accompanied by a young Friend from London, who had kindly agreed to go with her ;

they went in the " Ariadne," Captain Bazin's steam vessel. They had a rough passage, but a warm reception at D'Hautrée, Colonel (now General) Touzel's. By him and his family were they treated, not merely with hospitality, but with true Christian fellowship, as " beloved for their works' sake."

She had many interviews with persons in authority, but to little immediate purpose. Her desire was, that such buildings should be added to the prison, as should render it a House of Correction, and make it possible to enforce classification and needful discipline ; but great difficulty existed from many perplexing questions between the States of the Island and its Governor, Field Marshal Viscount Beresford, as to who was to pay the expenses that would be entailed. She found the District Society flourishing, and a committee of ladies visiting the Hospital.

On her return, she spent a few days at Guernsey, where the prison was in the same deplorable state in which she had seen it two years before. Thence she crossed to Weymouth, where she rejoined her party, who were rejoiced to welcome her again in safety. She was laden with fruits and flowers ; the rich produce of those fertile islands. Among other treasures, she bore with her a bunch of carnations and picotees of every colour ; scarlet, yellow bizarre, of an immoderate size.

They were some days at Plymouth. Occasional intervals of rest, with the addition of sunshine and fine scenery, were thankfully received by her. She prized the varied beauties in the material world, not alone as in themselves good and pleasant, but as types and emblems of the beautiful and good in the spiritual creation, and above all, in the spirit of Heber, she could appropriate his language—

> " If thus Thy meaner works are fair !
> If thus Thy bounties gild the span
> Of ruined earth, and sinful man,
> How glorious must the mansion be,
> Where Thy redeemed shall dwell with Thee !"

There was one day she often referred to with pleasure, when, with the Coast Guard Captain of the District, in his cutter, they visited some of the Stations, crossing Cawsand Bay, and landing at a romantic spot, where one of them is placed. At the Breakwater, on their return, they were met by several naval officers, their cutters or yachts, meanwhile, sailing about that beautiful harbour.

The contrasts in her life were great. This was rather a fresh variety: walking up and down the Breakwater, with her daughter, surrounded by naval officers of various ranks and different ages, but the one great aim of her life not forgotten. The conversation between the Quakeress and those sons of storm and strife, was of benefiting seamen, raising their moral condition, and the best methods of inculcating habits of piety and virtue.

At Falmouth, they were warmly welcomed by Mr. and Mrs. George Croker Fox, and by every member of that family. Mrs. George Croker Fox, and Mrs. Robert Were Fox, were among her oldest friends; their mother, Mrs. Barclay, was sister to her father. In childhood and youth the intercourse was frequent and delightful, between the two groups of sisters, seven in each family, alike left motherless in early life.

Here she heard much of the packets continually sailing from that port; she wished to have libraries for them also. In this she was seconded by Captain Clavell, R.N., of the "Astrea" flag-ship, and by many of the commanders of the packets, and their families. Grants from the Societies, and private subscriptions were raised, the Religious Tract Society gave their publications at half-price, and the Christian Knowledge Society presented books to the amount of ten pounds. These vessels were supplied with Bibles, Testaments, and Prayer-books, by Government. The library books were placed, as a depôt, at the office of Captain Clavell; each packet, when she sailed, took out a box containing thirty books, changed from time to time, so as to produce constant variety. The gratitude of the men was great, and the co-operation of their officers hearty: of fifty-one pounds, that this arrangement cost, twenty pounds were subscribed by them. A few months afterwards, from one of Captain Clavell's family, was received a communication, dated Falmouth, January 27th, 1835 :—

"I am sure you will be glad to hear our library is getting on with much success. The men appear more anxious than ever to read. * * I cannot tell you how much we all feel indebted to you for your great kindness, and benevolent exertions; but particularly our poor sailors."

A second letter, of a later date, stated—

"I have delightful accounts from all the packets; the men really beg for the books. I wish I could show you a box just returned from sea, the books well thumbed, a proof, I should think, of their being read."

The writer of these letters was not the only person engaged; Lieutenant Jennings of the "Tyrean," was also one of the warmest and earliest promoters of the plan, and so were the Fox family.

Accompanied by some of their relatives, the travellers proceeded, passing through the wild stern features of the Cornish coast, to Penzance and the Land's-End. The state of the lunatics at Penzance was very grievous. Elizabeth Fry could not permit such evils to remain without some endeavour to remedy them. She soon afterwards heard from a friend that— "the comforts of the poor lunatics at Penzance are likely to be increased. A wall is now building round a part of the garden, which is made expressly for them to walk in, and I hope the internal arrangements are also improved."

A few days were passed among the romantic beauties of North Devon. Thence they turned their steps homewards; but at

Amesbury she paused long enough to make arrangements for a library being established for the use of the shepherds of Salisbury Plain. An excellent individual, approved by the clergyman, and Sir Edward and Lady Antrobus, undertook the care of the books, and their circulation. After a few months' trial of the plan, he writes to Mrs. Fry that—

" Forty-five books are in constant circulation with the additional magazines. More than fifty poor people read them with attention, return them with thanks, and desire the loan of more, frequently observing, they think it a very kind thing indeed, that they should be furnished with so many good books, free of all cost, so entertaining and instructive, these long winter evenings."

From the different officers of the Coast Guard Stations, she received letters that gladdened her heart ; but far too numerous for insertion here, and to select would be most difficult, as all breathe the same spirit, and express their cordial approbation of the plan, and the pleasure felt by the men and their families. But something beyond pleasure was desired by her, with whom the idea originated ; that advantage and edification should accrue, to those who read. The seed she sowed has in truth wonderfully flourished ; and now it is, that the fruits may be discerned. If those, who visit our coasts for pleasure or duty, would make their way into the low-browed preventive houses, so continually recurring; in some apartment, frequently the room where the arms are kept, they may see, three or four shelves against the wall, filled with well kept, but evidently well read books. Let them enter into a little conversation, with the intelligent looking man, decently dressed, who sits reading, after a long watch ; and they will find, whether or not these books are appreciated ; or let them address a few words to the wife, and hear her estimate of their value. Exceptions of course there are, and degrees in the estimate put upon the opportunity for improvement, but the former

are few, and the amount of interest and pleasure afforded by the
books, far beyond any thing that was anticipated, even by the
most sanguine supporters of the plan.

Upton, Tenth Month 13*th*.—I returned home yesterday with
my dear husband from a very affecting and unexpected visit
into Norfolk, in consequence of the severe illness and death, of
my beloved sister Mary Gurney, my brother Joseph's amiable,
devoted, and superior wife. She was in the prime of her day,
only thirty-two years of age, a spiritually minded and lively
minister, a very intellectual person, and highly cultivated, generous and remarkably cheerful, a wonderful helper to my brother,
adapted to his wants. When I heard how ill she was, I could
hardly believe she would die, she had such an apparent call here
below, but our ways are not the Lord's ways, nor our thoughts His
thoughts. He took her, thus early to Himself, but we apprehend,
as the shock of corn fully ripe. Our dearest Joseph's resignation
and patience are great indeed, and his even cheerful acquiescence
to the will of his God, is instructive. The funeral was deeply
affecting. After dinner we had an extraordinary time. Our dear
brother Francis being here, prayed—his dear Richenda spoke.
Joseph in the most striking manner enlarged on the character of
the departed, on his loss, and his consolation, the day went on,
and ended well in a reading, with the poor neighbours ; but words
fail me, to tell of the solemn, holy, loving feeling over us. Oh !
what a blessing is family unity in the Lord—my children who were
present, and many others were deeply and powerfully impressed.
May it be lasting—may the same spirit that has so remarkably rested upon us, rest on them, the same love, the same peace,
the same unity of spirit, the same freeness of spiritual communication. Such a day is almost like being raised above the things
of this world ; all appeared sanctified, all blessed, even the very
beauties of the place. How did I feel called upon to entreat, and
to warn, how did I seek to bear testimony to the very truth—and
how did dearest Joseph in his affliction beseech all to come to
Christ, for salvation.

23*rd*.—Since my return home, I have had very satisfactory
letters from the island of Jersey, saying that great alterations and

improvements are taking place in the Hospital. The Prison Committee have also acted upon many of my suggestions, I am now in communication with Lord Beresford, the Governor of the Island, in the hope of accomplishing an entire alteration in the prison ; new buildings, &c. &c.

In our home prison cause, it is really marvellous to me to observe the openings of Providence, in the good effected by the members of the Ladies' British Society. I feel rather bound to record these things—not by way of boasting, but as a proof that all comes from the Lord, who blesses in the labour, and who strengthens for the work.

Eleventh Month 25th.—After a beautiful drive over the Forest, to see Robert Barclay and his children, after their heavy loss ; I inclined to express a little of the feelings of my heart. I have in my drive, admired the various works of creation. I have felt in missing dear Elizabeth Barclay at Knotts Green—how many are departed from amongst us—how much we have in our circle, seen, felt and known. I have observed the marvellous changes and various deliverances, and how some tenderly-beloved departed ones have been very gently dealt with, provided for in time, and we believe redeemed, so as to be prepared for eternity; and when I looked at the various difficulties, temporal and spiritual, that some amongst us have passed through : the low places they have been brought into, and then again raised up ; provided for naturally, their sins, as we humbly believe, forgiven and blotted out, through the Saviour : and snatched as brands from the burning. My conclusion was, not to be too anxious, not to be too fearful ; but to have my heart more fixed, trusting in God.

Twelfth Month 11th.—I returned last evening from a visit to my dear brother Joseph, who was so very low and unwell, that I was unexpectedly sent for ; my visit was interesting, and I trust satisfactory.

To her youngest daughter, who was ill during this absence, she wrote.

Earlham, *Twelfth Month* 7th.

I have thought of thee with much tender interest since we parted, and have felt being separated from thee in thy present

delicate state of health.   In thinking of thee yesterday, it
occurred to me, that this text would eventually apply to thy
condition : " I was brought low and He comforted me ; return
unto thy rest, oh my soul! for the Lord hath dealt bountifully
with thee." I believe it to be needful for us to be brought low,
to know what it is to be really helped of the Lord.   I wish for
thee and for myself, and for all of us, to have our hearts fixed,
trusting to the Lord.   There is nothing like committing ourselves, and our ways, and our all, to Him, who is our Helper, and
who orders every thing for us, in wisdom, love and mercy.   I have
not been very well since my arrival here ; but I do not feel uncomfortable, and expect soon to be better.   I long to return to
you all again, although I hope this little turn out is a right one.
I hope my love, if a little better, that thou wilt get into the air
in the garden.

I am, thy tenderly attached mother,
ELIZABETH FRY.

Upton Lane, First Month.—I have had a hope that the last
year has, notwithstanding all our short comings, drawn some near
to God ; but may we all remember, that we cannot stand still in
our religious course, and if we do not go forward, there is very great
danger of going backward.   I have felt unusually bound to encourage all my most tenderly beloved family, to a full and entire surrender of themselves, to the service of the best of Masters, to be
willing to be taught of Him, by His Holy Spirit, through the
Scriptures, and through the dealings of our Heavenly Father
towards us.   I want all my children to partake of the same delightful spiritual union that we have partaken of, as a family : that
they may be each other's joy in the Lord.   I think there is much
in the observation of Rogers : " It is a rare thing for any man, so
to use prosperity, as to have his heart drawn by it nearer to God.
Therefore we have need in that state, to watch diligently, and
labour to walk humbly."   I desire in our intercourse with each
other, that we should increasingly partake, not only of temporal
enjoyments, but also of intellectual pleasures, and above all, of
spiritual communion, which gives so lively a relish to all the gifts
of God.   As to outward religious callings, at present, there
appears some diversity amongst us ; sweet as it would be to me,

to have some led in the same path as myself, yet I may in truth
say, my first desire is, that my dearest children may seek to be of
God, in Christ Jesus; (as it is easier to join ourselves to a sect
than to be joined to Christ) and may know their Lord's will
respecting them; may seek to be conformed to it; may be fully
persuaded in their own minds, and then hold fast, very fast, that
which is good; that here, they each may fill their ranks in
righteousness, as followers of a crucified Lord; and eventually
through Him, be saved with an everlasting salvation. Amen.

During the commencement of this year, Mrs. Fry encountered
some annoyance, not to say pain, from the animadversions of the
newly-appointed Prison Inspectors, on the state of Newgate.
She had long strenuously urged the necessity of appointing Prison
Inspectors for Great Britain, having seen the advantage accru-
ing to the prisons in Ireland from their superintendence.

At the close of the preceding year, the Rev. Whitworth
Russell and William Crawford, Esquire, were appointed Prison
Inspectors to the Home District; Captain Williams. to the
Eastern; and Dr. Bisset Hawkins to the Southern. Mr.
Frederick Hill was named Inspector for Scotland. Mr. Russell
and Mr. Crawford commenced a searching investigation into the
state of Newgate. Having studied the subject of Prison Discipline, with the advantage of personal inquiry, on the part of
Mr. Crawford, in his visit to America; and personal experience,
on that of Mr. Russell, whilst Chaplain of the Millbank Penitentiary, they saw, without making fair allowance, the unavoidable
defects existing in Newgate. Mrs. Fry had always herself represented Newgate, as a most defective prison, allowing no room
for proper classification or arrangement. She had never approved,
as a permanent system, the admission of Visitors to the Readings
there on Friday; but during the infancy of the question of
Prison Reform, whilst public interest had still to be aroused, she
believed it a useful and allowable means towards a desired end.

The Inspectors appear altogether to have overlooked the fact, that this was done for the purpose of making known how much might be accomplished by kindness and moral influence, without authoritative enactments, rather than to gratify any morbid curiosity on the part of the visitors, or love of display on that of the ladies.

It is not now worth while to dwell on what was deemed discourteous or unkind by the ladies, at the time; or the means they adopted to rectify the inaccuracies which appeared in the First Official Report of the Inspectors, in reference to their proceedings. The differences between them soon died away, and on subsequent occasions, the ladies felt themselves under obligation to these gentlemen for the attention paid to their requests on behalf of the Transports. The reader may judge from the perusal of the following letter from Mr. Russell, how completely their minds were freed from all misapprehension of the motives or conduct of the Ladies' Committee.

LETTER FROM THE REV. WHITWORTH RUSSELL TO THE SECRETARY OF THE LADIES' CONVICT SHIP COMMITTEE.

"26, Cumberland Street, 14*th July*, 1843.

"My dear Madam,

"As there was no Board of the Inspectors of the Millbank Prison until yesterday afternoon, your very valuable and interesting letter could not sooner be brought under their notice. I am commissioned by them to convey to you their best thanks, and to assure you, how much they desire to promote the objects to which your letter refers, and to carry out the many excellent suggestions it contains. I am going to-day to make inquiries of the different departments, in order to ascertain what has been done with reference to the fitments of the Woodbridge, and the clothing of the convicts who are to go out in her. I am almost afraid we shall not be able to alter the existing arrangements, so as to bring them to bear on the Woodbridge; we shall, however, try what can be effected.

"We shall not only be anxious to communicate to Mrs. Fry

any arrangements we may succeed in making, but shall also be glad to benefit by her advice and experience. As, however, Mr. Crawford is now absent at Parkhurst, and does not return until the afternoon of Monday next, the interview proposed for that day must necessarily be postponed. When our arrangements are more matured, we will ask Mrs. Fry to fix any time for an interview which may be convenient to her. We also beg to offer our thanks to the ladies of the Convict Ship Committee, for their kind co-operation in a work, for which they have already done so much, and in which they will prove such valuable assistants. Let me again thank you, my dear madam, and be assured, we shall gladly receive any communication you may be so good as to make to us.

"I am, my dear Madàm,
"Yours very faithfully,
"WHITWORTH RUSSELL."

Thus, through a measure of evil report, and through many difficulties, did Mrs. Fry pursue her way ; but her aim being singly to serve Him whose service she had deliberately chosen, wherever and however that service might lead her, she could not be "greatly moved." She dealt with Him who "looketh not at the outward appearance," but at "the heart." It was from within that she sought consolation, and there she found the Reward of peace ; for her heart was "fixed, trusting in the Lord." From His hands she received success with gratitude ; checks or impediments, she knew, were equally of His sending, and to be alike received with thanksgiving.

Upton Lane, Second Month 16*th.* Yesterday, I had the real satisfaction of meeting our Coast Guard Library Committee ; Government gave us £300 ; and Captain Bowles, who was present (the Comptroller of the Customs, or head of all the Coast Guard Stations) gave £20 ; through which grants, we paid for all the books, bought for our District Libraries ; about 20,000 volumes ; we gave our secretary, T. Timpson, a present of £50, and had £10 over. When I remember the many difficulties I had to encounter

in it, first, at the Custom House, the wearisome walks to the top
of that great building, to see Captain Bowles.   My protracted
correspondence with various members of the Government, many
committees, besides some rebuffs and humiliations to go through.
I think, hardly any public engagement has occupied so much
of my time; but, now, thanks to my Holy Head, and merciful
Helper, I think my part in it is finished.   I desire to be very
watchful how I put my hand to any other fresh public work ;
for I see much care needful, lest my attention should be too
much turned from my own heart, my own family, or even my
duties to the religious community to which I belong : but, on
the other hand, if ever called again by my Lord, into fresh service
of this kind; may I be enabled, promptly, diligently and faithfully
to attend to it.

At this time, Mrs. Fry had the gratification of making the
acquaintance of Miss Anley,* then about to proceed to Australia,
to reside for a time with her cousin, Mrs. Dumaresq.   This lady
entered warmly into Mrs. Fry's views ; the observations she
made during her sojourn in that distant land are highly interesting, though the picture she draws is very sorrowful, of the almost
unavoidable crime and misery existing there.

Colonel Dumaresq, had as many as one hundred prisoners in his
employ, and it was his aim in every way to promote their moral
and religious welfare ; but his difficulties, though great, could not
have equalled those of his predecessor, Sir W. Edward Parry,.
who, with his lady, spent some years at Port Stephen, devoted
not more to the secular interests of the company he so effectively
served, than to the good of the wretched convict population
around him.

Upton Lane, Second Month 25th.—On the 23rd instant, I
thought it right to lay before my Monthly Meeting, my belief,
that it was my duty to have some religious services in Sussex,
Kent, and my own Quarterly Meeting.   I can hardly express

* Authoress of the "Prisoners of Australia," "Miriam," and other
works.

the sweetness and peacefulness I felt, in making this small sacrifice, to what I believe to be, the call of duty. The near unity and sympathy expressed with me, by my friends, was also very encouraging and comforting. My dearest brother Samuel offering to take me this expedition, was quite a help and comfort.

Third Month 13th.—I returned from my journey on Sixth-day last, having been out a week. I felt low, in fact, almost ill with the serious weight of the prospect of the Public Meetings. The first Meeting I wished to have, was at Hastings, the second at Rye; a curious interesting place, towards which I had felt much attracted in my last journey. We found a meeting-house there. Grover Kemp, a valuable young minister joined me at my request, which was a great satisfaction to me.

At Hastings, several of the Coast Guard men and officers were at the Meeting. I had many proofs of the use and value of the libraries, sent to them ; to my comfort and satisfaction : proving it not to have been labour " in vain in the Lord." Real kindness, almost affection, as well as gratitude was shown to me, by several of the men and officers and their families. We hope a Bible Society will be formed at Rye, in consequence of our visit, and a Prison Society at Dover. But to come to one of the most interesting parts of our expedition ; we went to Sheerness, to visit the women and children in the ships in ordinary. Captain Kennedy had them collected at my request ; it was a fine sight, in a large man-of-war, instead of bloodshed and fightings, to see many naval officers, two chaplains, sailors, soldiers, ladies, numbers of women and children, all met to hear what two Quakers had to say, more particularly a woman, and to listen to any advice given by them. We examined the children, as to their knowledge, then gave them advice, afterwards we addressed their parents, and lastly, those present generally—we were received with great cordiality by Captain Kennedy, and his wife.

23rd.—I laid before our Monthly Meeting on Third-day, my belief of its being my duty to go to Ireland, and take Liverpool and Manchester in the way. I had the unity of my friends—I say in my heart ; unless Thy presence go with me, take me not up hence. May my Lord answer this prayer in His tender mercy.

Fourth Month 12*th.*—My beloved niece C—— G—— is to be married this morning, to my dear nephew E. N. B——. My prayers have been offered up on their behalf, may the Lord be with them, bless them, keep, prosper and increase them !

14*th.*—Just about leaving home for Ireland, oh dearest˜Lord ! bless I entreat Thee this act of faith, to my family, myself, and those amongst whom I go, and be, I most humbly pray Thee, my Keeper their Keeper, my Helper their Helper, my Strength their Strength, my Joy and Peace, and their Joy and Peace, Amen ! Grant this for Thine own name sake, oh ! most gracious Lord God, cause also, that we may meet again, in love, joy, peace, and safety.

The motives of Elizabeth Fry for undertaking this journey were two-fold. To attend the Meetings of Friends in Lancashire, and be present at the Dublin Yearly Meeting ; and to visit the prisons at Dublin, and make a renewed effort for their amendment. She cared especially for the large female prison, in Grange Gorman Lane, then in contemplation, she had long earnestly wished to see a prison devoted to women. This being the first in the kingdom, it was likely to prove a sort of model, should the example be followed in other places : she therefore considered it of great importance, that the arrangements should be as complete and effective as possible. Lord Mulgrave (Marquis of Normandy) the Lord Lieutenant, she had reason to believe was earnestly anxious to carry out, a wise, and yet merciful system of prison discipline. Mr. Spring Rice (Lord Monteagle) kindly furnished her with a letter of introduction to him, but in a note to herself, assures her that any introduction to that nobleman was unnecessary, which indeed she found verified, for the attention Lord Normanby gave to her suggestions, was not greater than his personal kindness and courtesy to herself and her friends, during their stay in Ireland.

The Grange Gorman Lane prison was completed early in 1837. After the lapse of ten years, it is thus mentioned in Major

Cottingham's Report.   Appendix to Twenty-fifth Report of In-spectors-General of Prisons in Ireland.

" Visited, February 18th, 1847.—Although I made my annual inspection of this prison on the 18th February, 1847, as a date upon which to form my report, yet I have had very many oppor-tunities of seeing it during the past and former years, in my duties connected with my superintendence of the convict depart-ment. The visitor may see many changes in the faces and per-sons of the prisoners, but no surprise can ever find a difference in the high and superior order with which this prison is conducted. The Matron, Mrs. Rawlins, upon whom the entire responsibility of the interior management devolves, was selected some years since, and sent over to this country by the benevolent and philan-thropic Mrs. Fry, whose exertions in the cause of female prison reformation, were extended to all parts of the British Empire; and who, although lately summoned to the presence of her Divine Master, has nowhere left a more valuable instance of her sound judgment, and high discriminating powers, than in the selection of Mrs. Rawlins to be placed at the head of this experimental prison, occupied alone by females ; and so successful has the experiment been, that I understand several other prisons, solely for females, have lately been opened in Scotland, and even in Australia. In this prison is to be seen an uninterrupted system of reformatory discipline in every class, such as is to be found in no other prison, that I am aware of."

The following extracts are from a letter, written by the Matron, Mrs. Rawlins, dated September 1st, 1847.

" It is perhaps needless for me to tell you, that Mrs. Fry had long wished to have the trial made of an exclusively female prison. That Mrs. Fry's plan has completely succeeded, every authority, both city and government, have borne ample and unqualified testi-mony, but I regret to say, she never personally saw the fruit of her labour, not having visited Ireland since my residence here, but to her wise, judicious, and maternal counsel (under Provi-dence) I entirely ascribe the success that has attended our oxertions. I never took any material step at the commencement, without consulting her, and at her own request, at least every week, I wrote an account of my movements ; and many obstacles that at first arose, she settled in her own quiet way, by her influence with the government."

There was another subject which occupied Mrs. Fry's attention in Ireland, the state of the National Schools there ; she visited some, and obtained minute reports of the state of many others. The result was, that she believed them to be falling rapidly under the power of the Roman Catholic priesthood, and that instead of affording scriptural instruction generally, these schools gave but a fresh opportunity for inculcating the spirit of popery. That even the Bible lessons so strongly recommended by the Commissioners were in most cases very little used, and then without the children being told from whence they were taken, or led to reverence the Bible as the word of God. It was not Mrs. Fry's wish to take a prominent part in any thing which she did not consider as an absolute duty, encumbent upon herself, to perform. She communicated, upon her return to England, her observations to Lord Morpeth, but it was through her brother-in-law, Mr. Buxton, that she endeavoured, to bring forward the dangers which she detected, in the working of the system. That she was most liberal, almost too liberal, no one who knew her will deny ; but this very liberality caused her to disapprove of the expenditure of public money in the support of schools, professedly intended for the good of all, and to favour no sect or party ; but in point of fact, excluding by their practical arrangements and internal government, the children of pious Protestants ; and the superintendence of pious Protestant ministers, of every name.

Upton Lane, Fifth Month 13th.—I returned home safely yesterday afternoon. I think I never had so happy and so prosperous an arrival—I wept with joy ; the stream appears to be turned for a while, my tears have often flowed for sorrow, and now my beloved husband and children have caused them to flow for joy. I found not only all going on well, and having done so during my absence, but to please, comfort, and surprise me, my dearest husband had had my rooms altered and made most comfortable, and my children had sent me nice presents to render them more complete. Their offerings of love quite gladdened my heart, though far too good for me ; I felt utterly unworthy of them, I may say peculiarly so. I have seldom ⌐d home more sensible of the hidden evils of my heart. ⌐ ⌐nstances have unusually made me feel this. I fully believe ⌐is going out, much help has been granted me in various ⌐⌐s ; my understanding has appeared to be enlightened more fully to see and comprehend gospel truth, and power has been given me to utter it boldly, beyond what I could have supposed. The fear of man was much taken away in Ireland, when I had to tell them what I believed to be home truths ————. I may say I am brought down under a very deep feeling of utter unworthiness ; and earnestly desire and pray, that whatever of our labours have been acceptable in the sight of our heavenly Father, they may be truly blessed to many, and not be in vain in Him ; and that whatever may have been in any way not according to His will, that He would in His own power prevent any harm from it arising to others.

The kindness shown us by James and Hannah Doyle, Elizabeth Doyle, and their mother, is I think never to be forgotten, during our long stay with them ; also by our much valued friends Jonathan and Eliza Pim, and many others dearly loved in the Lord. My desires and prayers are strong, that being returned home, I may profit by the deep experience of this expedition. May my holy Redeemer cause me by His Spirit to walk very closely to Himself, keeping to the Truth in His Spirit ; and by His power preserving me from impetuous zeal in holy things. In this Yearly Meeting, may very sound discretion be my portion. As for my home duties, my longings are indescribable that I may perform them in deep humility, godliness, holy fear and love ; that I may be a preacher of righteousness in all things and in all ways.

Sixth Month 12*th,* *(First-day morning).*—We, yesterday, had
our British Society Meeting, and it was to me striking to observe,
how much our various labours had been blessed, and to hear how
many poor women from various parts have been induced to forsake their evil courses, and are now either leading good lives, or
have died happy Christian deaths.

18*th.*—I have felt a good deal pressed in spirit, the last few days.
The day before yesterday I counted twenty-nine persons who came
here, on various accounts, principally to see me ; there are times,
when the tide of life is almost overpowering. It makes me
doubtful, as to our remaining much longer in this place, which
from its situation brings so many here. I have several things
which rather weightily press me just now. I desire to lay my
case before the Lord, trusting in Him, and casting myself and
my whole care upon Him. Dearest Lord, help, supply all our
needs, through the riches of Thy grace, in Christ Jesus ! Amen.
I yesterday accompanied General Campbell, the Lieutenant-
Governor of Jersey, to Lord John Russell, our Secretary of State,
to settle the difficulties respecting the prison in that island. May
our efforts be blessed.

23*rd.*—I much regret to say that last evening, I had an account
that my dearest sister Louisa ruptured a blood-vessel on the chest
and is very poorly, she had a similar attack last summer. She
has in addition, ever since the loss of her son, three years ago, been
much tried by nervous depression, so as to cast quite a cloud over
her, still she is lively in spirit, walking humbly and watchfully
before the Lord ; but I consider her affliction to be a heavy one,
and one that claims in no common degree, our deep sympathy and
prayers—may our Lord, heal, help and sustain her ! whether her
course here be for a longer or shorter time !

In June, Mrs. Fry had the gratification of receiving the printed
Report of the Committee, acting under the sanction of His
Majesty's Government, for furnishing the Coast Guard of the
United Kingdom, with libraries of religious and instructive books ;
announcing the completion of the project with a short account of
what had been effected.

" The committee, acting under the sanction of His Majesty's Government, for furnishing the Coast Guard of the United Kingdom with libraries of religious and instructive books, and also with school books for the families of the men employed on that service, having, by the blessing of Divine Providence, completed that object, it becomes their pleasing duty to lay before the subscribers a Report of their proceedings.

" In the commencement of this duty, it is proper gratefully to acknowledge, that the idea of furnishing these libraries first suggested itself to the benevolent mind of Mrs. Fry, whose active and charitable exertions on all occasions affecting the benefit of mankind are too well known, and too highly estimated, to need further remark on the present occasion, and who having previously succeeded in inducing His Majesty's Government to establish libraries for the use of the patients in the naval hospitals, was induced by the observations she had made on the subject, to endeavour to extend the same beneficial measure to the Coast Guard Service, and after several unsuccessful efforts, arising from the expense which it would occasion, a sum of £500. was obtained in 1835, from the first lord of the treasury (Sir Robert Peel) for this purpose, which munificent donation has since been followed by subscriptions from many charitable individuals, and grants from several public book societies, but as the whole of these funds were not sufficient to meet the object in view, the present chancellor of the exchequer (Mr. Spring Rice) kindly granted two further sums amounting together to £460. to effect its completion.

" The means thus so liberally afforded, have enabled the committee to provide and forward to the coast,

498 Libraries for the Stations on shore, containing	25,896 vols.
74 Ditto Districts	12,880
48 Ditto Cruizers	1,867
School books for the children of the crews of stations	6,464
Pamphlets, Tracts, &c.	5,357 in Nos.
Making a total of	52,464 vols.

and thereby to furnish a body of deserving and useful men and their wives and families, (amounting to upwards of 21,000 persons) with the means of moral and religious instruction, as well as˜profitable amusement, most of whom, from their situation in life, have not the means of procuring such benefits from their own resources, and who in many instances, are so far removed from places of public worship and schools, as to prevent the possibility of themselves or their families deriving advantage from either."

This work was now accomplished ; and dismissed from her mind as a point gained, and a blessing granted.

Her active exertions in behalf of the prisons of the United Kingdom generally, were drawing to a close. She had been an eminent instrument, in calling attention to the subject—but attention was now fully aroused, and the Prison Inspectors were pursuing their scrutinies with great and good effect.

Other matters, however, pressed upon her attention ; nothing so much as the state of the Prisons in Guernsey and Jersey ; in the latter prison, the difficulties of remedying the existing evils appeared almost insurmountable.   Dr. Bisset Hawkins had visited both these gaols, and carefully investigated their state ; he had also given his attention in Jersey to the points in dispute between the States and the Governor, Field-Marshal Lord Beresford.   In his report to Lord John Russell, he describes the prison as in the most neglected state, exhibiting almost every defect in arrangement, which a prison is capable of displaying, and suffering under the absence of many common essentials, such as " clothing, suitable bedding, soap, washing, white-washing ; while the keeper appears to be almost his own master, and is appointed by the Bailiff of the Island, although he derives his emoluments from the Governor."

Dr. Hawkins recommended to have the question settled, of maintaining the prisoners, by an equal portion being borne by the Governor and the States.   He proposed that a House of Correction should be built on the grounds on which the present prison is situated, which affords ample space for the erection of such a building, without disturbing the already existing gaol. With respect to the expense of building it, he shows, that the Grant of King Charles the Second, by which the States are empowered to raise an Impôt on Liquors, expressly enjoins, " Three Hundred Livres Tournois," out of the revenue so raised, " shall be yearly employed for the erecting and building a couvenient House, and for and towards raising and maintaining of a Stock of Money, to be used for the setting to work, and orderly governing of Poor and Idle people, the relief of decayed Tradesmen, and the Correction and Restraint of Vagabonds and Beggars within the said Isle."

From this fund, he considers, that the States, by the payment of £1000. for two successive years, could, without difficulty, meet the expenses of erecting a building, in all respects sufficient for the required purpose. He recommended a Prison Board for the superintendence, not only of the work, but of the prison afterwards, to consist of the following five high functionaries of the Island ; namely, the Lieutenant-Governor, the Bailiff, the two Law-Officers of the Crown, and the Sheriff or Deputy Sheriff, (usually denominated Vicomte or Deputy Vicomte) ; the Secretary and Treasurer to be the Greffier of the States.

Dr. Hawkins' propositions met with the concurrence of Lord John Russell, who recommended their adoption to the States. By that body Lord John Russell's communication was very fairly received, and the alterations they suggested were unimportant. Mrs. Fry took a lively interest in the subject as it proceeded. She was urged by many of her island friends, again to go to Jersey, before the contemplated buildings were begun.

Lord John Russell had favoured her with an interview on the subject, and she had frequently communicated with Lord Beresford. On this, as on many other occasions, her knowledge of the subject, and her facility in devising expedients, occasioned her not merely to be listened to with attention, but not unfrequently her counsel to be sought. And it is due to men of different parties, who successively guided the helm of State, to acknowledge, that her remarks were invariably received with courtesy, and where (as was generally the case), the subject matter approved itself to their own judgments, her advice as invariably followed. How much of this was owing to her extreme caution in forming opinions, and her nice discretion in bringing them forward, will be discerned by those, who whilst they read the history of her life, observe and comprehend her mental qualities. She considered that her presence might prove serviceable in Jersey; she was earnest that the arrangements about to be made there should be as complete as possible, especially for women. She wished again to inspect the Hospital, and to see the working of the District Society. Similar objects attracted her in Guernsey. She believed also, that it was her duty to visit the Island of Alderney, where hitherto she had not been.

To her husband and daughter the idea of a renewed tarriance in Jersey was entirely agreeable; but in her heart, an impediment existed, which occasioned her no little conflict, many doubts, and much distress, before she could determine upon the allotted path of duty.

Her sister, Mrs. Samuel Hoare had never recovered the loss of her eldest son. She bowed in submission to the blow; but never recovered the shock, and though she was enabled to persevere in all her duties, with much true Christian cheerfulness, it was evident to those who loved her, that the serious injury her constitution had received, was slowly but surely undermining the powers of life. Never, perhaps, had a son been more to his mother than her first-born son, had been to Mrs. Hoare: never the tie of affection or sympathy stronger. She had reared him with a firm, but most tender hand; he had passed through the slippery paths of youth, and early manhood, singularly intact, and had distinguished himself at College, which he quitted with high credit, to enter with equal diligence a business-career with his father in London.   He had only left the home of his parents, when united to one, as much their choice as his own.   Blessed as husband and father with all outward prosperity, suddenly, the message came, " Thou shalt die and not live."   He returned to his father's house, for a few weeks of deep illness and sedulous nursing; there, in perfect, acknowledged and most simple reliance on the wisdom and goodness of God his Saviour, in all His dealings with the children of men ; he left his father's house, on earth, for the eternal home, prepared for him by his Father in heaven.

At the time that Mrs. Fry was preparing to leave England, it became obvious that her sister was approaching that " country from whose bourn no traveller returns."   There are many who believe that they " acknowledge God in all their ways," trusting in Him, " to direct their paths ;" but there are not many who carry this belief into the practice of life, or are from experience, able to unite with Judge Hale in his assertion, that—

" They who truly fear God, have a secret guidance from a higher wisdom than what is barely human, viz., the Spirit of Truth and Godliness : which doth really, though secretly, prevent and direct them.   Any man that sincerely and truly fears Almighty God, and calls and relies upon him for his direction, *has it* as *really as a son has the counsel and direction of his father;* and though the voice be not audible, nor discernible by sense, yet it is as real as if a man heard a voice saying, ' This is the way walk in it.'

" Though this secret direction of Almighty God, is principally seen in matters relating to the soul ; yet it may also be found in the concerns of this life, which a good man that fears God and begging his direction, will *very often* if *not at all times* find.   I can call my own experience to witness that *even in the temporal concerns of my whole life,* I have never been disappointed of the best direction, when I have, in humility and sincerity implored it."

Elizabeth Fry was one of the few, who sought this guidance, and there probably, lay the secret of her strength. She watched for opportunity, she waited for occasion, she listened for the Father's voice ; but when heard, unhesitatingly pursued her way.

She believed it her duty to go to Jersey, at any sacrifice of personal feeling, and this view was confirmed, by knowing that by her suffering sister she was not needed ; every thing that love or skill could effect, being done for Mrs. Hoare, by her own family and her other sisters. Another circumstance tended to satisfy Mrs. Fry as to the rectitude of her decision ; her sister-in-law, Elizabeth Fry, then in very delicate health, having been advised again to visit the Channel Islands, where she had before derived much benefit from the mild sea air, and she, with Mr. and Mrs. Fry, and their daughter, embarked at Southampton, on a calm fine evening, with every prospect of a favourable voyage ; but about four o'clock in the morning, all on board were roused by the sudden stopping of the vessel. A dense fog had come on, when passing through the intricate passage between the Caskets and the Island of Alderney. They remained many hours entangled among rocks, which the sinking tide rendered more and more dangerous ; with the fog so thick, that it was not always easy to see the length of the vessel ; much apprehension was entertained by many on board, in which Mrs. Fry partook, though preserving her wonted calmness of demeanour.

Happily, may it not be called providentially, there was as passenger in the steamer, the old Guernsey pilot, who had brought Lord de Saumarez, and two frigates under his command, into Guernsey, in the presence of a superior French force, by piloting them through a passage, generally considered impracticable. Of his advice and assistance, the Captain himself a skilful pilot, took advantage, and after a time of careful navigation, the joyful tidings spread among the passengers, that the jeopardy was over, that they were through the Channel, and once more in the open sea. The spirit of her mind was exemplified in Mrs. Fry's remark to her daughter, at this instant, "I have felt it very doubtful whether this was not to be for us the dawn of the eternal, instead of the earthly Sabbath ; I thought it rather the Church above, than the Church below, we were to join to-day."

Jersey, Eighth Month 6th.—My husband and I have been here rather more than a week. I left home on Fourth-day, the 27th, accompanied by my dear sister Gurney, leaving my husband and the rest of the party to follow on Sixth-day, because I believed it my duty to attend the Quarterly Meeting at Alton, in my way to Southampton. In tender mercy, I was permitted to part from my beloved family in peace, in love, and in good hope that our Heavenly Father would bless and protect them. On Second-day, before leaving home, we had our dear children and grandchildren, for a sweet cheerful evening, drinking tea and having straw-berries, in the garden, a little farewell frolic—it was a lovely sight. From Alton, I proceeded to Southampton, where we all met, and were favoured with a favourable passage till early in the morning, when so awful a fog came on, just as we were in the midst of the rocks, between Alderney and Guernsey, that the Captain and the crew appeared to be much alarmed. We all felt it very seriously, and I experienced something of my own infirmity and fearful nature, still I was quiet, and I think trustful. It was delightful once more to see land, and to have the sun shine upon us. I can hardly express the feeling. We were detained about four hours in this fog. I must describe our arrival, the sun breaking out, showing us the Island of Guernsey, Herm and Sark. Castle Carey, the place of our destination, on the top of the hill, sur-rounded by trees, looking beautiful, we met with the most cordial reception from our friends and their children—the place delight-ful—my room commanding the finest view of the sea and islands, our comforts abundant, far above our deserts. I had apprehended, previously to leaving home, that I should feel it a duty to visit the island of Alderney, but I became discouraged, the danger of the sea having been so much brought home to me ; and the passage very difficult. But I found upon weighing the subject, that I was not satisfied to omit it, and therefore if a favourable opening occurred, resolved to make the effort, and to go on

Fourth-day, the 11th.   We tried for a conveyance in vain, till
the very morning when we found a vessel going.   The sun shone
brilliantly, the wind fair ; every thing prospered our setting off,
and we appeared to have the unity of all our party.   My beloved
husband, Edmund Richards, Sophia Mourant, and myself.   We
had a very favourable voyage, though these little sailing vessels
are unpleasant to me, and give me an uncomfortable sensation.
We arrived at this curious island, which is rocky, wild, not generally cultivated, covered in parts with a carpet of lovely wild
flowers, and scantily inhabited by an interesting people.   No
inn of course, but we had a very nice lodging, where we might
truly say, we wanted for no real comfort, so the Lord doth provide.   I was low and poorly, the first part of our visit ; but like
the fog on the voyage, my cloudy state was suddenly dispersed, as
from a ray of the Sun of Righteousness.   We held some meetings, we also formed a Ladies' Charity to visit the poor, we
proposed sending a library, and Edmund Richards formed a
temperance society.   We were received with great kindness, by
numbers of the people, and by Major Baines the Governor, and
his wife.   We found no opportunity for our departure, at the
time we had proposed leaving Alderney, and were literally confined there, until the end of the following week, when the way
appeared to be as clear to return as it had been to go.   A vessel
to take us—the wind fair, and the sun bright.   We arrived safely
at Castle Carey, on the evening of the 24th of the Seventh
Month, and found good accounts from home, and from the party
who had preceded us to Jersey ; thanks be to my Heavenly
Father!   My too anxious and fearful mind having been disposed
to much anxiety.   I had not much public service in Guernsey.
Meetings as usual on First-day.   I went to see many families of
Friends and others, and besides some of the poor, visited the
Hospital, and urged the great need of a Lunatic Asylum.   The
evening before our departure, I had a very solemn Public Meeting, with many interesting persons, afterwards several joined us at
Castle Carey ; where we had a time of much interest, pleasantly
partaking of natural friendship ; afterwards we were read to by a
clergyman, and then I had a very solemn occasion of thanksgiving
and prayer, greatly doubting my ever seeing most of their faces

again. The next morning, John and Matilda Carey, their children, the clergyman, and our friends the Richards', all accompanied us to the shore, some went with us in a boat to the ship, which I entered in peace and comfort; under the belief, that I had been in my right allotment in that island, and Alderney. We had a beautiful passage here, calm, and lovely weather, I had the blessing of finding the party well.

Jersey, 19th.—In this place I find much to occupy me, in the Hospital, the District Society, and in the Prisons. We receive much kind attention from the inhabitants of the island. I had much to say in a large District Society Meeting, yesterday—I hope usefully. I entered it prayerfully, but not enough so. I have enjoyed some delightful expeditions into the lovely country, where we have sometimes taken our cold dinner, and spent the day in the rocky bays. We have also joined two large parties of the same kind, which were pleasant to me; my nature leads me to be social, and rather like general society, but I wish all to be done in the right spirit. Innocent recreation, I believe, is profitable as well as pleasant. Our Lord desired His servants to rest, and He evidently felt for them when they had hardly time to eat; (6th chapter of Mark, 31st verse) but this rest was after labour. I believe our recreations are right, as far as they fit us for our Master's service, and wrong, if they enervate and disqualify us for it. I have deeply felt my sister Hoare's state. I may say in measure, I bear her burdens with her,—she has my frequent prayers, and my tears often rise in remembrance of her. My heart is also much at home, most tenderly interested for all my children, more particularly my boys. I think I have cause for much thankfulness in the accounts from them.

23rd.—The letters on First-day brought us the affecting intelligence that my much loved sister Hoare was worse; her decline has been rapid the last week or two. My sister Cunningham wrote to beg me to set off to her directly; this proved a stunning blow—the low estate of this tenderly beloved sister, the difficulty of getting to her, the doubts as to what I ought to do, the disappointment that we should again lose our time of refreshment and recreation in France, all upset me, as I say, stunned me. What could I do, but pray in this emergency to be helped and directed aright; that I might faithfully do my duty to all, and that my poor dear afflicted sister might be so helped immediately by her Lord Himself, that no other help might be really needful to her, yet the infirmity of my heart led me to pray also, that if right for us I might see her again and be some little help and comfort to her in her last hours.

Mrs. Hoare was to Mrs. Fry a beloved sister, a faithful and unfailing friend, and often a wise counsellor—she being a woman of a large and comprehensive mind, excellent in judgment, and of very uncommon cultivation. Besides, it was again a lessening of the band; another taken of the seven sisters, who had entered life together; and, as such, an event to affect and alter it, to those who were left.

In the early days of Earlham, Louisa Gurney is described by one who shared with her their interests and pleasures, as "a noble girl, and the most talented of any of them, possessing a fine understanding, great energy, and a taste for excellence, which produced a high stimulus in her pursuits, and success, for the most part, in all she undertook ; but, in case of failure, an equal degree of disappointment and vexation : a heart warm and generous, a glowing disposition, very benevolent, active and effective in her habits ; rising early of her own accord, full of her own objects, and fond of learning and cultivation of every kind."

As a mother nothing more need be said of her, than that the principles inculcated in her writings,* she carried out in daily practice, enlarging and expanding as her children advanced in life.

After the death of their son, Mr. Hoare's family removed to their residence at Cromer. Thence she wrote to Mrs. Fry—

" How kind of you, my dearest sister, to write again so fully to us ! With your tender hand, never be afraid of touching us, in

* Hints on Early Education, and the Workhouse Boy.

our present low estate. You well know the secrets of real and deep grief; few have been taught like yourself to minister to the afflicted. I always feel a difficulty in describing our present state; I do so long to be thankful, and enabled to acknowledge the mercies received, and the manifestations that have been vouchsafed to us, of the beauty and efficacy of grace, received in humble faith and obedience! such simplicity of faith, humility, meekness, fortitude, and deep resignation of spirit as we were permitted to witness! But the loss is indescribable; and the conflict has been greater and sharper than I was prepared for. There is a natural sinking, too, after strong and continued excitement; and I believe I am suffering from the shake to the nerves, as well as the great trial to the feelings. How do we need, in the season of deep trial, to refrain our souls and keep them low! to be made willing to suffer, till the time of revival and refreshment is ordered for us! ' He will command His loving kindness in the day-time, and in the night His song shall be with me.' May this be our happy experience, and your dear R——'s too, in her long sickness! What an exercise of long suffering day after day! But what a provision for us—'Give us day by day our daily bread!' We must learn to live as little children, our eye continually fixed on our God and Saviour, seeking for nourishment from Him, and that precious anointing, which can heal our deepest wounds, and shed abroad in us the consoling and constraining love of Christ! Oh, for more of that love, to elevate and sanctify our natural affections, and gradually to swallow up the sense of sorrow and mourning, in the view of the love and faithfulness of Him who hath promised eternal life to all that believe in Him! How I long to drink more deeply of this living stream! for all our fresh springs are in Him, and our times of mourning and of joy in His hands."

The accounts of Mrs. Hoare becoming rapidly worse, and Mrs. Fry's objects in the Channel Islands being accomplished; she prepared for her departure.

A Committee of Ladies was established for visiting the Hospital in Jersey, with the Lady of the Lieutenant-Governor

General Campbell at its head. The District Society was increasing in usefulness, the new House of Correction was likely to be established on the best principles; and she had the comfort of knowing, that all these objects were left under the skilful and efficient superintendence of her kind friend Lieutenant-General Touzel, who had been with other Jersey gentlemen, faithful co-adjutors in her various labours. Her visits to Alderney and Guernsey had been accomplished to her own satisfaction.

Jersey, Eighth Month 25th.—Since I last wrote, I have passed through much conflict; K—— too unwell to allow of my leaving her; indeed I have been strongly drawn two ways. I now expect to cross to-morrow; but some discouragement attends it. I am about going to a Public Meeting of importance, to finish, as I suppose, such services here. Be pleased, most gracious Lord, to be with me in this straitened place; help me through this service, by Thine own Spirit to glorify Thee; edify, comfort, and help this people, and those dear to me. Show me, I pray Thee, for Thy dear Son's sake, this token for good in my low estate—and if it please Thee, make my way quite clear before me; if I am called to my beloved sister, oh dearest Lord, be Thyself with me, and by the openings of Thy Providence outwardly, and the light of Thy Spirit inwardly; make my way clear before me, and all of us, that we may part in peace, love, and joy in Thee. Amen. In Thy love and pity in Christ Jesus, hearken to my unworthy cry.

Upton Lane, Ninth Month 13th.—I was favoured to get through this Meeting well. By the close of that day I had very much concluded the various duties that I was called to perform in that island. My daughter was better, and the time to depart seemed come, though I minded having to get up in the night, for we had to be in the vessel before four o'clock, A.M. When the morning came the wind was favourable, and we, not the worse for getting up so early. I felt peace, in going at that time, and not waiting for the next post, and prayed for preservation for us all. We then set off, found a comfortable small vessel, a good captain, rather a moderate sea, at first weather doubtful ; by degrees the day cleared, the sun shone upon us, and though the wind became high and the sea rough, yet it did not make us unwell, and we had altogether a pleasant and prosperous voyage.   I left my sister Elizabeth Fry at Weymouth, and travelled on to London on First and Second-day, as in a case of this kind, I consider it allowable to travel on the Sabbath.   I arrived at Hampstead on Third-day morning, the 29th, and found my much-loved sister in a very affecting state ; her malady, whatever it is, having made rapid advances.   From extreme reduction, her mind appears unable to form more than one sentence at a time ; she therefore can express but little of her mind religiously, but, even in this very low tried state ; we perceive her high Christian principle.   No complaining, no irritation ;   kind and grateful, yielding to our requests, whilst a word or ·two, now and then, show us her mind.   When I said, "How suffering illness is," and "what it is to suffer"—she added, "to reign," referring to the text, those who "suffer with Christ will also reign with Him in glory."   Being tried by pain, I expressed that "all was right" that was ordered for us ; she replied, "perfectly right."   I was plunged into deep feeling and conflict on entering the scene, the transition being great from the one in Jersey ; and my foolish, fearful, doubting mind was full of misgivings at having left my husband and daughter, and not going with them to France; but, thanks to my Heavenly Father, my spirit became gradually more at rest.

I had the inexpressible comfort of being permitted a few days with her, and she evidently liked my company.   I particularly observed, how gently I was dealt with, by her reviving a little after I arrived, so that I had not the bitterness of her at once sinking.   The affliction was thus mitigated to me ; I was enabled to show her some marks of my deep and true love, and to be with, and earnestly pray for her, in·the hour of death.   I was helped to be some comfort to many of her family, and (utterly unworthy as I know I am of it) I believe in my various ministrations, I was enabled to prove the power of the Spirit to qualify for his own work, and amongst them all, particularly with my dear nephew, who has just entered the Church, deeply to impress the necessity of the work of the Spirit being carried on in the heart; and of having Christian charity towards others of every denomination. My beloved sister Hoare's death has made a deep impression on me. I do not like to enter life or its cares, or to see many, or to be seen. I like to withdraw from the world, and to be very quiet. I have naturally much felt the event, though supported and comforted under it.

To her Sister Mrs. Buxton, and her Family then
in Scotland.

Upton Lane, *Ninth Month* 14*th*, 1836.

To the dear party at Rennyhill,

The accounts of you and from you, have deeply interested me this morning. I desire, my tenderly beloved ones, to hand you a few words of encouragement, more particularly my dearest sister. I feel our loss a deep one indeed; but I also see much wisdom, mercy and love in the heavy trial,—in the first place, as it respects herself. Her very susceptible mind was so acutely sensible of the trials of life, that her Lord saw she had had enough; more might have overwhelmed her, therefore she was taken in the accepted time. I see also, that her many preservations and deliverances, and her being kept as she was by the power of God, in soundness of faith through her sore conflicts, a cause for deep thankfulness: and then, to look upon her, really and fully at rest—in and with the Beloved of her soul, with her Lord, and also with the just made perfect; this brings to my feelings, as well as to my mind, much rest, peace and refreshment on her behalf. Then I consider ourselves, and our great loss; but I also see a something of gain, in her being taken in so much freshness, in the midst of her usefulness; it causes her death to speak so loudly, the very vacancy makes it stimulating; I have not unfrequently observed Christians being called away in the midst of their labours, much blessed to those who remain, in leading them to look more simply to Him, who can work with or without His instruments; in making them more diligent, seeing that the Lord is at hand. Again, by encouraging to patience, hope, and trust, as we know not how soon the warfare may be accomplished with any of us ; and further, the holy lively example of such, is so present with us, and so encouraging, to strive to follow them, as they followed Christ. But after expressing so far, the bright side of the question, I know and feel the other but too well, to have one so tenderly beloved gone from our present view—to see her place vacant—to miss her delightful influence and tender watchful care over all, is bitter, causing many a heaving of the heart. I am very anxious for thee, dearest Hannah, that thou mayst be comforted ; remember all our time is short, and that it is well to have some, safely landed beyond the reach of every storm.

Upton Lane, Ninth Month 22nd.—On Third-day I dined with J—— and A—— ; thirteen of my children were there, and no one else. I have seldom enjoyed a visit anywhere more. We had a solemn reading and time of prayer, before we parted.

To her Daughter Mrs. F—— C——.

Upton Lane, *Ninth Month.*

My dearest R——,

I fancy you arriving to-morrow from Cresswell, and I write for a letter ; in my quiet home it would be a treat to hear from thee. I much value and enjoy the true kindness I receive from all my married children. I have lately daily dined with one of them ; it has made me think of thee, my loved child, and thy dear husband, particularly when the other day at J——'s, on his birthday, I sat surrounded by all the married pairs. I am much disposed to pay you a visit. I deeply feel, in the loss of my beloved sister, the shortness of the time that I may be with you. No remaining duty has dwelt so much on my mind as my relative duties, that I may be enabled to minister to my beloved husband or children, brothers or sisters, as they may want it, either spiritually or temporally. May we all do our part faithfully towards each other, seeing how little we know how soon we may part ! I have written to Harrow, to ask your dear F—— to come and see me ; I think it right he should do so after my long absence ; I have requested him to ask Dr. Wordsworth to let him come on Seventh-day, to stay over the Sabbath. Our

R 2

garden is lovely, and house pleasant; so our Heavenly Father deals very kindly with his unworthy servant.

I am,

Thy tenderly attached mother,

ELIZABETH FRY.

Tenth Month 2nd, First-day.—On Second-day morning, when going into the Select Quarterly Meeting, with my brother Samuel, my son William came to tell us, that a serious accident had happened to my husband and daughter in Normandy. They had been thrown down a precipice, the carriage broken to pieces, and although they had experienced a very Providential deliverance, in their lives being spared and no dangerous wound received, yet K—— was so much hurt, and my dearest husband so much shaken, that they wished me to go to them immediately. I gave up the Quarterly Meeting of course, and set off with my much-loved son William to Dover, so as to cross by the first packet to France. I remembered my sorrow, and perhaps undue disappointment in not accompanying them to France. It seemed almost as if my Heavenly Father had heard my murmurings, as He had heard the children of Israel in the Wilderness, and had taken me to France ; when I did go—against my inclination, alas ! I received it as a lesson to have but one prayer and desire in all things, " that the Lord's will be done on earth as it is in Heaven." The accident was most serious ; such an escape, I think, I never heard of: the carriage, in the first instance, fell with one horse (the driver and the other horse being separated from them before) about four yards perpendicularly ; then the carriage was dragged down about twenty-six yards more. The poor peasants came to assist, and fetched the village doctor for the body, and the priest for the soul.

Calais, Ninth Month 26th, 1836.

MY DEAREST J——,

William and I reached Dover soon after twelve o'clock last evening. We were settled by one o'clock, and off about half-past seven this morning. Our journey was an anxious one, until as the evening advanced, I became more quieted, and trustful that all was ordered for us in mercy and wisdom. We had a very favourable passage of three hours; and to our great satisfaction, found your father looking for us on the quay. We found our dearest K—— exceedingly bruised, and very grievously hurt altogether. Your dear father looks, I think, shaken and aged by all that he has gone through. Mary has been a very attentive nurse. She looks also jaded, but from her excessive fright, when they were going down the hill, she knelt down and put her head on K——'s lap, by which means her face was perfectly saved. And so I have at last touched French ground. William and I have not been idle; we have already visited the Prison and Hospital. We hope it may please Providence, in tender mercy to permit us all to arrive at home next Seventh-day, probably by a packet that leaves this place that morning for London.

Upton Lane, Tenth Month 15*th.*—William and I went *one day* to St. Omer, and stayed till the next. We had a very interesting expedition; his company was sweet to me.

I was a good deal instructed as well as interested, in visiting the Roman Catholic charities. The sacrifice that must be made to give up the whole life, as the Sisters of Charity do, to teach and bring up the poor children and attend to the sick in their hospitals is very exemplary; and the slackness of some Protestants and coldness of too many led me to think, that whilst on the one hand the meritoriousness of good works may be unsoundly upheld by the Roman Catholics, yet, that it stimulates to much that is excellent; and a fear arose in my mind, that the true doctrine that teaches that we have no merit in any thing that we do, is either so injudiciously represented, or so misunderstood, that in too many cases it leads to laxity as to sin, and a want of diligence in works of righteousness and true holiness. I was much interested in attending High Mass, but here I thought I saw something of the work of true religion under what appeared to me, the rubbish of superstition and show. But I also thought, that much of the same thing remained amongst Protestants. I long to see true religion in its purity and simplicity, spread more and more to the glory of God and the peace of men.

Eleventh Month 6*th, First-day.*—It has pleased our Heavenly Father to permit much trial within the last two or three weeks. My dearest C—— has had a very serious, I may say dangerous illness, one of great suffering. This day week her medical attendants were much alarmed, and wished to have a third called in ; I deeply felt her state, but very earnestly desired to have no will in it, seeing I knew not what was best for her. My prayer was most earnest for her salvation, that whenever taken hence she might be ready, being washed and made white in the blood of the everlasting covenant.

During C——'s illness, I had very affecting accounts from Lynn, of dearest R—— : her little Willy and his nurse, all in the scarlet fever ; the little boy very dangerously ill.

From amongst almost daily letters, written from the sick chamber of one daughter, to cheer and soothe the sorrow and sufferings of the other, the following extracts are taken :—

Upton Lane, Eleventh Month 11th.

The very affecting account from you is just arrived ; to think of that lovely boy laid so prostrate ! Still sweet babe it is good to remember "that of such is the kingdom of God," and the encouraging delightful idea that their angels or ministering spirits, are always before the face of our God. I am afraid of asking for his life, lest he should be contaminated in this evil world, but I can ask, if in the mercy of our Heavenly Father, He should see meet to keep him in the world, that He would preserve him from the evil ; and that should he be raised up, it may be for purposes of His own glory. But it is a trial indeed, to flesh and blood—I have found it a bitter one, to see these little ones suffer—but as thy dear husband truly says, we must in all things learn to say, "not my will but Thine be done."

Eleventh Month 15th.

Your time of trial has been a deep one, surely you must both have been deeply afflicted to see the poor little one's sufferings. I have a sweet hope for these little ones, that the Lord comforts and supports them by His Spirit in their afflictions, though their understandings may not be enlightened to know the hand that sustains, but that it is felt, though not known by them.

Twelfth Month 17th.—I went to the Great Mill Bank Penitentiary, to meet a committee of gentlemen, with some of our ladies afterwards ; and found, to our great satisfaction, that through the Secretary of State, Lord John Russell, our way was fully open to visit this prison, which we had long desired to do, but never before had gained access to it. Now I think, every criminal prison in London, is visited by us. I see much encouragement and cause for thankfulness, in our way thus continuing to be made in this work of Christian love. I went to Hampstead in the evening, truly affecting was it to find the real great loss in that dear family. I felt much love towards them, but did not see religiously or naturally, that I was very likely to be able to help them.

We had a very interesting Quarterly Meeting yesterday, though the ministry of our dear friend —— —— tried me much in parts, more particularly her applying to us as a people, those blessed hopes and promises, that I apprehend simply belong to the members of the living Church of Christ, gathered out of all administrations and nations. I doubt not the living members of our body, from their first rise, have been in many instances bright and shining lights in their day, and have peculiarly had to uphold the simple pure spirituality of gospel truth ; but I see no authority for our supposing ourselves to be more of a chosen people, the select few, than all who are redeemed by the blood of the Lamb ; though I think our calling a high and important one, in the Militant Church of Christ. May our Holy Head establish by His own power, all that is true and of Himself, amongst us, and entirely bring to nought all that is contrary to His will. This I earnestly desire, and may I not say pray for myself individually, as well as others.

31st.—Late in the evening, alone,—I feel it a rather solemn close to this year, not a time of brightness though abounding with causes for thankfulness—which I desire more deeply to feel. May my Lord grant for His dear Son's sake, that the Holy Spirit may more abundantly rest upon me and mine, as our Guide, Sanctifier and Comforter. May I more faithfully, watchfully, and humbly perform all my duties to my Lord, my family, my friends, the church generally and the world ; and to myself—and in afflictions may my soul be possessed in patience and watchfulness ! and may every day draw us nearer to God and His kingdom !

CHAPTER XX.

Earlham, First Month 4th, 1837. It is rather striking to begin my new year here. The drawing of my mind led me this way, and I ventured to leave all, in faith, after offering many prayers for their help and preservation during my absence. My prayers have been expressed in public, in my family, and in private, upon entering this new year. There are cries from the depth of my heart, unutterable ; but He who is my advocate with the Father, will I trust, availingly present them before the throne. I may say, Help Lord, or I perish ! Grant through thy love, pity and grace, that I may know Thee always, in all places, and at all times, to be my Defence—my Help—my Counsellor. Enlighten my darkness, cause me, in all things, to choose the good and refuse the evil ; lighten mine eyes always lest I sleep the sleep of death, and Satan in any way blind mine eyes. Pour forth more fully, and more freely, Thy Spirit upon me, that I may be qualified for Thy work, in my family, amongst my neighbours, in the church, and wherever Thou mayst call me.

5th.—I am much struck, by observing in our spiritual course, how different are the lines we are led in ; even those who may be under the same outward administration. We observe in nature both animal and vegetable, there are different classes, orders, genera, and species ; so I think, I see it spiritually, as the flowers of one species differ a little in colour or size ; so in the Church of

Christ, those who may be said to be of one species, differ in some small things, no two quite alike. May these differences in no degree separate us from each other.

Upton Lane, 25th.—My heart and mind have been much occupied, by my brother Joseph writing to inform me, that he apprehends it will be his duty to go to America this year, upon religious service. The subject is deeply important and weighty, yet I desire to rejoice in his willingness to give up all for the service of his Lord. Though some fears have arisen from a sort of floating apprehension I have had for many years, that I ought or might go with him, if ever he visited that land. Upon viewing it, as it respects myself, I believe I may truly say, I do not at present see any such opening. As far as I can see, *home* has my ·first call of duty, what the future may produce, I leave ; but as far as I know my own heart, I very earnestly desire to feel continually that I am not my own, but bought with a price, therefore, I am my Lord's servant, and must do as I am bidden, even if the service called for, appear to me unreasonable. But I must further observe, that in condescending mercy, I have generally found in services really called for, there has been a ripeness, that may be compared to the fruit come to maturity. For this service for the present, I see no way.

29th.—The present time of sickness and death is almost unprecedented. We hear of one or other continually. Two of our dear friends are taken.

Second Month 11th.—Yesterday, when I went to town to visit Newgate, I was stopped by F—— R——, saying, that he had sad tidings for me ; which proved to be,—that my beloved sister Harriet was most suddenly taken, leaving eight young children and my poor dear brother. Still, I trust not " left," because surely his Lord will be near, to help him in this very deep sorrow. Of course, we are brought very low by this fresh family affliction. Deeply do I desire, that it may be sanctified to us all. The same post brought yesterday, the account from my brother Joseph, that he had laid his concern to visit America before his Monthly Meeting. So one brother is called to do, the other to suffer ; may our Lord's will be done, by and through them both.

15th.—The funeral of my much loved sister takes place to-day. What a scene of unutterable sorrow at Runcton, where, a few days ago, all was in no common degree, joy, peace and great prosperity. Oh! what occasions are these, where families meet together for the affecting and solemn purpose of committing the remains of a beloved one to the silent grave!

May the Lord Himself lift up the light of His countenance upon them, bless them, and keep them in a sound mind and sound faith. Be pleased, oh gracious Lord! to help, pity, and comfort these afflicted ones this day.

No event could be more startling or more touching than this. Lady Harriet Gurney had entered the family, when many of the elder members had reached the meridian of life. She had come, not alone to gladden her own domestic hearth, but to diffuse of her bright, loving, hopeful spirit amongst her husband's relatives. For fourteen years she had in an exemplary manner, fulfilled the duties of wife and mother, friend and mistress—

> "A spirit, yet a woman too."

Her brother-in-law, Mr. Buxton, wrote on the day of her funeral:—" In seeing her coffin committed to the vault, I could not but feel, that it contained all that remained of as much beauty and true loveliness of mind, body, and spirit, as we ever saw removed from this world!"

Upton Lane, Third Month 12th.—I, yesterday, went to the Colonial Office to meet Sir George Grey, on subjects respecting New South Wales, and the state of the female convicts; to the Irish Office, and saw Lord Morpeth respecting National Schools and Prisons, and then to the Home Office, about Jersey Prisons, &c. In every one I met with a most cordial reception. So the Lord yet makes my way with those in power.

Sixth Month.—The King died last Third-day, the 20th. Our young Queen was proclaimed yesterday. My prayers have arisen for her, that our Heavenly Father would pour forth His Spirit upon her, guide her by His counsel, and grant her that wisdom which is from above. I was with Lord —— yesterday, who told me, that she behaved with much feeling and remarkable propriety, when meeting the Privy Council. She was supported by her uncles the new King of Hanover, and the Duke of Sussex. I have received a long letter from the Duchess of ——, containing a very interesting account of her, and of the death of the late King.

25th.—Being wounded in spirit, the grass-hopper becomes a burden,—still my causes for thankfulness much more abound. Yesterday, I went to my son J——'s, and saw his lawn, sprinkled over with my lovely grandchildren and their parents, so as to remind me of these words, " The Lord shall increase you more and more, you and your children. Ye are blessed of the Lord which made Heaven and earth."—Psal. cxv. 14, 15. I believe that the blessing of the Lord is with us ; blessed be His most holy name, for this gracious and unmerited mercy !

Seventh Month 20th.—I returned home yesterday evening from Lowestoft, after having accompanied my brother Joseph to Liverpool, in his way to America. Our time at Earlham was very interesting ; I believe I was helpful to my brother in a large Meeting that he held, to take leave of the citizens of Norwich. It was a highly interesting occasion, and I trust edifying to many. I am very sorry to say, my mind has too much the habit of anxiety and fearfulness. I believe this little journey would have been much more useful to me, but from an almost constant cloud over me, from the fear of being wanted by some of my family. I think it would be better for myself and for them, if they did not always cling so closely round my heart, so as to become too much of a weight upon me.

My beloved brother's leave-taking of Earlham and the family there, was very affecting ; still there was peace in it, and joy in the Lord, inasmuch as there is delight in doing what we believe to be His will. Of this, I think we partook with him. We went from Earlham to Runcton, there we dined. Shall I ever dine with my three brothers again ? the Lord only knows : my heart was tendered in being with them.

I rejoice that I proceeded with Joseph, for I did not before that feel that I had come at his mind, he had been so much engaged, but on the journey I did so very satisfactorily. Samuel, Eliza-

beth, Joseph and myself, thus had a time together, never to be
forgotten. We had much interesting conversation respecting
things spiritual and things temporal, ourselves and our families.
We proceeded to Manchester, where we met our dear Jonathan
and Hannah Backhouse, their children, and Eliza P. Kirkbride;
also, William Forster. We were a very united company. That
evening, William Forster read the 54th chapter of Isaiah, expressing his full belief, that our dearest Joseph would experience
the promises contained in the last few verses. The next day we
went to Liverpool, and spent much of the morning in his very
comfortable ship; we felt being in it, for it was very touching
parting with one so tenderly beloved. We made things comfortable for him; I attended to the books, and that a proper library
should go out for the crew, passengers and steerage passengers.
However occupied or interested, I desire never to forget any
thing that may be of service to others. We had a delightful
morning with Joseph, but the tears often rose to my eyes; still, I
desire to be thankful more than sorrowful, that I have a brother
so fitted for his Lord's service, and willing to give up all for His
name's sake.

That evening again we had an interesting religious time in
prayer. The next morning there was a solemn calm over us—
the day of parting was come. After breakfast we all assembled
with some of our friends. We read the 4th of Philippians. Our
spirits were much bowed and broken; the chapter encouraged us
to stand fast in the Lord, to help one another in Christ, even the
women who laboured in the gospel. To be careful for nothing,
that the Lord would supply all our need.

After her brother had ministered to them, and prayer had been
offered, she adds:—

Soon afterwards we went to the ship. I saw the library arranged with some others to help me; then went and devoted myself to my beloved brother, put sweet flowers in his cabin, which
was made most comfortable for him. It was announced that the
ship was going; we assembled in the ladies' cabin, I believe all
wept. William Forster said, the language had powerfully im-

pressed him—" I will be with you always, even to the end of the world ;" therefore we might trust our beloved ones to Him who had promised. I then knelt down with these words—" Now, Lord, what wait we for, our hope is in Thee," and entirely committed him and his companions in the ship, to the most holy and powerful keeping of Israel's Shepherd, that even the voyage might be blessed to him and to others. In short, our souls were poured forth before and unto the Lord, in deep prayer and supplication. Joseph almost sobbed, still a solemn quiet and peace reigned over us. I believe the Lord was with us, and owned us at this solemn time. We left the ship, and walked by the side of the Pier until they were towed out, then we went away and wept bitterly ; but not the tears of deep sorrow, far from it; how different to the grief for sin, or even disease, or the perplexities of life. It appeared the Lord's doing, though long marvellous in my eyes ; yet I now trust and believe it is His call, and therefore it is well, and there is more cause to rejoice than to mourn over it. We remained at Liverpool till Second-day morning ; went by the railroad to Birmingham, meeting with an accident by the way which might have been serious, but we were preserved from harm. I became at last very poorly, and one morning nearly fainted. I was much sunk, and brought once more to feel my deep infirmity in illness or suffering. By the time we arrived at Lynn, I was too ill to go on to Earlham, and there remained to be most affectionately cared for by my beloved son and daughter, and their servants. I afterwards went to Earlham, and from thence to Lowestoft. I much valued my visits, only my foolish nature was too anxious, to enjoy them as I might have done, fancying I was wanted at home. We truly partook of the unity of the Spirit in the bond of peace. I am favoured on returning home, to find my children unusually well, and receive good accounts from my husband and sons on the Continent ; so that, once more it has pleased the Lord to permit me to rest as beside the still waters. He restoreth my soul !

Upton Lane, Eighth Month 6th.—I am much occupied about the great Female Prison in Ireland, also the one at Paramatta. Government is wonderfully kind, and I believe much good likely to be done by the steps now being taken.

The Factory at Paramatta, in the first instance was intended as a prison for women, and arranged for the reception of refractory as well as unassigned prisoners. It was well disciplined, and the inmates divided into three classes; a distinction being very properly made in the treatment of the different classes. Gradually, the establishment, from mismanagement fell into great confusion; so that from being a place of punishment, it had become a home and refuge for the idle and profligate, preferred by them to service and hard work. In the Factory they were fed and clothed, and lived in idleness among congenial companions, and having once incurred the disgrace of being sent there, soon lost all sense of shame; and after being released, again offended, for the express purpose of returning thither. It was a great satisfaction to the ladies of the British Society, to learn that a system so subversive of every hope of moral improvement, had been altered. By the introduction of hard labour and strict discipline, the Factory was re-converted into a place of punishment, and other measures were in progress likely to conduce to the reformation of the prisoners. Sir Richard Bourke endeavoured, not only to reform the Factory arrangements, but to induce ladies suitable for the office, again to visit it. Immense advantage had accrued to the institution, from the regulations and occasional inspection of Lady Darling, supported by the authority of Sir Ralph. Lord Glenelg and Sir George Grey paid the subject every attention, not meeting the case as one merely of business routine and political expediency; but with kindness of heart and real philanthropy they entered into details, and endeavoured to obtain information from every available source. Mr. Clapham as Superintendent, and Mrs. Leach as Matron, were sent out to take the charge of the Factory, with full and minute directions for their own conduct, and supplied in England with every thing required for the occupation and instruction of its inmates, or furnished with orders for them on the Government stores there.

About the time that some improvement appeared likely to take place amongst the wretched inmates of the Paramatta Factory, the long debated question of the Jersey Prison was brought to a close, by the accession of the States to the proposals of Lord John Russell: and arrangements being entered into for commencing the building without further delay. Mrs. Fry never again visited Jersey, but she had the pleasure of cheering reports, from time to time, of the alterations effected there.

On the 12th of July, an event took place in her family, which afforded Mrs. Fry peculiar satisfaction, the marriage of her fourth son at Frankfort-sur-Maine, to the daughter of her valued friend, Dr. Pinkerton.

Upton Lane, Eighth Month 18*th.*—I have believed it right to have the poor invited, to attend the Evening Meeting at Ratcliff to-morrow. These are weighty engagements ; may the Holy Spirit be poured forth, for the comfort, help, and encouragement of the hearers, and to my own peace.

Second-day 20*th.*—Yesterday, we were favoured to get well through the Meeting ; the people were very attentive, and some appeared in tears. Christ was preached as the " Way" to the Kingdom of Heaven, the sacrifice for our sins, and the healer of our wounds. He appeared to me to be exalted through the power of the Spirit. May I be faithful in every call of duty, trusting in Him who can qualify me by His own power.

Ninth Month 2*nd.*—Since this Meeting, the interest that others have taken with me in the poor of Ratcliff, has led us to look into their deplorable state. We have formed a committee to visit them at their houses, see their state, provide a library for their use and probably an infant school. So one thing springs out of another !

Last Seventh-day, my brother and sister Gurney and I went to Crawley to attend the little Meeting at Ifield, to go to William Allen's, and to Linfield. My brother said, that any serious persons who liked to attend the Meeting might do so, and to our surprise, we found a large congregation of the labouring classes ; I should think nearly a hundred men in smock-frocks ; it was quite a sight. I felt low, empty, unworthy and stripped in spirit ; but my Lord helped me. We certainly had a solemn Meeting ; the people were very attentive ; we also had a very satisfactory reading with the people at the inn. In the evening we attended another Meeting at Linfield, in which William Allen very acceptably united. Other Friends were there. We also called upon some poor, sorrowful, destitute ones. This little excursion appeared blessed to our comfort, refreshment and peace, and I believe had the same effect on those whom we visited. I observe, with those who may think they differ in sentiment, there is nothing like bringing them together ; how often it is then found, that the difference is more in expression than reality, and that the spirit of love and charity breaks down the partition walls.

I have for many months past, deeply felt the wish for more religious intercourse with my children, and more uniting with them upon important and interesting subjects. I have turned it in my mind again and again, and at last have proposed making the experiment, and meeting this evening—first, to consider different subjects of usefulness in charities, and then to close with serious reading and such religious communication as way may open for.

Thou Lord only knowest the depth of my desire, for the everlasting welfare of my children. If it be Thy holy and blessed will, grant that we may be truly united to Thee, as members of Thy Militant Church on earth, and spiritually united amongst ourselves, as members of one body, each filling his different office, faithfully unto Thee. Grant that this little effort may be blessed to promote this end, and cause that in making it, we may experience the sweet influence of Thy love shed abroad in each of our hearts, to our real help, comfort edification and unity !

Upton Lane, Eighth Month 15th, 1837.

MY DEAREST CHILDREN,

Many of you know that for some time I have felt and expressed the want of our social intercourse at times leading to religious union and communion amongst us. It has pleased the Almighty to permit, that by far the larger number of you, no longer walk with me in my religious course. Except very occasionally, we do not meet together for the solemn purpose of worship, and upon some other points we do not see eye to eye, and whilst I feel deeply sensible that notwithstanding this diversity amongst us, we are truly united in our Holy Head, there are times when in my declining years, I seriously feel the loss of not having more of the spiritual help and encouragement of those, I have brought up, and truly sought to nurture in the Lord. This has led me to many serious considerations how the case may, under present circumstances, be in any way met.

My conclusion is, that believing as we do in one Lord as our Saviour, one Holy Spirit as our Sanctifier, and one God and Father of us all, our points of union are surely strong; and if we are members of one living Church, and expect to be such for ever, we may profitably unite in some religious engagements here below.

The world and the things of it occupy us much, and they are rapidly passing away; it would be well if we occasionally set apart a time for unitedly attending to the things of Eternity. I therefore propose that we try the following plan, if it answer, continue it, if not, by no means feel bound to it. That our party in the first instance, should consist of no others than our children and such grandchildren as may be old enough to attend. That our object in meeting, be for the strengthening of our faith, for our advancement in a devoted, religious, and holy life, and for the object of promoting Christian love and fellowship.

That we read the Scriptures unitedly, in an easy familiar manner, each being perfectly at liberty to make any remark or ask any question; that it should be a time of religious instruction by seeking to understand the mind of the Lord, for doctrine and practice in searching the Scriptures, and bringing ourselves and our deeds to the light, that it may be made manifest if they are wrought in God. That either before or after the Scriptures are read, we should consider how far we are really engaged for the good of our fellow-men, and what, as far as we can judge, most conduces to this object. All the members of this little community are advised to communicate any thing they may have found useful or interesting in religious books, and to bring forward any thing that is doing for the good of mankind, in the world generally.

I hope that thus meeting together may stimulate the family to more devotion of heart to the service of their God, at home and abroad to mind their different callings, however varied ; and to be active in helping others. It is proposed that this meeting should take place once a month, at each house in rotation.

I now have drawn some little outline of what I desire, and if any of you like to unite with me in making the experiment, it would be very gratifying to me, still, I hope that all will feel at liberty, to do as they think best themselves.

I am indeed, .

Your nearly attached mother,

ELIZABETH FRY.

The plan was tried and found to answer exceedingly well. Some of the collateral branches of the family afterwards joined these little réunions, they proved occasions of stimulus in "every good word and work." Some important good has resulted from the combined exertions consequent upon them, they continue to this day under the name of "philanthropic evenings ;" and are always concluded by a scripture reading, and occasionally by prayer.

Twelfth Month 20th.—I have laid before my Monthly Meeting my prospect of visiting France for a few weeks, and obtained the concurrence of Friends. Oh ! for help, daily, hourly,—and may a sound mind, love and power be granted to me and to others, to our own peace and the glory of God.

First-day, Afternoon, 24th.—An accident about carriages keeps me from Meeting, which I much regret. The Morning Meeting was solemn. After it, my certificate was read in our adjourned Monthly Meeting, which was exceedingly encouraging to me, it expressed great unity with me as a minister, and much concurrence in my concern to go to France. It appeared to be signed by nearly the whole of the Meeting.

To a near Relative.

North Repps Hall, *First Month 2nd*, 1838.

I have trusted that if right for thee, this year may bring thee some deliverances from thy trying and exercising states. At the same time we must not desire the fire to cease burning, until the dross is burnt up ; but we may ask, that it may never be heated so as to hurt the pure metal. I have a strong apprehension that all the ordeals thou hast lately had, are sent for a purpose, I am ready to believe to fit thee to receive more of the enduring riches of Christ, and not only so, but to fit thee to enrich, comfort and help others. I can assure thee that it is deeply interesting entering the new year with my only three remaining sisters. We much value and enjoy being together ; but we feel like a few remaining autumnal fruits, at the close of no common summer, of family love and unity. We had a very solemn time together this morning, in which our children and our children's children, with ourselves were remembered at the throne of grace. The day is very fine, and all looks bright. May happy accounts from home complete the brightness of the picture.

Upton Lane, First Month 6th, 1838.—I returned yesterday from a visit to Norfolk. Before going there, I laid my concern to go to France, before our large Quarterly Meeting, and had the very great encouragement of such a flow of unity, as I have seldom heard expressed upon any occasion.

24th.—I expect to leave home to-morrow for France. My spirit has been very much brought down before the Lord ; some causes of anxiety have arisen, still in this my going out, love abounds in no common degree, and a portion of soul-sustaining peace underneath. These words comforted me this morning, 2 Timothy i. 12. "I know whom I have believed, and am persuaded that He is able to keep that which I have committed unto Him against that day." I therefore, in this going out, commit myself and my all to my most blessed and holy Keeper, even to the Lord God of my salvation, my only hope of real help and defence, and of eternal glory.

Mrs. Fry was accompanied in this journey, by her husband, their friend Josiah Forster and Lydia Irving, the same young friend who had kindly gone with her to Jersey, in 1835.

Abbeville, *First Month* 28*th.*

My DEAREST CHILDREN, AND BROTHERS AND SISTERS,

As I know your kind interest in all that concerns us, I go on whilst I can, with our journal letters myself. We left Boulogne yesterday morning, in a very comfortable French carriage after some delay in our departure, from various difficulties with luggage, we enjoyed our reading and conversation, until we arrived at Montreuil, where we were refreshed by a little boullion, and then proceeded to this place ; but the cold was bitter, and neither French fires, nor tea, nor any other means proved sufficient to warm us. As the following morning advanced, my sense of mercy and peace was great. I remembered what some devoted Christian expressed, " where the God of peace is, there is home." After breakfast we read as usual, then Josiah Forster went out ; but he could hear of no protestants nor of any place of worship for them ; nor of any place desirable for us to visit, excepting one hospital, one convent, and one prison. These we visited, after having had a very solemn and sweet meeting in our own room. That text was feelingly brought to our minds, " where two or three are met together in my name, there am I in the midst of them."

I find my small knowledge of the language very valuable, I can read to the fille de chambre, and in some degree convey my feelings and sentiments, enough to produce sympathy and interest. In our visit to the prison, convent and hospital, I found this the case.

To go now to minor points : picture us,—our feet on some fleeces that we have found, generally wrapped up in cloaks, surrounded by screens, to keep off the air ; the wood fire at our feet. We have just finished an interesting reading in French, in the New Testament, with the landlady, her daughters and some of the servants of the hotel ; they appeared very attentive, and much interested.

Farewell, my dearly beloved ones.　May the Lord be with you, and keep you, and bless you !

Your tenderly attached,
E. F.

In Paris, comfortable and commodious apartments were prepared for them at the Hotel de Castille, by the kind attention of M. Francois Delessert.　They arrived there very tired and very cold, on the 30th of January.　The morning of the 31st was opened with solemn, united prayer, offered for wisdom from on High to direct, and strength to perform whatever might be called for at their hands.　Then came a visit from Madame Francois Delessert ; two notes from Lord Granville, our Ambassador at Paris ; a call at the Embassy, and in the evening the company of M. and Madame de Presseusé, the Secretary of the Bible Society.

In a letter to her children at home, Mrs. Fry not merely describes their rooms at the Hotel, and gives a plan of them, but sends a little sketch, drolly characteristic of the femme de chambre and waiter.

February 1st, they attended the small Friends' Meeting held in the Faubourg du Roule, and afterwards called on La Baronne Pelet de la Lozere.　In her Mrs. Fry found a friend and sister in Christ.　They then paid a visit to Count Montalivet, Minister of the Interior, by whom they were most kindly received, and promised all needful admissions to the different prisons.

Afterwards, at the Hotel, they received visits from the Duchess de Broglie and other ladies.　The following day found Mrs. Fry oppressed and feverish, and evidently suffering from the cold she had endured on her journey.　Her new friends all displayed the liveliest sympathy, whilst Madame Pelet, in particular, neglected no kindness or attention that could add to her comfort.

The 3rd, though too unwell to go out, Mrs. Fry received in the evening M. de Metz, Conseiller de la Cour Royale, and had the pleasure of much important conversation with him on the subject of Prisons, in which he was greatly interested. On the 4th, she paid pleasant visits to Lady Granville and to Madame Pelet. On Sunday, the day began with seeing a school conducted by M. Pressensé, for two hundred children ; a most cheering and delightful sight. At twelve o'clock they attended the Friends' Meeting: there were assembled French, English, a Pole, and Americans. Among this motley group might be found Roman Catholics, Presbyterians, Episcopalians, various Dissenters, and Quakers.

Monday, the 5th, they visited the St. Lazare Prison for women, containing nine hundred and fifty-two inmates, a very melancholy sight. An American lady invited the party to her house in the evening, where she received about fifty individuals, mostly English and American. The conversation turned upon the general state of European society ; but especially in France, and what means were the most likely to benefit its polished, refined, but dissipated and irreligious capital. The fearful writings of the day, "many too bad to read," were discussed, and what might be the root of a tree, the branches of which bore fruit of such deadly nature. There was present, on that occasion, a young medical student, who addressed himself to Mrs. Fry on the fearful contamination to which young men in his position were exposed—no domestic home to retire to, none of that indefinable but potent influence around them of public opinion, in favour of virtue and morality, their studies all tending to materialism, and to the lessening of that dependence upon an unseen superior Power, which lingers even in the unregenerate heart of man ; and, above all, little or no opportunity afforded them for the commonest religious advantage. This large gathering concluded by solemn exhortation and prayer.

On the 6th, accompanied by Madame Delessert, the travellers visited a French Protestant school, for two hundred children, on the British and Foreign system, admirably conducted by a valuable committee of ladies. They dined at M. Presseusé's, where was a large party afterwards. Mrs. Fry spoke of this occasion as very encouraging to her, when she compared it with the state of things in France during her youth, and how unlikely it then seemed, that such a dawn of better things would ever appear there.

The 7th, they received many guests, both morning and evening, and in the course of the day accompanied the Duchess de Broglie to the Prison des Jeunes Détenus, a good new building, the inmates well ordered, but still capable of improvement.

The following day was occupied by attending their Meeting in the morning, and in the evening receiving a party of ladies to consider how they might, in the best manner, promote good in the city, in Prisons, Schools, District Societies, and similar objects. The evening was finished by reading the 15th chapter of St. Luke.

On the 9th, the Prison for men (La Force) was visited. A dinner at M. Pelet's, and a very large party there in the evening.

The 10th, they inspected the Military Prison at St. Germains, which appeared to them to be upon the whole well conducted, and in tolerable order; books they found to be greatly wanted. Afterwards they saw the Central Prison at Poissy, but whilst they admired its good order, they considered it not sufficiently penal, too much like a large manufactory for different trades, instead of a place of punishment.

The following day, the Sabbath was indeed welcome, for its rest was greatly needed by Elizabeth Fry. She desired that it might be free from company, and prove a season of refreshment, the press of people being so great and the subjects for consideration so many and so exceedingly important. The Meeting was not a very large one ; in it their certificates were read. They appeared much to interest those who heard them, and opened the way for a little explanation of Friends' principles. There were a few callers in the evening ; amongst others, a gentleman interested about prisons, who remained during their Scripture reading, at which some of the servants of the Hotel were also present.

On the 12th, they visited the Prison of the Conciergerie. There they saw the room where the unhappy Marie Antoinette was confined. They took tea at Mr. Toase's, successor to Mr. Newstead, the Methodist minister, and passed an interesting evening with a large party of his congregation.

The next morning they went to some schools ; one, an Infant School, was particularly attractive, the superintendents appearing well adapted for their important post ; money was given to purchase the little creatures each a bun, which highly delighted them, their happy faces showing how pleased they were. Also an Hospital, and the Enfans Trouvès, were visited. Mrs. Fry's maternal experience, led her to give some advice about the poor babies' dress, that it might be less complicated, and afford them more liberty of movement. The nuns appeared kind. The Hospital they found very close, and wanting ventilation. In the evening to Mr. Sutteroth's, where between fifty and sixty persons were present, a " charming company," " many amongst them truly serious."

On the 14th, another visit was paid to the Women's Prison of St. Lazare. There, after going over the building, the women were collected at Mrs. Fry's request, that a portion of Scripture might be read to them. She chose the parable of the prodigal son. It was beautifully read by a French lady, from the Roman Catholic Prayer Book. A pause ensued, then Mrs. Fry commented upon it, the same lady translated for her, sentence by sentence. It was exceedingly well done, losing little or nothing of its solemnity. The women were touched and impressed. She then asked them whether they would like ladies to visit them, read to them, and sympathize with them. The offer was eagerly accepted. " Oui, oui," " Eh moi, aussi !" came from all sides ; nor was it only these poor outcasts, or those accompanying Mrs. Fry, who wept, the jailor and turnkeys who had entered the room, contrary to her wishes, were so affected that tears ran down their cheeks. " Elles ne sont pas pire que nous, ces pauvres femmes," (said an excellent lady for the first time brought into contact with such as these,) " seulement les circonstances sont toutes pour nous, et toutes contre elles."

This reading occasioned quite a sensation in Paris, for it had been said, that the wonderful effect of Mrs. Fry's readings in Newgate arose from her peculiar voice and manner, her skill in arresting the attention of her auditors, and her power to touch their hearts. She and others attributed it to the simple indwelling power of the word of God, and asserted that it would be found the same whatever national differences might exist, or by whomsoever the inspired word might be presented. The result on this occasion was decisive.

They saw, on the 15th, a school for about forty-five Protestants, many of them training for servants. To find attention paid to this class afforded them much satisfaction. In the evening, Mr. and Mrs. Fry dined at the English Embassy. · Throughout their stay in Paris the kindness and attention of Lord and Lady Granville were unfailing.

The next day, some more " delightful schools" were inspected, and a prison for debtors.

In the evening, the party for the promotion of philanthropic objects, which had been adjourned the preceding week, again met ; much interesting conversation took place. As on the previous evening, the party concluded with reading a portion of the Holy Scriptures, and solemn prayer.

On the 17th, Mrs. Fry had an interview with the prison officers, and obtained much information respecting the state of

St. Lazare Female Prison. Madame Pelet and Madame Jules Mallet interpreting for her. They saw M. Toase on the subject of fitting up a room as a library for the benefit of English and American students ; and in the evening they went to Mr. Baird's, the American clergyman, to meet some of them, who are invited there every Saturday to read the Scriptures, &c., &c. A young Englishman present expressed himself strongly ; warning his cotemporaries, first, on the awful prevalence of taking the sacred name in vain ; secondly, the desecration of the Sabbath ; and thirdly, against the literature of modern France, poisoned as it is with infidelity and licentiousness.

The 19th, was devoted by Mrs. Fry to writing observations on the prisons which she had seen ; to making some calls : and in the evening receiving several gentlemen to consider and talk over prison subjects.

On the 20th, they visited the Salpétrière and Hospital for the old, infirm, epileptic, idiotic and insane. The building stands on nine acres of ground, and the whole occupies ninety-eight. There are five thousand inmates. They were exceedingly struck with the kindness manifested towards them, particularly towards the insane, so much liberty being given them. Formerly, these un-happy creatures were chained and cruelly treated ; many of the inmates followed the party about, pleased at being noticed. One thing, however, occasioned real pain to the visitors : amidst the good order which prevailed, the absence of all religious instruction. Proved, as it has long been, that this unfortunate class of persons are helped and soothed by the blessed promises of Scripture, and capable in many instances, notwithstanding their mental infirmity, of feeling and appropriating the Christian's hope.

A third visit was paid on the 21st to the St. Lazare, in company with Lady Granville, Lady Georgiana Fullerton, and two other ladies. From what was witnessed in these visits, it was obvious, that great good would result from the regular attendance of a

Ladies' Committee, though no easy matter to arrange it. In the evening, went to M. De Metz's. Great had been the kindness of this gentleman and his brother-in-law M. Pirou, in going about with them to the different prisons.

On the 22nd, M. Berenger came to breakfast, when the conversation was almost entirely on subjects referring to prisons. The Friends' Meeting that morning was an important one ; the ministry leading all to Christ ; and many strangers and persons of different denominations being there. Afterwards, Mrs. Fry met several ladies at the Duchess de Broglie's, to consider the possibility of forming a Committee for visiting prisons. They dined at M. Rumpff's, Minister of the Hanse Towns. The Duke Decazes was there, with whom Mrs. Fry had much conversation.

The 23rd, they breakfasted at Mr. Wilk's at Passy, where they had the gratification of meeting M. David the sculptor. Afterwards they called on Madame Pelet and Madame de Pastoret, concluding the day by a dinner at the Duke de Broglie's.

The following day they visited a convent, and some schools conducted by Sisters of Charity. Dined at M. Jules Mallet's, about twenty to dinner, and saw nearly a hundred in the evening ; a most interesting company—several hitherto unknown to them—many young people, which was " delightful" to Mrs. Fry.

On the 25th, was their last meeting at Paris, a very large and solemn one it proved.

The 26th was devoted to the discussion of prison subjects with the Prefect of Police. They dined at M. Dutrone's.

The 27th, they paid some important calls, and had a large Committee of Ladies to consider prison subjects, though there were too many present to effect much. The party that day dined with the veteran philanthropist, the Baron de Girando.

During the 28th they received many callers, paid leave-taking visits, and dined at the Duke Decaze's.

The 2nd, was the day appointed for them to wait upon the King and Queen, and the Duchess of Orleans. They dined at M. de Salvandi's, Minister of Public Instruction, and were quite delighted in accompanying him to see a large library and room fitted up for the use of the middle classes.

Their two last days in Paris were occupied by winding up their different objects, and preparing to depart.

The result of her observations on the state of the prisons, Mrs. Fry embodied in a letter addressed to the Prefect of Police, but as it contained little beyond her opinions, so frequently stated, as to arrangements, classification, female officers for women, and instruction, it is not inserted here.

She also addressed a memorial to the King, touching on the subject that so deeply occupied her thoughts ; but beyond every other thing, urging a more extended circulation of the Holy Scriptures, and their free use in all public institutions in France.

From St. Germains she wrote to her children.

Third Month 5th, 1838.

We arrived here last evening, after quitting the most deeply interesting field of service, I think I was ever engaged in. My first feeling is, peace and true thankfulness for the extraordinary help granted to us ; my next feeling, an earnest desire to communicate to you, my most tenderly beloved children, and others nearest to me, the sense that I have of the kindness and goodness and mercy of my Heavenly Father, who has dealt so bountifully with me; that it may lead all to serve Him fully, love Him more, and follow more simply the guidance of His Spirit.

I mean now to tell you a little of my reflections upon this important period, the last month at Paris. I was at first very poorly, very low, and saw little opening for religious usefulness, though some for charity and benevolent objects. Soon my health revived, and we had full occupation in visiting prisons and other institutions, and saw many influential persons. This opened a door in various ways, for close communication with a deeply interesting variety of both philanthropic and religious people, and has thus introduced us into a more intimate acquaintance with the state of general society. Religiously, we find some, indeed we may say a great many, who appear much broken off from the bonds of Roman Catholic superstition ; but with it, I fear, have been ready to give up religion itself, though feeling the need of it for themselves and others. To these I think we have been helpful, by upholding religion in its simplicity, and most strongly expressing our sense of the necessity of it, and that nothing can alter and improve the moral character, or bring real peace, but true Christian principles. To this we have very faithfully borne testimony, and most strongly encouraged all to promote a more free circulation of the Scriptures, particularly the New Testament, and a more diligent reading of the Bible in institutions and families. I have, in private circles, introduced (frequently by describing what poor criminals wanted in prisons) the simple truths of the Gospel, illustrated sometimes by interesting facts, respecting the conversion of some of these poor women prisoners ; and have been thus enabled in numerous parties, to show the *broad, clear,* and *simple* way of salvation, through our Lord and Saviour, for *all.* It has been striking to me in our dinner visits, some of them splendid occasions, how curiously way has opened without the least formality, or even difficulty in conversation, to "speak the truth in love," especially one day, as to how far balls and theatres were Christian and right ; the way in which Roman Catholic priests appeared to hinder the spread of the Gospel—the importance of circulating good books (this has been a very common subject) and above all the New Testament. At our own Ambassador's, Lord Granville's, several were in tears during the conversation. I think our dinner visits have been an important part of our service, so much has been done by these communications after, and at them. In many instances, numbers have joined us in the evening, particularly the youth. With these, it has pleased my Heavenly Father to give me some influence. Last First-day evening, I had a very large party of them to a reading, which appears to have given much satisfaction. It has been a most curious opening with persons of many nations. Many have lately flocked to our little Meetings ; I wonder how I could feel easy to go away from such a field of

service, but I did, and therefore went. On Third-day, when we
went to the King and Queen, and therefore could not attend our
little week-day Meeting, they said eighty persons came to it who
went away. I have found unusual help at these times, to speak
the truth with power ; my belief is, that there are many unsettled and seeking minds in this country.

We have had much intercourse with the Minister of Instruction, and he gives me leave to send him a large number of books
from England, to be translated into French. My full belief is,
that many Testaments and valuable books will circulate in consequence of our visit.

The efforts made to form a Ladies' Society, to visit the prisons
of France, and particularly Paris, (whether they succeed or not)
have been important. First, by my taking many ladies to visit
the great Female Prison of St. Lazare, and there reading, or
having read, small portions of Scripture, and my few words
through an interpreter, producing (far beyond what I could have
expected) such a wonderful effect upon these poor sinners. The
glad tidings of the Gospel appeared to touch their hearts, many
wept exceedingly, and it was a fresh and striking proof of the
power of the truth, when simply told. In the next place, the
large number of ladies that have met at our house upon the
subject, has afforded so remarkable an opportunity to express to
them my views of salvation by Christ alone, of the unity that
should exist amongst Christians, and must do so, if sanctified by
the Spirit, and deeply to impress the simplicity and spirituality of
true religion. I think something important in the prison cause
will eventually come out of it, but it will take time.

We have had very large parties of English and Americans,
and some French, at the houses of the Methodist minister, the
American minister, and at another serious person's. Also we
joined the French Wesleyan Methodists in their chapel, and
had a precious meeting with them. Of the highly evangelical
Episcopalians and Independents, we have had very large parties
at different houses. In all these, we have had solemn religious
service. The Episcopalians have been brought into very close
union with us. In our own house, we have had two large parties
of a philanthropic and religious nature, attended by many. Lady

Olivia Sparrow has often been quite a comfort to me; and many others I may say have proved true helpers, French and Americans, and more than these—the Chargé d'Affaires of the Hanse Towns and his wife, also Russians and Swiss. The Greek Ambassador, Coletti, came to me for advice on some points in the state of Greece, in which I believe I shall be enabled to assist him. A Captain B—— thinks of having my sister Hoare's " Hints for the Labouring Classes" translated, for the parents of the children who attend the schools upon the mountains in India. We have also seen many of the medical students, English and American, and are anxious to have some efforts made for their moral and religious good, in Paris, where so many come.

Our visit to the King and the Queen was interesting; but alas! what in reality is rank? The King I think in person like the late Lord Torrington, the Queen a very agreeable and even interesting woman. I expressed my religious interest and concern for them, which was well received, and we had much conversation with the Queen and the Princess Adelaide, before the King came into the room. We strongly expressed to the Queen our desire to have the Sabbath better kept, and the Scriptures more read. She is a sweet minded merciful woman. There were present Madame Adelaide, the King's sister, one of the young Princesses, the Marchioness of D——, principal Lady of Honour to the Queen.

We then proceeded to the Duchess of Orleans'; there we had a delightful visit, and the sweetest religious communication with her, and other interesting conversation. We found her an uncommon person; my belief is, that she is a very valuable young woman.

The Queen appeared much pleased with my Text-book; and the Princess Adelaide said, she should keep it in her pocket and read it daily. Indeed no books have given the same pleasure as the Text-books, both in French and English. I think we have given many hundreds of them, and next in number my sister Louisa's books on Education; they delight the people; also a great many of Joseph's Letter to Dr. A——, of which we have a beautiful edition in French, and his Sabbath; of these we expect to give many hundreds, and one or two other tracts, upon

Christian Duties, and the Offices of the Holy Spirit. Our
various books and tracts have had a very open reception, but we
have been very careful when, where, and what to give ; although
in some of the newspapers it was stated that I distributed con-
troversial tracts, which is not true.

I began in my letter to say what a variety we have seen, but
I did not say what deeply interesting and delightful persons we
have met with ; amongst the Protestants particularly, some first-
rate ladies, who have been as sisters to me, so abundant in
kindness and love. One has truly reminded me of my sister
Rachel, in her person, her mind, and her excessive care over me ;
she has felt me, I believe, like her own. We have indeed increased our dear and near friends by this visit, much as it was
in Jersey and Guernsey, only in far greater numbers. I think
nothing could be more seasonable than our visit ; as it respected
the prisons, and I believe the influence of our advice has been
very decided, with many persons of consideration. The schools
we have also attended to, and I have encouraged a more scriptural education ; some schools of great consequence, kept by
serious Protestants in a district of Paris, much want help.
There are seven hundred children, and we hear that the Head of
the Police in that neighbourhood, says the people generally are
improved in consequence.

The want of the language, I have now and then much felt,
but not very often, so many speak English well, and many
understand it who cannot speak it. Also I blunder out a little
French.

The entreaties for us to stop longer in Paris have been very
great, but my inclination draws homeward ; I am a very great
friend to not stopping too long in a place. And as I believed I
saw a little light upon our departure, we thought it best to leave
all for the present, and go, if we even have, before many months.
more, to return for a short time. We have been a united, and
often a cheerful little party. At times I have carried a great
weight, never hardly having my home party out of mind for long
together, however full and occupied. At other times our business
has been so great, as almost to overwhelm us—callers almost
innumerable, and most of them on important business, and out

and in almost constantly ourselves, so that I have sometimes felt as if I could not long bear it, particularly when I could not obtain some rest in the afternoon.   Through all I must say, He who I believe put me forth, has from season to season restored my soul and body, and helped me from hour to hour.   This day week, I sat down upon my chair and wept ; but I was soon helped and revived.   I long for every child, brother, sister, and all near to me, to be sensible how very near my Holy Helper has been to me ; and yet I have exceedingly and deeply felt my utter unworthiness and short coming, and that all is from the fulness and freeness of unmerited mercy and love, in Christ Jesus.   I can hardly express the very near love I have felt for you all.   My prayers very often have risen for you ; and if any labour I have been engaged in has been accepted *through the Beloved*, may you my most tenderly beloved ones, partake of the blessing attendant upon it.   My dearest husband has been a true helper ; and Josiah Forster and Lydia I——, very kind and useful companions.

I forgot to say, I think the few Friends in Paris have been greatly comforted and stimulated by our visit.

I end my account by saying, what I trust is true, " The Lord is my Shepherd, I shall not want."   We are now quietly at St. Germains.   We hear most interesting accounts of the state of Normandy, and have many letters of introduction to the places where we propose to go, if not wanted home, I shall be glad to go there.   We propose being at Rouen to-morrow.

I am,

Your most tenderly attached,

ELIZABETH FRY.

At Rouen they were much interested by meeting with a respectable woman in humble life, who had lived nurse fifteen years in a gentleman's family, a Roman Catholic, but his wife a Protestant. There she had been so much impressed by religious truth, (though still a Roman Catholic herself) that she felt it her duty where she resided, to circulate the Scriptures and religious tracts.   Her master told them, it was surprising the great influence she had obtained in the neighbourhood.   Mrs. Fry supplied her with six Testaments and a Bible, from the Bible Society Depôt.   From the same Society she obtained Testaments for the school in the prison, where the Testament was habitually read, but the supply very inadequate.   This school was under the care of the Abbé Gossier, M. du Hamel and other religious gentlemen, who themselves daily instructed the young prisoners.

At Caen, they found some excellent and devoted Methodists amongst the French, and, that through the efforts of one young English lady, an orphan residing in a gentleman's family as governess—many copies of the Scriptures had been purchased ; and at the shop of a Roman Catholic, more than a hundred of de Sacy's Testaments sold since the beginning of the year.

The Prison of Beaulieu near Caen, they visited with much satisfaction, nearly a thousand prisoners were confined there : they found it admirably regulated, and a serious Roman Catholic clergyman devoted to the good of those under his care.   He gladly welcomed the gift of fifty Testaments.   ·

At Hàvre, the Ladies' Bible Society had sold during the former year, four hundred and twenty-six Testaments, and thirty-three Bibles, and had given to soldiers fifty Testaments, who were in the habit every evening of reading them to their comrades in barracks.

At Boulogne, they made arrangements for the sale of the Holy Scriptures, and took a lively interest in the District Society, thence crossed to Dover, and the following day Mrs. Fry had the comfort of finding herself again with her family at home.

The effect on her mind, of this her first introduction to France was very powerful.   She was greatly attracted by the life and facility of the French character ; in a letter she speaks of them as " such a nation—such a numerous and superior people— filling such a place in the world—and Satan appearing in no common degree to be seeking to destroy them—first, by infidelity and so called philosophy—secondly, by superstition, and the priesthood rising with fresh power—thirdly, by an extreme love of the world and its pleasures—fourthly, by an unsettled, restless, and warlike spirit—yet under all this, a hidden power of good at work amongst them, many very extraordinary Christian characters, bright, sober, zealous Roman Catholics and Protestants, education increasing—the Holy Scriptures more read and valued, a general stirring to improve the prisons of France. The Government making fresh regulations for that purpose, but great fear of the priests prevailing, from the palace downwards; and they alas! resisting all good wherever or however it may arise."

Upton Lane, Fourth Month 27th.—Yesterday was the largest British Society meeting I ever remember, partly collected to hear my account of our French journey, there must have been some hundreds of ladies present, many of them of rank. In the desire not to say too much, perhaps I said too little upon some points, although I do not feel condemned, yet I am ready to think if I had watched and prayed more, I should have done better—my prayers have arisen, that however imperfectly or unworthily sown, the seed scattered yesterday, may be so prospered by His own free power, life and grace, that it may bear a full crop to His praise!

Fifth Month 8th.—I have just had a serious faintness for a short time, at times I think I may be suddenly taken off in one of these attacks: they appear to have so much to do with the heart. If perfectly ready, by being washed and made clean in the blood of the Everlasting Covenant, then, I think that a rapid translation from time to eternity, may save much pain and sorrow. But all these things, I am disposed to leave wholly to the Lord, who has through His unutterable mercy, been remarkably with me in life, and will I believe, be with me in death. So be it Lord Jesus, when Thou comest, even if it be quickly, through Thine own merits receive me unto Thyself!

20th.—To-morrow I am fifty-eight, an advanced period of what I apprehend to be not a very common pilgrimage, I now very earnestly desire and pray that my Lord may guide me continually,

cause me to know more of the day of His power, that I may
have my will wholly subjected to His will. What He would have
me to do, that may I do, where He would have me to go, there
may I go—what He may call me to suffer for His name sake, may
I be willing to suffer. Further, may He keep me from all false
fears and imaginations, and ever preserve me from putting my
hand to any work, not called for by Him, even if my fellow-
creatures press me into it ; as I think some are disposed to do
about America. Be pleased to grant these my desires and
prayers for Thine own Holy and Blessed name's sake.

Seventh Month 8th.—This day I enter with much fear and
trembling, as we are looking forward to a very important Meeting
to be held at the Westminster Meeting House, at the request of
Hannah Backhouse, to which foreigners of rank and our own
nobility are invited. The weight is great—very great from various
causes, partly from my fears and doubts, as to women's holding
Public Meetings.

14th.—The Meeting was attended by many high in rank.
Soon after we assembled, William Allen spoke for some time,
then I knelt down and felt much unction and power in prayer for
the Queen. After Hannah Backhouse had spoken, in a lively,
simple, powerful manner, preaching the truths of the gospel,
several went out. I then rose, first endeavouring to show that
truth must not be despised, because it came through weak instruments. I mentioned, how Anna in the Temple spoke of our
Lord, to all who looked for redemption in Israel, how the women
first told of our Lord's resurrection, and that their fellow-disciples
called it " idle tales." After thus showing that the Lord might
see right to use weak instruments, I expressed my feelings towards
those present. First, from Scripture, I showed that God is no
respecter of persons, that from the palace to the very dungeon, I
continually saw this. Then I showed, the important and responsible situation of those, who fill high places in the world. Either
they would be blessed themselves, and be a blessing to others, as
a city set on a hill, their light shining before men ; or they would
be of the number of those, through whom, offences come, and
therefore with the " curse of the Lord" resting on them. I
showed them some of their peculiar temptations, in being clothed

in purple and fine linen, and faring sumptuously every day ; and warned them, seeking to lead them to Christ, and to eternal glory through Him. At the close, I had a few words to express in the way of exhortation, as to their example in their houses, amongst children and servants, reading the Holy Scriptures, family worship and other points.

There was a subject at this time weighing heavily upon the mind of Elizabeth Fry, which she turned again and again before she dare dismiss it ; and then, it was more that other calls of duty appeared immediately required of her, than that she deliberately abandoned the idea. Her ˙brother Joseph John Gurney was pursuing his labours in America, as a minister of the Gospel ; and she doubted, whether it might not be her duty to cross the Atlantic, in order to join him for a time in his visits in the United States, and to accompany him to the West Indies. There were those who thought she ought to go ; but, on the other hand, she knew how entirely it would be against, not only the wishes, but the judgment of her own family. She had learned to trust very little to the opinions of any of her fellow-mortals, and these conflicting views only served to bring her in deeper dependence and more entire self-resignation, to the footstool of her great Master, to learn His will, that she might fulfil it. Whilst she pondered these things, a strong conviction arose in her heart, that there was a present duty for her to fulfil : once more to visit Friends and their Meetings in North Britain ; again to inspect the prisons there, and to communicate with the magistrates and men in authority ; whilst the Bill was still pending, which had been brought before the House the preceding Session of Parliament, to improve prisons and prison discipline in Scotland.

She laid this concern before her friends, and receiving the assurance of their unity, she left home the 11th of August, with her constant companion, her sister-in-law Elizabeth Fry, and her husband's old and valued friend, John Sanderson. They stayed a night at Birmingham, and on the 14th of August, arrived at Glen Rothay, in the vale of Rydal, where the kindest reception awaited them ; but the kindness of their host and hostess ceased not here. Elizabeth Fry's onerous and multiplied objects requiring more assistance ; William Ball, a minister among Friends, though not at the time travelling in that character, and peculiarly suited for the undertaking, was prepared, upon her particular request, to leave that beautiful home and accompany them on their way. They left Glen Rothay on the 15th, Mrs. Ball going with them the two first stages.

As Mrs. Fry's occupation and great fatigue made it almost impossible for her to write fully to her home party, or to keep a journal of their proceedings ; Mr. Ball undertook both offices. He had never travelled with, or known her so intimately before, and his journal is interspersed with observations on her objects and habits. From it, the account of this journey is chiefly taken.

" After being kindly received at G. H. Head's, Rickerby Hall, we left Carlisle : posted four stages to Hawick ; attended a Meeting that was appointed for that afternoon, in which our dear friends were enabled to ' labour in the Gospel ;' went on two stages to Torsance Inn, where we slept.

" On the 17th, left Torsance about nine o'clock ; arrived at Edinburgh to dinner, at our dear aged friend Alexander Cruickshanks ; came on to Kinross to tea, and arrived at Perth in the evening. A fine drive this day; the approach to Edinburgh very striking, also the neighbourhood of Perth ; but the free course of interesting and profitable conversation on the part of our beloved friend, the chief charm of a charming journey. How instructive is her regard to the comfort and the feelings of others, even in little things !

" 18th.—In the carriage about half past six o'clock. From Perth to Cupar Angus to breakfast, in the hope of being at Aberdeen, in time for the Meeting that is held the evening previous to the General Meeting of Friends of Scotland. At Forfar, visited the prison ; it is in very bad order. Changed horses at Brechin ; but did not allow ourselves time for dinner, which we took in the carriage. At Stonehaven, finding it vain any further to attempt to reach Aberdeen by six o'clock, we rested awhile, and had tea at a very pleasant inn. The drive from Stonehaven to Aberdeen, over hills in view of the sea, is very fine. But we had no time to stop at Ury, (the seat of the Barclay family) which is passed on this route. Arrived at Aberdeen at eight o'clock, and took up our abode at the Royal Hotel.

" These journeys are, I trust, not lost time ; we have two Scripture readings daily in the carriage, and much instructive conversation ; also, abundant time for that which is so important, the private reading of the Holy Scripture. This is very precious to dear Elizabeth Fry, and I have thought it a privilege to note her reverent ' marking and learning' of these sacred truths of divine inspiration. Often does she lay down the Book, close her eyes, and wait upon Him, who hath the key of David to open and to seal the instruction of the sacred page. Truly, it helps to explain how her ' profiting appears unto all,' when she is thus diligent and fervent, in ' meditating upon these things, and giving herself wholly to them.' "

The first two days at Aberdeen were devoted to attending the Meetings ; and visits to Friends. Among others, one to a very old and valued friend, John Wigham. He had been to her as " a nursing father" in the early part of her religious course.

" It was much like the meeting and interchange of parent and child, after long separation and many vicissitudes ; and these last, as they had affected our dear friend in the interval, were freely spoken of by her, with that deep feeling, chastened into resig-nation, which so remarkably covers her subjected spirit, in relation to these affecting topics.

" Some of the serious inhabitants, a clergyman and others, called on us this evening.

" 21st.—An agreeable breakfast-visit to Principal Jack, of Old Aberdeen College, and his amiable family ; where we were privileged to partake both of friendly hospitality and Christian

fellowship. Visited the prison, in company with our friends
A. and M. Wigham, the Provost, Sheriff, Town Clerk, and Baillie
Blackie. The Baillie is a valuable man, who has done a great
deal for the improvement of the gaol, which Elizabeth Fry finds
very materially mended ; in fact, in excellent order. The authorities here, are most anxious to facilitate Elizabeth Fry's inspection, and to forward her views ; well knowing them to be
the result of the enlarged observation, and long experience of a
practical judicious mind, as well as of close and heartfelt interest
in the subject.

"A meeting with the ladies of Aberdeen this evening at our
Hotel, when prison matters were discussed, and things put in
train for forming a regular association, ere we leave the city.
Elizabeth Fry's capacity for various successive engagements, all
of an important nature, is astonishing. Surely, it is because she
dwells mentally in the 'quiet habitation,' to which she continually resorts, for the renewal of that calming influence of the
Spirit, which purifies the heart, clears the understanding, and
rectifies the judgment ; bestowing upon the truly devoted follower of the Lamb, ' the spirit of love and of power and of a
sound mind.' She is both lovely and wonderful on close acquain-·
tance ; such energy, combined with meekness, and so much power
with entire teachableness, are rarely found.

" 22nd.—We went to Kinmuck—setting out quite early ; had
much satisfaction in being among the Friends there, who seem
a kind, serious, simple-hearted people. Returned to Aberdeen
late.

" 23rd.—After a morning engagement, we were occupied with
the principal officers of the gaol who visited us, desiring to have
some private conversation with Elizabeth Fry. Then came on
the large meeting of ladies ; nearly two hundred assembled. She
had only meant to receive them in our drawing-room, but they
flocked in to such degree, that a large assembly room in our
Hotel, was got ready on the spur of the moment. There was
much reading from reports, &c., as well as valuable communication from Elizabeth Fry, to this interesting assembly. Her
excellent tact and remarkable facility on these occasions, are
admirable. A society was formed for the prisons of Aberdeen

and its vicinity. The Countess of Errol is Patroness; the Lady of the Provost, President; very respectable persons take the other functions. The Provost, Sheriff, and many other gentlemen were in attendance, but, to their evident disappointment, were most politely dismissed by our dear friend, who feels it important, as a woman, not to overstep the line which restricts her public addresses to those of her own sex, excepting only in the exercise of the spiritual gift of the Ministry.

" Between the formation of the association, and proceeding to select the various officers, Elizabeth Fry read a psalm, spoke very nicely upon it to the ladies, and was then engaged in prayer. This meeting satisfactorily over, we went, accompanied by a large party of gentlemen, magistrates, and others, and many ladies also, to visit the Bridewell. A thorough inspection was made, indeed this visit employed an hour and a half; all met afterwards in the Committee-room, to hear what Elizabeth Fry had to remark upon the state of this large and important establishment; she made an excellent address."

Embodied afterwards in a letter,—

To the Provost and Magistrates of the City, and Sheriff Depute, and Sheriff Substitute of the County of Aberdeen.

On visiting the prison of your city, I had much satisfaction in observing the great improvement in the construction of the building, and the arrangement of the yards, since I was last at Aberdeen. The diet also is improved; but I am of opinion, that the addition of a portion of animal food once a week, is very desirable, and likely to conduce to the preservation of the health of the prisoners.

I observe, that the separate system is adopted for tried and untried prisoners, that attention is paid to their instruction, that some employment is provided for them ; and that, upon their dismissal from prison, they are allowed to partake of their earnings.

It is satisfactory also, to learn, that a medical man and a chaplain attend the prisoners, but above all, that it is intended to appoint a female officer to have the oversight and care of the female prisoners. This arrangement is, under any circumstances, important, but peculiarly so when the prisoners are separately confined. There is an obvious impropriety, in women so circumstanced, being under the sole care of men, both as it respects the prisoners and the persons who have the custody of them. The indelicacy and moral exposure are great, and have been found, from experience, to lead to injurious consequences to both parties ; so much so, that by the last Prison Act of George the Fourth, in England, no male officer, not even the Governor or Chaplain, is allowed to visit a female prisoner except in company with a female officer.

The appointment of women to the care of prisoners of their own sex, would moreover prove an economical arrangement, inasmuch as the salaries of women are less than those of men ; but one female turnkey will prove insufficient for the gaol. A Matron will be wanted to instruct the prisoners daily, and to have a constant superintendence over them; and one female turnkey under her. They should both reside in the prison, and no male officer, except the Governor and Chaplain, should ever enter the women's side. The choice of these officers is of the utmost importance ; they should be women of good principles, should possess good sense and discretion, and combine gentleness with firmness. The system of separate confinement, although it has many advantages, requires great care in its administration, in order to make it productive of good effects on the mind of the prisoner, who should frequently be visited by serious judicious persons, to read the scriptures, and carefully mark and cherish any returning good impressions. This practice of regular visiting has been adopted in America, as well as our own country, with great advantage.

The opinion that I had previously formed, as to the peculiar care required in applying this system, was confirmed by learning, on visiting your prison, that no less than two of the prisoners, now in confinement, had attempted self-destruction.

With respect to untried prisoners, several months of separate confinement before trial and before conviction of any crime, is certainly severe discipline. These prisoners therefore, besides having the above-mentioned advantages, should be allowed to receive food from their friends, and occasionally to be visited by them.

The introduction of a prison dress has my entire approbation. It tends to promote the comfort of the prisoners during their confinement, and they have the advantage of taking away their own clothes in an unimpaired state, when they are discharged. Without this provision, they frequently leave the prison in a most destitute condition.

In the Bridewell of your city, I was much satisfied with the general order that prevails, and especially with the very desirable provision of two cells for each prisoner. The want of female officers appears the great and important deficiency of this institution.

I beg to press on your attention, in conclusion, the great benefits that I believe will result to the female prisoners (and to the community at large) from the visits of respectable and discreet ladies, who have formed themselves into a Society for this purpose, and who will be subject to regulations, which will be submitted to you for your approbation. The good that has been produced by similar associations in England, and also in some places in Scotland and Ireland, is so great and obvious, and so fully acknowledged by persons in authority, that I need not enlarge upon it ; but respectfully entreat you to extend to the ladies, who have undertaken this work of charity in the city of Aberdeen, your kind assistance and patronage.

I feel greatly obliged by the kind attentions which I have received from you in my visit to your city, for which be pleased to accept my thanks.

I am, very sincerely,
Your friend,
Elizabeth Fry.

" On our return from the Bridewell, the Sheriff, Dr. Duar, Principal of Mareschal College, and another gentleman of influence, came to attend at a private discussion of certain points, especially of the new Prison Bill for Scotland."

From Aberdeen, Mrs. Fry and her companions went to Rennie Hill, and remained for three days with Mr. Johnston and her niece. A large party of magistrates, lairds, and their ladies, met on Saturday at Rennie Hill, when prison subjects were discussed. The history of the Sunday must be told in Mr. Ball's own words :—

" First-day, 26th.—Our little party sat together after the manner of Friends this morning. Dear Priscilla J—— joined us. I felt afresh, that it is a privilege to know that the worship of God is in spirit and in truth; and may be rendered acceptable, wherever contrite hearts are reverently turned toward Him, in dependence on the mediation of His beloved Son, who is ever near to those, if only ' two or three,' who are met to offer this worship in His name." * * * " Elizabeth Fry and her sister had desired to meet with the fishermen about Anstruther this evening ; but we were all taken by surprise on going down to the town, to find that this simple, religious gathering, turned out to be a very large and crowded Meeting. The room we had arranged for, not having proved nearly capable of containing the people, they had flocked to a chapel near ; the service of which (and of some others I believe) was put off to give place for a Public Meeting of Friends. We had expected to sit down with the poor fishermen in a much more private way. John Sanderson stated to the assemblage, that we began with a pause of silence. Then Elizabeth Fry explained our views on worship, rather in the way of an affectionate introductory address. Her sister E. Fry bent the knee in prayer. After which, Elizabeth Fry was strengthened, in a very striking manner, to proclaim the glad tidings of the gospel of life and salvation : truly an awakening ministry ! Her sister followed, enlarging on the nature and fruits of true repentance ; then Elizabeth Fry addressed the sea-faring men, most appropriately and feelingly, warned the sinners emphatically ; and was afterwards engaged in fervent prayer. At the close of this memorable Meeting, Andrew Johnston briefly addressed this large assembly of his neighbours, acknowledging the kindness of the minister and attention of the people ; and enforcing, with great seriousness, his desire, that the novelty of the occasion, might in no degree be suffered to divert solemn attention, from the infinite importance of the Gospel truths delivered."

" After primary attention to religious engagements among
Friends in Edinburgh, on the 28th, 29th, and 30th ; there was
a party assembled to meet Elizabeth Fry, at the house of our
valued and hospitable host, the late Alexander Cruickshank, on
the evening of the 30th ; when her conversation on the important
subject of the condition and care of prisoners, greatly interested
a large company, including some distinguished individuals and
some foreigners.

" 31st.—Having arranged on our arrival, in concert with the
active members of the Scottish Society, for a large meeting of
ladies at the Royal Hotel. It took place this day, Andrew and
Priscilla Johnston having joined us the evening before. It was
a good and serviceable Meeting. The ladies of the Scotch Committee proved their efficiency in conducting business, and deve-
loping the state of prison affairs in their city, as well as their
diligence in the details of self-denying exertion on behalf of the
cause ; and the leading object of this meeting, in extending the
sphere of interest on behalf of poor prisoners, through the personal communications of Elizabeth Fry, among the ladies of
Edinburgh, seemed to be fully obtained.

" Afterwards, in company with Elizabeth's Fry's much valued
coadjutors, the sisters Mackenzie (of Seaforth) Eliza Fletcher,
and others, we visited the Refuge ; also a house, where they think
of establishing a Penitentiary, to see if it met Elizabeth Fry's
ideas of the requisites for such an Institution. There was an
interesting reunion at the dinner-table of Lord Mackenzie at
Belmont, this evening; where continued interchange of sentiment
upon the subjects so near to the heart of our devoted friend,
was pursued and enjoyed.

" Ninth Month 1st.—A party of about twenty, at a _déjeûner_
at Augusta Mackenzie's, where the same profitable conversation
freely flowed. Elizabeth Fry opened out on the prison objects of
her journey, very instructively, and was listened to with deep
attention. Visited the Sessional Schools, among other engagements this morning ; and Elizabeth Fry, with the sisters
Mackenzie, went to inspect the solitary wards of the prison,
where no gentlemen are admitted. In the evening we received
at the Royal Hotel, a number of gentlemen, magistrates, and

others, when the new Scotch Prison Bill, in particular, and the general subjects of Prison Discipline and Reformation were fully discussed."

Mrs. Fry was at this time extremely anxious as to the extent to which Prison Discipline was carried in Scotland. She greatly feared the enforcement of solitary confinement, and felt it her duty to make a sort of appeal against its possible abuses.

She had therefore invited this large number of influential gentlemen, whose attention had been given to the subject, magistrates, lawyers, members of the Prison Discipline Society, and others, to meet her on this occasion—an appalling audience—as they all sat round, to the number of fifty. She gently engaged in conversation with some, who were seated at the most distant part of the room, and, by degrees, fell into an account of her experience, and a full exposition of her mind on the subject.

As an abstract principle, she doubted the right of man to place a fellow-creature under circumstances of such misery, if his offences were not of a very heinous or aggravated nature. She could not believe that it was accordant with reason or religion, thus to isolate a being, intended by his great Creator for social life, unless necessary for the safety of the community at large ; nor did she consider continual solitude, as the best method of reforming the offender. Very many hours, she thought, might be passed alone with advantage, and the night always ; but she recognised a vast difference between useful and improving reflection, and the imagination dwelling upon past guilt or prospective evil. Her conviction was, that with the greater number of criminals left to feed upon their own mental resources, the latter state of mind was highly probable, the former very unlikely. Confinement, that secluded from the vicious, but allowed of frequent intercourse with sober and well-conducted persons, would have been in her view perfect. But where could funds be obtained to raise the prison, or maintain its discipline on such a system ? Some intercourse for a few-hours daily, among prisoners carefully classed, diligently employed, judiciously instructed, and under most vigilant and unceasing superintendence, with the remaining hours of the twenty-four passed in separate, but not gloomy seclusion ; was in her opinion the best and the most likely method of benefiting the criminal, and thus eventually diminishing crime. She shrank from the abuses to which the solitary system is liable. How soon might the cell become an oubliette ; how short the transition from kind and constant attention, to cruelty and neglect ; how entirely the comfort, nay the existence of a prisoner, must depend upon his keeper's will ; and what was human nature, to be trusted with such responsibility ? With an active magistracy, a zealous clergyman, and careful medical attendant, all might be well ; but who could ensure the continuance of the advantages ? and were the activity and benevolence of the present day to pass away, why might not the slumber of indifference again cover the land ? Nor was this her only fear—" They may be building, though they little think it, dungeons for their children and their children's children, if times of religious persecution or political disturbance should return." Cell within cell, as in some prisons, in others the light and air of heaven admitted through a crooked funnel, but the glorious sun shut from their eyes ; with no sound to reach them ; and,—but a keeper withdrawn, or a wire broken,—no sound to be heard *from* them, however deep the need of assistance.

" On the evenings of the 2nd and the 3rd, large Public Meetings for religious worship were held ; the former at Edinburgh, the latter at Leith, in which Elizabeth Fry was greatly strengthened to declare the truths of the everlasting gospel of our Lord and Saviour Jesus Christ. Many calls were made on distinguished persons, and some visits also received, on the 3rd ; especially one from the late Dr. Abercrombie, which will long be remembered with interest.

"4th.—We came to the George Hotel, Glasgow, and on the 5th and 6th, Elizabeth Fry and her sister were occupied in their religious engagements, among the Friends of that city. Our valued friends and most efficient helpers, the sisters Augusta and Helen Mackenzie, arrived to our aid on the evening of the 6th, and joined us at our Hotel. The Lord Provost and other gentlemen visited Elizabeth Fry, and she went to the Bridewell. At seven o'clock the same evening, a large number of the ladies of Glasgow met at our Hotel, a very crowded, but as usual interesting occasion.

"7th.—The whole party went to Greenock. Elizabeth Fry and the sisters Mackenzie had a very important meeting with the ladies of Greenock this morning; about one hundred were assembled, and it proved highly satisfactory; Elizabeth Fry and these experienced companions entered into many particulars in regard to the visiting of prisons, a subject generally that excited lively interest. She was also engaged strikingly in prayer, with, and for the large company of ladies thus met together. We visited the Greenock gaol, when the women were collected, who were very affectionately addressed by Elizabeth Fry; we were glad to find this gaol a good one, and capable of much usefulness. A large Public Meeting for religious worship was held in the Seaman's Chapel this evening, it proved satisfactory, and was intensely crowded; the doctrine of the gospel was fully set forth, in the love and power of the truth, by our dear friend. An interruption by an advocate of the temperance movement, who embraced the occasion for speaking in favour of that cause, and was applauded by the throng, seemed to threaten the service of this Meeting. But Elizabeth Fry soon resumed, and the seriousness and weight of her manner happily restored solemnity.

"8th.—Invited the landlord of our Greenock Hotel, and his wife, and servants, to our Scripture reading this morning. They came in and we were favoured with an instructive season; another large Meeting of the Greenock ladies afterwards, who seem thoroughly desirous to render their aid to the poor imprisoned ones, too often tied and bound also with the chains of sin! Elizabeth Fry much interested, in arranging to bring into communication with the Religious Tract Society, a man who sells books to sailors on Greenock quay, and in visiting a large factory on the hill, where the work people were assembled and addressed by her. Returned to Glasgow, and visited the Bridewell the same day. The inspection there was truly satisfactory. It is an excellent institution.

" 9th.—Our usual Meeting for worship at Glasgow this morning, almost like a public one, so many of the inhabitants who were aware of Elizabeth Fry's presence, came in. We went to a very satisfactory Public Meeting for worship at Paisley, seven miles from Glasgow, this evening.

" 10th.—The ladies' large Glasgow Prison Meeting was held in the Friends' Meeting House, and an association was formed which we hope will work well. We received company this evening at our Hotel; some ladies as well as gentlemen of Glasgow, who were disposed to give their interest to our objects, conducted as usual. The Scotch Prison Act and similar matters discussed.

" 11th.—Our party made a hasty visit to Paisley, and there inspected the gaol. Here the magistrates met us and showed every attention to facilitate Elizabeth Fry's inspection, as well as in listening to her suggestions, which she was requested to leave in writing."

How sincerely these gentlemen desired to profit from her suggestions, was proved a few months later, when a local newspaper was sent to her, containing the following paragraph.

" PRISON REFORM.

" On Tuesday, the 1st, Janet Stewart of Glasgow was unanimously appointed by a committee of the Commissioners, Matron of the Paisley gaol and Bridewell. The duties of this office are new in the prisons of Scotland. The object of the appointment is, to put the whole of the female prisoners exclusively under the charge of one of their own sex, who is to perform the duties over them of teacher, turnkey, gaoler, &c. In fact, they are not to be seen by any other person but the female keeper, unless it be by persons visiting the establishment, and as far as possible these visitors are to be exclusively females also. It was at the suggestion of Mrs. Fry, at her late visit, that this plan of appointing an instructress and keeper, for the females of their own sex, who should be constantly beside them, was adopted ; and we have the pleasure of adding, that several of the other improvements which were then in contemplation, and which had been recommended by that lady and the Government Inspector, Mr. Hill, have now been carried into effect."

From Glasgow by Carlisle, Penrith, and Patterdale, where meetings for worship were held, this united little band travelled on, till again at Glen Rothay. There, they passed a day of rest and refreshment. With Mr. Ball's account of it, must close the extracts from his narrative.

" 15th.—A day of unwonted quiet. After writing and such restful avocations were done, Elizabeth Fry enjoyed a ramble into the mountain air of Loughrigg Fell, though she did not reach the summit. Amidst many secret exercises of soul, and so much laborious exertion for the temporal as well as spiritual good of others, our dear friend largely shares in the sweet experience that " He giveth all things richly to enjoy." Her love of nature, from the mountain to the field-flower, is signal ; and admirably preserved through atmospheres unfavourable, in general, to the maintenance of a taste for simple and retired pleasures. Yet, where the love of religious retirement is in lively exercise, probably such a taste is less endangered ; it harmonizes with that frame of spirit, which seeks the valley where the dew remains. Precious indeed, is a childlike and watchful spirit, submissively eyeing the chief Shepherd, and waiting His leading."

They attended some meetings appointed for them, in Westmoreland and Lancashire. Mr. Ball accompanied them as far as Liverpool ; from whence Mrs. Fry and her sister returned immediately home.

Upton, Ninth Month 26th.—We arrived at home last Seventh-day, and to my great comfort I found all my family going on well and comfortably. I ventured to ask, or at least to desire, if my goings out were acceptable to the Lord, and if I were to be called to further, and perhaps still more weighty service, that I might find the blessing of preservation extended to those most dear to me at home, as well as to myself in going. Through mercy, this sign has been rather unusually granted me. What can I render unto my Lord for His tender and unmerited mercies?

After leaving William Ball's (Glen Rothay), we spent First-day at Kendal. This meeting is in the most critical state, some of its most valuable members, young and old, leaving the Society. I can hardly express how much I felt in attending it; fears got hold of me; however, I experienced much help. I had simply to preach the Gospel, until the close of the Afternoon Meeting, when I believed it my duty to express my conviction, that we, as a Society, fill an important place in the Church of Christ; and having found it myself a blessed administration of the truth as it is in Jesus; I felt that where so many seeking minds were about leaving the Society, I was bound to bear my testimony to that which I believed to be true. We afterwards attended some very interesting Meetings at Lancaster, Yelland and Ulverston. These places had been long on my mind, I think at least ten years. So things rest with me, until I see the time come to work in them.

Tenth Month 28th.—I have been a satisfactory visit with my husband, and partly accompanied by Peter Bedford and John Hodgskin, to Croydon and Ifield. Our Meeting in Sussex was a very satisfactory one; and a reading we had the next morning at a cottage on a Common, belonging to a dear Friend, where we had been before. The libraries we established, appear to have been much read and valued. It is cause for much thankfulness, to find that our labour has not been in vain in the Lord. How sweet are His mercies! May all become His servants, saith my soul!

I have also left home accompanied by my beloved husband and my sister Elizabeth, to visit a few Meetings in Essex.

Twelfth Month 6th.—This morning I deeply feel the seriousness of laying before my Monthly Meeting, my belief, that it may be my duty again to visit France and some other parts of the Continent of Europe. It is after much weighty consideration that I have come to the conclusion, that it is right to do this. I have long thought that this summer my course might be turned either to my dearest brother Joseph in America, or to the Continent of Europe; after much weighing it, I have believed the latter to be the right opening for me. I laid my prospect before the Friends of our Monthly Meeting, this morning. Several Friends were there, not members of it. We had a very solemn Meeting—for worship first. My sister and I returned our certificates for visiting Scotland, and then I asked for one for Europe; having very earnestly prayed for help, direction and protection. When under a fresh feeling of its being right to do it, I simply informed Friends that I looked to paying a visit to Paris, then to the Friends in the south of France; and should probably in returning visit some other parts of Europe. Much unity and sympathy were expressed with this prospect of religious duty, by our own members and those who visited us. There certainly appeared to be in no common degree, a seal set to this serious prospect of religious service.

I now desire to leave all to the further openings of Providence, as to when to go, who is to go with me, and where to go. I desire to leave it all to my most holy and gracious Head and High Priest, my All in All, my Lord and my God. Although I am very deeply sensible that it is only through the fulness and freeness of unmerited mercy, love and grace, that I dare call or feel my Lord thus to be my Head and my Helper. I may acknowledge in faith, my belief that through the help of the Holy Spirit, my Lord has been and is unto me "Wonderful, Counsellor, the Mighty God, the Everlasting Father, and the Prince of Peace."

28th.—Yesterday, excepting our dear F—— and R—— C——, all our beloved children dined with us. It really was to me a beautiful sight. Sixteen round our table, happy in each other, a strong tie of love amidst the brothers and sisters; and much united to us their father and mother. I felt the occasion serious as well as sweet, and very earnestly prayed to the Lord that I might be very faithful, if He called me to any religious service amongst them; whether it were to pray for them, or speak to them of His goodness. When the cloth was removed after dinner, I believed it my duty to kneel down, and very fervently-to pray and to return thanks to my God, for all these most tenderly beloved ones. Great help and deliverance has been granted to some of our circle ; the Lord has been very gracious, He has added to our number and not diminished them. I did from my heart return God thanks, earnestly asking in faith for a continuance of His mercies ; more particularly, that our souls should be satisfied more abundantly with the unsearchable riches of Christ ; and that we might be still more closely united in our Heavenly Father's love. I asked the Lord that it might please Him to grant us peace and prosperity, through His tender mercy in Christ Jesus ; and that wherever we might be, His blessing might be with us ; and that when the end came, it might crown all.

After this solemn time, thirteen of the sweet, dear grandchildren came in. We missed dearest F—— and R——, and their lovely group ; but they were not forgotten by us. We passed an evening of uncommon enjoyment, cheerful yet sober, lively yet sensible of the blessing and peace of our Lord being with us. I seldom if ever remember so bright a family meeting, it reminded me of our Earlham days ; but I could not but feel it a blessing, when a mother as well as a father is spared to watch their family grow up and prosper, and to see and enjoy their children's children.

When I remember all that I have passed through on their account ; above all the exquisite anxiety about their spiritual welfare, and now so far to see what the Lord has done for me and for them, What can I say ? What can I do ? ought I not to leave them all to His most holy keeping, and no longer " toil and spin" so much for them.

CHAPTER XXI.

First Month 12th.—I returned from Lynn last evening. I was a good deal with my beloved sister Catharine, who was there. Before parting, we had a deeply interesting time together, when the spirit of prayer was remarkably poured forth upon us. I prayed for them each separately, and believe that access was in mercy granted to the Throne of Grace. My dearest sister offered a solemn prayer for us before we rose from our knees. I felt, as I have often done, an earnest desire, that we may none be in spiritual bonds. I think Satan, in hardly any way mars the Lord's work more, than in putting persons in the stiff bonds of High Churchism. He attacks all professors in this way, and leads them to rest in their sectarianism, rather than their Christianity. I do not mean that this is the case with those I was amongst, but I see it a frightful bait, thrown out to all professors of all denominations. Few things I more earnestly desire, than unity in the Church of Christ, and that all partition walls may be broken down. Lord, hasten the coming of that day, for Thine own name's sake !

16th.—I have had the pleasure and satisfaction of meeting at dinner, at my son Foster Reynolds, my beloved brother Gurney, three of my sons, one of his, and my nephew Edward Buxton, previous to attending a Bible Meeting. Surely it is a cause of deep thankfulness to have my children, and others so near and dear to me, engaged in so excellent a cause. I consider it to be an honour of which we are all unworthy, to promote in this or any other way, the knowledge of the everlasting Gospel. On Second-day, I laid my concern to go to France, before the

Morning Meeting.   I feel encouraged by all the testimonies from the Lord's servants, and the real help and excellence of the arrangement, that we should thus, in such weighty and important duties, have the sanction of that section of the Church to which we belong.

I have received very encouraging accounts from Scotland as to the results of our last journey.   Several refuges are likely to be formed, and women prisoners to be visited.   The accounts from France have also been in many ways encouraging.   My dear and valued friend, the Duchess de Broglie, who died some little time ago, expressed that her faith had been strengthened by our visit. Many important alterations have taken place in the prisons ; the New Testament is now circulated in some of them, and the hospitals.   So I may take courage, and return God thanks.

There was one subject of anxiety pressing upon the mind of Elizabeth Fry, which she knew to be so important, that with all the preparations for her long journey, and arrangements to make for her family at home, she resolved to remove it if possible— the low state of the funds of the British Ladies' Society.

Money was not only wanted in carrying on the Prison Visiting, to furnish employment in many cases, and to supply books and little rewards as encouragement for good behaviour ; but there were also to be assisted the valuable Refuges that had been established ; one for little girls at Chelsea, and another for young women at Manor Hall Clapham.   There were, besides these demands, heavy and continual calls upon their funds, to meet the melancholy cases of liberated prisoners, or accused but destitute females, who could not be received into either of these institutions.   A sub-committee had been formed, under the name of the Patronage Committee, and at this time was actively at work, to assist such cases ; once a week the ladies met (and continue to meet), to receive applications.   Fearful details of misery and guilt are constantly brought before them—frequently may be seen a police officer with some poor creature in his custody, (or

voluntarily under his care,) come to implore shelter and opportunity of existence, without living in sin. Besides this, the Convict Ships continued a heavy demand upon the funds of the British
Society.   Some expedient to meet these emergencies was become
essential.   Mrs. Fry had no taste for Bazaars and Repositories ;
but, conducted in a sober quiet manner, she did not believe them
wrong ; under these circumstances, therefore, and after full con-
sultation with her friends and coadjutors, she determined upon
having a sale for this purpose.

There is an ancient building in the city of London, called
Crosby Hall, still beautiful, though fallen into decay.   It had
become the property of a lady, desirous of restoring it ; she had
already begun the work, and willingly granted the use of it, as a
means of carrying on some of the repairs.   A few days however,
before the sale was to take place, the needful preparations were
found not even commenced.   Two rooms, formerly part of the
ancient palace, absolutely necessary on this occasion were still a
ruin.   Skilful workmen were called in ; a magical change passed
over the scene, the worm-eaten timbers were covered and floored,
the arched windows through which the wind had howled, and the
rain beaten three days before, were glazed, and where cobweb
waved upon ruined walls, hangings were suspended, with at
intervals armorial boarings, to enliven the whole.   By the day
of sale all things were ready to receive the public.

Paris, Third Month 17th.—Before leaving home, we were
much occupied by a very large sale, for the British Society, held
in Crosby Hall.   I felt it an exercising time lest any should be
exposed to temptation by it, and I see that there are two sides to
the question respecting these sales, as there is an exposure in
them that may prove injurious to some.   However, I think I saw
in this instance many favourable results, and particularly in the
kind and capital help my children gave me in it, and the way
in which it occupied them.   One day I had fifteen children, and

several grandchildren helping me to sell. A sweet and Chris_
tian spirit appeared to reign in the room. There were more than
a thousand pounds obtained by it, clear of all expenses, which
will be a great help to the British Society. The marks of kindness shown me by numbers, in the things sent to the sale, were
very encouraging to me. My brothers and sisters, my nephews
and nieces, were also very kind, in aiding me in many ways.

Previous to our departure, I had the servants of our different
families meet me at Meeting ; it proved quite a large number,
almost filling our Meeting House. I believe it was a time of
real edification and comfort to some who were there.

Josiah Forster, an elder among Friends, accompanied Elizabeth
Fry on this journey. Her husband and a daughter were also with
her ; her youngest son was to join them at Paris. Difficulties
attended their first starting, which gradually yielded, and they
left home on the 11th of March.

Scarcely had Mrs. Fry reached the Hotel at Boulogne, before
so many came to seek her, that with difficulty she found time to
breakfast or change her dress. She visited the prison, which was
in a very deplorable state ; and in the evening received about
forty at the Hotel, chiefly the ladies of a little district Society
she had been instrumental in forming on her previous visit. The
results of their labours were very satisfactory ; many of the poor
French were subscribing for, or buying New Testaments, as well
as eagerly reading the tracts circulated amongst them. The state
of the resident English poor was also considered as decidedly improved, through this means.

On retiring to her room at night, Mrs. Fry's maid could not
refrain the expression of her astonishment, at the eagerness of the
servants of the Hotel for Testaments, " The people here are
craving Testaments Ma'am ;" it appeared that they lent them
to their friends, who carried them into the country, where they
were so eagerly read and re-read, that it was difficult for the
rightful owners to regain possession of them.

On the 14th, en route to Abbeville, the party stopped at
Samer for an hour, to give Mrs. Fry the opportunity of visiting
a poor sick Englishman in great affliction.   At Montreuil-sur-
Mer, she gave a tract to a man whilst changing horses ; the
carriage was soon surrounded by people begging for books ; it was
curious to see their energy to obtain them.   The same thing
occurred at the Hotel at Abbeville, where those, to whom she had
given them on her previous visit, begged for more, and came
creeping up to her apartment to prefer their request.   Her Text-
books, " Les petits livres de matin," were the decided favourites.
In the morning, the people of the Hotel again gathered round
her.   The Sunday she had spent there on her former visit to
Paris—the reading they had in the evening—the prayer she
offered for them, had made a deep impression.   They beguiled
her into the kitchen, where she told them in broken French,
which however they contrived to understand, a little of her wishes
for them as to faith and practice ; then all would shake hands
with her to the portly " chef de cuisine."

Paris, Third Month 17th.—Here we are once more in this
most interesting city, after a favourable journey, and calm
passage.   Leaving home was very touching to our feelings ; I
never saw my children feel a separation so much.

I am not high in spirits on my arrival here.   At Meeting, and
in a time of prayer with some of my dear friends, I felt the
springs very low, but I trust through the tender mercy of my
Heavenly Father, they will rise by degrees.   It was sweet on our
arrival, to see some beautiful flowers and other things all ready
for us, provided by our dear kind friends as marks of their
love, particularly from the Baroness Pelet, it cheered my heart ;
sweet visits from Sophia D—— and Emelie M——, were also
comforting.   How earnestly do I desire and pray, that my Lord
would clearly point out my work in this place ; that He would
enable me by His own Power and Spirit, to perform it in simplicity to His praise, the good of others, and my own peace.

Lord, regard Thy servant in her low estate, and if it be Thy holy will, give some token, by Thy presence, Spirit and Power, that Thou art with us ; and more abundantly fit and prepare for Thine own work, as Thou hast often blessed and abundantly increased that which may appear small in the eyes of man, to the help of numbers : so, oh Lord ! bless, prosper, and increase the weak labours of Thy unworthy servant, to the good of numbers, and the promotion of Thy cause in this place; where " the world, the flesh, and the devil," appear so powerful. Answer this cry, I beseech Thee, and give Thy poor servant a quiet, patient, trustful spirit, only dependent upon the fresh pourings forth of Thy Spirit, and the incomings of Thy love.   Amen.

24th.—In mercy my cry was heard. We went to our little Meeting, where were some seeking minds ; and to my own feelings, we were remarkably bound together by the presence of our Lord. I also may thankfully say, that I was enabled to preach the word and to pray. I felt it an encouraging, edifying time, and an answer to prayer. After Meeting, we called at our Ambassador's, and met with a very cordial reception. In the evening, we went to an evangelical party which I was glad to be at, although I thought part of the service flat. I had a few words only to say.

On Sixth-day, we visited a large French Methodists' school ; it was a very encouraging sight : there were about a hundred children, who appeared well taught. I had a good deal of advice to give them and their parents, and felt peace in the service ; but the place was so exceedingly cold, that I left it with severe tooth-ache, which lasted all day, and brought me down in body and spirit.

Having invited a large company for philanthropic and religious objects for the following evening, I felt anxious ; but when the time came, I was enabled, though the party was very large, to speak a little on the subject of Negro Slavery : Josiah Forster also expressed himself very agreeably upon the subject. We finished with a short, lively Scripture-reading, and to my own feelings, strength was in a remarkable manner given me in the needful time.

This morning, I paid a most interesting visit to a Roman Catholic lady,—a young widow,—her little children, and her friend. I have seldom seen the Christian life more exemplified.

So we see and "perceive that God is no respecter of persons; but in every nation, he that feareth Him, and worketh righteousness, is accepted with Him."—Acts x. 34, 35.

Thus began this second sojourn in Paris: the same friends gathered round her, the same institutions were revisited, with some others which she had not seen before; the same objects of interest occupied her attention. The mornings were thus spent; the evenings generally at the houses of their many kind friends, or in receiving guests at the Hotel for profitable conversation and intercourse.

Mrs. Fry had not before visited the hospitals generally; now she did so, accompanied by the Baron de Girando. The enlarged religion and benevolence of this excellent old man was delightful to her: his being a member of the Roman Catholic Church in no way preventing their Christian unity.

He was endeavouring to found a Penitentiary, or Magdalen, in Paris; but complained, that people are so easily influenced through their senses, that it was comparatively easy to induce them to feed the starving, clothe the naked, and administer to the sick; whilst moral reforms, the benefit of which are less immediately obvious, but of such infinitely greater importance, are too often neglected.

The first visit was to the Hospital of the Hôtel Dieu, a vast pile built on either side of one of the branches of the Seine, over which is a communication by a covered bridge. It is an extremely ancient foundation, and contains 1260 beds, of which a hundred or a hundred and fifty, are placed in each of the immense wards. These, notwithstanding their size and the cleanliness of the beds, linen, and floors, were offensively close. The mortality in this hospital is at all times great: partly to be attributed to the severity of the accidents and other cases brought to the Hôtel Dieu, but even more to the defective ventilation. This is proved by the singular fact, that the greatest number of deaths occur on the third and highest story, less on the second, and the fewest on the ground-floor.

This hospital is under the care of a lay director, and nuns of the Order of St. Augustin; there are forty of them divided between the Hôtel Dieu and the Hospital of St. Louis.

The Superior spoke feelingly of the trials to which they were exposed, in fulfilling their arduous and distasteful labours; that only as a duty to God could they endure it. The nuns appeared very kind to the poor creatures under their care, but take no part in ministering to their mental necessities and religious state.

The following day, accompanied by the Baron de Girando and M. Valderuche, Mrs. Fry visited the Hospital of St. Louis, founded by Henri IV., for plague, leprosy, and other contagious complaints. It was entirely built in his time, and contains all that was then considered necessary to prevent or check contagion; it is now used for cases of cutaneous disease. The Hospital of St. Louis is a noble pile of buildings, placed amongst gardens, in the outskirts of the town. It encloses within itself, five large courts laid out in gardens; the wards each containing as many beds as those in the Hôtel Dieu, but being lofty, vaulted, and with the finest ventilation from a double tier of almost unnumbered windows, they were perfectly fresh and pleasant. The nuns said the rate of mortality was very small.

A poor English maid-servant was among the sufferers; she had been there for months, having been left by an English family with whom she had been travelling. She spoke of the kindness she had received in the Hospital as great. Her heart bounded at the sound of her native tongue; nor was she left without arrangements for her future comfort.

The establishment of baths of various descriptions is very complete, and available for out-door as well as house patients. The appearance of the hospital was highly gratifying as to every outward arrangement, but not so as to any opportunity for moral and

religious improvement. Before quitting the establishment, Mrs.
Fry asked to see the Chaplain (L'Aumonier.) After some
general discourse on the state of the institution, she addressed
him on the subject of her concern for the souls of these poor
people, the reply was, " Nons avons les sacramens de l'Eglise,"
which closed the conversation ; the priest accepting a Text Book,
and parting from his visitors in a friendly manner.

Two days afterwards, the same party went to the Hospital
des Enfans Trouvés. This monument of St. Vincent de Paul
is an affecting sight, from the miserable state of the wretched
infants, and the fearful mortality that prevails among them.
Their sufferings must be greatly increased by the unnatural practice of swaddling, from which thraldom they are only unloosed
once in twelve hours, for any purpose ; the sound in the ward
could be only compared to the faint and pitiful bleating of a
flock of lambs. A lady who not unfrequently visited the institution said, that she never remembered examining the long array
of clean white cots that lined the walls, without finding one or
more dead. In front of the fire was a sloping stage, on which
was a mattress, and a row of these little creatures placed upon it
to warm, and await their turn to be fed from the spoon by a
nurse. After much persuasion, one that was crying piteously,
was released from its swaddling bands, it stretched its little
limbs, and ceased its wailings. Mrs. Fry pleaded so hard for
them with the Superior, that their arms have since been released.
The Sisters of Charity professed to be desirous of doing justice to
the children ; but the conduct of the whole institution wanted
vigour and deliverance from the prejudices which consigns
infancy to so much suffering and untimely death.

The medical attendants were alive to the defects of the
management, but professed themselves unable to effect any
change in the old-established usages of the place. These
appeared to Mrs. Fry and her party to be almost confounded in

the minds of the Sisters with the regulations of their religious order ; at all events, if not belonging to it, very naturally arising from the "invincible immobilité" of monachism, as a strict Roman Catholic lady, but a keen observer of all around her, expressed it to Mrs. Fry many years before.

If these infants survive the first few days, they are sent into the country to be nursed. There is also a sort of Orphan Asylum attached to the Enfans Trouvés for children of all ages, but they are seldom there a month before removal into the country to be brought up by the ignorant peasants to whom they are consigned.

Mrs. Fry saw at a glance, how vast an opportunity of national good was here lost ; multitudes of children belonging to the State, and ignorant of any other parentage, would if properly trained and educated, act as a leaven among the mass to raise the tone of good feeling and principle, and increase the attachment of the lower classes to their country and its institutions.

From the Enfans Trouvés they proceeded to the Hospice de la Maternité, this building is full of recollections, being the Porte Royale of Paris—now so changed ! The cells used for the patients still retain their cellular divisions, so that complete privacy is enjoyed by each poor woman, with all the convenience of wards. Mrs. Fry thought this, the best Lying-in Hospital she had ever seen ; the Matron and the Superintendent appeared enlightened and intelligent, the whole condition of the place vigorous and sound. It is entirely under secular care. In this as in all the other Paris hospitals, no tickets of admission are required, a person has only to prove herself poor and ill, to be admitted as a patient.

Third-day.—Visited an hospital, and dined at Lord William Bentinck's, I trust to some good purpose, but I fear for myself in many ways on such occasions.

Fifth-day.—A very solemn Morning Meeting, numbers there, mostly women, some ladies of rank, some very interesting persons, I was afresh enabled to pray and to minister.

Her ministry on this occasion was wonderful, chiefly addressed to the afflicted, and seemed to find an echo in many hearts. She afterwards called on Madame Guizot, mother of the Minister ; a charming old lady eighty years of age, taking charge of her three little grandchildren.

We dined at our dear friends the Mallets, where we met a large family party, and had much interesting conversation. There was a blessed feeling of the love of God over us ; I believe this service was called for, and was blessed to many present.

Mrs. Fry again visited the St. Lazare prison. She found some improvements effected, and female officers introduced. Many of the prisoners knew her again and seemed delighted to see her. In one ward (Salle) they told her that since her last visit, they had thought and talked so much of religion, that they had subscribed to purchase " Celle-la" pointing to an image of the Virgin placed against the wall.

The St. Lazare Prison is only for women, and often contains 1200 at one time ; to it is attached a sort of compulsory lock hospital.

She also saw La Roquette, or the prison for " Les Jeunes Detenus" a very fine establishment for boys. By the laws of France, a boy is not held responsible for his actions under sixteen years of age, and therefore if he commits a crime, he is detained and confined, but not sentenced. Fathers in France have the power of confining sons under this age.

La Roquette is built upon the plan of a prison, and contains between five and six hundred inmates ; there is a regular school for their instruction in reading, writing, and arithmetic. Several of the classes were reading the New Testament, (De Sacy's translation). Each boy has a copy, and they may have the book to read if they wish it in their hours of recreation. There are various workshops where they learn trades. Of their earnings they receive one-third at the time, one-third when they leave the prison, the remaining third goes to the establishment. They have no other punishment than solitary confinement. The boys under "Correction Paternelle" were in cells, where their education was carried vigorously forward, according to their rank in life, no other difference is permitted—the same little bed, table, chair, and shelves in each, and the same diet and costume. It was to Mrs. Fry's feelings a highly interesting and satisfactory establishment. Not so the prison of La Force, into which she ventured, and saw six hundred untried persons crowded together in a state of total idleness, vice and neglect, without even on Sundays, or fête days, the service of the Roman Catholic Church being performed.

About this time the party was joined by several of Mrs. Fry's family, it was highly interesting to them, thus to be together under such novel circumstances, and to be permitted for once to witness and partake in the scenes, incident to their beloved mother's labours in the cause of benevolence and religion.

Fourth Month 7th, First-day.—Last evening about a hundred persons spent the evening with us. The subject of prisons was brought forward, Newgate, &c., I endeavoured to show the state of prisons formerly, and many of their improvements. But above all, to inculcate Christian principle as the only sure means of improving practice. I sought in every way, in the cases brought forward, to uphold the value of the Scriptures, and to show the blessed results of faith and repentance. We finished by reading in a solemn manner the 15th of Luke, as the chapter so greatly blessed to poor prisoners. I made little comment, there was very great solemnity over us. There were Catholics and Protestants, and, I believe, some of the Greek Church. There were Greeks, Ionians, Spaniards, a Pole, Italians, Germans, English, Americans and French. Several of the English and French, persons of rank ; the Marquis de Brignolles Sardinian Minister, and Prince Czartorinski. Thus this week has run away! may it

have been for the real good of others, and the glory of God.
Most merciful God, I perfectly know that I am unworthy to present myself before Thee on the bended knee of my soul. But I
come boldly to the throne of grace, through the merits of Thy
dear Son, our Mediator with Thee our God. Grant Holy Father,
that the iniquity of my holy things may be blotted out, and that
in my efforts to serve Thee, and promote the cause of truth and
righteousness, my infirmities and the unworthiness of the instrument may not have cast a blemish on Thy truth. Grant also,
Holy Father, that the word spoken may through Thy blessing
comfort, strengthen and edify Thy followers, and be a means
of bringing many to repentance and faith in Thy beloved Son
Christ Jesus our Lord. Dearest Lord, be near to keep, to help,
and direct all my steps, as I go on in this cause, for Thy glory,
the good of others, and my own edification and peace. Permit
Thy servant also to commend to Thy special keeping all most
near to her, left in her own land, and all everywhere, beloved by
her, and for whom she travails in spirit, and spread the knowledge
of Thyself, and of Thy Son, and Thy righteousness, through the
Holy Spirit, everywhere on this earth. Amen!

Paris, 21*st.*—I feel that, under a lively sense of peace
and rest of soul, I may record the mercies of the Lord this last
week.

Our First-day was very satisfactory, a large Meeting, five of our
children with us. I now mention the events of the week without
stating the days.

I had a very serious, interesting and intimate conversation
with the Duchess of Orleans.

I visited and attended to some prisons, formed a Ladies' Society
to visit the Protestants in prisons and hospitals, met a very influential company at dinner at Lord Granville's, much interesting
conversation in the evening ; the same twice at Baron Pelet's, and
we had an agreeable dinner at Lord William Bentinck's. I have
paid some very interesting private calls, spent one morning with
my children ; our great philanthropic evening largely attended,
about a hundred and forty present. Josiah Forster gave a concentrated account of our former evenings, and added other things
very agreeably. I strongly impressed upon them the extreme

importance of the influence of the higher, on the lower classes of society, by their example and precept; mentioned late hours, theatres, and other evils. Then advised; giving the poor, Christian education, reading the Holy Scriptures in their families, lending Libraries, District Societies and other objects: we finished with a very solemn Scripture reading, the greater part of the third chapter of Colossians, and 20th and 21st verses of the last chapter of the epistle to the Hebrews, "Now the God of peace that brought again from the dead our Lord Jesus, that great Shepherd of the sheep, through the blood of the everlasting covenant, make you perfect in every good work, to do His will, working in you that which is well pleasing in His sight, through Jesus Christ; to whom be glory for ever and ever. Amen."

Previous to reading this, I had expressed some solemn parting truths, and our party broke up in much love and peace.

May the Lord of the harvest, Himself cause that some of these may be gathered into His garner, and may He bless, prosper, and increase the seed so unworthily scattered.

On Fifth-day, we dined with some sweet, spiritual, and delight-ful people, the de Presensés and de Valcours; in the evening to Mark Wilkes', to meet a very large party of ministers from different parts of France, come to attend the Meetings of the various Societies.

Fontainbleau, 28th.—The day before our departure from Paris we visited the Prefét de Police, took in our report of the state of the prisons, and obtained leave for the Protestant ladies to visit the Protestant prisoners; we had much interesting con-versation. We have the great satisfaction of hearing, that a law is likely to pass for women prisoners, throughout France, to be under the care of women.

In the evening and during the day, numbers came to take leave of us; a good many Greeks, who appeared to feel much interest in and for us, as if our labours with them had not been in vain.

On parting with my beloved children, (to return to England) I could not refrain from many tears. Our beloved friend Emilie Mallet joined us very early in the morning, also our kind friend John Sargent, our friend de Béranger, and one or two others.

My soul was particularly humbled within me, and, before parting we assembled with our friends, and poured forth deep prayer and thanksgiving unto the Lord; thanks for the help granted to us, and for the kindness shown us by our Christian friends, and the love and unity we have partaken of with them; prayer that our labours might be blessed, and the seed scattered, prospered and increased, and that no reproach might have been brought by us upon the cause nearest to my heart; earnestly did I ask a blessing upon our friends, ourselves, the tenderly beloved ones just parted from, and those at home. After this we took an affectionate leave of all, including our host, hostess, and the Hotel servants.

Among other topics connected with penal legislation, the solitary or separate system was frequently debated in the conversations at Paris. Mrs. Fry was continually called upon to give her opinion. M. de Béranger and she discussed it frequently, and on leaving Paris she employed her husband to address to him the following letter:

The subject of separate confinement is one presenting many difficulties, from the diversity of views taken by so many persons of talent and humanity; and my wife has thought that I could not better convey her ideas than by simply stating the arguments that appear to her to bear with the most weight, favourably or unfavourably, on the question.

The following she considers the most prominent reasons in favour of separate confinement:—

First,—It prevents, with the most certainty, all contamination from their fellow-prisoners.

Secondly,—It prevents the formation of intimacy, or acquaintance, with persons who may prove highly injurious associates in future life.

Thirdly,—It affords more opportunity for serious reflection, and should any become religiously disposed for prayer and meditation, and being much cut off from their fellow-mortals, it may lead to a greater dependence on God, and to having their hearts more devoted to Him.

Fourthly,—The privacy of the confinement may prevent that loss of character, in the estimation of the world, which is the general consequence of imprisonment, as now inflicted.

The following reasons may, on the other hand, be strongly adduced against the system being generally adopted :—

In the *first* place, the extreme liability to its abuse, and to its being rendered an unduly severe punishment, *or the reverse,* according to the will or caprice, partiality, dislike, or neglect, of the persons who have the management of them.

Secondly,—The very great difficulty of obtaining a sufficiency, of either men or women officers, of that high and upright principle, as, by their impartiality and firmness, with proper kindness and due attention to the welfare of the prisoners, would be *fit* persons to be entrusted with so weighty a change. This opinion is strongly corroborated by that of the experienced Governor of the Great Central Prison of Beaulieu, also by the Governor of the House of Correction, at Cold-Bath Fields, in London.

Thirdly,—Prisoners so confined are rendered almost *irresistibly* subject to the moral contamination of officers, which is the case only in a very limited degree, when allowed to associate daily with their fellow-prisoners.

Fourthly,—Although, when the moral good of the community is concerned, expense ought to be a very secondary consideration, yet it ought not to be overlooked. The expense of providing proper cells, and a sufficient number of properly qualified officers, for so large a number of prisoners, would be enormous ; and the difficulty, of so building as to prevent the communication of sound, very great, and its attainment uncertain, besides the liability of the prisoners not being able to make themselves heard, in case of necessity, arising from sudden illness or accident.

Fifthly,—Although for short periods, neither the powers of the mind nor body might suffer essentially, yet after a long and too solitary confinement, there is *unquestionable danger for both.* Too much silence is contrary to nature, and physically injurious both to the stomach and lungs ; and as regards the faculties, we are credibly informed of the fact, (in addition to what we have known at home,) that amongst the monks of La Trappe, few attained to the age of sixty years without having suffered an absolute decay of their mental powers, and fallen into premature childishness.

Sixthly,—That whilst, on the one hand, it affords to the penitent an opportunity for salutary reflection, there is reason on the other hand to fear, that a large proportion of those who are confined in jails, are so deeply depraved, that when left to themselves they would be *more likely* to consume their hours in ruminating over past crimes and exploits, and in devising and planning schemes for the commission of new ones; the heart becomes more hardened, the character and temper more sullen and morose, and better prepared for fresh crimes upon their dismissal from prison.

The *seventh* and most weighty objection of all, is this, that as the vast majority of those who enter a prison, are likely to be returned into the bosom of society, it is a most important and paramount consideration, that as man is a social being, and not designed for a life of seclusion, such a system of prison discipline be adopted, as may best prepare those under its correction, for re-entering active life, and all its consequent exposures and temptations. This can never be effected in solitude or separation: it can only be achieved by such regulations, brought to bear upon every day prison life, as may most easily, and with the best chance of success, be afterwards carried out and realized in daily practice, upon their restoration to liberty. Of course, this view embraces all useful labour, and excludes such as (like the Tread-wheel) can in no way facilitate the future means of an honest livelihood.

Having thus briefly stated the reasons for and against the separate confinement of prisoners in the day-time, and the result of which is the conclusion, that it is inexpedient to bring it into general practice: I will endeavour to represent Mrs. Fry's opinion, as to the best line of conduct to be adopted towards untried prisoners, not only with a view to prevent the commission of such offences, as would subject them to punishment, but fundamentally to improve their principles, and regulate their whole future conduct and life, which is the one grand point to keep in view.

In the first place, from the instant that any individual is

placed under restraint, charged with the commission of an offence against the law, the grand preliminary object ought to be, to preserve, by every possible means, the morals of the person thus detained, from being *deteriorated* by the process ; and that, at all events, the *law* *itself* should not become the instrument of the most cruel and fatal of all injustices,—that of demoralizing, by every species of exposure and contamination, the wretched being whom it sooner or later may have to consign, as the consequence of its own action, to infamy and punishment.

A man,—a youth, perhaps,—is charged with a crime. He may be innocent, he may be a trembling beginner : his education, his previous habits, may have been good. He knows little of crime, and has few or no associates in it. He is now turned loose into a den, amongst the most hardened criminals, and in one short month, all remaining scruples, all remaining tenderness of conscience, are gone too probably for ever. But it is not only one short month ; but in France, and in most English counties, it is many months' opportunity which is thus afforded to the profligate villain, to harden, to season, and to embue the mind of his unpractised victim, for re-entering society depraved, debased, and ripe for the commission of crimes, at which he would have shuddered, when the act of the law, by placing them in public detention, first exposed him to irretrievable degradation and ruin.

But let us suppose the case of those, wholly innocent of the crimes laid to their charge, the victims of false accusation, malice or mistake. Suppose them, by the aid of religious and moral principle, to have withstood all the baneful influences to which a cruel and unjust law has exposed them ; and to go out of prison justly acquitted, and worthy to be replaced in the esteem and confidence of their fellow-citizens. What follows ? why, they go forth blighted and blasted. Their involuntary association, with the companions the law has chosen for them, has for ever destroyed their characters ; they are shunned, and become the objects of most reasonable suspicion ; they have no means, no hope left, of gaining an honest living,—the law has effectually prevented that, —they are driven to dishonest, dishonourable, or violent means of obtaining a morsel of bread ; they are again arrested, and the same law that made them what they are, pours forth its heaviest judgments on the victims of its own injurious policy.

Heartily, therefore, should every friend to humanity hail the day, when arrangements are made for the separate confinement of all untried prisoners, with liberty, daily to see some of their own friends, to consult their legal advisers, to improve their own accommodation in their bedding or their diet, to be visited by such benevolent persons as may seek to promote their present and everlasting welfare ; and, joined to this, every practicable arrangement made by the Government of their country, for the shortest possible period, elapsing, previous to their trial, both for the good of the prisoners and its advantage to the country, by lessening essentially the prison-room required, and the many expenses attached to the confinement of prisoners.

If found guilty on their trial, and if their first offence, Mrs. Fry's views are simple, and are given in her own words :—

I believe nothing so likely to conduce to the real improvement of principle and conduct in delinquents, and to render them fit for a return to society, as a limited number of them being regularly instructed, and working together in small companies— say, from ten to twenty—under faithful, constant, and strict inspection by day, and at night always sleeping in separate cells. The mode of instruction and its subjects, should be very simple, and if possible, be rendered agreeable to them. The Scripture-readings, (and reading the Scriptures ought never to be omitted) should be short and well-selected, adapted to their generally dark and very ignorant state, and calculated to give them a taste for something superior to their former low and depraved habits. Books of a moral and religious tendency, that amuse whilst they instruct, are also very desirable, and especially so, in the cases of separate confinement. I consider religious instruction, given in a kind and judicious spirit, the most powerful and efficacious means of deterring from crime, and inducing good conduct, resulting from improved principles. Some advantage may occasionally arise from this instruction being given privately ; but it is more generally likely to be well received in companies, because, very close and cogent advice may be thus given, without danger of hurting individual feelings, as they receive the advice, without supposing it directed immediately to themselves. I consider, also, that employment in companies, is more likely to be well and industriously performed, as there is a stimulus in trying who can do the best, and who can do the most, in the shortest period of time.

If, after the plan of being associated in small companies has been tried on any prisoner, he returns to undergo the penalty of a second condemnation, a more rigorous system had better be adopted. I think, they should then be confined separately, having instruction and employment, and a certain number of visits daily, from the officers of the prison, or persons allowed or appointed for this special purpose ; thus preventing the (now) old offender from associating with the novice in guilt, and suitably proportioning the punishment to the offence. But it is necessary to add, that in no case should women be separately confined, unless placed under the care of officers of their own sex ; nor should any man, not even the Chaplain or Physician, be allowed to visit them under any pretext, unless accompanied by a female officer.—I remain, &c.

Just before Mrs. Fry left Paris, she was informed that the Archbishop was annoyed at her proceedings, that he had expressed dissatisfaction at the alterations she had recommended in the St. Lazare Prison, and had gone so far as to speak with regret, if not displeasure, of the Baron de G——'s having accompanied her in her visits to the hospitals. But the secret of the Archiepiscopal opposition lay not here : it was the more general knowledge of the Holy Scriptures which he dreaded. It was, that the reforms, Mrs. Fry recommended, were all based upon Scriptural authority, that it was to those sacred writings she referred for rules of active obligation, as the only source from whence to learn all that is due from man to man ; and above all this, that she lost no opportunity in all companies, and on all occasions, where it could be done with propriety, to urge their perusal and general circulation.

But whilst she did this, believing it to be an absolute duty, she had no tendency, where she deemed the great foundation of religious truth secure, to oppose the opinions of others, or introduce her own.

The party left Paris on Saturday, the 27th of April, and proceeded through Melun to Fontainbleau. Mrs. Fry was furnished with a letter from the Minister of the Interior, granting her, Mr. Forster, and her husband, permission to visit all the prisons in France. This important document was first made use of at Melun, and on this occasion, as on every succeeding one, Mrs. Fry was received with respect, and every facility afforded her and her party, for inspecting the prisons.

The Prison at Melun contained upwards of a thousand men, thirty of whom were Protestants, and visited by their own minister, who supplied them with copies of the Scriptures; but on inquiring of the Chaplain (l'Aumônier) whether the Roman Catholics were allowed to possess the Bible, he evaded the question, by replying, " They have religious books."

In Lyons, where they arrived on the 4th of May, many objects of interest presented themselves. In the Prison of La Perrache, they saw a hundred and thirty-two lads under the care of fifteen of the Brethren of St. Joseph.

They also visited the Maison d'Arrêt or La Roanne, where they saw with pleasure, the beneficial effects of women being placed under the care of persons of their own sex ; ten or twelve Sisters of St. Joseph are here devoted to this work. Mrs. Fry expressed a few words, through an interpreter, exhorting them to repentance and faith, and speaking of the joy in heaven over one sinner that repenteth, which appeared to touch them.

They saw an institution under the care of the same Order of nuns, called La Solitude, where, as in the former instance, they were pleased with the Superior. The women were out for recreation ; the young persons " at a simple dance, for their amusement." The building commands a very fine view, and extensive garden ; and orchard attached to it. The inmates, about eighty in number, are either discharged prisoners, or vagrants; they are employed in washing, spinning, &c. Some were being trained as novices, eventually to enter the Order. The whole effect was neat and orderly.

Avignon, Fifth Month 9th.—We had no particular calls of duty until we arrived at Lyons, where there was a great press of engagements: prisons and refuges to inspect, besides many schools, of which I only had time to visit one—a woman's adult school. We had a large company of the poorer French Protestants on two different evenings, when we read with them. We also visited several of their houses; but it was more for serious conversation amongst them, than absolute religious engagement. We had one *very* important Meeting of influential people, in which I desired to speak the Truth in love. It was introduced by the Prison subject. I endeavoured to show, that change of heart could only be produced by Christian principles, as revealed to us in Holy Scripture, through the power of the Holy Spirit. This, I very boldly attested, and then strove to impress the importance of Christian example, and of religious duties being faithfully performed, both public and private. Then I entered upon useful societies, charities, and schools, with Christian instruction. We had much attention paid to us, much kindness shown to us, and I humbly trust, an impression made on many minds, and some humble valuable Christians comforted by our visit.

LETTER FROM ELIZABETH FRY.

Nismes, *Fifth Month 12th,* 1839.

My much loved Children,

I have been considering which is best, to write one full letter to you, or several notes, and I am come to the conclusion, now we are so far from home, and have so much to do, that it is better to write to you collectively: —— —— —— ——. We may thankfully say, we feel peaceful, and in our right place, although separated from many so very dear to us.

We paid a very interesting visit to Lyons, and found a good deal

new in the Prisons and Refuges. An order of Catholics, called the
Brethren and Sisters of St. Joseph, believe it their duty entirely,
to take care of prisoners and criminals generally. They do not
visit as we do, but take the entire part of turnkeys and prison-
officers, and live with the prisoners night and day, constantly
caring for them. I thought the effect on the female prisoners
surprisingly good, as far as their influence extended. But the
mixture of gross superstition is curious, the image of the Virgin
dressed up in the finest manner, in their different wards. I
feared, that their religion lay so much in form and ceremonies, that
it led from heart work, and from that great change which would
probably be produced, did these Sisters simply teach them Christianity. Their books appeared to be mostly about the Virgin ; not
a sign of Scripture to be found in either prison or refuge. I
felt it laid on me as a weighty, yet humbling duty, before I
left Lyons, to invite Roman Catholics and Protestants, who
had influence in the prisons, to come to our Hotel, and there,
in Christian love, to tell them the *truth* to the best of my
belief, as to the *only* real ground of reformation of heart, and
the means likely to conduce to this end. It was the more fearful,
as I had to be entirely interpreted for. My heart almost sank
within me as the time approached. It was about three o'clock in
the day, about sixty people came of the very influential Catholics
and Protestants, and I was enabled, through a most excellent
interpreter, to show them, that nothing but the pure simple
truth, as revealed in Scripture, through the power of the Holy
Spirit, could really enlighten the understanding or change the
heart. My husband and Josiah Forster also, took a very useful
and valuable part. *Much* satisfaction was expressed. We afterwards dined at a gentleman's, who lived in a lovely situation, on
the top of a hill near Lyons. Our invitations began to flow in,
and we should, I doubt not, had we stayed longer, soon have been
in as great a current as at Paris, or greater. We met with some
very interesting, devoted Christian characters : a cousin of
the Baroness Pelet's almost like herself ; her notes and flowers
coming in every morning. The last day was most fatiguing ;
we had to rise soon after three in the morning, for Avignon, to go
a hundred and fifty miles down the Rhone.

We have passed through the most delightful country I ever saw. Lyons, with the Rhone and Soane, is in its environs beautiful, and the passage from Lyons to Avignon really lovely ; mountains in the distance (parts of the Alps,) their tops covered with snow ; vegetation in perfection, the flowers of spring and summer in bloom at once, grass just ready to be cut, barley in the ear, lilacs, laburnums, syringas, roses, pinks, carnations, acacias in full bloom, yellow jessamine wild in the hedges. It is a sudden burst of the finest summer, combined with the freshness of spring. The olive groves, intermixed with abundant vineyards and mulberry groves, all beautiful from their freshness. The ancient buildings of Avignon, the ruins on the banks of the Rhone, the very fine and wonderful Roman remains of the aqueduct, called the Pont du Gard, really exceed description. This place also abounds in curious buildings. Here, or in the neighbourhood, we expect to remain some time.

We find the poor Friends delighted to see us, and the Protestants give us a hearty welcome. All these interests do not prevent our hearts being with you, and I am longing to know all about you —— —— —— ——.

I am,
Your most loving mother,
E. F.

At Avignon, Mrs. Fry's order to see the Prison, did not avail with the gaoler, when first presented to him. The guard-room was reached, but no further was she permitted to enter. But in the evening, at the Hotel, the Préfet was announced, with whom it was arranged to visit the prisons on the morrow. Mrs. Fry was accompanied by him, the Mayor, the Procureur du Roi, and several gentlemen. The prison once formed a part of the Papal palace : it is only one of passage for untried prisoners, or before removal to the Maisons Centrales. Like all old prisons, especially those not originally intended for the purpose, it is ill adapted to its present use ; but the rooms were clean, large, and airy. Excellent cells, for separation by night, were in process of construction. In the workroom, every operation of picking old rope, was being carried on, carding, spinning, and weaving it, until - it became a coarse strong wrapping-cloth, used to pack the madder grown in Provence for the English market.

From Avignon, the party proceeded to Nismes.

Nismes is perhaps more the centre of Protestantism, than any other place in France. There, Mrs. Fry made a longer tarriance than usual. For a week, she remained exceedingly interested by the various objects that presented themselves to her notice, and by the persons she met with. There exists at Nismes and in the neighbouring villages, a scattered body of people professing the principles of the Society of Friends. She and Mr. Forster visited with much interest all who resided at Nismes, and attended their Meetings. This simple, but interesting body of people are the descendants of the Camisards, who took refuge in the mountains of the Cevennes and fought valiantly for their faith, during the persecutions subsequent to the revocation of the Edict of Nantes. The Camisards were of the old stock of the Albigenses. The continual loss or imprisonment of their ministers, induced their ministering one to the other. At the cessation of hostilities, many of them persevered in a system, which, in the first instance, had resulted from circumstances. Towards the close of the last century, a man, named Paul Codognan, formed the project of giving a positive form to the belief and customs of this his little community, and prepared a work, though very imperfectly, on the subject. It was taken by one of the body to Holland, to be printed, and there he heard, for the first time, that in England and America there existed a people, who entertained . many of the same opinions as himself.

He proceeded to England, and became acquainted with the

Society of Friends ; to whom the existence of this little body of fellow-believers was thus made known.   Since that period, but more especially of late years, the community at Congenies has become an object of much interest to Friends in England, and has been visited from time to time by ministers and other members of that Society.

The Protestant pastor at Nismes, M. Frossard, with his lady were to Elizabeth Fry as providential helpers, such excellent interpreters, such true sympathizers!   Much kind attention was paid them by Dr. Pleindoux, who entertained them sumptuously, in his kindness óf heart thus marking his welcome.   After dinner, a still better entertainment awaited them, in interesting, important, and edifying conversation, amongst a large party of excellent persons.   Mrs. Fry took a lively interest in the great Maison Centrale at Nismes, containing about one thousand two hundred prisoners.   It is built on the site of the old citadel, from which, in the time of Louis XIV. the Protestants were attacked whilst holding their assemblies for divine worship.   In her first visit, besides Mr. Forster, Mrs. Fry was accompanied by M. Frossard, the Protestant chaplain, and M. Castelnau, the Surgeon of the prison.   The men were employed in vast workshops, in which silence was maintained.   In passing through two or three of these, she expressed her interest for the prisoners, her pity for them, and her desire for their repentance and amendment of life. She particularly desired to see the Cachots.   In the first were eight men ; they were placed there as a punishment for exacting usury of their fellow-prisoners ; for instance, lending them a franc when they came out of the infirmary, or when, from any other cause, they were without money, and receiving eight sous weekly as interest.   This practice had existed to a great extent, and is one of the many evils resulting from the cantine system. These men were discontented and clamorous, their appearance fierce and depraved.   Five armed soldiers were introduced into the cell with the visitors, to protect them from their violence. In the second cell, were eighteen men without employment. Into this, the visitors requested to be admitted alone. In the third, which was entirely dark, two were placed for refractory conduct ; one was chained both hands and feet. Mrs. Fry said to them, that she had sometimes, when she had seen men thus circumstanced, pleaded for their liberation, on the promise of future good behaviour, if she believed their promise to be sincere. The fettered prisoner immediately volunteered this promise, and was promptly released.

In this prison, besides the Roman Catholic chapel, served by the Aumônier, who resides in the prison, there is a Protestant chapel, in which daily service is performed by a pastor of that faith. This is attended by any prisoner who desires it ; besides the professed Protestants, about a hundred among the Roman Catholics, from preference, worshipped there. On occasion of Mrs. Fry's second visit, she was accompanied by her family party, as well as some of her particular friends ; the object being, to attend the religious service of the Protestant prisoners. The chapel was small, and the middle filled by depraved-looking men in their rough prison dress. At the top, in a semi-circle, sat the party of ladies and gentlemen, six or eight in number, with the Governor (Directeur) and Protestant Chaplain. At the bottom of the room, and around the door, clustered the gens-d'arms and gardiens (turnkeys) in their smart, soldier-like costume, to the number of ten or fifteen. The service commenced with singing a hymn. Then M. Frossard read beautifully the 24th Psalm ; after which, Elizabeth Fry spoke to the audience in one of her most impressive strains—translated for her by M. Frossard with such spirit and force, that it hardly lost in the change of language. She began in the most touching tone of voice, on the conversion of poor Mary Magdalene, her loving much, because forgiven much, her washing her Lord's feet, her being with Him at His death, watching at His tomb, and permitted first to see Him after His resurrection. It was the strongest encouragement to the repentant sinner. She then turned, and spoke in a strain of awful entreaty and solemn warning to the hardened and profane. The listening expression of all countenances showed how deeply her words impressed them. Many tears were shed; and she heard afterwards, that among these hardened men, a few instances of real repentance and amendment of life had occurred. On leaving the chapel and crossing a corridor, a gendarme brought two men out of a workroom to Mrs. Fry; they began to speak eagerly to her, one told her that he should never lie down in his bed without praying for and blessing her, whilst the other echoed the sentiment. They were the two men for whom, on her previous visit, she had interceded, that they might be liberated from the dungeon.

After that, she again visited the cells, accompanied by M. Fossard and a venerable grey-headed pasteur, one of the fathers of the French Protestant Church. They went without guard. The visit was interesting and satisfactory, and ended in a condign apology being offered by the culprits, and forgiveness granted by the governor; though so desperate were these men, that the governor of the prison had thought it prudent, unknown at the time to them or to the prisoners, to place soldiers in concealment near.

A few days afterwards, Mrs. Fry received this letter from one of the prisoners:—

"Nismes, *le* 19 *Mai*, 1839.

" Très-honorée Dame,

" La visite que vous avez bien voulue faire a de malheureux prisonniers, a été pour beaucoup de nous un grand sujet de consolation. Les paroles, pleines de bienveillance et de bonté que vous nous avez adressées, se sont profondément gravées dans nos coeurs.

" Nous sommes si peu accoutumés à voir des personnes étran- gerès et jouissant d'une considération si distinguée, et en même temps, si bien méritée, plaindre notre sort et nous offrir des conso- lations, que nous regrettons bien vivement de ne pouvoir souvent être honorés de vôtre visite.

" Ah ! s'il vous était possible, madame, de nous voir encore une fois, et d'assister dimanche prochain au service divin, vous nous combleriez de joie.   Car nous pensons que vos prières, jointes aux nôtres, ne pourraient manquer d'être agréables à Dieu, et qu'il nous donnerait la force et le courage nécessaires pour imiter nôtre Sauveur Jésus-Christ, qui s'est immolé pour nous en supportant les plus affreux tourmens avec patience, et en priant son Perè de pardonner à ceux qui le faisaient mourir.

" Daignez, honorée Dame,
          " Recevoir mes humbles respects,
               " Vôtre très-obéissant serviteur,
                    " M———.''

Congenies is a retired village, to the west of the road from Nismes to Montpellier ; about four leagues from the former place.

To abandon hotels, towns and high-ways, and diverge amongst lanes and cross roads, to spend a fortnight in a country village in France, amongst its simple inhabitants, was an event not without its great interest, and even amusement.   As it was considered necessary to take provisions, hampers well stocked with coffee, sugar, candles, &c., were piled upon the carriage, or the attendant van, which was also the Congenies and Cordognan diligence. The country became less and less interesting, although well culti- vated ; a group of grey flat roofs in a little hollow among the hills, was the first appearance of Congenies.   After passing some distance through the village street, the carriage stopped at the door of a large, dull, prison-like house, the windows barred with iron and the door at one side up a flight of eight or ten steps.

This was the house prepared for the reception of the travellers. A hall with no one single article of furniture ; an ante-room containing a buffet, a fire-place, and a couple of chairs ; and a saloon with white curtains to the windows, a table, and some rush-bottomed chairs ; all these vaulted, white-washed, and floored with stone, formed the suite of reception rooms.

Other rooms of the same character, communicated with the hall of entrance ; from which ascended a dark, wide stone staircase, leading to suites of rambling comfortless chambers. Various needful articles were willingly supplied by the friendly peasants—spoons were lent by one, by another a bed-side carpet for Mrs. Fry. A second table was arranged in the saloon, and after a day or two, a sort of homely comfort prevailed. The finest anchovies from the neighbouring Mediterranean, a cask of olives of the village produce, and sweet wine, made expressly at the last year's vintage, were prepared by these kind people.

The hostess had good store of white household linen, her kitchen was in high activity ; though provisions were uncertain and had to be obtained from Calvisson. The Savoyard waiter, who had accompanied them from Nismes, superintended the cooking. The day's bill of fare, hung by him on a nail in the kitchen, was an inexhaustible source of amusement to the village women, who were perpetually gossiping with the hostess, and watching with curiosity the proceedings of her foreign inmates. There was one peculiarity in this ménage, the usual operations of a scullery being carried on in the entrance hall ! where an old woman and girl had established themselves, with a broken down table and chair, perpetually flooding it, in process of cleansing all manner of pots and pans, iron and copper, and earthenware, red, yellow and green. The houses were mostly entered by cartgates, under an archway, beyond which a court-yard, filled with dust and straw, with chickens and rabbits running about. On one side of this court, or yard, was the sitting room, with a vine covered porch, under

which the women sate and knitted silk gloves and mittens.
An open outside flight of stairs led to the chambers. A stable
opposite the entrance, a well in one corner, and a cart under the
gateway,—such was the style of most of their dwellings. These
cottagers all possessed abundant supplies of table linen, and in
every house where Mrs. Fry dined, she found dinner napkins provided. Soup, one or two entrées, a roast of lamb or a fowl, salad
and vegetables composed the dinner.

Although there are no horned cattle, the villagers possess a
good many sheep and some goats, which gather a scanty subsis-
tence from the herbage of the rocky hills, where the vine cannot
grow. Their milk is excellent, and so is the butter made from it.
The flocks are invariably attended by a shepherd and strong dogs,
to protect from the wolves of the Cevennes mountains ; after
watering them at the fountain in stone troughs, a most picturesque
sight, they are folded in the village at night.

The Friends, in Congenies and the neighbouring villages,
appeared to be a respectable well-conducted body of people. Louis
Majolier was a valuable minister amongst them. Accompanied by
her friend Josiah Forster, Elizabeth Fry visited them all in their
families ; and regularly attended their Meetings for worship and
discipline, by which she became exceedingly interested in their
welfare. Their Meeting House was neat, and abundantly adequate to the needs of the congregation.

The women Friends wear their caps and peasant costume with,
perhaps, a graver shade of colour over the whole. The men in
their peasant dress. In all the villages round, there seemed a
most eager willing ear to hear the truths of the gospel. The
Meeting held at Congenies, on the last Sunday evening, was
crowded—the people clustered up to the top of the doors, in all
the open windows, and on the walls outside, yet in perfect
quietude and order. At Calvisson, on the following Sunday, it
was the same, the Meeting there was held in the Protestant

Temple. The party broke up from Congenies on the 27th, and after, again partaking of the abounding hospitalities of Doctor Pleindoux, at Nismes, proceeded by the ancient city of Arles to Marseilles.

Congenies, Fifth Month 22nd.—Yesterday was my birth-day, and it pleased my Heavenly Father in His love and pity, to cause it to be a day of remarkable peace, from the early morning to the evening. I felt it was not for works of righteousness, that I had done, but of His grace and His mercy, that I have thus known my soul to be refreshed in the Lord. Lord, continue to be with us ! lift up the light of Thy countenance upon us, and bless us all, absent and present ; and particularly at this time, I ask Thee to bless our labours among this people, to their solid good and Thy praise, Amen !

Sixth Month 2nd.—We found a great deal of what was highly-interesting in Congenies. A peculiar and new place to us. The country remarkable, much cultivated in parts, and planted with vineyards, mulberry, olive, and fig-trees, with but little corn. There is a very delightful air ; the hills rather barren and singularly grey, with fine ruins upon some of them, and here and there a peep at the Mediterranean. The little dull villages, much strewed about, thickly inhabited, mostly by Protestants, who appear generally in a low neglected state ; we visited some of these villages, and had larger or smaller Meetings in them. We found a great inclination in the people to hear the truth, and I believe there is a real thirst after it. I humbly trust that the blessing of the Lord was with us, as I have seldom felt more peace or more sense of this blessing, than when engaged in these labours of Christian love at Congenies, or a more clear belief that I was in my right place.

At Marseilles, Mrs. Fry visited several of the institutions. The first of these was described to her, as a refuge for female penitents. It was not without considerable difficulty, that she obtained permission to enter. She was accompanied by a Roman Catholic lady, a stranger to her, who consented to be the medium

of her introduction, and was called one of the Directresses. It
proved to be a regular convent, under the control of nuns of
the strict monastic order of St. Charles, who, in addition to the
three ordinary vows, add that of converting souls, and therefore
admit poor young women, under the name of " Pénitentes,"
into the convent. The lady Directresses were no longer permitted to see the penitents, or even to enter the building, with
the exception of the one charged with its repairs. She is
allowed to see the dilapidations, but not any of the sisters or
inmates. Mrs. Fry and her companions were introduced into a
large, comfortable parlour, plainly furnished : on one side was a
close double grating, painted black, with black shutters behind,
extremely gloomy looking. Chairs had been placed for them
in front of the grating. After Mrs. Fry and her companions
had waited some time, the shutters were opened by the " Supérieure," a handsome woman of about thirty years of age. The
object of Mrs. Fry's journey was explained to her, which led
to a long and interesting conversation, in which the talents of
this lovely Abbess were abundantly displayed, and she proved
herself thoroughly mistress of her subject. She informed them,
that the number of penitents admitted are a hundred and five,
that they are not permitted to become Nuns in that Order, but
when the vocation is very strong, they may do so in others—
that more than half are converted, that most become servants,
and if well-behaved, are still cared for by the nuns. None
are compelled to enter or are retained against their will, although
encouraged by every means to stay. Some have remained nine
years.

They are not taught to read or write ; neither is the least
morsel of paper, pencil, pen, ink, or any other possible material
for writing, permitted, from the fear of their communicating with
people without. The day is spent in a perpetual round of
work, embroidery, recreation, recitation of prayers, psalms, &c.

The nuns were in number forty. They came from Tours about eighteen months previously, to take charge of this establishment. Upon Mrs. Fry's speaking of the importance of the Gospel for such persons, she informed them, that it was in parts read to them, and admitted that the history of Mary Magdalene, and the parables of the prodigal son, the piece of silver, and the lost sheep, were fit and good for them ; she added, that she found parts of Isaiah and all the Psalms suited to them ; but then went on, as Roman Catholics are wont to do, to urge the unsuitableness of the Scriptures, as a whole, especially parts of the Old Testament, for people in general. Mrs. Fry spoke of the sufferings of Christ for sinners, and salvation through Him : all which the nun united in. Indeed, to judge from her report, nothing could be better conducted than this institution.

The Abbess related a long history of one of the Pénitentes, who had died, only an hour before, the " death of an angel and a saint." But who, that has read the human heart, or traced the history of mankind individually or in collective bodies, has not detected a love of power, and an abuse of that power when obtained, which renders a system of secrecy and seclusion, with absolute authority, an evil liable to terrible abuse. Nuns directed by churchmen. Woman always extreme for good or ill, guided by superstition—herself a slave, employed to enslave others. If prisoners or penitents are committed to the care of monastic orders, justice assuredly demands the oversight and superintendence of the magistracy, and that these unhappy persons should be never placed beyond the reach of the secular arm.

From this establishment of darkness and mystery, Mrs. Fry went to a very different one, called " La Maison des Orphelines du Cholera." It was under the especial care of the Abbé Fisseaux, an active, intelligent young man, apparently devoted to doing good. The children were in excellent order. He accompanied the party to an interesting and prosperous little institu-

tion, founded by himself, called "La Maison des Jeunes Détenus, or Nouvel Pénitentiaire," for twenty-eight young delinquents, boys. They had all been committed for theft, and
collected from the different prisons of the department. They
appeared very kindly cared for by the Abbé; they sleep separately at night, with the exception of some, who, for good conduct, are permitted to be together in one apartment. The town
prison contained more than sixty prisoners; the women in a
separate part of the building; but there was no further classification, not even the tried from the untried, nor any employment.
After this, Mrs. Fry visited a large Hospital, in which were four
English sailors from ships in the port. One of these recognised
her, having seen her on board a female convict-ship, in the
River Thames, and greeted her as though she were an old and
valued friend. He informed those, who accompanied her, who
she was, which they had not previously understood. This
fatiguing day was concluded by dining at Monsieur Rabat's.

Hyères, *Sixth Month 2nd.*

My much-loved Children,

I now mean to sit quietly down and communicate with you.
Orange groves in flower, with here and there a little fruit, in
abundance around me, and a lovely blue sea with hills and islands
before me. We are at a small pleasant hotel, where we walk out
of our bed-room and saloon on-to a sort of brick terrace, part of
which, has vines and roses over a lattice-work, and an awning.
Here we take our meals, and with the abundance of fruit and
vegetables our tastes have been rather uncommonly gratified. The
beauty of the scene, the fragrance of the orange flower, the nice-
ness of the fruit; the air also, so warm, fresh and delightful:
that we could not but wish that you could have taken a peep
at us when seated round our table. This is the farthest distance that we expect to be from home; therefore, I hope to-
morrow, that we may feel we are turning our faces thitherward.

On Monday, June 3rd, Mrs. Fry returned from Hyères to

Toulon. The next morning, accompanied by the Protestant pastor and a naval captain, appointed to do so by the Préfet de la Marine, she and her companions visited the Bagnes; on their way seeing the Arsenal, at one extremity of which is the Bagnes, or prison for the galley-slaves (galériens); they work hard, sleep on the boards, eat only bread and dry beans, with half a bottle of wine to those who work. Many of them die. The returns are considerable, as from the close communication, the contagion of evil is fearful. A man, who is vicious when he goes in, inevitably comes out more so. They sleep in vast galleries, a hundred or two hundred in each, chained to a long iron rod which runs the whole length of the foot of the sleeping board. There is a salle, which contains four hundred, for those who have improved in conduct, and to them mattresses are allowed and rugs. In their leisure hours they are allowed to make and sell little carved toys and netting. Their look is generally unhealthy. The dress— a red cap and jacket, and the greater number fastened two and two by heavy chains; notwithstanding this, they often escape. One Englishman, taken on board a slaver was amongst them.

This was a day of extraordinary fatigue. Mrs. Fry went in the afternoon to see the town prison. Some poor Algerine women were confined there. She was accompanied by the Sous Préfet and his lady, who is a regular prison visitor.

From Toulon to Aix,—once the centre of Provençal song, and where King Réné held his court surrounded by his Troubadours. There, her heart was attached by a lively little Protestant congregation, under a zealous and apparently spiritual pastor. A great contrast to the scene which met her view, on turning into the Course on her arrival,—the procession of the Fête Dieu in all its tinsel finery.

From Aix, the travellers returned to Nismes. The subject of a District Society was much discussed. Sunday, the 10th, was passed there.

Sixth Month.—Our First-day at Nismes was deeply weighty in prospect, so that I rested little at night, as I had ventured to propose our holding one Meeting in the morning, in the Methodist chapel, that whoever liked might attend it; and in the evening, to do the same in a very large school-room, that all classes might attend, as I believed that all would not come to a Methodist Meeting. I went prostrated before the Lord, to this Meeting in the morning, hardly knowing how to hold up my head; I could only apply for help to the inexhaustible Source of our sure mercies, feeling that I could not do it, either on account of myself, or because it was the work in which I was engaged; but I could do it for the sake of my Lord, and that His kingdom might spread. Utterly unworthy did I feel myself, but my Lord was gracious. My dear interpreter, C. Majolier, was there to help me in a very large Meeting, and I felt power wonderfully given me to proclaim the truths of the Gospel, and to press upon the point of the Lord Himself being our teacher, immediately by His Spirit, through the Holy Scriptures, and by His Providences and works; and to show, that no teaching so much conduced to growth in grace, as the Lord's teaching. There was much attention; at the close, I felt the spirit of prayer much over us, longed for its vocal expression, and felt a desire some one might pray, when a Methodist minister, in a feeling manner, expressed a wish to offer something in prayer, to which, of course, we assented; it proved solemn and satisfactory.

We dined at our dear friends, the Pasteur Emilien Frossard's; he and his wife have been like a brother and sister to us; we were also joined by a Roman Catholic gentleman and his daughter. He has, I think, been seriously impressed by our visit, and it has led him to have the Scriptures read to his workmen. There were also Louis Majolier, his daughter, and a young English friend. I think I have very seldom in my life felt a more lively sense of the love of God, than at his table. I may say, our souls were animated under its sweetness. I think we rejoiced together, and magnified the name of our God.

In the evening, we met in a large school-room that would contain some hundreds, where numbers assembled, principally the French Protestants and some of their pastors. There, again, I was greatly helped, I really believe, by the Holy Spirit, to speak to them upon their very important situations in the Church of Christ, and the extreme consequence of their being sound both in faith and practice. I also felt it my duty to show them, as Protestants, the infinite importance, not only in France, but in the surrounding nations, of their being as a city set upon a hill that cannot be hid. I showed them how the truth is spreading, and how important to promote it, by being preachers of righteousness in life and conversation, as well as in word and doctrine. There was here also much attention ; and our dear and valued friend and brother in Christ, Emilien Frossard, prayed beautifully, that the word spoken might profit the people, and particularly, that the blessing of the Lord might rest upon me. It was no common prayer on my behalf. Thanks to my Heavenly Father, the Meeting broke up in much love, life, and peace.

The next morning Josiah Forster and myself held a large meeting, partly in the open air, at the village of Codognan. I was pleased to see many of our dear friends from Congenies and the neighbourhood, at this our last meeting in this part. We separated from them under a lively feeling of true peace and much love, and concluded our services under a strong confidence that our feet had been rightly turned amongst them : a pastor, a stranger to us, closed the Meeting in solemn and beautiful prayer.

After this, we proceeded on our journey to Montpellier, where important service opened for us. A Protestant Ladies' Committee was formed to visit the great Female Prison there ; much important advice offered to the Governor upon the changes now being made in the prison, and female officers being appointed ; we appeared to go in the very time wanted, and obtained the liberation of several poor women from their very sad cells. The Préfet was most kind to us, and thus, our way was easily made, the Mayor and all with us. Help was given me to speak religiously to the poor women, before all these gentlemen.

This was a Maison Centrale, and contained five hundred women, for whom it was exclusively used. The prisoners were employed in work-rooms ; some resistance had been shown on their part to the introduction of the female officers, so that this visit was useful and timely. Mrs. Fry visited this prison again the following day, and had a long conversation at her Hotel, with the Director and the new Matron, on their important duties. After this, she met a number of Protestant ladies at the Pastor Losignol's, who had waited for her arrival to form themselves into a regular Committee for visiting the Protestant women, both in the Prison and Hospital; this Committee was then regularly organized, and was, as well as that formed at Marseilles, to correspond with the Committee in Paris. In the evening she returned to the Pastor Losignol's, as she supposed, to spend a quiet social evening, but found instead, a large congregation assembled for a religious meeting. There were rich and poor, all ages, and the place so crowded, that the windows were lined with listeners, and boys perched upon the trees beyond.

The day the party left Montpellier, Mrs. Fry diverged to Cette, and crossing the Lagune of Thon, in the boat of an English merchant's vessel, rejoined her companions at Meze, a little fishing village on its banks; the British Consul and his lady came with her, and the captain of the merchantman. It was a temperance ship, and he a serious man. Whilst waiting at Meze, to avoid the mid-day sun, Mrs. Fry wrote to her friend John Carey, Esquire, in Guernsey, to interest him on behalf of the British seamen frequenting the port of Cette.

To JOHN CAREY, ESQ., CASTLE CAREY, GUERNSEY.

Meze, South of France, *Sixth Month* 13*th*, 1839.

MY DEAR AND VALUED FRIEND,

In a tour that my husband and myself, accompanied by our friend Josiah Forster, are taking, we have had the satisfaction of meeting with Richard Ryan and his amiable wife; he is British Consul at Cette; I understand that they are friends of yours, therefore, the application I am about to make appears to be almost needless, as they could represent the case better than I am likely to do it. I understand that there are several ships from various countries that call at Cette, in which many of the crews speak English, therefore, it would be highly desirable for them to be well supplied with English Testaments and Bibles, and tracts ; and it is so difficult to get them here from England, that I venture to propose, a few of our Guernsey friends inducing their different Bible Societies each to send some copies of the Holy Scriptures ; and I also thought, with your usual kindness, some of you would give some English tracts. I believe my dear friend Sophia Mourant would do her part, and by several others, each doing a little, much would be accomplished. I thus apply to my dear friends, because I find that ships not unfrequently visit Cette from Guernsey.

We are deeply interested in our visit to France, where we find many devoted characters, and we do believe that truth is spreading in this interesting land. We find the weather very warm, and are rather oppressed by it, but we are generally favoured with health.

I think of our dear Guernsey and Jersey friends with much gratitude and love, and desires for their present and everlasting welfare. I wish to be affectionately remembered to those in Guernsey.

And am, with dear love to thy wife and family, and also to Sophia Mourant, and affectionate remembrance to all thy brothers and sisters whom I know.

Thy affectionate and obliged friend,

ELIZABETH FRY.

In the evening, of this fatiguing day, when resting and refreshing themselves at the Hotel at Béziers, the Sous-Préfet was announced, he having been requested by the Préfet at Montpellier, to show Mrs. Fry attention during her visit to Béziers. He was anxious she should see the prison and hospital, but all arrangements had been made to set off again at five in the morning, and therefore, fatigued as she was, she consented to accompany him to the prison. It had become quite dark as this little band threaded its way through the narrow winding streets of Béziers,—how altered since those streets ran blood, at the time of the first crusade against the Albigéois, when the papal legate gave order to the Roman Catholic chieftains "to kill all, for God knows those who are His."

The astonished gaoler, candle in hand, followed by his myrmidons, answered the thundering rap of the Sous-Préfet, and the mastiffs which were prowling in the yards having been chained up, the prison, (a badly constructed and ill-arranged one), was inspected.

In returning to the Hotel, they paid a visit to the Cathedral, a vast, lofty, gothic building of one aisle and transepts, which had been lighted up to receive them. The effect was magnificent, illumined by a glare of partial light from the various altars, and the lamps carried by the attendants.

Saturday the 15th, was a cloudy day and travelling comparatively easy. Quiet, cool rooms at the Hotel de France, at Toulouse, afforded the travellers a most welcome retreat, for the heat had become extreme, the sun pouring down his rays, with overwhelming intensity, and adding greatly to fatigue, whilst the nature of their engagements forbade rest during the mid-day hours. The early morning, or cool of the evening being unsuited for visiting prisons and hospitals.

On Sunday evening, Mrs. Fry and her party went to the Scripture-reading, held at the house of M. Chabaut the pasteur, which is attended regularly by many of his congregation. Amongst others, a captain in the French army, a captain in the British navy, and a sergeant belonging to one of the regiments quartered there—all devoted Christian characters. They heard with pleasure of many really serious soldiers in the regiments then in Toulouse; so many, that at the Scripture-readings which took place, two evenings in the week, at the house of the

Messrs. Courtois, two long benches were often filled by them ; three or four more being occupied by young men inquiring after religious truth.

There are about six hundred Protestants at Toulouse, in the midst of a population of seventy thousand Roman Catholics. So lately as 1760, a Protestant was martyred there having first been broken on the wheel. The sentence and report of his execution are still to be seen in the archives of the town.

M. Chabaut considered, that from the time the British army occupied Toulouse in 1814, the Protestants had been held in higher estimation. Instead of taking possession of the Cathedral, as was generally anticipated at Toulouse, the victorious army worshipped in the humbler temple of their Protestant brethren, those hours being chosen when the French service was not going forward. The English regiments were seen marching to the Temple, headed by their officers, where the service of the Anglican Church was performed for them, by the chaplains of the army.

JOURNAL RESUMED.

We proceeded from place to place until we arrived at Toulouse, on Seventh-day evening, the 15th of the Sixth Month. On First-day evening, we met a large number of Protestants at one of their Scripture-readings. We took part in the service ; at the close, a solemn prayer was offered for us by Francis Courtois, one of a very remarkable trio of brothers, (bankers there) all three of whom are given up to the service of their Lord, and appear to have been instruments greatly blessed. Their kindness to us was very great. In Toulouse we visited two prisons ; had one important Prison Meeting, and one exceedingly solemn and satisfactory Scripture-reading and time of prayer, with the Courtois family, one or two pastors, and other religious persons.

I left my husband who was unwell from the heat at Toulouse, and went in faith and somewhat in the cross to Montauban ; the place, where the ministers of the Protestant Church of France are educated ; but I believed it right to go : Josiah Forster accompanied me.

Mrs. Fry's determined perseverance had surmounted every obstacle as long as her physical powers permitted ; but they were beginning to fail. Rest, and some cessation from mental and bodily labour, had become indispensable, and she yielded, though not without reluctance, to her husband's wish for a short tarriance in the cooler atmosphere of the Pyrenees. Speaking of this retreat, she says,—

We went from Toulouse to Bagnères de Louchon, a most lovely place, where we had a sweet, quiet lodging. I went two wonderfully fine excursions with my husband and children, (Josiah Forster partly with us,) which I rather enjoyed, particularly going into Spain.

One of these expeditions was to the Lake D'Oo. The gentlemen of the party, who were on horseback, having gone on, Mrs. Fry and her daughter found themselves, when about half way up a steep ascent, on a little level of green sward, shadowed by a huge rock. They left their chairs for the carriers to rest themselves. A group of wild-looking peasants were reposing near. Mrs. Fry sate down by them, and entered into conversation : they assured her they " adored the Virgin in those parts ;" she took out her French Text-Book ; the eight bearers joined the party. She read some words of Scripture, then drew their attention to the wonderful works of God in creation, in the beautiful scene around them ; from thence, she led to His infinite mercy in giving a Saviour to die for them. They listened with earnestness and respect, and thankfully received the little books she offered.

To her children in England.

Bagnères de Louchon, *Sixth Month* 23*rd.*

Here I sit before breakfast, with a most lovely scene before me. On entering this solemn Sabbath morning—my soul and body refreshed, not only in admiring the wonderful works of the outward creation, and being revived by the delightful air, fresh from

the snowy mountains before me; but what is more, my soul
refreshed. I have been enabled to lift my heart to my Heavenly
Father, for every brother, sister and child individually, and for
my dear husband; and collectively, for my many beloved ones;
committing all to His holy keeping. I feel rest. And now
my beloved children, I will tell you a little how we go on.

My attraction homewards grows stronger and stronger, but
I desire patiently to wait the right time: the openings for
religious service are greater than I expected, more particularly
amongst the Protestants, at Montpellier, Toulouse, and Montauban. At Montauban, without expressing any other wish,
than to have an evening party at one of their houses, to meet
some of the professors and students of the College (the only one
in France for educating Pasteurs for the Reformed Church).
We found, to our dismay, all arranged to receive us in the
College; and on arriving there, imagine how I felt, when the
Dean of the College offered me his arm, to take me into
the chapel. There, I believe, the whole of the collegians were
assembled, in all at least a hundred. It was fearful work. There
were also numbers of the people of the town; we thought about
three hundred. Josiah Forster spoke first, explaining our views
at some length. Then I rose, with an excellent interpreter, one
of their pasteurs; I first told them something of my Prison experience, and the power of Christian principle and kindness; then,
I related a little of the state of their prisons in France; then,
my ideas as to the general state of France; and afterwards,
endeavoured to bring home to them the extreme importance of
their future calling, as pasteurs in their church. I reminded
them of that passage of Scripture, "the leaders of the people
caused them to err." I endeavoured to show them how awful
such a state of things must be, and the extreme importance of
their being sound in doctrine and practice. Simple duty led me
to Montauban. Josiah F. was my kind and useful companion.
We were united in much Christian love to many there. I forgot
to say, that at the close of the occasion, the pasteur who interpreted for me, prayed beautifully and spiritually, that the words
spoken might profit the people; he also prayed for us: this has frequently occurred at the close of some of our interesting meetings,

a pouring forth of the spirit of prayer has been granted. My not knowing the language has obstructed my offering it, and it has appeared laid upon others instead. I have seldom felt sweeter peace in leaving a place than Montauban. At Toulouse, we were deeply interested by the Courtois' brothers : they appear, body, soul, and spirit, devoted to the service of their Lord ; quite a bright example to all of us. The world appeared as nothing to them. I have seldom seen men so wholly given up to the good and useful objects ; they were most kind to us. We had various calls of duty in that town, and I had a most excellent interpreter in François Courtois. We arrived here yesterday evening, after serious consideration, believing it the best to pursue this course. A certain time of quiet appears really needful to make representations to the French government, and to those in authority, of the various evils that want remedy in prisons, &c. We understand there are many seeking, serious minds, to whom we may be of some comfort, which helps to reconcile us to the measure.

During this recess, Mrs. Fry, assisted by Mr. Forster and her husband prepared a long memorial for the Minister of the Interior, and a shorter one for the Prefet of Police, embodying her observations on the state of the prisons she inspected, and her recommendation for their improvement.

The evils of the Cantine system, and the large sleeping apartments, affording every facility for evil and unrestricted communication, were the points on which she most strongly insisted ; though she also entered into various details of particular prisons requiring alteration.

From Bagnères de Luchon, they went to Bagnères de Bigorre.

Wednesday the 3rd, they left Bagnères de Bigorre, entering the gorge that leads to Luz and St. Sauveur. They passed the ruined castle of St. Marie, built by the English ; the Templar's Fortress-church at Luz, and pursued their way to St. Sauveur. There they remained some days, amidst the shadowy mountains which surround the town, and the rushing waters not alone of the Gaves, or rapid rivers of the district, but of the hundred little rivulets which feed them, tumbling and foaming from the heights above.

On the 8th, they departed for Pau. The drive was beautiful, the country familiarised by Froissard's descriptions, through the valley of Argellez, and by the old castle of Lourdes. Pau delighted them. In the birth-place of one, for a time the hero of the Protestant Faith, there is still a small body of Christian believers, untainted by the errors of Romanism, and adhering to the pure and simple faith of their forefathers. A few Protestants were found at Tarbes. With them Mrs. Fry had a Meeting, and was exceedingly interested by them and their pasteur M. Doudret.

St. Sauveur, Seventh Month 4th.—We left Bagnères de Bigorre, on the 3rd of the Seventh Month. I had a painful journey, having met with rather a serious accident, falling backwards, from a stool slipping from under me; besides this, my throat was very sore, but I desired to be patient and thankful that I was not worse. We arrived at this most beautiful place in the evening, I felt better, and to-day am quiet, peaceful and in great degree refreshed.

Very little service opened in the last places we were at. I formed a fund to assist the poor afflicted persons who come to the baths at Luchon, and at Bagnères de Bigorre, visited the prison; two poor sick prisoners were liberated in consequence, and placed in a comfortable hospital. I also had a serious reading of the Holy Scriptures, with many English who came to see us at our hotel, and a time of prayer; but the openings for service were small, which was a discouragement to me. I may however say, that through every discouragement, I commit myself, my all, and my work to the Lord, and believe that I may go on quietly and hopefully, trusting that day by day, and hour by hour, my Holy Head will not forsake me, but be my Guide and my Guard, and be with us all even unto the end. Our returning home through Switzerland, I still view very doubtfully. Unless Thy presence go with us, oh Lord! take us not there or to any other place.

z 2

Grenoble, 22*nd.*—We remained a few days at St. Sauveur, which was refreshing and satisfactory, with some sweet Christian friends. We visited the great military hospital at Barèges, and obtained leave to introduce the New Testament and I hope a library also. The men appeared much pleased with our visit.

By permission of the Directeur, the party distributed about two hundred tracts that day among the patients. They remained over the following Sabbath at St. Sauveur, holding a little Meeting in their room in the morning, whilst an English clergyman had service in his parlour. In the evening most of the English (two clergymen among the number), assembled in Mrs. Fry's rooms and a very solemn religious meeting was held. Meanwhile at the Catholic Chapel, a sermon was preached, warning the people against the little books that the Protestant visitors might distribute, especially "one lady, who went up even into the mountains to give them away." These were all to be given to the priest, or committed to the flames, unread, on pain of excommunication. This allusion, probably, did not relate to Mrs. Fry, as it so happened, that she had not distributed books there, or ascended the mountains.

I felt best satisfied to stay over First-day, that such of the English as might incline, should join us in our worship in the evening, a good many came, we were I believe really helped together; and I was enabled to speak the truth to them in Christian love. We set off the next morning for Canterots, another of these beautiful places, taking it in our way to Pau. There we were much interested and pleased, visited three little bodies of Protestants, serious, agreeable people, who appeared glad to see us, and, we trust, are a little helped by our visit. From Pau we returned to Toulouse, where we spent a Sabbath, and had a farewell Meeting with the Protestants. We parted with them in uncommon love and unity, and the prayers offered for us in this Meeting, and on other occasions have been to me very encouraging and comforting. May our Lord in His love and pity answer them !

We left Toulouse last Second-day, and have been travelling rather hard through the south of France, the heat very oppressive. Little religious service opened on the way. But at Montpellier and Nismes, we again met some of our dear friends, and there appeared reason to believe that our labour had not been in vain in the Lord, particularly at Nismes and Congenies. Oh, may our Heavenly Father, bless and prosper the seed scattered by us His unworthy instruments ; and may He in His tender and unmerited mercy, guide and guard us to the end ! Answer I pray Thee, the deep cries of Thy servant for Thine own name sake, and cause Thy love and peace to abound in our little circle until we separate.

Bönigen, near Interlachen, Switzerland, Eighth Month 11*th.* —I believe that my gracious Lord has guided our steps to this place,' blessed be His name. Now to go on with my journal. At Grenoble, where I felt rather pressed in spirit, to spend a First-day, I had a curious opening for religious service, and I believe an important one with several enlightened Roman Catholics, several Protestants, and a school of girls. It was a time of spiritual refreshment, by which many appeared helped and comforted. The next day was occupied in important prison visits, and in the evening a Meeting with influential Roman Catholics.

The prison at Grenoble, is an old and ill-constructed building, but kept very clean, and its defects and the wants of the prisoners as much remedied as possible, by an active Committee of ladies and gentlemen, who pay much attention to the bodily wants of the prisoners. The moral and religious instruction did not appear so well cared for, although they saw one man reading de Sacy's New Testament. The funds of these Committees are chiefly derived from money dropped into a box at the gate, by the peasants and lower class of persons, to obtain the prayers of the prisoners, which are considered by them peculiarly efficacious in releasing souls from purgatory : it often amounts to as much as eighty francs in a fortnight, which is chiefly expended in linen for the prisoners' use. The chaplain occasionally employing some of the better sort of prisoners, to say the prayers for the souls.

The Government and authorities have tried to put this system of the " tronc" entirely down, but have been successfully opposed by the Committee, on the ground that they have neither power nor right to interfere with private almsgiving, its purpose or appropriation.

Josiah Forster having left us to go by diligence to Geneva, we travelled alone through Savoy, and had a pleasant journey through a lovely country ; but the darkness of the Roman Catholic religion, and the arbitrary laws not allowing even a tract to be given away, were painful (we found that a Swiss gentleman had lately been imprisoned for doing it, and confined with a thief.) We arrived at Geneva, the 25th of the Seventh Month, in the evening. Here we passed a very interesting time, from various and impor- tant openings for religious service, in large parties, in prisons, &c. My belief is, that we were sent to that place, and amidst some trials, from different causes there was a pouring forth of spiritual help and spiritual peace. Many of the pasteurs came to us, and not a few expressed their refreshment and satisfaction with our visit ; before we left, several of the most spiritual, in a very striking and beautiful manner preached to us, particularly to myself, and prayed for us all, a time, I think, never to be forgotten by us. We had one of the most beautiful entertainments I ever saw, given by Colonel Tronchin, at a lovely place, a few miles from Geneva, the fine snowy mountains about us, the lake within sight. In an avenue, in the midst of a fine wood, we had a handsome repast, to which about a hundred persons sat down. The gentleman who gave it, is a devoted Christian, a man of large property, and this blessing sanctified by grace. I visited a delightful institution for the sick of his establishment and on his grounds ; to return to our entertainment, grace was very solemnly said before our meal, and very beautiful hymn-singing afterwards. Then we withdrew into the house, where I believe the anointing was poured forth upon me, to speak the truth in love and power. I had an excellent spiritually minded interpreter ; many appeared to feel this occasion. A young English gentleman came up to me afterwards, and expressed his belief that it would influence him for life ; and a lady came to me, and said, how remarkably her state had been spoken to. Much love was also shown to us and unity. Indeed, I felt how our Lord permits His servants to rejoice together in love, and even to partake of the good things of this life, in His love and fear, with a subjected spirit rejoicing in His mercies, temporal and spiritual. We had very great kindness also shown us by many, among others, by our dear friend Mary Ann Vernet and her family, including her daughter, the Baroness de Stael, with whom we dined at Coppet. The Duke de Broglie and his family were with her ; we had a very interesting visit. We went from Geneva to our dear friend Sophia Delessert, her husband was out ; they have a beautiful place on the banks of the Lake of Geneva, near Rolle ; here we had the warmest reception, and were refreshed and comforted together, she is truly loved by me.

Mrs. Fry was much struck with the completeness of the " Maison Penitentiaire" at Geneva. There were only fifty prisoners under a Directeur, Sous Directeur M. Grelet, brother of Stephen Grelet, and many guardians. The prisoners are divided into four classes, perfectly separated from each other, and their treatment varying in severity. They work and eat in common, each class in its own atelier ; they also recreate each in the yard of the class, but sleep in separate cells ; in every cell is a bed, a chair, table, shelf and some books. For the Protestants, Ostervald's Bible is provided ; for the Catholics, the Manuel du Chrétien : they are here for long terms of imprisonment. The returns, fourteen to the hundred ; but the health fails after the first or second year.

The second time she visited it, the prisoners were assembled in the chapel, for Mrs. Fry to have a religious opportunity with them. The Catholic priest however did not allow his flock to be present.

The same thing occurred at the Evéché, an old bad prison,

about to be pulled down ; the priest was there, purposely to prevent the four or five Roman Catholic women being present,
should Mrs. Fry speak to the women, unless she would promise
only to enforce " morality," and not touch on religion or Christian faith. She assured him she never touched upon the
" dogmes" of religion, only on the great principles of faith and
practice. This would not do, and the Catholic women were
withdrawn ! !

At Lausanne, we met with a kind friend, Charles Scholl,
whom we knew in England, a valuable pasteur. We visited the
prisons ; and with the women I had a religious time, one that
appears to have made a considerable impression upon some of
them. I have had very comforting accounts since I was there.
A good many ladies and some gentlemen, met Josiah Forster and
myself at a lady's house, where the subject of prisons was entered
upon. In the evening we met a very large party, numbers of
pasteurs, &c., at a gentleman's beautiful place on the banks of
the lake ; here again we had a deeply interesting time. I had
to speak for some time, showing the effect of Christian principle
and kindness on prisoners. I was well interpreted for, by my
friend Charles Scholl. In conclusion, one valuable pasteur read,
and another prayed ; and prayed much for my preservation in my
peculiar situation, and that I might not be entangled by the many
snares that surrounded me. Much love and real unity we felt
with many of these dear people. We then proceeded to Berne
by Friburg ; at Berne I again visited the Prison. These Penitentiaries at Geneva, Lausanne, and Berne, interested me much,
as excellent ; still there are some things wanting. At Berne, I
had also a religious time with all the female prisoners. We
visited the large and interesting institution of Dr. Fellenburg
for boys, with which I was much pleased ; but I desired more
reading of the Holy Scriptures, and spoke and wrote to him on
the subject. We had a very hospitable reception to dinner, invited for half-past eleven, from a gentleman and his lady. At
the prison, I was at first badly interpreted for, when a young
lady, Sophia Werstemburger, came forward, as she has since told

me, from believing it a duty, and offered to assist me. It was striking to me to observe, how remarkably she appeared helped to do it, and to convey my meaning.

The subject of this address was afterwards embodied in a German tract, and has been extensively diffused in prisons.

After this visit, we parted from our dear friend Josiah Forster, in love and unity, and I may add, grateful to him for his constant kindness, and faithful and industrious endeavour to help me in my various duties. May it please the Lord to grant him his reward, in a further knowledge of Himself, and of the rest, peace and liberty that He gives His children and people. We went from Berne to Thun, and then to this beautiful, delightful and interesting country, where I have almost entirely devoted myself to my dearest husband and children. We have had some sweet and refreshing times together. I have rested as beside the still waters, at times refreshed in body, mind and spirit, so as to be able to rejoice in my Lord, and glory in the God of my salvation.

In the midst of mountains and waterfalls.

Eighth Month 18*th.*

MY DEAREST H——,

We are come here for thy father, K—— and H——, to see one of the finest waterfalls in Europe. After a curious walk with a boy, my guide, who only spoke German, I have come to our pretty Hotel, where we are to have luncheon ; and happily I have found ink and paper. I often long for you to see some of my droll and entertaining communications with those to whom I cannot speak. By small papers and little tracts, that I have in German, I manage to show some interest in those around me ; at least a certain degree of pleasant feeling is excited, and they bring little presents of flowers in return for tracts and marks of kindness. I was amused just now in my walk, at being joined by three girls, as well as my boy guide, who began to chatter to me in German, and some things we at last made each other understand.

Switzerland is certainly a wonderful country, and very attrac-

tive, but I think not more so than the Pyrenees. Sweet as it
is, the flats of East and West Ham look to *us* sweeter.

I have much felt on this journey, that life itself is but a
journey, and how important to feel it so much so as to keep
the end constantly in view; not over anxious respecting the
changes to which we are subject, but going steadily forward
through clouds and sunshine, ups and downs, trusting to the
wisdom, love and mercy of our Guide, and His power to aid us
when walking through dangerous places. I also desire to commit
more constantly our "fellow-pilgrims" to the same holy and
sufficient Helper. I want to be more without carefulness, and
to have more hopefulness.

But in the midst of rest and relaxation, Mrs. Fry did not forget her objects ; she called on the pasteur at Grindenvald, found
his flock large, scattered, and she feared, ignorant. The Bible
Society's operations did not appear to have reached this place ;
Bibles being scarce amongst them.

When on the Lake of Brienz, a poor boy who rowed the boat
told her his mother lay sick in a cottage which he pointed out.
It rested on her mind, and when crossing the lake, she landed
not without difficulty ; the wife of the pasteur of Brienz was
with her. They found the poor woman very ill on a mattress
spread in the gallery of her cottage, with her Bible by her
side ; she was an afflicted discouraged Christian woman, to whom
the few words of encouragement offered were very timely, to
strengthen that which, through bodily suffering, seemed almost
ready to die.

Zurich, Eighth Month 25*th.*—We left our sweet little home
at Bönigen, on the banks of the Lake of Brienz, last Fourth-day.
I felt refreshed by our visit to this lovely country. I think my
prayers have been heard and answered, in its being a very uniting
time with those most tenderly beloved by me. We have had
some interesting communications with serious persons in the
humble walk of life, who reside in that neighbourhood. We have

desired to aid them spiritually and temporally, but the difficulty of communication has been very great, from want of suitable interpreters ; still, I trust, that some were edified and comforted. I also hope our circulation of books and tracts has been useful, and the establishment of at least one library at Brienz, for the use of the labouring classes. We have travelled along gently and agreeably by Lucerne, and through a delightful country.

Ludwigsburg, (a few miles from Stuttgard), Ninth Month 1*st.*—On the evening of the day that I wrote at Zurich, we went with our very dear friend La Baronne Pelet, afterwards joined by the Baron, to the house of that ancient devoted pasteur, Gesner. His wife was the daughter of that excellent servant of the Lord, Lavater. We met a large number of persons, I believe generally serious. I had proposed to myself speaking on the Prison subject, but my way opened differently ; to enlarge upon the state of the Protestant Church in France, to encourage all its members to devotedness ; and particularly in that place, where deep trials have been their portion, from their Government upholding infidelity and infidel men. At the close of the Meeting, our venerable friend, Gesner, spoke in a lively, powerful manner, and avowed his belief that the Lord Himself had enabled me to express what I had done, it was so remarkably " the word in season." I paid, also, a satisfactory religious visit to the female prisoners in the afternoon. The next morning I visited the head magistrate ; represented the evils I had observed ; and saw some ladies about visiting prisons. We afterwards went a sweet expedition on the Lake, with our beloved friends the Baron and Baroness Pelet. Early in the evening, I set off with a dear girl—great-granddaughter to Lavater, and grandaughter to Pastor Gesner—Barbara Usteri, in a curious little carriage to pay some visits, and to spend an evening at the house of the aunt of Matilda Escher, another interesting young woman, with whom I had become acquainted, I believe providentially, at an inn near Interlachen. I had no one with me but strangers, as my dear family stayed with the Baron and Baroness Pelet at my desire ; but I felt not among strangers, because those who love the Lord Jesus are dear to me, and in our holy Head we are one. I can hardly express, on this journey, how much I have found this to be the case. The

love, the unity, and the home feeling, I have had with those I
never saw before; and I have also found how little it matters
where we are, for " where the God of peace is, there is home."

The morning of their departure from Zurich, the venerable
Mr. Gesner (Antistes, or Prelate of the Canton), and many others,
called to take leave. This apostolic old man pronounced a wonderful blessing on Mrs. Fry, to which she replied in terms that
caused the bystanders to weep aloud. A tedious journey of four
days, through very wet weather, brought the travellers to Stuttgard; here the impediment of the language was great: few of
those to whom their letters were delivered speaking either French
or English. They proceeded to Ludwigsburg for Sunday.

A letter to Mr. Klett, resident Inspector of the Prison, was
delivered, and half-past seven o'clock the next morning, appointed
for her visit to that place. There a Swiss lad of eighteen years
of age, was in waiting to act as interpreter. The women, though
it was Sunday, were engaged in needlework by order of the King,
—a sad sight in a Protestant country. They also visited an
Orphan Asylum; and in the evening again went to the prison.
The women are well instructed, by a devoted lady who spends her
life in this service. They appeared in a tender, feeling state
of mind, and a solemn reading of the Scriptures impressed them
much.

Cologne, Ninth Month 8th.—At Frankfort, we met with a
most cordial reception from our dear friend Dr. Pinkerton and his
family; they treated us in the most handsome manner, and with
true Christian kindness. Their warm-heartedness, their piety,
and their cultivated minds, rendered their society delightful.
We had one evening a large party at their house, where much
passed of an interesting nature, and I fully believe that we were
blessed together. I also visited the prisons: all sad, (with one
exception). I hope the prisoners will be visited in consequence,
and a stall opened in the town for the sale of Bibles and tracts.

A rapid journey from Frankfort brought the travellers to Ostend. They landed at Dover on the 12th of September.

Upton Lane, Ninth Month 22nd.—We arrived here in the evening of the 13th, in health and peace, and found the numerous members of our beloved family generally well and prospering. Nothing appears to have suffered from our absence ; for this, we may reverently return thanks.

Lynn, Tenth Month 20th.—I am sitting in R——'s little sitting-room, on the Sabbath morning. I am thankful it has pleased my Heavenly Father to direct my steps to this place at this time. I did desire and pray to be directed, as to the time of coming here.

First-day, Eleventh Month 10th.—My time at Lynn was spent very satisfactorily with my beloved children and grandchildren, and my attention particularly occupied by the intention they had, of our dear eldest grandson going into the army. My prayers were first offered in secret, that my Lord would open some way of escape from a life, that I felt to be so unchristian and fearful a one. At first I said little, but kept my heart much lifted up on his account ; but afterwards, I fully represented my views to him and to his parents, and I found they had great weight with them. I partook of rather unusually sweet spiritual unity and intercourse with these dear children, much as they outwardly differ from me in many things, still we are, I believe, united in some most essential points of religious truth. My dear grandson Frank and I visited Earlham together, where I highly valued the company of my sisters, Catherine and Richenda, also of the rest of the party. I travelled home with my dear niece, Catherine B——.

Upton, First-day, Twelfth Month 8th.—I, yesterday, had some intimate conversation with Captain ——, who has just joined, or is about to join the Plymouth Brethren ; with a young lady, a follower of Edward Irving ; with another lady, a high Church woman ; and with Josiah Forster, an elder in our portion of the church. I cannot say, but that it is at times an exercise of my faith, to find the diversities of opinions existing amongst the professors of Christianity, and not only the professors, but those who I believe really love their Lord ; but my better judgment tells me, that there must be a wise purpose in its being so. These divisions into families and tribes may tend to the life and growth of religion, which, if we were all of one mind, might not be the case. But whilst I see these differences, I perceive that there is but one Christianity, one Body, one Spirit, one hope of our calling ; one Lord, one faith and one baptism ; one God and Father of all. All true members of the Church of Christ are, and must be one in Him, and the results we see the same everywhere. Love to God and love to man, manifested in life and conduct ; and how strikingly proved in death, as well as in life, that victory is obtained through the same Saviour, that in the dying hour, death loses its sting and the grave its victory. Therefore, if we believe and know our hearts to be cleansed by the blood of Christ, and through the power of the Holy Ghost live to His glory, bearing the fruits of faith, it matters little, in my estimation, to what religious denomination we belong, so that we mind our calling, and fill the place our Lord would have us to fill, in His Militant Church on earth.

I have had very satisfactory letters from the Continent, in which it appears, in various ways, that our visit has been blessed in many places ; Committees formed to visit prisoners ; Prisons improved. The minds of prisoners appear to have been seriously impressed, encouragement given to some who wanted it, and, I trust, by what I hear, many stimulated in their progress heavenward.

I visited Lord Normanby, our Home Secretary, a few days since, and met with a most cordial reception ; and found, in consequence of some suggestions that I had offered, a material improvement likely to take place in the arrangements for our female convicts ; that they are to be sent from the country, after trial, to the Millbank Penitentiary, to be employed and instructed, previous to their going abroad. He also very kindly attended to some other things of secondary importance, about which I was anxious to communicate with him.

CHAPTER XXII.

1840, 1841.—Audience of the Queen—Meeting in London—Leaves home for the Continent—Ostend—Brussels—Antwerp—Amsterdam —Zwolle—Minden and Pyrmont—Hanover—Berlin—Leipzig—Dusseldorf—Return home—Yearly Meeting—Anti-Slavery Society Meeting—Dying hours of a relative—Isle of Wight—Parkhurst—Nursing sisters—Illness of a son—Niger Expedition—Silent and Solitary System—Dangerous illness of a daughter.

First Month 26th, 1840.—An eventful time in public and private life. Our young Queen is to be married to Prince Albert. She has sent me a present of fifty pounds for our Refuge at Chelsea, by Lord Normanby. Political commotions about the country—riots in Wales—much religious stir in the Church of England, numbers of persons becoming much the same as Roman Catholics—Popish doctrines preached openly in many of our churches—infidel principles, in the form of Socialism, gaining ground.

The prospect of returning to the Continent, with my brother Samuel Gurney, is rather bright to me. William Allen and Lucy Bradshaw's company will be very desirable, and I fully expect to find them all true helpers in the Lord. The only real drawback that I know of, is the state of health of some of my children; but I leave it all to my Heavenly Father, who governs all in Mercy, according to the purpose of His own will; and I desire, as Leighton advises, to roll all my cares upon Him, more particularly the cares appertaining to duty. We have many and very great causes for thankfulness; and surely our latter days are our brightest days. In the midst of dark and heavy trials, I used to believe this would be the case.

Under a sweet feeling of Thy merciful and providential care over us, and Thy gentle dealings towards us, most gracious Lord God, I humbly return Thee thanks, and ask Thee in faith, and in the name of our Redeemer, to continue to be with us, to keep us, and bless us, and more abundantly to bestow upon us the gifts of

Thine own Holy Spirit, that we may faithfully fill the office Thou mayst call us into, to Thy glory, the good of others, and the spreading of the Truth as it is in Jesus ; also, be pleased, not only to bestow on us the gifts, but also the graces of Thy Spirit, that in meekness and deep humility, and much patience and long-suffering, we may walk worthy of Thee, who hast called us to Thy kingdom and glory. And now, Holy Father, under a fresh feeling of Thy love, Thy pity, and Thine unmerited mercy towards us, I commend my husband, my self, children, grandchildren, brothers, sisters, and their children, and all my beloved friends at home and abroad, and all who love Thy name and fear Thee, particularly the afflicted and tempted, to Thy most Holy keeping ; and I also pray Thee, for the sake of Thy beloved Son Christ Jesus our Saviour, who tasted death for every man, to regard for good the world at large, especially those who yet sit in darkness. Lift up the light of Thy blessed and holy countenance upon these and all wanderers, that they may behold Thy beauty and excellency, and come to the knowledge of Thyself and Thy dear Son. So be it, most merciful Lord God, that the day may hasten forward, when the knowledge of Thyself and Thy Christ, through the power of Thy Spirit, may cover the earth, even as the waters cover the sea ! Amen.

Mrs. Fry had not returned the certificate which she had received from the Meetings of Friends for her Continental journey in 1839. She had, when she asked for it, some expectation of prolonging her travels into Germany, but her objects in France occupied so much more time than she had anticipated, that she was under the necessity of returning to England. But she did not abandon the idea, and the time seemed now approaching, when she might again leave home with satisfaction. Her brother Samuel Gurney, his daughter Elizabeth, and her friend William Allen, with his niece Lucy Bradshaw, accompanied her.

Upton, Second Month 1st.—I am called to visit our young Queen to-day, in company with William Allen, and I hope my brother Samuel also.

We went to Buckingham Palace, and saw the Queen. Our
interview was short. Lord Normanby, the Home Secretary, presented us. The Queen asked us where we were going on the
Continent. She said it was some years since she saw me. She
asked about Caroline Neave's Refuge, for which she had lately
sent the fifty pounds. This gave me an opportunity of thanking
her. I ventured to express my satisfaction that she encouraged
various works of charity ; and I said it reminded me of the
words of scripture, " with the merciful Thou will shew Thyself
merciful." Before we withdrew, I stopped and said, I hoped the
Queen would allow me to assure her, that it was our prayer
that the blessing of God might rest upon the Queen and her
Consort.

Our beloved daughter L—— was confined on Fourth-day.
The babe, a lovely girl, breathed for twenty-four hours, and then
died. They had the child named and baptised. I happened to
be present, and certainly some of the prayers were very solemn,
and such as I could truly unite with ; but part of the ceremony
appeared to me superstitious, and having a strong savour of the
dark ages of the Church. I have for some time believed that
duty would call me to have a meeting in London and the neighbourhood, previous to leaving home. I see many difficulties
attached to it, and perhaps none so much, as my great fear of
women coming too forward in these things, beyond what the
Scripture dictates ; but I am sure the Scripture most clearly and
forcibly lays down the principle that the Spirit is not to be
grieved, or quenched, or vexed, or resisted ; and on this principle
I act, under the earnest desire that I may not do this, but that
whatever the Lord leads me into by His Spirit may be done
faithfully to Him, and in His name ; and I am of opinion,
that nothing Paul said, to discourage women's speaking in the
Churches, alluded to their speaking through the help of the
Spirit, as he clearly gave directions how they should conduct
themselves under such circumstances, when they prayed or
prophesied.

In a letter written a few days afterwards, a lady who was
present, not a Friend, described that Meeting : " It was really

a most impressive occasion—the large fine circular building filled
—not less, I should think, than fifteen hundred present. She
began by entreating the sympathy and supplications of those
present. I cannot tell you how mine flowed forth on her behalf.
After her prayer, we sat still for some time, then William Allen
spoke, and then she rose, giving as a text, 'Yield yourselves
unto God, as those that are alive from the dead;' and uncom-
mouly fine was her animated yet tender exhortation to all
present, but more especially the young, to present themselves as
living sacrifices to the Lord,—to be made of Him new creatures
in Christ—the old things passed away, and all things become
new as those alive from the dead. This change she dwelt and
enlarged on much ; its character, and the Power that alone can
effect it ; the duty demanded of us—'Yield yourselves ;' and its
infinite and eternal blessedness. I was astonished and deeply impressed ; the feeling was, 'surely God is amongst us of a truth.'"

In the carriage on board the steam-boat going to Ostend :—

Second Month 26th, 1840.

MY DEAREST HUSBAND AND CHILDREN,

Here I am by myself, none of our companions liking the
carriage; my brother Samuel and Lucy Bradshaw near me on the
deck. The sun shines brightly,—the wind and tide quite contrary to us,—the sea not very rough,—Calais in sight,—the
birds delighting themselves on the waves, and I feeling much
refreshed.

I desire to recount my mercies to you, inasmuch as at this
moment separated from so many so dearly beloved, I am quiet,
peaceful, hopeful, and well in health, neither faint nor sick with
the sea, but my quiet time alone in the carriage refreshing and
pleasant to me.

I think I must not say more, therefore farewell for the present.
Surely goodness and mercy have thus far followed me.

Ostend.—Here we may thankfully say we are, after a not unfavourable voyage of eleven hours. I feel the water separating

us, but we are united in heart, and I may gratefully say `I believe
I am in my right place ; every thing most comfortable for us.
I send what I wrote in the packet, hoping you can read it.

Farewell in nearest love,

ELIZABETH FRY.

Ostend, Second Month 27th, finished Ghent, 29th.

MY DEAREST R——,

We are favoured with a bright morning, and we may thankfully say that our spirits are permitted to partake of the same
brightness. I have a sweet feeling of being in the right place.
An order is come from the Belgian Government for us to visit
their prisons. So the way opens before us ; and though I give
up much to enter these services, and feel leaving my most
tenderly beloved ones, yet there is such a sense of the blessedness
of the service, and the honour of doing the least thing for my
Lord, unworthy as I am, that it often brings a peculiar feeling
of health, (if I may so say) as well as peace to my body, soul
and spirit.

My brother Samuel is a capital travelling companion, so
zealous, so able, so willing, so generous ; and I find dear E——
sweet, pleasant and cheering. Bruges is a beautiful old town ;
such exquisite buildings—they delighted my eye. Here we
visited the English Convent, where, to our surprise, we could
only speak through a grating. We had a good deal of conversation with dear S. P——'s sister and the Superior. They
appeared very interesting women. We talked about their
shutting-in system. I expressed my disapprobation of it as a
general practice, and one liable to such great abuse. I sent
them some books, and mean to send more. We also visited a
large school, to the great pleasure and amusement of the
children, your uncle gave them all a present. They could not
the least understand our language, as they speak Flemish.

We have been much interested, this morning, in visiting the
Maison de Force ; it is a very excellent prison of considerable
size, but wants some things very much. We have since been
occupied with the numerous English here. They are without
pasteur or school, and quite in a deplorable state. We propose

2 A 2

having a meeting with them of a religious and philanthropic nature, and hope to establish some schools, &c., amongst them.

May the blessing of the Most High abundantly rest on you all. Yours, in a close bond that I trust will never be broken.

E. F.

Brussels, *Third Month 1st.*

MY DEAREST HUSBAND AND CHILDREN,

We left Ghent on Seventh-day, about half-past two o'clock, after visiting a most deplorable prison, where we found a cell with the floor and sides formed of angular pieces of wood, so that no prisoner could stand, lie down, or lean against the wall, without suffering. We also visited a lunatic asylum, so beautifully conducted, that I more took the impression of how happy such persons may be made than I ever did before. They are cared for by the Sisters of St. Vincent de Paul. After rather a slow journey, we arrived here to dinner, at six o'clock.

Ghent, Third Month 3rd.—Here we are once more : we have visited another large prison for the military ; and had a very interesting Meeting with the English workmen, their wives and children. I am glad to say, they conclude for us to send them schoolmasters. We had flocks after us last evening, English and Belgians—I suppose about seventy : they appeared to be touched by our reading. I observe how much the English appear impressed on these occasions. Our little party are very comfortable, and each has plenty to do.

Farewell, yours indeed,

ELIZABETH FRY.

Antwerp, *Third Month 6th.*

MY DEAREST HUSBAND AND CHILDREN,

Upon our return to Brussels from Ghent, we visited the great prison of Vilvorde, where we were met by Count Arrivabene, a very interesting Italian, who has been our most kind and attentive friend in Brussels. He is a great philanthropist, and is likely soon to visit England. We gave many of our little Scripture extracts to the prisoners. We got home to dinner, and spent the evening at the Baron de Bois', where we met several pleasant persons. The pictures were beautiful: the Dutch and Flemish masters are to me very attractive. The next day we visited many large institutions. We had company to dinner; and a considerable number of Belgians, poor and rich, came to an Evening Meeting at our hotel. The next day was one of no common interest. After some engagements in the morning, breakfasting out, &c., we visited the King, who held out both his hands to receive me with real kindness, and appeared quite pleased to see me again. Our party were William Allen, my brother Samuel, J. Forster, and myself; and before we left, Lucy Bradshaw and dear E—— were admitted to see him. We first had a very interesting conversation on the state of the prisons, and your uncle read the King our address to him upon the subject, when the part was read expressing our desire for him, the Queen and his family, he appeared to feel it. We had open, interesting communication upon many subjects. We remained nearly an hour. The Queen was unwell, and the children asleep, therefore I did not see them. We gave the King several books for himself and the Queen. After we returned home we had engagements until near dinner time. We were invited by Count Arrivabene to dine with one of the first Belgian families. I felt it rather fearful, when, to my surprise after dinner, I was seated by the Dean of Brussels, surrounded by the company, and told that I was permitted to speak openly upon my religious views. Indeed, I think the wish was, that I should preach to them. This was curious, because I was warned on going to say nothing about religion. Preach I did not—as I do not feel that, at my command; but I spoke very seriously about the Scriptures not being read in the prisons; and endeavoured to show in few words what alone can produce change of heart, life, and conduct, and the danger of resting in forms. We parted in much good-will, and we sent the Dean and the ladies books. In the evening we had a philanthropic party at our hotel. The next morning, a large, very solemn and interesting religious Meeting, also at the hotel. We left Brussels in much peace, (rejoicing would not be too strong a word). In nearest love,

E. F.

From the journal of her niece, Elizabeth Gurney :—

" Brussels, March 6th.—We expect to end our very interesting
visit in this place to-day.   Had I a hundred times more power
of writing, I could not initiate you into our life here.   A great
Meeting is now assembling in the Table d'Hôte salon, fitted up
by our landlord for the occasion.   This is to be our farewell
Meeting.   We have had a very full morning, partly employed in
distributing books.   The servants at the palace sent an entreaty
that they might not be overlooked.   I wish you could have seen
us looking out a good variety for about sixty of them.

" Yesterday began with a full tide of business.   They were to
see the King at twelve o'clock.   My aunt looked beautifully.
He is a particularly pleasing-looking man, rather older than I
expected.   The Duchess of Kent had kindly written to the King,
to say, that my aunt was likely to visit Brussels.

" I must tell you about our dinner at M. le Comte de ——,
the first Roman Catholic family here.   We were taken there by
our kind friend Count Arrivabene.   The party consisted of
fifteen persons, only two speaking English.   Amongst them was
the Dean, the head of the Church here, under the Bishop of
Malines.   Much that was interesting passed.   The Dean and
our aunt seated themselves in a corner of the room, and by
degrees the whole party gathered round ; the Count and Josiah
Forster interpreting by turns.   It was a critical thing to know
what to say, as the conversation became more and more of a
religious nature.   She began on the prisons—prevention of crime
—how much the upper classes are often the cause, by example, of
the sins of the lower ; related a few of her prison facts as proofs,
and finally ended by saying, ' Will the Dean allow me to speak
my mind candidly ?'   His permission being given, and that of
the Count and Countess, she began by expressing the sincere
interest that she felt for the inhabitants of this city, and how
much she had been desiring for them, ' that as a people, they
might each place less confidence in men and in the forms of
religion, and look to Christ with an entire and simple faith.'
The priest said nothing ; but turned the subject, and asked what
the views of the Quakers were ? upon which Josiah Forster gave

them a short account in French, which appeared to interest them all."

My DEAREST HUSBAND AND CHILDREN,

I think you have not heard of our departure from Brussels, and of the great kindness of our dear friends, who shed tears at parting. At Antwerp we visited a prison in a deplorable state, where much evil, I fear, is going on; and two excellent institutions, one for old women, under the care of Sisters of Charity. Their comfort, order, and cleanliness, were great indeed; and I think I never saw so much appearance of religion in a Roman Catholic institution. One poor old woman took up her rosary, and pointed to the beads that were to be prayers for me after I was gone; they almost all appeared to be meditating, praying, or working. My dear brother and myself then visited a Refuge for poor girls, in the most beautiful order, kept by ladies (not nuns) who give up their time and fortune to attend to this Christian duty. Such perfect arrangements for moral good, I have seldom, if ever, seen in a Refuge. It is inspected day and night by the ladies. The girls are well employed, and receive some instruction, but, sad to say, the Scriptures forbidden.

Our journey to Rotterdam was over one continued marsh; the road raised considerably above the level. Rotterdam appears half water and half land; it has a curious effect. John Mollett met us, a valuable, cheerful and bright old man. On Thirdday we visited a large Prison for boys, capitally taught by gentlemen, who daily visit them, and by an excellent schoolmaster. Your dear uncle and I gave them an exhortation, to which they were very attentive.

Mrs. Fry's observations on this prison were as follows :—

It contains about two hundred and forty boys.
The building not suitable.
An excellent school, and good master.
Visited daily by a gentlemen's committee.
Proportion that returns to the prison small.

They appear to be well fed and clothed.

A hammock for each boy, two rows one above another.

No inspection by night, except an officer watching round, and looking through a grating into the lighted rooms.

Divided into three classes.

Three courts for them to walk in.

Good employment when not at lessons.

They do not go to bed until nine o'clock.

Medical attendant and infirmary we thought not very good.

Attended by Protestant and Roman Catholic chaplains.

There was another prison, under the same roof, for women, but solely under the care of men. A considerable number of highly-respectable Dutch gentlemen and ladies came in the evening, and a few English ; amongst them a delightful clergyman. We closed our evening much as at Paris, with a short reading.

The next morning Sir Alexander Ferner, our English Minister, visited us. We then went over land and water to a great female prison, about twelve miles from Rotterdam. Such country not only I never saw, but hardly could have imagined ; small pieces of land, evidently raised out of a bed of water by the art of man ; a field, perhaps fifteen or twenty yards square with water round it, perhaps four yards wide, and a little further off a body of water quite a large lake on one side, and a river on the other. They have good farm-houses on these pieces of land, and bridges made to turn round ; so they are thrown across the water by day, and turned on to the land by night. I really liked the perfect novelty of the scene. Gouda, the place of our destination, is a curious old Dutch town, with a church of great beauty and celebrity, said to contain the finest painted glass in Europe. We went to the female prison ; there were three hundred prisoners under the care of two women, lately introduced, and five men, and never watched at night by any one. They are visited by two very interesting ladies, (Madame veuve Van Meerten, and Madlle. H. M. de Graves), and some gentlemen. We were received, by about six gentlemen and these two ladies, with the greatest kindness ; coffee ready for us at the prison. Such a curious place I never saw ; we had to ascend story upon story, by stairs little better than ladders, and at the very top we found three great rooms in the roof, where the women worked ; two were attended by a female officer, the other was without. We spoke to them, which they appeared to feel, their tears running down their faces. It was most evident, through every disadvantage, that great good resulted from the ladies' visits, and their labours had been much blessed. The next morning we went to the Hague, and dined that day at the English Minister's Sir Edward Disbrowe. We became acquainted with a very superior Dutch family, and a good many other persons. We visited a sad prison, in company with several gentlemen, in the morning ; and a considerable number came to us in the afternoon, trying to form committees to visit prisons. The Secretary of the Interior came in the morning, and we had a thorough prison conversation with him. In the evening we went to a large religious party, at the house of the French pasteur ; here I took a part which appeared to be very well accepted ; the pasteur prayed for us. We then drank tea in a very beautiful Dutch house, with a rich, but excellent gentleman, his wife, and some other choice persons. The next morning we set off for this place, visiting the large military prison at Leyden, where we saw the excellent effect of the Scriptures being freely read. Our Sabbath ended highly satisfactorily ; we had a very large Dutch company, an English clergyman and Scotch minister ; after our reading, and William Allen and myself had spoken, a gentleman got up, and in a powerful, encouraging and beautiful manner, expressed his unity with us, and satisfaction in our visit. He is, they say, a very pious, devoted and learned man, a merchant here. We then ended in prayer.

I am yours, in tender love and desire that the best of blessings may be with you.

E. F.

Although so many circumstances occurred to encourage her, Mrs. Fry often went heavily on her way, feeling delicate in health, and oppressed in spirit. A letter from Dr. Bosworth, with whom she had become acquainted at Rotterdam, was very consoling to her.

" Before I answer your questions, let me discharge a debt of gratitude, which I and my wife owe to you and your friends, for your benevolent exertions in Rotterdam. You have excited amongst us, and have left, I trust, an abiding Christian affection. We feel we are brethren, united in the same good cause of our adorable Saviour, that of promoting ' peace on earth, and good-will to men.' How soon will the wood, hay, and stubble of party be burnt up, and what is built on the Rock of Ages remain, &c. &c. We are here in a parched wilderness, but your visit has brought a refreshing dew, and may it abide with us."

To her youngest Son.

Amsterdam, *Third Month* 19*th.*

My dearest H——,

We find this a very interesting place. How amused you would all be at some of our curious Meetings. The other evening we went to drink tea at the house of a converted Jew, where we met numbers of the Pietists ; he read the 14th chapter of John in French, I spoke, and gave a little advice on Christian love and unity ; then the Jew spoke, and another Jew prayed, and after-wards William Allen. The serious, the sweet, the good, and the ludicrous were curiously mixed up together. Yesterday was very full : first company, breakfast and reading, then preparation for two meetings, one for prisons in the afternoon, and one in the evening for philanthropic objects, &c. ; at three o'clock about twenty gentlemen came to discuss with us the state of the prisons of Holland, an excellent meeting. A gentleman named Surengar was present, who has followed us from Rotterdam, and has kindly invited us to his house in the North of Holland. Your uncle is very clever in his speeches, and real knowledge of the subject. I received blessing and thanks from many, far too much ; our visit appears most seasonable here, so much wanting to be done in the prisons, and other things.

Fifth-day morning.—We went to our Friends' Meeting, when we arrived the numbers round the door were so great that we doubted whether we could get in, however, way was soon made for us, and we found a large and highly respectable congregation needing no interpreter. We had certainly a flowing Meeting in every sense, I think the cup flowed over with Christian love. I believe it has been a most unusual thing the way in which hearts have been opened towards us. I then went off to the prison to launch the Committee of Ladies in visiting it, several gentlemen also with me. I had just time to come home, rest and dress, and set off to a dinner at our friend Van der Hope's, where there are the most exquisite paintings by the Dutch masters. I think I never saw any so much to my taste.

I can assure thee, my dearest H——, when I see how ripe the fields are unto harvest every where, I long and pray that more labourers may be brought into this most interesting, important, and, may I not say, delightful service, but there must be a preparation for it, by yielding to the cross of Christ, and often deep humiliations and much self-abasement are needful, before the Lord makes much use of us, but above all, we must yield ourselves to God, as " those that are alive from the dead ;" He will then fit us for His own work in His own way.

Dearest love to all of you,

I am, thy most tenderly attached mother,

Elizabeth Fry.

Zwolle, Third Month 22nd.

My dearest Husband and Children,

Since I sent my long letter to Harry, we have visited Utrecht. We had invited different persons to the hotel, but as none appeared likely to come, we sat down industriously in our travelling trim to our employments, when to our surprise, gentlemen and ladies began to assemble, and we had quite a large party, who were so much interested that we agreed fully to open our doors the next evening to any one who liked to come. We had indeed a very full day in prospect, and could only look upwards for help, mentally and bodily. First we visited a Lunatic Asylum, a very interesting and superior one, then we went to Zeist, a large Moravian settlement, about five miles from Utrecht ; here we remained some hours, and had some weighty business to lay before the elders ; my desire for them is, that they may turn their powers to more account. In the evening we went to tea with a lady and found about twenty to meet us. When I followed my brother and E—— to the hotel about eight o'clock, you may suppose I felt scarcely equal to encounter a party of eighty-two persons, whom I found assembled in the large room. My heart was almost ready to sink ; however we began by a capital speech of my brother's on slavery, showing them the importance of liberating the slaves in their colonies ; then John Mollet spoke in French ; afterwards my poor self, first upon prisons, with all appertaining, then their schools, little or no scripture being allowed in the public ones, about this I spoke most strongly. We ended with Scripture reading and exhortation : there was great attention paid, and much love shown to us.

Believe me, your most tenderly attached,

E. F.

From Zwolle, the travellers went to Minden, to visit a small body of Friends resident there, as well as the larger congregation at Pyrmont.

Minden, Third Month 28*th.*—We left Zwolle on Second-day, the 23rd, and slept at a true German inn—neither carpet nor curtain. Our night was disturbed, still we did well. The next day we set off in good time, and travelled until twelve o'clock ; we did not settle till two in the morning. I think I have not yet recovered the fatigue, not having slept well one night since. We have been interested by the Friends, who are much like those of Congenies, but more entirely Friends ; we have visited them in almost all their families, and had two Meetings with them. We have been brought into much sympathy with them, for they are a tried, and I believe a Christian people. We have this evening had three pastors with us, two of them I think spiritual men. Our Meeting was largely attended this afternoon, and I can assure you my heart almost failed me, being interpreted for in German is so difficult, but we have in Auguste Mundhenck, a well educated young Friend, a capital interpreter. The Meeting ended well. In my wakeful nights I feel solitary, and have you very present with me ; but I humbly trust He that sleepeth not is watching over you with tender care.

Pyrmont, 29*th.*—In our way here we visited at Hameln, a large prison, under the King of Hanover,· almost all the poor prisoners, upwards of four hundred in number, heavily chained. I told them a little of my deep interest for their present and ever-lasting welfare ; they appeared to feel it very much ; one poor man, a tall fine figure, with heavy chains on both legs, sat weeping like a child. I am just come in from visiting the families of Friends ; they are really a very valuable set. I longed to take a picture for you of an old Friend with a plain skull cap, either quilted or knitted, a purple handkerchief, a striped apron, and the whole appearance truly curious ; but she was a sweet old woman full of love. I am really amused, the old and young are as fond of me as if I could fully speak to them ; the little ones sitting on my lap as if I were their mother, and leaning their little heads upon me. A little child about four or five said, what happy days they should have when we went to see them. We expect à large party this evening.

30*th.*—We had our party, and I understand there were present some of the first persons of the town, besides the master of the hotel, his wife, the doctor, the post-master, the bookbinder, the shoemaker, &c., &c., &c. ! We discussed the state of their poor, their not visiting them, or attending to them; for it appears that visiting the poor is not thought of here. I hope and expect our coming will be useful in this respect. How curious is the variety we meet with, and the different things there are to occupy our attention !

Hameln—ended Hanover, Fourth Month 2nd.

MY DEAREST HUSBAND AND CHILDREN,

Whilst stopping at a small inn, I mean to finish my account of our visit to Pyrmont. After I wrote we went shaking on such bad roads from house to house, to see the Friends, that I almost feared we must break down. We twice dined with them, in their beautiful spot at Friedensthal, (or the valley of peace) surrounded with hills, and a river flowing through it. Roebucks wild from the woods abounding. We were very pleasantly received. I must describe the dinner. Many Germans were present, young and old, and our English party ; the table was well covered with

cakes, and dried and stewed fruits, the produce generally of
their grounds. The soup on the table,· and one large Westphalia ham. We had veal handed round afterwards in different forms ; and plum puddings, of course for us, in the middle
óf dinner. I much liked the true German hospitality, and also
seeing the mode of living in the country. Our visits were very
satisfactory to these valuable and agreeable people. Tears and
kisses abounded at our departure. I must tell you of an interesting event :—I went to buy something for little John at a shop,
where a very agreeable lady spoke to me in English, and I was
so much attracted by her, that I requested her to accept a book,
and sent a work on the rites and ceremonies of the Jews. I
asked her to attend our Meeting on Second-day morning. She
proved to be a Jewish lady of some importance ; she came to
Meeting with several other Jews, and truly I believe her heart
was touched. I invited her to come and see us the next evening,
when we expected several persons to join our party. The following day we agreed to form a District Society, to attend to the
deplorable state of the poor. ·The Jewish lady capitally helped
us, she then appeared in a feeling state ; but this morning when
the ladies met to finish our arrangements, and I felt it my place
to give them a little advice, and my blessing in the name of the
Lord, the tears poured down her face. I then felt it my absolute
duty to take her into my room to give her such books as I thought
right, and to tell her how earnest my desires were that she should
come to the knowledge of our Saviour. I think in our whole
journey no person has appeared to be so affected or so deeply
impressed ; may it be lasting, and may she become a Christian
indeed !

Your much attached,

E. FRY.

Hildesheim, Fourth Month 6th.

MY MUCH LOVED FAMILY,

We left Hanover to-day about five o'clock, after rather a
singular visit. We arrived there on Fifth-day evening. On
Sixth and Seventh-day our way did not open quite so brightly as
some times. We saw a deplorable prison ; poor untried prisoners

chained to the ground until they would confess their crimes, whether they had committed them or not, and some other sad evils. Several interesting persons came to see us. Seventh-day evening we spent at a gentleman's house, where we met some very clever and superior persons, and had much important communication upon their prisons, &c., &c. On First-day we had our little Meetings ; such a tide on a Sabbath I think I hardly ever had ; it was like being driven down a mighty stream ; we had allowed persons to come to us, supposing it would be the last day there. I made some calls of Christian love. The principal magistrate came for an hour about the prisons, and very many other persons. In the evening we had also a party of a select nature to our Scripture reading, and after a very solemn time we represented many things wanted in Hanover. I forgot to tell you, amongst other visitors, the Queen's Chamberlain came to say that the Queen wished to see our whole party on Second-day at one o'clock. We had proposed going that morning early, but put it off on this account. I think I never paid a more interesting visit to royalty—my brother Samuel, William Allen, and myself. In the first place we were received with ceremonious respect, shown through many rooms to a drawing-room, where were the Queen's Chamberlain and three ladies in waiting to receive us. They showed us some pictures of the family, until Prince George and his half-sister came in to us ; he appeared much pleased to be with me again. His sister appeared a serious and interesting young lady. After some little time we were sent for by the Queen ; the King was too ill to see us. She is a stately woman, tall, large, and rather a fine countenance. We very soon began to speak of her afflictions, and I gave a little encouragement and exhortation. She was much affected, and after a little while requested us to sit down. We had very interesting and important subjects brought forward : the difficulties and temptations to which rank is subject—the importance of their influence—the objects incumbent upon them to attend to and help in, Bible Societies, Prisons, &c. We then read our address to the Queen, wishing her to patronise ladies visiting the prisons ; it contained serious advice, and our desires for her, the King, and the Prince ;

then I gave the Queen several books, which she accepted in the kindest manner. —— —— —— —— ——

I am indeed,
Your most tenderly attached,
E. F.

At Berlin the travellers found a cordial welcome from all ranks of persons. A wonderful field of usefulness appeared open, and many hearts ready to receive them. Much service of various descriptions awaited them, some of a peculiarly interesting nature. Her gracious and cordial reception by the Royal Family was very gratifying to Mrs. Fry, and in the Princess William, sister to the late King, she found a zealous co-operator in her labours on behalf of the prisons. This eminent and truly Christian lady had been as a mother to the younger members of the Royal Family after the death of Queen Louisa, and in her exalted station she was an example of every good word and work.

From a letter written by her niece :—

Hotel de Russie, Berlin.

" Our dear aunt's first evening for philanthropic purposes took place on the 13th. There is a splendid room in the hotel, capable of containing two hundred persons, where we have our réunions. At one end is raised a low platform ; on this platform sat my aunt, William Allen, Lucy Bradshaw, papa, and Professor Tholück (a very noted scholar) as interpreter. A fine company of the higher classes filled more than half the room.

" It would be impossible to describe the intense interest and eagerness which prevailed when our aunt rose. Papa having introduced her to the assembly, she commenced with the deplorable state of the London Prisons when she was young—her own first entering these horrid abodes—the clamour that was raised by all parties on her venturing to go in alone and unprotected— the shocking state of filth and depravity that the prisons were in, and the violence of the prisoners, the females especially, so great, that even the turnkeys hardly dare venture amongst them

then ; she related the quiet way in which she and her companions were received, their taking clothing for the children, and
the respect with which the prisoners treated them.   She went on
to express her own feelings about introducing Christian doctrine
amongst them.   ' Could it be possible to touch their hearts by
religious truths ?   Shall I venture to read the Holy Scriptures
to them ?   What effect will it produce ?'

  " The attention of the whole assembly seemed completely
rivetted by her address.   Those that could not understand a
word, could at least watch her and listen to her voice.   She then
mentioned a few instances of the good that had been effected, and
the changes that had been brought about through the means of
the visiting ladies ; such as, commencing public worship amongst
the prisoners, and instituting matrons over them, &c.   She
ended with a most earnest and eloquent appeal to all to come
forward in the work, and lend their aid to seek to turn these
poor sinners from the error of their ways, and to take an interest
in their everlasting welfare.   William Allen had previously told
them the object of their mission, and a little of what they had
been doing since our arrival in Berlin.   Every one wants to
know about our aunt's history.   ' Where does she live ?'   ' Is she
married ?'   And their astonishment is great, when I tell them of
five and twenty grandchildren ; this seems to add to the respect
paid to her.

  " The Princess William has been very desirous to give her
sanction, as far as possible, to the Ladies' Committee for visiting
the prisons that my aunt has been forming ; and to show her
full approbation, had invited the Committee to meet her at her
palace.   So imagine about twenty ladies assembling here, at our
Hotel, at half-past twelve o'clock to-day, beautifully dressed ;
and further, fancy us all driving off and arriving at the palace.
The Princess had also asked some of her friends, so we must have
been about forty.   Such a party of ladies, and only our friend
Count Gröben to interpret.   The Princess received us most
kindly, and conducting us herself to the top of the room, we
talked some time whilst waiting the arrival of other members of
the Royal Family.   The ladies walking about the suite of rooms
and taking chocolate, for about half an hour, waiting for the

Crown Princess, who soon arrived. The Princess Charles was
also there, and the Crown Prince himself soon afterwards entered ;
I could not but long for a painter's eye, to have carried away the
scene. All of us seated in that beautiful room, our aunt in
the middle of the sofa, the Crown Prince and Princess, and
the Princess Charles on her right. The Princess William,
Princess Marie, and the Princess Czartoryski on the left. Count
Gröben sitting near her to interpret, the Countesses Bohlen
and Dernath by her, I was sitting by the Countess Schlieffen, a
delightful person, who is much interested in all our proceedings.
A table was placed before our aunt with pens, ink, and paper,
like other Committees, with the various rules that our aunt and
I had drawn up, and the Countess Bohlen had translated into
German, and which she read to the assembly; our aunt then gave
a clever concise account of the Societies in England, commencing
every fresh sentence with ' If the Prince and Princesses will
permit.' When business was over, my aunt mentioned some
texts, which she asked leave to read. A German Bible was handed
to Count Gröben, the text in Isaiah having been pointed out,
that our good aunt had wished for, ' Is not this the fast that I
have chosen,' &c. The Count read it, after which our aunt said
' Will the Prince and Princesses allow a short time for prayer,'
they all bowed assent, and stood, while she knelt down and offered
one of her touching, heartfelt prayers for them—that a blessing
might rest on the whole place, from the King on his throne to the
poor prisoner in the dungeon, and she prayed especially for the
Royal Family. Then for the ladies, that the works of their hands
might be prospered in what they had undertaken to perform.
Many of the ladies now withdrew, and we were soon left with the
Royal Family. They all invited us to see them again, before
we left Berlin, and took leave of us in the kindest manner."

Among other most onerous matters, Mrs. Fry felt it her duty
to inquire into the actual state of the Lutheran Church, in the
Prussian dominions, and whether it was still exposed to persecution. She found, that although more leniently dealt with than it
had been, great oppression existed ; confiscation of property and

imprisonment being not unfrequently resorted to, to compel sub-mission. Mrs. Fry could not feel justified without endeavouring to bring the subject before the King. Lord William Russell, our Ambassador, her kind and constant friend, and the Baron Humbolt, discouraged her attempting to do so. She had a strong inclination to consult the Crown Prince, when the unexpected meeting at the Princess William's, afforded her the desired opportunity. After earnestly petitioning the best Help, and wisdom from above, she opened the subject. His Royal Highness gave her most attentive hearing, and entirely encouraged her to act as she believed to be right. A petition had been beautifully drawn up by William Allen, this was translated into German, and presented through the official channel to His Majesty. It was no light matter doing this; but in faith she committed it to Him, who had put it so strongly into her heart, to bless the measure. The following day the King's Chaplain was the bearer of the delightful intelligence, that the petition had been graciously received, and that the King had said that "he thought the Spirit of God must have helped them to express themselves as they had done." She told this gentleman what a subject of prayer it had been with her; to which he rejoined, that "like Daniel her petition had been answered before she had ceased praying."

To a Daughter.

Leipzig, *Fourth Month 30th.*

My dearest L——,

The deeply weighty exercises at Berlin had so much expended all my powers, that I concluded to remain here alone, with my maid and our young friend Beyerhaus, whilst the rest of our little company went to Dresden. I have had a quiet time, and am much refreshed. I enjoy this fine weather. How beautiful is the breaking forth of spring! It is almost hot in the middle of the day, and the country very pleasant.

We have been particularly interested in visiting Luther's abode at Wittemberg, being where he was, and sitting where he sat by his table. Though in an old monastery, he appears to have had very comfortable apartments. We saw a beautiful painted ceiling in his sitting room, though now much defaced. I hope you have all read Merle D'Aubigné's History of the Reformation, we have found it so very interesting, we expect to visit many of the places mentioned in it, and to see the castle in which Luther was confined.

When left alone here I really was amused to find how kind friends gathered round me ; one brought me beautiful flowers and oranges, another books, another a very fine print of prisoners in their place of worship. In the morning of Second-day I took a little recreation, accompanied by two gentlemen, and drove about to see this pretty town and environs, the longest excursion for pleasure I have had. I spent the evening at the house of one of these gentlemen where were many to meet me. Two or three spoke English, some French, I am absolutely obliged to communicate my ideas in French, when by myself, and visitors come to see me, who cannot speak English, I managed to hold much communication with them, although no doubt in a very blundering manner. It often surprises me how little real obstruction the want of knowledge of languages has proved to me ; but it makes me long for my children and grandchildren thoroughly to know the modern languages. What should I have done, had not numbers here known English. Indeed, every well-educated person abroad appears instructed in English and French. As to French, our young people ought to know it as well as they do English, for it is a passport everywhere. I hope the greatest pains will be taken with it, with all the grandchildren, both girls and boys. I must now say, in much near and tender love, farewell.

Farewell in the Lord, every one of you,

Your most tenderly attached,

E. F.

Frankfort, Fifth Month 4th.—I felt very unwell yesterday, and low in spirits. My dearest brother and sweet niece were most kind to me ; all that I required I had, so "the Lord doth provide." I almost dreaded my night ; but through tender mercy the Comforter was near to comfort and help my great infirmity, so that I rested in my Lord, and feel revived in body and soul this morning. This text has been present with me, " I am the Lord that healeth thee."—Exodus xv. 26. Such fears presented themselves. How could I get home ? How could I bear the sea ? should I not be much burdened, not having finished what I thought I ought to do ? and so on ; but now my most gracious and holy Helper delivers me from my fears. Thanks to His most blessed and holy Name.

At Düsseldorf, Mrs. Fry was able to ascertain many particulars, she wished to know, of the Association for the improvement of prisoners in the Prussian Provinces of the Rhine and Westphalia. She found it to be composed of nine connected societies : those of Düsseldorf, Aix-la-Chapelle, Cologne, Cleves, Coblentz, Treves—in the Rhineland ; of Münster, and Herford —in Westphalia.

The society of Düsseldorf is the principal or leading society (Haupt-Gesellschaft), the other are of second rank. All these societies are established in places in which are a larger prison, and the object of their activity, is principally to maintain the order of this prison ; the classification of the prisoners ; to furnish work ; to procure the spiritual assistance of chaplains, and the use of the holy Scriptures and other religious books.

A General Meeting is annually held at Düsseldorf, where matters of common interest are discussed, and the reports of the different societies read. The general report is printed and distributed to the members of the association.

To every one of those nine societies are subjected Auxiliary-societies (Hülfs-vereine) in every place of the country, where a sufficient number of men, who are interested in the subject, are to be found. The care of those Auxiliary-societies is to provide work, and assistance of every kind, for the discharged prisoners of their neighbourhood. The society of the place, in which he has been imprisoned, gives a notice of his dismission to the Auxiliary-society, in whose compass he is likely to reside.

Düsseldorf, Fifth Month 10*th.*—Here we are, and thanks to my Heavenly Father I am much revived: my cough better; unfavourable symptoms subsided; sufficient strength given me for the various duties as they arise. I feel my prospect weighty; first, going to the prison to visit some prisoners whom I did not see yesterday. And then, we expect a large evening party to read the Scriptures and for worship, and this amongst strangers who know little or nothing of us or our ways, and our interpreter not accustomed to us; but our holy Helper can, through His own unmerited mercy and Almighty power, really so help us as to touch the hearts of those who come to us, to their true edification. O gracious Lord! be with us; help us and bless us. Thy servants have come in much fear; much weakness; and under a belief that it is Thy call, that has brought them here. Now, be Thyself present with us, in this our last occasion of the kind, to our help, consolation, and edification! I can only cast myself on Thy love, mercy, and pity!

Fifth Month.—In the afternoon I visited the prison, accompanied by my dear brother, William Allen, and Lucy Bradshaw. We first collected a large number of men in a yard, and I was, in my low state of body, strengthened to speak to them in the open air. Unexpectedly, a valuable man, the Pastor Fliedner, met us, who interpreted beautifully for me. We then visited several wards, and the prisoners appeared to feel a great deal. May its effect long remain. I also visited a very valuable lady, a Roman Catholic, who has visited the prison many years. We partook of Christian love, and, I believe, of Christian unity. In the evening we had a very large party to our reading and worship; I should think nearly a hundred persons. My Lord and Master only knows what such occasions are to me, weak in body, rather low in spirits—amongst perfect strangers to us—not able to speak to them in their own language. To whom could I go? I could say, " With God all things are possible ;" and so I found it. My brother Samuel read the 7th chapter of Matthew. One of the pastors read it in German. I soon spoke, and unexpectedly had to enlarge much on the present and past state of Germany: how it was that more fruit had not been produced, considering the remarkable seed sown in years past; the query, what hindered its growth? I expressed my belief—first, that it arose from a lukewarm and indifferent spirit; secondly, from infidel principles creeping in under a specious form; thirdly, from too much superstition yet remaining; fourthly, and above all, from the love of the world, and the things of it, beyond the love of Christ. After showing the evil and its results—the seed obstructed, as in the parable of the Sower, bringing no fruit to perfection; I endeavoured to point to the remedy—to look at home, and not to judge one another; to ask for help, protection, and direction; to walk in the narrow way; to be doers and not hearers of the word; and to devote ourselves to His service, who had done so much for us. William Allen followed with a satisfactory sermon. I then prayed very earnestly for them, and afterwards exhorted on reading the Scriptures, family worship, keeping the Sabbath, &c., and ended with a blessing—the attention was excessive; the interpretation excellent, by my dear friend the Pastor Fliedner; hearts much melted, and great unity expressed by numbers. It was a very solemn seal, set to our labours in this land, and one not to be forgotten. So our Lord helped us, and regarded me, His poor servant, in my low estate; afterwards, peace was in no common degree my portion. Blessed be the name of the Lord; all my dear companions, William Allen, my brother, and the younger of the party, Lucy Bradshaw and my dear niece, appeared happy and cheerful. I returned thanks on sitting down to a refreshing meal, after the labours of the day; and I think I may say we ate our "meat with gladness and singleness of heart."

We had a pleasant journey through Liege to Antwerp, where we were cordially received by some of our dear friends in that place, who appeared to have been deeply impressed by our last visit. We had a solemn time after our reading in the morning, at Ostend, the last reading we had of this kind, in which I very earnestly and fervently prayed for my most tenderly-beloved brother, that the sacrifice he had thus made in his Lord's service, and all he had so liberally done for us, as His servants, might

bring blessing to his own soul, and a large portion of the unsearchable riches of Christ. I prayed for his dear daughter,
that the experience of this journey might be greatly blessed to
her soul. I prayed for William Allen, that now in his latter
days, he might more and more be filled with, and spread the
glorious truths of the Gospel in their fulness, freeness, and
universality. I prayed for Lucy Bradshaw also, and for the servants, that the journey might be blessed to them ; and lastly
for my poor unworthy self, that I might be kept by my Lord,
humble, faithful, trustful, and more devoted to Him and His
service. It was as a spiritual farewell, and break up of this most
interesting expedition. Our voyage was calm and beautiful. I
return in a delicate state of health, and very weak in spirits, but
deeply feeling my Lord's mercies towards me.

Upton, 19th.—I attended the first Select Meeting yesterday.
My lot was to sit in silence. I saw many much loved by me.
May my most gracious Lord help me by His own Spirit this
Yearly Meeting fully, simply, and clearly to lay what I think
and feel before this people ; that which is right for the aged, and
more experienced before them, and that which is for the youth
before them. Gracious Lord, help me to do it in faithfulness, in
love, in truth, in deep humility and godly sincerity. Amen.
We have had altogether a favourable reply to our letter from the
King of Prussia ; he justifies the measure pursued towards the
Lutherans, but I believe our address will not be in vain. We
have had satisfactory reports of the Government, already acting
on our suggestions respecting the prisons in Prussia. The prisoners are to have more religious instruction, and more inspection.
I have had also a very interesting letter from the Queen of
Denmark, expressing real regret at our not going there, and not
only great desire to see me there, but much unity with my views
on many subjects.

There certainly is the most extraordinary opening in the hearts
of those in authority, on the Continent, to receive me. I felt
much drawn to go to Denmark, but the way did not open for it ;
if I am called still to go, may my Lord make my way plain
before me, though I do not see it now. My present position is
this : I consider my health has been almost in a precarious

state for many months ; I have not recovered my usual strength, and there is a feeling of delicacy throughout ; I do not think that I am nervous, but my spirits are low ; I am, however, so much revived and strengthened by generous living and a little care and quietness, that I rather look to a general revival of health. On the other hand, I query whether a step downwards is not taken, that I shall never fully recover ; at all events, I have been poorly enough to have the end of life brought closely before me, and to stimulate me in faith to do *quickly* what my Lord may require of me ; but above all, it leads me to desire to cast myself more entirely on the fulness of His love, mercy, and pity, and to entreat his care over me, not permitting more to be brought upon me than my extremely weak and infirm nature can bear, and that He will undertake for me at the last, and through the freeness of His grace, and the fulness of the merits of His dear Son, grant me a place within the gates of His city. I long, before I go hence, to have a clearer and more certain view of the Heavenly inheritance.

25th.—Before breakfast—I am in a strait. O, my gracious Lord ! be Thou my Helper, my Guide, my Counsellor, and my Defence ; keep me, I pray Thee, from the most weighty service before me, unless it be really and truly Thy call ; and if it be Thy call, fit me for it by Thine own Spirit, and Thine own power, and touch my lips, as with a live coal from Thine altar, that I may be qualified to speak the word in season to those who need it. Anoint Thou the tongue to speak, and the ear to hear. Grant this prayer for Thine own sake.

Fifth-day morning, 28th.—The Yearly Meeting has cordially united in William Allen and myself having a Meeting for the young people. It is appointed for this evening, which I much regret, as my children cannot attend it ; but I must commit all to my Lord.

I received this morning a most encouraging letter from the Crown Prince of Prussia, expressing great kindness and unity, his belief that a blessing has rested on our visit to Berlin, and requesting us to go again ; it contains an affecting account of the King's health.

In great weakness, in much lowness, and under some real dis-

couragement, and yet not without a sweet hope and feeling of
Thy love, most gracious God, and even Thy peace. I do ask
help of Thee this day, that through Thine own power, and Thine
own Spirit, Thou wouldest help me so to speak the truths of the
everlasting Gospel, that sinners may be induced to turn from
their evil way ; the wavering may be confirmed to give up all for
Thy Name's sake ; the mourners may be comforted, and the
weak strengthened. Take from me the fear of man, and help
me to do all singly and simply to Thy glory, and for the good of
others ; for Thine own Name's sake answer this petition. Amen,
and Amen.

First-day, Sixth Month 14*th.*—The King of Prussia died
this month, and his son the Crown Prince, our dear and valued
friend in the Lord, has succeeded him.

Our Young Queen and Prince Albert were shot at, a few days
ago, by a man with two pistols; but we may thankfully say not
injured.

I desire to commend those in authority, gracious Lord, to Thy
most Holy keeping. Be Thyself their Helper, in their very
difficult and dangerous circumstances, and grant them wisdom
and sound discretion, to reign over the people with equity, with
judgment, and with mercy.

21*st.*—Our British Society Meeting was, I think, well got
through, our reports, &c., &c., occupied so much time, that I could
not properly say all that I wished to say ; but I trust that the
short account I gave of our journey was satisfactory. I pressed a
few points about prisoners, also on having Patronage Societies for
discharged prisoners, and Sisters of Charity. I enlarged a little
on the great good the Bible Society had effected in Europe, and
the sweetness of Christian unity, as we had been enabled to maintain it in the British Society, and how I desired that the Lord
Himself might preserve this unity, for with advancing years
and increase of experience, I more and more feel myself a member of the Church Universal, and am less disposed than ever to
any sectarian spirit.

28*th, First-day.*—Since I last wrote I have called upon the
Duchess of Beaufort, and the Duchess of Sutherland. The
Duchess of Beaufort received me with much true Christian friend-

ship ; the Duchess of Sutherland, in a remarkably kind manner ; soon after I entered the room, the Duke and his daughters came in. We had much interesting religious conversation. I felt the spirit of Christian love and prayer arise in my heart for them, that the blessing of God might rest upon them, that as He had given them so liberally of the fatness of the earth, He would also cause the dew of Heaven to descend upon them. The next day, I wrote to ask the Duchess whether she wished to attend a Meeting, on account of the Anti-Slavery Society, at Exeter Hall, as I fancied she might like it, I had a cordial answer, saying that she would go. We sat near the Duke of Sussex and the French Ambassador. To find my poor unworthy self thus placed in the face of this immense assembly (I think three thousand persons) was rather fearful, and yet very interesting, from the cause we were engaged in, the numbers interested in it and the honour of appearing on the side of the afflicted slaves.

On the following, Mrs. Fry encountered one of those days, of extreme fatigue and overwhelming interest, which unquestionably were sapping the springs of life. The morning began with a meeting of Friends in London ; afterwards she waited upon the Duchess of Gloucester, had a short interview with the Duke of Sussex ; and returned to Upton to meet, at Ham House, the residence of her brother Samuel Gurney, the American Delegates, who had come to England on the subject of slavery. She describes her drive from London, with the Duchess of Sutherland, and Lord Morpeth " as pleasant and interesting."

We had much conversation on deeply important subjects, I endeavoured to show them the blessedness of the Lord's service, and its excellence ; and the beauty of the work of grace in the heart, how it strengthened, regulated, and gave power to enjoy the blessings of this life.

Upton Lane, Seventh Month 7th.—We had the French Ambassador, and a large party to dinner here yesterday, these occasions are serious to me. The query comes home, how far the expensive dinner is right to give, and further, whether good results from it, and whether, if death was approaching, we should thus spend our time ; on the other hand, after the extraordinary kindness shown us in France, and even by the French Government, some mark of attention was due from us. Also, to show hospitality to strangers is right and Christian, and in some measure to receive them as they are accustomed to live, does not appear wrong. My fear is, that the time was not turned to account, by the most important subjects being enough brought forward, I tried to do a little in this way, but I fear not enough. May my Lord keep us from in any way lowering the cause we love, may He help us by His grace more continually to exalt it, and may neither our omissions or commissions injure it. Grant gracious Lord that this may be the case.

15*th*.—I am just come from, what we believe to be, the deathbed of my dear cousin A—— C——, and a very remarkable scene it is. After a long illness of much suffering, and the birth of a child a few days ago, and after much deep conflict of spirit, and humiliation of heart, she appears, through grace, to have experienced entire pardon and reconciliation with God, which she has most clearly expressed ; besides, in the most remarkable manner, having exhorted her husband and children to serve the Lord with purpose of heart. She says, the world is a cruel, hard master, but the Lord our God is a most merciful Master, it appears as if spiritual things were in a very remarkable and powerful degree opened to her view. She wished once more to see W. Wigram the clergyman and me, but she added " I have ceased from man." When I went to her she said " I am washed." I replied, in the blood of the everlasting covenant. " I see my Saviour, and wish always to look to Jesus." I said, I believed I might say, thine eye will see the King in His beauty, and behold the land that is very far off ; she replied, " yes, I shall see the golden streets and the pearl gates of the city." I said, eye hath not seen nor ear heard, what the Lord hath prepared for those that love Him ; she replied, " God is love." I said, I believed that through mercy, the blessing of the Lord rested on her, and would rest on those nearest to her ; she added, " if they cleave to Him, and entirely serve Him without compromise."

First-day, 19*th*.—My attention much occupied by poor dear

A—— C—— and all nearest to her. To have extreme illness, suffering and death, brought so closely home, touches me and makes me feel my weakness on these points.

I also spent part of the afternoon with dear S—— S——, reading the Scriptures with her and her sisters, desiring, in her suffering state, to lead her to look to the Saviour simply and unreservedly ; so that my day was nearly devoted to the sorrowful, at the same time that I felt myself encompassed with infirmity.

26th.—I paid a very interesting visit to Lady Granville, and found the Duchess of Beaufort with her, that dear devoted spiritually minded lady.

Eighth Month 6th.—There has been some fear of a war with France, which has been really sorrowful to me ; I could have wept at the thoughts, so dear are the people of that country to my heart, and so awful is it to think of the horrors of war, which ever way we look at the subject, religiously, morally or physically. The longer I live, and the greater my experience of life, the more decided are my objections to war, as wholly inconsistent with the Christian calling. O may the Almighty grant, that through His Omnipotence and unutterable love and mercy in Christ our Saviour, the day may not be very far distant, when the people shall learn war no more,—when peace and righteousness shall reign in the earth.

16th, *First-day morning.*—After being unwell for some days, I set off with my dearest husband and H—— for Sea View, a lovely little spot on the Isle of Wight, where F——, C——, and their children are staying. We met with the kindest and warmest reception, and were, I may truly say, cherished and comforted by them. How the tide turns ; my dearest children, for whom I have felt so deeply, are in their turns becoming my helpers and comforters,—thanks be to my Heavenly Father. The place beautiful—the sea air very refreshing, and I almost like another person. On First-day morning we had a very solemn Meeting together ; and in the evening, a large number came to our reading, the gentry, sailors, &c. One day I visited Parkhurst, an interesting new prison for boys, which gave me much satisfaction. It was curious to see some of the very things that in early life I in part begun, carried out in practice. I have lived to see much more than I expected of real improvement in prisons. We are expecting our dearest brother Joseph home this week from America, and I mean to accompany him into Norfolk, if it be my Lord's will. May a blessing rest upon his return! I am increasingly of opinion, that these long separations are liable to serious objections; I think, where it is clear that the great Head of the Church calls any of us far off for a long time, it is most important to have those nearest to us, join us for part of the time, and I believe it would be according to the will of our God.

Earlham, 21*st.*—My dearest brother Joseph is safely returned home, after his absence of three years, on his religious visit to America and the West India Islands. I think I never saw any person in so perfectly peaceful a state; he says, unalloyed peace, like a sky without a cloud, and above all, enabled thankfully to enjoy his many blessings. We arrived at Liverpool on the 16th, and I first met him at my son G——'s, as he called there for me. We all went together to Upton, after our visit to G—— and S——, and a delightful time we had together. The next morning our dearest brother Joseph returned God thanks for his unspeakable mercies; his many deliverances, his great preservations spiritually and temporally, his labours of Christian love being blessed and prospered, and many fruits of it seen. He then returned thanks for my brother Samuel and his family, and earnestly prayed for them, that the windows of heaven might be opened, and blessings be poured forth upon them; he also returned thanks for our brother Fowell, and for his having been prospered in his work of Christian charity for the poor slaves, then for me, and for the blessing attending on me and mine; and lastly, for his own children, wholly giving them up to the Lord and to His service. After dinner the same day, he made a beautiful and striking acknowledgment of the mercies shown him; and what delighted me, he appeared to stand fast in true gospel liberty, and to feel true unity of spirit with all that love the Lord Jesus in sincerity. I also returned thanks for these innumerable mercies. We left home the next morning, and I had a very interesting journey here with dearest Joseph, Fowell and Hannah; but I was fatigued.

Twelfth Month 31*st.*—I deeply feel coming to the close of this year, rather unusually so, it finds me in a low estate, as from circumstances, my spirit is rather overwhelmed, although I am sensible that blessings abound through unmerited mercy. I think the prison cause at home and abroad much prospering, many happy results from our foreign expedition, and much doing at home. Among other things, the establishment of a Patronage Society for prisoners, by which many poor wanderers appear to be helped and protected, and a Society for Sisters of Charity to visit and attend the sick. I have had much to do with those in authority, in other countries and our own ; and have been treated with great kindness and respect by them.

I have been really interested for our Queen in her marriage with Prince Albert, and lately in her confinement with a little girl.

Mrs. Fry's habitual acquaintance with the chamber of sickness, and with scenes of suffering and death, had taught her the necessity that exists for a class of women to attend upon such, altogether different and superior to the hireling nurses that are generally to be obtained. Her communications with M. Fliedner, and all she learned from him personally, and by letter, of his establishment at Kaiserswerth, stimulated her desire to attempt something of the kind in England. Her own occupations being too urgent and numerous to allow of much personal attention, the plan was undertaken, and on a small scale carried into effect by her sister, Mrs. Samuel Gurney, with the assistance of her daughters, and some other ladies. When not engaged in nursing, the " Sisters" reside at " the home" in the City. They wear a plain, but inconspicuous dress ; they are maintained and paid by the institution, but are not permitted to receive any money or gift, under any circumstances, for their attendance in illness.

The funds of the society are small, partly depending upon subscriptions, and partly upon the liberality of those who have benefited from the institution, and have the means of so doing. To the poor the services of the Sisters are gratuitous.

The exertions of this little society have been hitherto greatly circumscribed, and it may be looked upon more as an experiment than as an object attained. The help of the nursing Sisters has been sought and greatly valued by persons of all classes, from royalty to the poorest and most destitute.

Mrs. Fry could imagine a still higher calling; one of a more spiritual nature, in which love to souls should be the leading, compassion to the suffering body the secondary motive for action. Perhaps the nearest thing in England, to that which she would have desired to see, is to be found in the German Hospital, lately established at Dalston, where Deaconesses from Kaisers-- werth perform their arduous duties in a spirit of meekness, perseverance, and love, that ensures, not only the tender and judicious care of the patient, but has been marvellously blessed, in leading many to the Fountain opened for sin and uncleanness.

Earlham, First Month 3rd, 1841.—I found my spirits much overwhelmed yesterday, by a very serious account from Champion S——, of an accident that they had met with in the Medi- terranean, by a vessel striking against their steamer, but in mercy they were saved by the hand of the Lord (we may say) though in the greatest danger. From the ship that ran against them a man fell into their vessel; and as he came direct from Constantinople, they became, in the eye of law, infected; there- fore, were obliged to perform quarantine for weeks, in a small dirty steam-vessel, in the harbour of Civita Vecchia. H—— being so extremely tried by the sea, I consider it an affliction; and yet so far greater an one has been averted, that I have only cause humbly and reverently to return thanks to Him, who has answered my prayers for them, that they might be kept safely in the hour of danger. Twice they have thus been exposed in steam-packets already; once in going to Havre, and now again.

Second Month 21st, First-day.—Our dearest son J—— had

been poorly a few days with influenza, and on Third-day last, A—— sent for me, saying, he was very unwell. I walked over with little delay, and found him, I thought, really ill. We sent for Dr. Elliot, who said his lungs were highly inflamed, and most evidently, blood constantly flowing or oozing from some vessels. Our eyes were suddenly opened to see this most tenderly beloved one in a state of real danger. My heart almost sunk within me, and with the exception of leaving him for a few hours to see the Queen Dowager, an appointment which I did not think it right to break, I have been constantly nursing him since, with the exception of sitting up with him at night. He has, at times, suffered a good deal ; at others, not so much as might be expected. I have felt deep anxiety, but generally a quiet and hopeful spirit has been my portion. His dearest wife has been greatly afflicted, and latterly much overcome; but the evident amendment of yesterday and to-day has comforted us much. It has closely brought home to the heart, the need of knowing Christ to be our Refuge, our Help and our Salvation ; it will not do to wait until the day of sickness comes upon us, when perhaps, the least excitement might cause danger and death, when the most solemn truths are felt, but must not be spoken ; when subjects of the deepest interest ought not to be named in the sick room, and often, if they are, the mind is not in a state to receive them.

Third Month 12*th.*—A few days ago, I went to meet the gentlemen going to Africa in the Niger expedition. Several naval officers Sir Edward Parry, Captain Trotter, Captain William B. Allen, Sir Robert Inglis, Sir Thomas Acland and many others. After our luncheon, my dear brother Buxton asked me, if I wished for a pause, when almost without my consent, there was silence. I had not a word on my mind before, although deeply concerned for them. I however felt then enabled to recommend all to keep a very single eye to their Lord ; not to depend on the arm of flesh, but continually to look upwards ; not to be discouraged at any difficulties or opposition for I had found it good to meet with these things, because they led us more constantly to Christ, as our Help, our Refuge and our Guide. There was a very solemn feeling over us, and I think, much unity of spirit felt. They wish me to go to see their ships, and meet the officers and men to have some religious time with them, previous to their departure for Africa.

28th, First-day.—This has been a very important week, and very exercising in part. In the first instance, our dearest L—— was taken very ill last First-day afternoon, not having been confined a week. I went to her after going to Tottenham Meeting, and I was very weightily engaged in ministry and prayer there; and the same in our Afternoon Meeting, so that, in addition to my anxiety and fatigue with our dearest L——, I felt really overdone. The next day, I closely nursed her until the evening, when I went to Ham House to meet again most of the naval officers going out on the African expedition, to endeavour to suppress slavery and promote free trade and missionary labours in that land. There were many naval captains, and a considerable number of other interesting persons. I should think, sixty or seventy. I felt it laid upon me to have a religious time with them, and spoke to them and prayed for them—to me a very deeply humbling service, much, very much in the cross; but my Lord helped me. I have to-day a very weighty prospect of duty, to go to the ships to see those who were not with us the other evening, and some who were. May my Lord be very near to me, fitting me for His own service, out of weakness making me strong. May He freely pour forth His own holy anointing upon me, and be unto me Himself wisdom, that His own praise may be really shown forth, and the people edified, comforted and helped, before they leave for their great undertaking.

Upton, Fourth Month 4th, First-day.—On the afternoon of last First-day, we went to the Wilberforce ship, my dear brother Buxton, my brother Gurney, and several of our young people. We found our valuable friend Captain Cook, and his wife there; Captain Bird Allen and many other officers; also, the chaplain going out with them. After a while, we all met together in a great hulk, as there was not suitable room in the ship. First, a considerable portion of the Church Service was read. Then Captain B. Allen opened the way for any present to speak; my brother Buxton rose and addressed all present, officers and crew. Further, he said, on behalf of any there of the Society

of Friends, he wished all to know that they did not come prepared, but entirely trusted to the teachings of the Holy Spirit;
and how earnestly he desired, that on that occasion the Holy
Spirit might be poured forth upon some present, and help them
to speak. He said to those going the expedition, how he prayed
for them, and should pray for them day and night, that their Lord
might be with them, keep them and bless them, (or to that
effect); we then sat in silence awhile, then I arose and ministered. I think the first text I had to speak was, " Put on as
the elect of God, holy and beloved, bowels of mercies, kindness,
humbleness of mind, meekness, long suffering." I had to show
the wonderful power and efficacy of the influence of a true
Christian spirit, and however humble a situation any might
fill, they would be preachers of righteousness if they were thus
governed by the spirit of Christ. I showed them how our Lord
made use of humble instruments, such as the poor fishermen;
then I endeavoured to encourage the most peaceable conduct
towards the heathen. I had some advice for the officers, and
afterwards knelt down, and had a very solemn time in prayer.
My brother Samuel spoke very acceptably, and then gave them
all a text-book, and we parted in love. Captain Bird Allen
accompanied us to the convict ship, where we found the poor
women on deck singing hymns. I spoke to them as a farewell exhortation. I had been with them some time the day
before; several of the poor women having become delirious,
from the excitement of the change from separate confinement
to the bustle of the ship. This must lead me to make further
and stronger efforts for an entire change of the system adopted
with them.

Mrs. Fry's dread of the solitary system was only augmented
by further knowledge of its consequences. As permanent and
a punishment for life, she considered it was too cruel to con-
template, even for the most heinous crimes. As a preparation
for returning into society, she could only suppose it desirable for
very limited periods to be followed by greater enlargement, and
gradually extended intercourse with their fellows. The eye after

being accustomed to total darkness is not more fitted for a burst of light, than, in her opinion, was the inmate of the solitary cell to be again exposed to temptation and unrestricted intercourse with his fellow-men.

Nor was the silent system, when carried to an extreme, approved much if at all more by Mrs. Fry, than the solitary or separate one—though her objections to it were on different grounds. She knew, that it was not liable to the same abuses, from neglect or cruelty, but she considered it little likely to benefit the criminal, and particularly adapted to harden the heart. Who that has reflected much, or marked the workings of the mind of man, has not found that without word or action, a spirit may pervade any collection of persons, either of resistance, opposition and defiance, or of comparative kindliness and subordination. No delusion did she consider greater, than that man can be treated as a machine, and remodelled, though having his conduct bent to obedience by strong ₊coercion and dread of punishment. To benefit a sentient being, his sympathies must be as much as possible enlisted on the right side, the spirit of opposition never heedlessly excited, nor his displeasure roused, against the circumstances he is under, and the authorities over him. Perhaps no scheme could be contrived by the ingenuity of man, more likely to petrify the little remaining softness of the heart, or aggravate his already rebellious passions, than to consign an individual to the companionship of others similarly circumstanced, submitting to in act, but resisting in spirit, the influences they are under. He and they may be so placed, as habitually, not even to see one another. But who will believe, that there are not moments and opportunities, when the evil glance can pass from man to man? When the concentrated malice that burns within, will show itself in the countenance? When the mighty power of the human eye can convey meaning, or circulate a watchword of mental resistance, without a sound escaping the lips? Men are not likely

to abhor evil from being driven to abhor the *method* by which it
is purposed to bring them to good. The more hateful the restraints of virtue in the aggregate become to any one, and the
stronger his dislike of the authorities by which they are enforced,
the more ready is he for the commission of fresh crime ; for no
mere dread of punishment, because a little more or less severe, or
under somewhat different modifications, in the hour of reckless
temptation will deter from guilt. To induce an inclination to
do better something of a taste for better things, a glimmer-
ing of light shed on the darkness of former depravity, were in
Mrs. Fry's estimation the great objects to be obtained. As a
loving parent mixes tenderness with unflinching and even stern
severity, so would she have had the State, the "·Powers that
be," deal with the offender as,

> " A father, whose authority in show
> When most severe, and mustering all its force,
> Is but the graver countenance of love."

With these views, she could not fail as occasion presented
itself, to urge her opinions upon others, and deprecate the attempt
at enforcing absolute silence amongst prisoners—for though she
approved of only partial and guarded intercourse, varying with
their guilt and character, and in no case without the presence
and oversight of the officers of the prison ; the endeavour absolutely to close all avenues of communication, where personal
contact remained, was in her estimation, in its practical working
as delusive, as the system in itself was harsh and untenable.

Upton, Fifth Month 23rd, First-day.—The last week has
been a serious one, attendance of the Yearly Meeting difficult,
from L——'s serious illness and other causes.

25th.—Yesterday, I accompanied Hannah Backhouse into the
Men's Meeting. When she had spoken, I rose saying, that I
feared to make any addition, but that I had a few hints to offer.
After expressing my earnest desire that they might all be washed

and sanctified, and justified in the name of the Lord Jesus, and by
the Spirit of our God, I began with my hints.   I said my views
of the state of the Society were not so discouraging as those of
many others.   I remembered, that our first Friends were gathered
out of various religious denominations, and from the most spiritual of these, therefore they were a spiritual and seeking people ;
but in our day, most were Friends from birth and education,
and not conviction ; though I believed there were really spiritual
ones amongst us ; but I saw much wanting, arising partly from
these causes, first, the tendency to be a formal people, resting
in a high spiritual profession ; like the foolish virgins with
lamps but no oil in them, this did much harm.   Then I feared,
being so much a commercial people, that there were too many
who bowed to the idols of gold and of silver, and this hindered
their serving only the living God ; but above all, I apprehended
that too many grieved, quenched and resisted the Holy Spirit of
God, and this was most injurious to us.   I feared an unwilling-
ness to be taught the first simple lessons of the Spirit, because
humbling to the human heart, and that this hindered arriving
at greater knowledge.   I thought our deficiencies in faith and
practice much to arise from this quenching the Holy Spirit.   I
believed if there was more faithfulness at all times and in all
places—in the Market place—in the Counting-house—they would
be preachers of righteousness, and there would be judges raised
up as at the first, and counsellors as at the beginning ; that we
should as a people, arise, shine and show that the glory of the
Lord had risen upon us, and that we should uphold our important
testimonies in the spirit of wisdom and meekness.   I also showed
those who were young, how gently our Lord dealt with us, how
He fitted us for His own work, how He gave us, not the spirit of
fear, but of love and of power and of a sound mind.   I also
expressed my desire for all those engaged in the discipline, that
their spirits might be covered with charity, that they might
seek to restore the offender, remembering themselves, lest they
should also be tempted ; and that they might be enabled to
strengthen the things that remain that were ready to die.   I
concluded by expressing my desire, that all might fill their
places in the militant Church on earth, and eventually join the

Church triumphant in Heaven in never-ending rest, peace, joy and glory.

To the daughter who was so ill, whom she was sedulously nursing, in a moment of agitation and distress, she administered a lotion by mistake for a draught, which was likely to be seriously injurious, unless the measures resorted to proved entirely successful.

Upton, Fifth Month 30*th.*—In the very depths of affliction, O Lord! I apply unto Thee, in faith, for help. Leave me not, nor forsake me in this awful time, and enable me to thank Thee for the mitigations permitted. Our dearest L—— being again extremely ill, I in my hurry gave her a wrong medicine of a poisonous nature : my fright at first was inexpressible. We sent for the Doctor, who gave an emetic. It was thought that she did not suffer materially from it, but in addition to her other sufferings and afflicted state, it was bitter to me, almost past expression ; but I sought to endure, as seeing Him who is invisible. The conflict of my mind is great indeed ; not I think so much in giving up this beloved one, if the Lord saw meet to take her to Himself into His kingdom, though it would be very hard to part, as I have perhaps too much encouraged her with the expectation of recovery. Still she has had a long time of preparation for many months past ; she has, I know, doubted her living, and I do believe that a very precious work of grace has been going on in her heart, and through infinite wisdom, mercy, and love, she has, through a Saviour's blood, obtained pardon and reconciliation with God.

Permit me, gracious Lord ! in this deep emergency, to entreat Thee to save my beloved child, with an everlasting salvation, and if it be Thy blessed will, grant her a little revival, that I may never have the weight of believing that her end was accelerated by my carelessness. Be very near to her, granting her Thy peace, and the joy of Thy salvation, and be very near to help her beloved husband, whose tender care over her is wonderful. Keep also, merciful Lord ! Thy poor servant, from losing her faith or her power of mind in this close trial of faith and patience.

Near one o'clock.—Our sweet L—— revived wonderfully out of a sleep, that looked almost death-like, and she has been quite lively ever since.

Sixth Month 5th.—Our dearest L—— decidedly mending, her state of mind highly favoured, so entirely resigned to her Lord's will. My spirits also are revived, and my bodily health much restored. I have seen the tender mercy and faithfulness of my Lord, in keeping my understanding clear and my faith alive during that awful night, when I made so sad a mistake.

The query now comes closely home, Am I called again to the continent or not? Gracious Lord, I earnestly pray Thee, for Thine own name sake, to make my way plain before me, and through the power of Thy own Spirit, to make me perfectly willing to go or to stay, to do or to suffer, to be something or nothing, exactly as Thou mayst see good for myself, or on account of others. I do commit myself, my all, and Thy cause which I love, to Thy most Holy keeping and direction. Amen.

CHAPTER XXIII.

From the time of Mrs. Fry's return from her journey the preceding year, she had continually received communications from the Continent, urging her going to some places which she had not visited, or returning to complete the work in others where she had already been. When she heard of these openings for usefulness, her heart responded to the call. Her daughter, whose fearful illness had caused her such extreme anxiety, had nearly recovered its effects; and another daughter, who had passed the winter in Italy with her family, was again in England. Her home party was provided for, having arranged to spend the autumn at Ramsgate; whilst her beloved brother, Joseph John Gurney, offered her the great advantage of his society and support; he believing it his duty to visit several places on the Continent, for various religious and philanthropic purposes, especially, to impart the observations he had made during his lengthened tarriance in America and the West Indies, on slavery, and slave-holding, to those potentates, who still permitted this evil to exist in their dominions. Mrs. Fry shrunk from the great effort of leaving home, and encountering the fatigue of travelling, from the shaken

state of her health ; for her sensations and symptoms induced the
belief, that her life of exertion and effort had told irremediably
upon her vital powers. But it was not because the shades of
evening were gathering round her, that she would slacken her
labours for the good of others. Whilst it was yet day, she desired
to work and accomplish all that her great Master might have for
her to do, before the night should come in which no man can
work.

(Previous to Ratcliff Monthly Meeting), Sixth Month 22nd.
—I most earnestly desire the direction of my Lord and Master,
through the immediate teaching of His Holy Spirit, that I may
really know and do His will, and His will only. For Thy Name
sake, O Lord ! lead me and teach me. Am I once more to lay
before the members of our little portion of Thy Church, my
apprehended call of duty to go abroad ? I earnestly pray Thee,
if it be Thy call, make it very clear ; if it be not, let me certainly
know it, gracious Lord, that not my will but Thine be done.
Amen.

27th, First-day.—After most deeply weighing the subject,
and after very earnest prayer for direction, I felt best satisfied to
inform my friends of my belief that it might be right for me to
accompany my dearest brother Joseph to the Continent, and to
visit some of the more northern countries of Europe. I had
very decided encouragement from the Friends, particularly the
most spiritual amongst them, which I felt helpful to me ; but I
was surprised at the degree of relief and peace that I felt afterwards, as from a voice before me, saying, " this is the way, walk
in it."

28th, Second-day.—I had, on Seventh-day, letters from the
Queen of Prussia and the Princess William. The first expressing much satisfaction at our proposed visit ; our way is clearly
open in her heart, and that of the King.

My sister Gurney, and our dear friend Charlotte Upcher, went
with me to the Bishop of London on Sixth-day, on the subject
of the Sisters of Charity. It has been a great pleasure to me
the Queen Dowager giving her name as Patroness.

Before leaving home, Mrs. Fry addressed this letter to Captain (Colonel) Jebb, on the subject of the Model Prison, at Pentonville :—

Seventh Month 22nd, 1841.

ESTEEMED FRIEND,

Thy letter, explaining the cause of our not having the pleasure of meeting thee at Newgate, followed me to this place. But not being willing to give up seeing the new prison that is building before I went abroad, my brother Gurney and two of his sons accompanied me there, after having waited sometime at Newgate, in the hope of seeing thee there.

We were much interested by our visit to this new prison. We think the building, generally, does much credit to the architect, particularly in some important points, as ventilation, the plan of the galleries, the chapel, &c. ; and we were also much pleased to observe the arrangement for water in each cell, and that the prisoner could ring a bell in case of wanting help.

The points that made us uneasy, were first, the dark cells, which, we consider should never exist in a Christian and civilized country. I think having prisoners placed in these cells a punishment peculiarly liable to abuse. Whatever restrictions may be made for the governor of a gaol, and however lenient those who *now* govern, we can little calculate upon the change the future may produce, or how these very cells, may one day be made use of in case of either political or religious disturbance in the country, or how any poor prisoner may be placed in them, in case of a more severe administration of justice.

I think no person should be placed in *total* darkness ; there should be a ray of light admitted. These cells appear to me calculated to excite such awful terror in the mind, not merely from their darkness, but from the circumstance of their being placed within another cell, as well as being in such a dismal situation.

I am always fearful of any punishment beyond what the law *publicly authorises*, being *privately inflicted* by any keeper, or officer of a prison ; for my experience most strongly proves, that there are few men who are themselves sufficiently governed and regulated by Christian principle, to be fit to have *such power* entrusted in their hands; and further, I observe, that officers in prisons have generally so much to try and to provoke them, that they themselves are apt to become hardened to the more tender feelings of humanity; they necessarily, also, see so much through the eyes of those under them, turnkeys and inferior officers, (too many of whom are little removed, either in education or morals, from the prisoners themselves,) that their judgments are not always just.

The next point that struck us was, that in the cells generally, the windows have that description of glass in them that even the sight of the sky is entirely precluded. I am aware that the motive is, to prevent the possibility of seeing a fellow-prisoner; but I think a prison for separate confinement should be so constructed that the culprits may at least see the sky; indeed, I should prefer more than the sky, without the liability of seeing fellow-prisoners. My reason for this opinion is, that I consider it a very important object to preserve the *health of mind and body* in these poor creatures; and I am *certain* that separate confinement produces an unhealthy state, both of mind and body, and that, therefore, everything should be done to counteract this influence, which, *I am sure,* is baneful in its moral tendency; for I am satisfied that a sinful course of life increases the tendency to mental derangement, as well as bodily disease; and I am as certain, that an unhealthy state of mind and body has generally a demoralising influence, as the mind in an enervated state is more liable to yield to temptation, than when in a lively powerful state; and I consider light, air, and the power of seeing something beyond the mere monotonous walls of a cell, highly important. I am aware that air is properly admitted, also light, still I do think they ought to see the sky, the changes in which make it a most pleasant object for those closely confined.

When speaking of health of body and mind, I also mean health of *soul,* which is of the first importance; for I do not believe that a despairing or stupified state is suitable for leading poor sinners to a Saviour's feet for pardon and salvation.

　　　　　　　I remain, with regard,

　　　　　　　　　　　Thy friend,

　　　　　　　　　　　　　　ELIZABETH FRY.

Upton, Seventh Month 30th.—All difficulties and obstructions, which have been serious and numerous, are removed, as far as I can see; the way is made plain and open before us, to set off to-morrow for our visit to Holland, Germany, Prussia, and Denmark. My brother Joseph, his daughter Anna, my dear niece Elizabeth Gurney and my own maid go with me, with the prospect of every comfort this life can afford; and, I humbly trust, the Lord Himself calling us into His service, that His blessing will be with those who stay, and those who go. Grant, gracious Lord, through the fulness of Thy love, that this may indeed be the case.

The travellers arrived at Rotterdam, July the 31st, and passed a tranquil Sabbath there. In the evening, they held a large Meeting in an apartment of the Hotel; the following day visited prisons; and on the 2ud of August proceeded to the Hague.

Returning a second time, they neither felt themselves, nor were received as strangers. They again visited the prisons, and urged upon the proper authorities the means of remedying the evils existing there. The gracious reception given to themselves and the objects of their mission, by the Royal family, Mrs. Fry describes in a letter to her home circle.

You will like to know that, through tender mercy, I was favoured to feel much rest, refreshment, and peace, at Rotterdam, and much evidence that I was in my right place. Our visits to the boys' prison at Rotterdam, and to the women's prison at Gouda, were highly interesting. I find a second visit to a place much better than a first. We had two meetings—one philanthropic, one religious—both well got through, and a large attendance. I felt in leaving the place much comfort and satisfaction.

When we arrived at the Hague, our kind friend Lady Disbrowe, (the wife of the British Minister), and Sir Alexander and Lady Malet, received us cordially. We divided our evening between Sir Edward Disbrowe and our hotel, having a party for us by

accident in each place; on the whole both passed off very
well, and many appeared to be very glad to see us again. We
sent our letters to the King from Prince Albert. On Sixth-
day, a message came to desire that we would wait upon the
King and Queen the next day, at half-past one o'clock, accompanied by Lady Disbrowe.

We remained with the King and Queen, and their daughter the
Princess Sophia, about an hour. As rather an interesting event in
my life, I mean to tell you particulars of this interview. Before we
went, we had a solemn, short Meeting for worship, with our dear
and valued friends of this town; afterwards we prepared to go.
I was decorated by my best garments outwardly, and I desired
so to be clothed with better ornaments spiritually, as to render
attractive that which I had to recommend. We all felt very
weightily our serious engagement, as we had much to represent
to the King respecting the West Indies, prisons, and religious
education for the people in his own country. The King, a lively,
clever, perfect gentleman, not a large man, in regimentals; the
Queen, (sister to the Emperor of Russia), a fine, stately person,
in full and rather beautiful morning dress of white; the Princess
much the same. After our presentation the King began easy
and pleasant conversation with me, about my visiting prisons. I
told him in a short, lively manner, the history of it; he said, he
heard I had so many children, how could I do it? This I explained; and mentioned how one of my daughters now helped
me in the Patronage Society. He appeared much interested, as
did the Queen. I then said, my brother had visited the West
Indies, and would be glad to tell the King and Queen the result
of his observations in these islands. This he did capitally, shew-
ing the excellency of freedom, and its most happy results; he
represented, also, the sad effects of the Dutch enlisting soldiers
on the Gold Coast, and how it led to evil and slavery, which so
touched the King, that he said he meant to put a stop to it. I
then began again, and most seriously laid before the King, the
sad defect of having no religious education in their Government
Schools, and the Bible not introduced. He said he really felt it;
but what could he do when there was a law against it? We then
endeavoured to explain how we thought it might be obtained.

Our very serious conversation was mixed with much cheerfulness. I felt helped to speak very boldly, yet respectfully; so did my brother. I concluded by expressing my earnest desire that the King's reign might be marked by the prisons being so reformed, that punishment might become the means of the reformation of criminals; by the lower classes being religiously educated; and by the slaves in their Colonies being liberated. The King then took me by the hand, and said he hoped God would bless me. I expressed my desire, that the blessing of the Almighty might rest on the King, Queen, their children, and their children's children. We gave them books, which they accepted kindly. It certainly was a very pleasant and satisfactory interview, that, I humbly trust, will not prove in vain in the Lord.

On Sixth-day, with my brother, I visited the Princess of Orange. We had open, free, pleasant communication on many important points. The same morning, I visited the Princess Frederick, sister to the King of Prussia, just out of her confinement. I found her like the other members of that superior family. My brother, also, had very satisfactory intercourse with the Princess of Orange. The Ministers of the Interior and of Finance have been very kind, and we hope and expect that real good will result. The Princess of Orange has a lovely little boy about two months older than our Princess. The girls went to see him; they accompanied me to the Princess Fredric, who wished to see them, from her knowledge of us through the Prussian Court.

The 7th, they reached Amsterdam, where they remained four days, visiting the prisons and various public institutions, and holding meetings for philanthropic and religious objects. The Lunatic Asylum they found in a deplorable condition.

Among other miserable objects, one unhappy woman unclothed lay grovelling in straw. Whether the look of compassion or the voice attracted her, cannot be known; but she dragged herself, as nearly as her chains would admit to her visitant, and endeavoured to reach her : the hand she desired to touch was yielded, she kissed it again and again, and burst into an agony of tears.

Will any one venture to assert that this poor creature was past all touch of human feeling, or the reach of gentle control.

It was a question, on leaving Amsterdam, whether to take the usual route to Bremen or to go by Wilderhausen, over desolate country, by a shorter, but not so good a road. The one which was chosen proved extremely rough and fatiguing, in places, the sand reaching to the axle-tree of the carriage; scarcely a bird or an insect, or any living thing to be seen. Miserable accommodation by night, and wearisome travelling by day. Mrs. Fry became much indisposed, and scarcely able to proceed, when, in the middle of the last day's journey, a sudden jerk broke the mainspring of the carriage; but happily, not far from a small inn, where rest and refreshment could be obtained. On Saturday the 14th, they had the happiness of finding themselves in excellent quarters, in the pleasant town of Bremen. The early part of Sunday was tranquil, but in the evening there was a very large Meeting held in the Museum, a noble building near the Hotel. Long before the appointed hour, well-dressed persons proceeded to secure places. Several of the pasteurs were present. One of them at the close arose and beautifully addressed the missionary brother and sister, expressing his desire that what had passed might be blessed to the people, and that they might be themselves blessed. To Mrs. Fry he said, your name has long been to us " a word of beauty." A Christian gentleman wrote to them afterwards, " Now I am more than convinced that you are sent to us by the Lord, to be and to become a great blessing and a salt to our city." The following morning they went to see the prison. Bremen being a Hans Town, the address afterwards forwarded by Mrs. Fry and her brother to the authorities necessarily varied in some respects from one intended for a sovereign power.

When the carriage came to the Hotel door, for their departure, crowds of the lower classes surrounded it, wishing them a prosperous journey, " bon voyage," thanking them for the good Meeting they had had the evening before, and begging for tracts ; whilst numbers could not be persuaded to move till Mrs. Fry had shaken hands with them.

Their little transit across the Elbe would have been delightful, with a glorious setting sun, but for a mob of persons returning from Harburg market, who having discovered Mrs. Fry and her tract bag, so pressed upon her, that she was glad to take refuge in the carriage, whilst their clever and devoted courier (Erançois) harangued the people, on his lady's various excellencies, but carefully prevented their approach. The time at Harburg was extremely full ; work was ready for them before their arrival. With Miss Sieveking with whom she had long communicated, though personally unknown till then, she attended with exceeding interest the Committee of Ladies, which had for years faithfully laboured in the female prison there. Prisons and public institutions again occupied the mornings. The evenings were devoted to social intercourse, when subjects of benevolence or religion were discussed, or to appointed Meetings for worship. They held two of this nature, the last, a very large one, took place in the Assembly Room, a splendid apartment fully lighted and well arranged with seats. · Many of the authorities and principal inhabitants of the place were present, the English Chargé d'Affaires, the French Chargé d'Affaires, their friend Colonel F——, and many others. They were conducted into the Meeting by the Syndic Sieveking, an eminently good man, who led them to a small platform. Mrs. Fry rose to explain her experience in prisons, and the principles upon which she had acted. The results of Gospel truth being taught, Christian kindness, change of habit and many similar topics ; she then spoke of the institutions of their city, and all she had remarked in them of a desirable or an undesirable nature. Mr. Gurney addressed the assembly upon what he had seen in the West Indies, Abolition of Slavery, Religious Liberty, &c. Great attention was paid, and the interpreters were excellent. At the conclusion, about fifty of their friends attended them to their apartment, when after partaking of refreshments, they parted with regret and affection on all sides.

The following afternoon saw them embarked on the Baltic, they had a brilliant moonlight night and an easy pleasant voyage to Copenhagen, where they remained a week.

On board the packet after leaving Copenhagen, Eighth Month 30th:—

My dearest Husband and Children,

We have been favoured to leave Denmark with peaceful minds, having endeavoured to fulfil our mission as ability has been granted us; a more important one, or a more interesting one, I think I never was called into. On First-day morning, when we arrived in the harbour, we were met by Peter Browne the Secretary to the English Legation, to inform us that the Queen had engaged for us apartments in the Hotel Royal. The appearance of the Hotel was, I should think, like the arrangements of one of our first-rate Hotels about a hundred years ago. ·

The next morning the Queen came to town, and we had a very pleasant and satisfactory interview with her, she certainly is a most delightful woman, as well as a truly Christian and devoted character: she is also lovely in person, and quite the Queen in appearance. She took me in her carriage to her infant school, it really was beautiful to see her surrounded by the little children, and to hear her translating what I wished to say to them. After staying with her about two hours, we returned to our Hotel; and that evening took a drive to see the beautiful Palace of Fredricksburgh in a most lovely situation, the beauties of land and sea combined, with fine forest trees around it. The following morning we regularly began our prison visiting, very sad scenes we witnessed in some of them. We saw hundreds of persons confined for life in melancholy places; but what occupied our most particular attention, was the state of the persecuted Christians. We found Baptist ministers, excellent men, in one of the prisons, and that many others of this sect suffered much in this country, for there is hardly any religious tolerance. It produces the most flattening religious influence, I think more marked than in Roman

Catholic countries. We were much devoted to this service of visiting prisons. Third and Fourth-days, we received various persons in the evenings, but saw as yet but few Danes. On Fourth-day we dined at Sir Henry Watkins Wynn our ambassador, and here we became acquainted with several persons, they live quite in the country, and we saw the true Danish country-house and gardens. The King and Queen were kind enough to invite us all to dine at their palace in the country, on Fifth-day, this was a very serious occasion, as we had so much to lay before the King—slavery in the West Indies—the condition of the persecuted Christians here—and the sad state of the prisons. I was in spirit so weighed down with the importance of the occasion, that I hardly could enjoy the beautiful scene. We arrived about a quarter past three o'clock ; the Queen met us with the utmost kindness and condescension, and took us a walk in their lovely grounds, which are open to the public. We had much interesting conversation, between French and English, and made ourselves understood ; when our walk was finished, we were shown into the drawing-room to the King, who met us very courteously, several were there in attendance. Dinner was soon announced ; imagine me, the King on one side, and the Queen on the other, and only my poor French to depend upon, but I did my best to turn the time to account. At dinner we found the fruit on the table ; first we had soup of the country, secondly, melons, thirdly, yams, anchovies, cavia, bread and butter and radishes, then meat, then pudding, then fish, then chickens, then game, and so on. The fashion was to touch glasses ; no drinking healths. The King and Queen touched my glass on both sides ; when dinner was over we all rose and went out together. The afternoon was very entertaining, the King and Queen took us to the drawing-room window, where we were to see a large school of orphans, protégés of the Queen. I took advantage of this opportunity and laid the state of the prisons before the King, telling him at the same time, that I had a petition for him which I meant to make before leaving the palace. After an amusing time with the poor children, my brother Joseph withdrew with the King into a private room, where for about an hour he gave him attention, whilst he thoroughly enlarged upon the state of their West India islands.

I stayed with the Queen; but after awhile went in to them, and did entreat the King for the poor Baptists in prison, and for religious toleration. I did my best, in few words to express my mind, and very strongly I did it. I gave also Luther's sentiments upon the subject. We slept at our friends the Brownes', a beautiful place by the sea-side. An agreeable serious gentleman, Julius Sehesteed, was our interpreter, and remained with us, helping us to prepare our document for the King, he has become our constant companion, and is now with us in the packet, going to Lubeck, to interpret for us there. On Seventh-day one of our fullest days, we drove into the country to visit the King's sister the Landgravine of Hesse Cassel, the Prince her husband brother to the Duchess of Cambridge, and the lovely Princesses her daughters. We endeavoured to turn these visits to account, by our conversation. In the evening, we held one of our very large Meetings, I may say a splendid one, as to the company, room, &c. I trust that we were both so helped to speak the truth in love on various and very important subjects, as to assist the causes nearest our hearts, for our poor fellow-mortals ; it did not appear desirable to allude to the persecuted Christians, as we had laid their case before the King, we might have done harm by it ; but I feel the way in which Protestant Europe is persecuting, to be a subject that cannot and must not be allowed to rest.

Where we now are, the same old Lutherans whom we found persecuted in Prussia are persecuting others. The way in which ceremonies are depended upon is wonderful, no person is allowed to fill any office civilly or religiously, until confirmed, not even to marry ; and when once confirmed, we hear that it leads to a feeling of such security spiritually, that they think themselves at liberty to do as they like, sadly numerous are the instances of moral fall ! These very weighty subjects so deeply occupying my attention, and being separated from so many beloved ones prevent the lively enjoyment I should otherwise feel, in some of the scenes we pass through ; but I see this to be well, and in the right ordering of Providence. I have the kindest attendants and everything to make me comfortable.

On First-day morning, we had a very interesting Meeting with the poor Baptists. We then again went into the country, to lay all our statements before the King and Queen. I read the one about the prisons and the persecuted Christians ; and my brother read the one about the West Indies : we had had them translated into Danish, for the King to read at the same time. After pressing these things as strongly as we felt right, we expressed our religious concern and desires for the King and Queen. I read a little to them in one of Paul's Epistles ; after that I felt that I must commit them and these important causes to Him who can alone touch the heart. We had a very handsome luncheon, when I was again seated between the King and Queen. I may say their kindness was very great to me.

On Second-day morning, we formed a Society for attending to poor prisoners—gentlemen and ladies ; and then paid a most delightful farewell religious visit to the Queen and Princess. I forgot to mention a very interesting visit to the Queen Dowager.

We arrived at Lübeck, after a calm voyage ; but I do not like nights in steam-packets. I believe that we were sent to Copenhagen for a purpose. May our unworthy labours be blessed to the liberation of many captives, spiritually and temporally.

May the God of peace be near to all of you and to us, as our continual Keeper and Helper.

Farewell, in most tender and near love to all.

Yours indeed, and in truth,

ELIZABETH FRY.

By Lübeck they returned to Hamburgh ; thence Mrs. Fry wrote to her family :—

Hamburgh, *Ninth Month 3rd.*

——— ——— ——— ——— ——— ———,

We last night finished our labours in these Hans Towns. We have laboured in them in various ways, particularly in this large and important town. We have boldly set our faces against religious persecution, and upheld religious toleration and Christian unity in the Church of Christ. We also have laboured about their prisons, and expect to have many evils mitigated. It is extraordinary, the good fellowship and love that we have enjoyed with numbers. In a spiritual sense, fathers, mothers, brothers and sisters given to us, and helpers most curiously and constantly raised up from place to place. ——— ———

From Hamburgh, by Minden and Pyrmont, they pursued
their way to Hanover.

TO HER YOUNGEST DAUGHTER.

Hanover, *Ninth Month 9th,* 1841.

MY DEAREST L——,

I cannot express the fulness of my love and interest for my
children in their different allotments, and how often I think of
you and your families before the Lord, in my quiet meditations.
We arrived here, after finishing our interesting and satisfactory
visits to our dear Friends at Minden and Pyrmont. I felt it
refreshing, being again with these dear simple-hearted people,
and I do think they are useful in their allotment. How much
I should like you to have seen us dining with them at Friedensthal ; such a numerous family, grandmother, children, grandchildren in a large room, with a beautiful and most hospitable
German dinner. We not only were favoured with outward
refreshment, but it reminded me of the disciples formerly, who
went from house to house breaking bread and giving thanks ;
and I desired that we might do as they did, " eat our meat with
gladness and singleness of heart." I hope there was something
of this spirit. The country lovely. I retired for rest on a little
German bed, whilst my companions took a ride on horseback
over the beautiful hills. We had a very interesting Meeting,
largely attended by the company who come here to drink the
waters and the Pyrmontese. At Minden, the Friends are in
more humble life. I could not but be struck with the peculiar
contrast of my circumstances ; in the morning traversing the bad
pavement of a street in Minden, with a poor old Friend in a sort
of knitted cap close to her head, in the evening surrounded by
the Princes and Princesses of a German court ; for, to our surprise, De Julius' sister followed us to Minden, to inform us that
in the town of Bückeberg, that we had passed through, there
was a desire expressed that we should hold a Meeting, and that
the reigning Princess wished us to go to the palace. After some
consideration we agreed to go, and upon our arrival in the town
found a large Meeting of the gentry assembling ; some time afterwards the Prince and Princess and their family came in. They

rule the state of Lippe Schonenburg, one of the small rich
German states. I endeavoured to speak the truth boldly in love,
drawing results from my experience in prisons, and seeking, as
ability was granted me, to bring it home to the hearts of those
present. Your uncle also spoke to the same purpose. Afterwards we had a very agreeable visit to the palace, where we
were most cordially received, and had tea at five o'clock; there
were many to meet us. After this singular visit, we proceeded
here, but did not arrive till past twelve o'clock at night, having
had two Meetings at Minden, and one at Bückeburg. We were
completely tired; almost too much so. To-day we are busy
here, and I am delighted to find the dear late Queen really
had the chains knocked off the poor prisoners at Hameln; it
was a delightful sight to see their happy grateful faces. They
looked as if they knew that we had pleaded for them. I think
it was one of the pleasantest visits I ever paid, and to find that
the prisoners had behaved so well since, and that the kindness
shown them had had so good an effect. We are now much occupied in answering an interesting letter from the King of Hanover
to me, and as we have many weighty things to say to him, I fear
I must leave off, being very tired, and expecting a large party
this evening.

The party in the evening proved particularly satisfactory. Mrs.
Fry and her brother, also met both the gentlemen and the
ladies' Committees for visiting prisons. A day of very hard
travelling brought them to Magdeburgh; and a second, by railroad diverging to visit Wittenburg, to Berlin. Numerous objects
awaited their attention in that city, not the less weighty to Mrs.
Fry, from having been there before and made so many acquain-
tances, besides the additional interest she felt in Institutions
already known to her.

The state of the prisons was of course her chief object of
attention. Mrs. Fry and Mr. Gurney prepared recommendations
to lay before General Thile Minister of the Royal House, embodying their observations and opinions, and urging the necessity
of many alterations before real improvement could be effected.

The Prussian Royal Family were at the time in Silesia; thither
the travellers had been invited to follow them, for there were
those amongst them who considered that the retirement and tran-
quillity of that place would be well suited for the consideration of Mrs. Fry's objects. After three long days' travelling,
they arrived at Hirschberg; but in a day or two moved from
there to Goldenstern, a lovely little hotel close to Fischbach. It
was not a light prospect to Mrs. Fry; she had naturally the fear
of man deeply implanted in her character. Religion had changed
its direction, but not eradicated it. It was no longer for herself
that she was afraid, it was for the cause sake to which her heart
was given; for amongst these royal and noble personages she
dreaded in either herself or her companions, any thing that might
not adorn the doctrine of God her Saviour: but she soon discovered that she had come amongst Christians, many of them
devoted as herself to the service of their Maker. Amongst the
members of the House of Brandenberg, she found many intellectual and excellent persons. In the noble head of that royal
House, one, who with a spirit indomitable as the great Frederick's,
showed equal moral courage in carrying out all that he believed
likely to conduce to the temporal and eternal good of his subjects,
as his predecessor, had displayed in self-aggrandisement and war.
In the beautiful retirement of the Reisenberg, she saw Royalty
retaining all the grace and finish that appertains to it; but freed
from the encumbrances of a city court. Her reception was more
than kind, honoured for her "works' sake," she found herself
by all, and on all occasions, treated with Christian affection and
consideration. No record of this time, singular and important
as it was, exists of her own writing, but a letter to her grandchildren.

Fischbach.

My much-loved Grandchildren,

Instead of writing my private journal, I am disposed to write
to you from this very lovely and interesting place. I am not very

well in health, but I may thankfully acknowledge, that although
tried by it for a while, such sweet peace was granted me that I
was permitted to feel it sleeping as well as waking; so that I
may say, my Lord restored my soul and I fully expect is healing
and will heal my body.   I think a more interesting neighbourhood
I never heard of, than the one we are in.   These lovely mountains have beautiful palaces scattered about them.   One belonging
to the King, others to Prince William, Prince Frederic, and other
Princes and Princesses, not royal, besides several to the nobility ;
but what delights my heart is, that almost all these palaces are
inhabited by Christian families : some, of the most remarkable
brightness.   Then we find a large establishment, with numerous
cottages in the Swiss style, inhabited by a little colony of Tyrolese.
They fled from Zillerthál, because they suffered so much on account
of their religious principles, being Protestants.   The late King
of Prussia allowed them to take refuge in these mountains, and
built them these beautiful cottages.   We therefore rejoice in the
belief, that in the cottages as well as the palaces, there are many
faithful servants of the Lord Jesus Christ.   This evening we
are to hold a Meeting for such as can attend, at the mansion of
the Countess Reden, who is like a mother in Israel to rich and
poor.   We dined at her castle yesterday.   I think the palaces,
for simple country beauty exceed any thing I ever saw ; the
drawing-rooms are so filled with flowers, that they are like green-
houses, beautifully built, and with the finest views of the mountains.   We dined at the Princess William's with several of the
Royal Family ; the Queen came afterwards, she appeared much
pleased at my delight on hearing that the King had stopped
religious persecutions in the country, and that several other things
had been improved since our last visit.   It is a very great comfort to believe, that our efforts for the good of others have been
blessed : may we be thankful enough for it.   Yesterday, we paid
a very interesting visit to the Queen, then to Prince Frederic
of Holland and his Princess sister to the King of Prussia, with
her we had much serious conversation upon many important
subjects, as we had also with the Queen.   Dined early at the
Countess Reden's.   The Princess William and her daughter the
Princess Mary joined us in the afternoon, with several others.

How delighted you would be with the Countess and her sister ; they show the beauty of holiness. Although looked up to by all, they appear so humble, so moderate in every thing. I think the Christian ladies on the Continent dress far more simply than those in England. The Countess appeared very liberal, but extravagant in nothing. A handsome dinner ; but only one sort of wine, and all accordingly. To please us, she had apple-dump- lings, which were felt quite a curiosity : they really were very nice. The company stood still before and after dinner, instead of saying grace.

Afternoon.—We are just returned from Prince William's, where we have had a Meeting of a very interesting nature. Many ladies were assembled to meet us, that I might give them some account of my experience in prisons. Your uncle added some account of his journey in the West Indies. We expressed our desire that the blessing of God might be with them. Great love was shown us ; indeed, they treat me more like a sister than a poor humble individual as I feel myself to be. On our return, we met the King, we rather expect he will be at our Meeting at the Countess Reden's this evening.

Second-day morning.—We returned from our interesting Meeting at the Countess' about eleven o'clock in the evening. The Royal Family were assembled, and numbers of the nobility ; after a while the King and Queen arrived : the poor Tyrolese flocked in numbers. I doubt such a Meeting ever having been held before any where—the curious mixture of all ranks and con- ditions. My poor heart almost failed me. Most earnestly did I pray for best Help and not unduly to fear man. The Royal Family sat together, or nearly so ; the King and Queen, Princess William, Princess Frederick, Princess Mary, Prince William, Prince Charles, brother to the King, Prince Frederick of the Netherlands, young Prince William, besides several other Princes and Princesses not royal. They began with a hymn in German. Your uncle Joseph spoke for a little while, explaining our views on worship. Then I enlarged upon the changes that had taken place since I was last in Prussia, mentioned the late King's kindness to these poor Tyrolese in their affliction and distress ; afterwards addressed these poor people, and then those of high rank, and felt greatly helped to speak the truth to them in love. They appeared very attentive and feeling. I also, at the close of my exhortation, expressed my prayer for them. Then your uncle Joseph spoke fully on the great truths of the Gospel, and showed that the prince as well as the peasant would have to give an account of himself to God. In conclusion, he expressed his prayer for them. They finished with another hymn. It was a solemn time. We afterwards had interesting conversation for about an hour. When the King and Queen were gone, we were enabled to pray with the Countess, for herself and her sister, that all their labours in the Lord's service might be blessed. Now, my much loved grandchildren, let me remind you that we must be humbled and take up the cross of Christ, if we desire to be made use of by our Lord; "He that honoureth me, I will honour." May you confess your Lord before men, and He will then assuredly confess and honour you. I can assure you, when surrounded by so many who are willing to hear me, I feel greatly humbled.

I wish dear Frank to read this, as my eldest grandchild, and one in whom I take so tender an interest. Indeed, my beloved grandchildren, you dwell very near my heart; may the same Holy Spirit who has helped and guided your grandmother, help and guide you!

May the Lord bless you and keep you, and raise you up for His own service, for it is a most blessed service. Dearest love to your fathers and mothers,

I am,

Your most loving grandmother,

E. F.

Erdmansdorf, *Ninth Month* 20th.

My DEAREST H——,

I wish thee, as my beloved youngest son, to have the account of the conclusion of our visit to the beautiful mountains and valleys of Silesia. I wrote a long letter to the grandchildren, which I hope thou wilt see, as it gives an account of our adventures yesterday and the day before. This morning we visited the King and Queen, after our very interesting Meeting last

evening which they attended, at the Countess Reden's ; a
Meeting never to be forgotten. This morning we went with a
long document to the King and Queen about the prisons, and
various other subjects ; we were received with the utmost kindness, and remained with them nearly two hours and a half. We
had also a reading in the Holy Scriptures, and I prayed for them.
We párted in love. We then went over the lovely country, past
the little beautiful Swiss cottages built for the Tyrolese by the
late King, and proceeded to Fischbach to dinner, to take leave
of our much valued friends in these parts. We had a cheerful
pleasant dinner, and afterwards, when thy uncle and the girls went
a drive, I sat down with Prince and Princess William, and the
Countess Reden and her sister, and told them the history of all my
children. When your uncle and the girls came in with the young
party we had a serious time: afterwards I prayed for them. With
many tears we parted, and left this lovely country and family
and friends. I go on with my letter :—This morning we left
Hirschberg between six and seven o'clock, and sad to say, our
careless postilions ran us violently against a cart, and broke our
pole ; we were none hurt, as it was on level ground. Here I am
in a little German pot-house, disposed to finish my history to
thee. I wish thou couldest see us, I think it would make thee
smile—having a sort of breakfast in the same room with the poor
labourers, and such a singular set of people. Thy uncle would
have me get into a cart to come here ; picture me laid down in
a curious German waggon made of basket work, lying on sacks
and straw, but the jolting rather trying, as I am very far from
well. I wish I could fully describe the deep interests we have
had in this journey, and how marked has been the kindness of
Providence towards us in many ways, and how blessed His service
is. I certainly think the inhabitants of the mountains of Silesia
the most interesting and curious assemblage of persons that I
ever met with. We from this place see those beautiful mountains the Reisenberg in their splendour, the morning being
very fine and bright ; probably the last time I shall ever see
them—though the King and Queen begged me to return ; but
this I never expect to do, for I find the roughs of the journey
are, with all my numerous indulgences, far too much for me, and

I often feel very nearly ill. I think through all, I have seldom had more reason to believe that I have been called to any service; but we have been so much limited for time, as to make the press in travelling too great for my strength. We hope to be in England next Seventh-day week. How often and how tenderly I think of thee, my dearest youngest son.

I am thy loving mother,

E. F.

Cassel, *Ninth Month 26th.*

My most tenderly beloved Husband and Children,

I am glad, and I trust thankful, to be so far on our way homewards, and I hope and expect that we may this day week have the inexpressible consolation of being once more in England; my longings for it are almost inexpressible, and I have to pray and seek after faith and patience not to be too anxious, or in too great a hurry. I have continued very far from well, with latterly a considerable stiffness in my limbs, so that I am obliged to be assisted to walk up stairs, and helped into the carriage, sometimes by one or two men. I might have had the same attack at home; but one thing is certain, we may fully trust in our Heavenly Father, who is constantly protecting us under the wing of His love, and who knows what is best for us. I have sometimes thought that after being so helped on my way, from the palace to the prison, it was likely that the poor instrument should need a little further refining and purifying, for our works are to be tried as by fire. I have very earnestly desired not to repine, or to be unwilling to drink the cup that may be given me to drink. We travel with six horses to make the greatest speed home. I have a board in the carriage, that when your uncle and Anna are outside, I can quite rest and make a real sofa of it, when I need it, which I do for one or two stages in the day. Mary and François are very attentive and kind; indeed how differently am I cared for to many poor missionaries. I wish you to feel for me, but not to be too anxious about me; commit me entirely to Him who only knows what is best for me. Your aunt Elizabeth's letter was very seasonable and acceptable. I wish her and all my children to know how it is with me, for I need their sympathy and prayers, at the same time that I feel best help to be near, and the Power that says to the waves, " So far shall ye go and no further." Often in my wakeful and at times distressing nights, a sweet peace comes over me to calm my troubled spirit. We hear from newspapers, that the poor Baptists in Copenhagen are to be released from prison, a small sum being paid by way of fine. What a comfort! and the poor Lutherans in Prussia say they are now so well off, that they do not wish us to ask for any more liberty for them of the King.

I am indeed yours most faithfully and lovingly,

ELIZABETH FRY.

From Cassel they pursued their rapid journey to Ostend, and landed at Dover on the 2nd of October. There Mrs. Fry was met by her husband, who was little prepared for the sorrowful state in which she was brought back to him. At Ramsgate, where her eldest daughter awaited her, she remained till she could be moved without material suffering. Her son William was at that time residing at Upton Lane, whilst his own house (Manor House) was undergoing some alterations. She stayed a few days with him and his family, and then, with great difficulty, she was conveyed into Norfolk, where, for many reasons, she was particularly anxious to go.

Lynn, Tenth Month 21st.—At Ramsgate, I met with the utmost love and kindness, constant and faithful care, which were very useful to me until the time of my departure.

My visit to Upton Lane, to our dearest William and J——, has really been cheering to my heart; the day appears come, that my beloved children (for whom I have passed through such deep travail of spirit, and for whom I have exercised such tender care, and felt such wonderful love) are to take care of me; indeed, their kindness has been delightful and very comforting, quite enlivening and consoling. I see in this an advantage in coming home so broken in health. I have fallen upon them for care, first at Ramsgate, then at Upton Lane, ministering to my wants in the kindest way, K—— doing all she can for me; and now

F—— and R—— are abundantly kind. I already feel better for their care over me, and that my suffering is more than made up to me, by the tender love and sweetness it has drawn forth from my most beloved ones.

I yesterday received a letter from my husband, saying, that my dearest brother Joseph was married to Eliza P. Kirkbride, on Fifth-day the 21st. On the morning of their marriage, my heart was poured forth in prayers and tears on their behalf, that the blessing of the Most High might rest upon them.

Earlham, Eleventh Month 1st.—We had a very delightful reception here. This is our dearest H—— and F——'s birthday nineteen. We have cause for deep thankfulness on behalf of these dear sons; they have known many deliverances, and are, I trust, alive unto God as well as alive naturally. I humbly trust they may this year grow in grace, in the knowledge of God and of Christ our Saviour. Grant, gracious Lord! for Thine own name sake, that it may be so.

Warley Lodge, 5th.—We had a most satisfactory visit, and parting from Earlham and my beloved brother Joseph. His dear wife met me as a sister, and was most kind to us all. We had a very interesting Sabbath. I accompanied them to Meeting in the morning, wishing to be with Eliza at her first entry to Norwich as Joseph's wife. Our Meeting was very solemn, many very dear to us there. My brother spoke first, after I had knelt down and poured forth my heart in thanksgiving and prayer, for surely we had deep cause for thankfulness for his marriage, our remarkable journey, &c. ; and indeed, we may say, our many great and wonderful deliverances. I also prayed for a continuance of blessing. Joseph's was one of his excellent and instructive sermons, particularly on the certain guidance of the Holy Spirit of Truth. Mine was rather a song of praise to our Lord as the Lamb of God who taketh away the sins of the world, the Physician of value who healeth all our diseases, our Guide through this wilderness, as a cloud by day and a pillar of fire by night, who had brought some of us through very dark places ; so that through the fulness of His love, " the wilderness" had become at times as " Eden, and the desert as the garden of the Lord : joy and gladness being found therein, thanksgiving and the voice of melody." I also impressed upon all, how we were encompassed with so great a cloud of witnesses of the redeemed ones, who were gone, and of those who remained here; and how we ought to accept and rejoice in so great salvation, "laying aside every weight, and the sin that so easily besets us, running with patience the race set before us, looking unto Jesus the author and finisher of our faith." My sister Eliza followed in very solemn thanksgiving to the same purpose. In the evening we had another very interesting religious time together, in which our dear friend Robert Hankinson, prayed for our brother. and sister and all of us.

On Second-day, our sister Catherine, our brother and sister Cunningham, and others dear to us, joined our party, and we had a large wedding-dinner, being refreshed together. We parted, and no common parting it was.

I much enjoy my beloved children of this place, and desire to be enabled to minister to them spiritually before we part, according to their needs. I leave them, as I have done the other places, in much love and peace.

Upton, Twelfth Month 5th, First-day morning.—I have been favoured to be much better the last few days,—far more easy,—thanks to my Heavenly Father; though I suffer still at times. I look upon this late indisposition as a very privileged one, and have felt, and deeply feel, the mercy extended towards me, in all my wants being so wonderfully provided for. The luxuries of life and generous living that. I have had, I accept as gifts from a gracious and merciful Providence, that have been greatly blessed to my help, and, I believe, have greatly promoted my recovery. I exceedingly regret what I consider the intemperate and unchristian views some take of these things, judging all who feel it right to take stimulants in moderation. I believe Christians may use and not abuse these outward blessings, and that we have the highest authority for doing so; as He who set us a perfect example, and exactly knows our wants spiritual and temporal, certainly took wine. May He guide me in this and all other things, and guard me from being injured myself, or injuring others. Grant that this may be the case, gracious and most adorable Lord God and Saviour!

The infirm state of Elizabeth Fry's health precluded at this period much active exertion ; but her time was fully occupied, and her interest not at all diminished in those subjects to which she had so long devoted her attention. Her correspondence was extensive, both at home and abroad—the latter especially, much of it arising from her late journeys on the Continent. She had the happiness of hearing of the beneficial results of her exertions in different places ; from others, she received details of the obstacles which had occurred to delay or preclude improvement. To the Minister of the Interior in Holland, she wrote :—

Upton Lane, *Twelfth Month 7th*, 1841.

DEAR FRIEND,

I hope thou wilt excuse the liberty that I take, in communicating a little further with thee, on the subject of your prisons in Holland, and making some observations on the state of your lunatic asylums, as I presume such objects all come under thy notice, as Minister of the Interior. Since my return home, I have felt such a strong interest in the welfare of your prisons and lunatic asylums, that I cannot be satisfied without again addressing thee, respecting these important subjects.

I feel that our time is short ; I therefore am very anxious that whilst the present King reigns, and whilst thou art filling thy important post, such measures should be adopted as may conduce to the real welfare of the community, in the reformation of criminals, in the prevention of crime, and in mitigating the sorrows of the poor lunatics. One point I feel peculiarly bound to press, that women in all your prisons should be under the care of their own sex ; and that no men, not even the governor, chaplain, or medical man, should be admitted, unless a female officer be present, as experience has proved to me the absolute necessity of this measure, for the moral preservation of the female prisoner. I consider this a most important point. I am also very desirous that ladies should visit your prisons wherever women are confined, as their influence is highly beneficial, both to the prisoners and officers, and tends greatly to raise the standard

both of religion and morals amongst them. I have been gratified
to observe, the beneficial results of such visits at Gouda and
Amsterdam ; I have also had favourable reports from the ladies
who visit the prisoners at Zwolle. Excuse my reminding thee
again, that the number of guardians (turnkeys) in most of the
prisons in Holland is not adequate to that of the prisoners. I
have sometimes thought that Gouda is not the best situation that
might be found for a female prison, and that if the one which it
has been proposed to build, near Amsterdam, were large enough, it
might accommodate a considerable number of women. One or
two more prisons are much wanted, and it is very desirable that
all these new prisons should have separate night cells. I also
feel it very important, that men and women should be placed in
separate prisons entirely. The building of prisons for women is
less expensive than those for men, as they need not be so strongly
constructed ; and the expense of female officers is also smaller
than that of men. I think it best to inform thee, that I was
greatly shocked by the state in which I found the lunatic asylum
near Amsterdam, as its inmates appear grievously neglected ; and
such humane measures are not adopted, as experience has proved
not only tends to the comfort, but to the recovery of patients
thus afflicted. I am rather anxious to know whether the King
has attended to the subject of the Scriptural education of the
lower classes, as I believe the greatest advantage would result
from the Holy Scriptures being daily read in your different public schools, at the same time I am not a friend to the Bible being
used as a common class book, in which children are taught to
read. If thou thinkest me very urgent on these subjects, I am
inclined to hope the deep interest I take in the present and everlasting welfare of the people of the Netherlands will plead my
excuse for being so. Pray present my kind regards to thy wife ;
and with true desire that wisdom from above may be granted
thee, to direct all thy steps in thy important position, I remain,
with regard and esteem,

Thy obliged friend,

ELIZABETH FRY.

Count Schimmelpennick.

From her beloved and valued friend, the Countess Reden, she received heart-cheering communications ; the King of Prussia having urged upon General Thile, Minister of the Royal House, the necessity of effecting various reforms in prisons. The Countess Reden's letter enclosed an extract from a Prussian newspaper, giving an account of Mrs. Fry's visit to the great prison at Jauer, translated by one of her nieces with so much feeling and simplicity, that although retaining something of the German idiom, it is presented here.

"*Jauer, the 8th of October.*

" Our town has been rejoiced soon after the presence of the many military persons assembled here on occasion of the great review, by the visit of a stranger, whose object was very different, but well worth our attention. This was Mrs. Elizabeth Fry, who has for more than twenty years given her chief attention to try how the poor prisoners, who are almost all sunken so deeply, could be saved from the wretchedness of their souls, and rendered useful again in common life. Having found, during many years, that the doctrines of the Bible, of the sinfulness and corruption of mankind, and of the salvation through the bloody death of Jesus Christ, were the only means of arriving at it ; she has now been driven by Christian love, to make known her experiences in Germany. After having been last year at Berlin, where she directed the attention of several persons in high stations to this point, she visited our prisons, coming from Berchwald, where she stayed during the sojourn of his Majesty the King, at Erdmanns-dorf, on the 21st of September, accompanied by her brother, Mr. Gurney. She went through the work, and bed-rooms, as well as through the isolated rooms, and the other apartments of the house, and denoted by her questions, her deep knowledge and acquaintance with everything which tended to the welfare of the prisoners. The female prisoners, and a great part of the men, were now assembled in the praying room ; and after singing some verses, and a speech of the clergyman of this institution Mr. Feldner, Mrs. Fry spoke to them with the aid of a very good interpreter, Mr. Wirnsahe from Nisky. The impression this˙ made was extremely deep and striking ; not only the women wept, but even a great number of the men could but ill conceal their emotion produced by her appearance. Several stories of female criminals who had been converted in prison, and lived now (being set at liberty), a christian and honourable life, seemed to make great impression upon all. This very remarkable meeting was finished by a very serious address by Mr. Gurney ; and we may hope that this visit will be blessed, and made useful in many respects to our prison."

A few weeks later, a delightful account came from the Pasteur Feldner, chaplain to the prison at Jauer, of the improvement amongst the prisoners. A hundred and three Bibles, and a hundred and twelve Prayer Books, had been purchased by them ; at the price of much self-denial, out of their small earnings, besides many copies of the Scriptures and tracts having been distributed amongst them. M. Feldner, amongst other cases, instances " a poor female prisoner, who, longing to possess a Bible, took the firm resolution to lay apart her very small gains till she was able to procure one by them. On the birth-day of our beloved King, the Director delivered to her, as a reward for her good behaviour, a fine Bible ; I have seldom witnessed a more touching emotion of joy than she manifested, when stretching out her hand she received the precious treasure. Another prisoner, careless and ripe in sins, who had long ago repulsed all my warnings, by assuring me that he was not worse than other persons, and hoped for eternal blessing as well as they, came on a sudden to beg for a Bible ; when I asked him what he intended to do with it, he answered, that he wished to com- pare himself, if what he heard in my sermons and lessons was really so. I gave him a copy, with the serious advice, never to read in it without praying God fervently, to bestow on him the grace to understand what he was reading ; and if he found difficulties, to come and beg me to explain them to him ; and I can but state the most satisfactory result in his behaviour and feelings. He is persuaded now he is a sinner, and implores grace. One prisoner acquainted me with surprise, that in the beginning, he could read whole chapters without interruption, but that now a single verse could put him in so deep a reflection, and in such thankful adoration for the divine grace shown him, a poor sinner, that he frequently could not read further."

A letter from Mademoiselle Nauti told her of admission being obtained for ladies to visit the prison at Lübeck, though not without difficulty, and under strict regulation. The permission to visit prisons at Hanover was not so readily granted ; but whilst awaiting the desired leave, several ladies there—amongst the most active—Lady Hartman, with Miss Ida Arenhold as President, established a Society for visiting and relieving the sick poor.

Mrs. Fry had also almost endless letters, asking for assistance or advice, and requiring more time and thought than she had power to give. The liberality of her brothers, and some of her other relatives, enabled her to administer to the claims and distresses of many persons, in a manner which would have been otherwise impossible. She was at this period much with her own family, welcoming them to Upton Lane, or paying little visits at their respective houses. A small but commodious close carriage, given to her by her faithful brother Joseph John Gurney, and kept for her own particular use, afforded her the power of moving easily about, and greatly added to the comfort of her declining years.

Sir John Pirie had been elected, the preceding autumn, Lord Mayor of London. Lady Pirie had been one of Mrs. Fry's most indefatigable helpers in Newgate, and in all her public objects. Sir John and she, being both persons eminently devoted to the service of God and the good of their fellow-men, resolved to use their year of power in doing everything within their reach to benefit others, and exalt the cause of truth and righteousness on earth. Amongst other things, they were bent upon assisting the cause of prison reform; and in their partial kindness looking upon Mrs. Fry as a sort of impersonation of the subject, they desired to bring her into communication with such persons as were likely to forward her views, for they believed, that her persuasive arguments were founded on such indubitable truth, that they required but to be understood, to carry conviction to the minds of those who heard them.

Upton, First Month 11th, 1842.—The Lady Mayoress has been here again to-day, to see if there is any prospect of my going to the Mansion House, according to the warm desire they have expressed to meet Prince Albert, the Duke of Wellington, and our different Ministers. I feel it a very weighty matter for my body, mind, and spirit, and do very earnestly crave direction and preservation in it, that if I go, my way may be made very plain, and that my Lord may be with me there.

14th.—As the time approaches, I much feel this prospect. Gracious Lord, for Thine own Name's sake, keep me from doing anything in this, or any other thing, that is not right in Thy sight; and if right, be with me Thyself in it, clothing me with the beautiful garments of Thy righteousness and Thy salvation, touching my tongue as with a live coal from Thy altar, so to speak the truth to those around me, that it may tend to good and edification. Grant me wisdom from above, to do all in wisdom and discretion.

The last week I have been generally better. We had an interesting visit from the Chevalier Bunsen, (the Prussian Minister), and his wife, in which I was enabled to relieve my mind, by speaking to him on some weighty subjects after a solemn Scripture reading, and in prayer. I felt relieved by it, as I had borne him much in mind, believing him to be a sincere and Christian man.

17th.—Be pleased, oh Lord, to be very near to us this

day, and help us to adorn Thy doctrine, and to speak the right thing in the right way, that the cause of truth, righteousness, and mercy may be promoted !

18th, Third-day.—Through condescending mercy, I may say, I found this prayer answered. I had an important conversation on a female prison being built with Sir James Graham our present Secretary of State, upon the Patronage Society, &c. I think it was a very important beginning with him for our British Society. With Lord Aberdeen Foreign Secretary, I spoke on some matters connected with the present state of the Continent. With Lord Stanley our Colonial Secretary, upon the state of our penal colonies, and the condition of the women in them, hoping to open the door for further communication with him on these subjects. Nearly the whole dinner was occupied in deeply interesting conversation with Prince Albert and Sir Robert Peel. With the Prince, I spoke very seriously upon the Christian education of their children, the management of the nursery, the infinite importance of a holy and religious life ; how I had seen it in all ranks of life ; no real peace or prosperity without it. Then the state of Europe ; the advancement of religion in the Continental Courts. Then prisons ; their present state in this country—my fear that our punishments were becoming too severe—my wish that the Queen should be informed of some particulars respecting separate confinement, &c. &c. We also had much entertaining conversation about my journeys, the state of Europe, habits of countries, mode of living, &c. &c. With Sir Robert Peel, I dwelt much more on the prison subject ; I expressed my fears that gaolers had too much power, that punishment was rendered uncertain, and often too severe—pressed upon the need of mercy, and begged him to see the New Prison, and to have the dark cells a little altered.

To her Sister, Lady Buxton.

Upton, *First Month* 22nd.

My Dearest Hannah,

I feel really grateful for thy letter, for deeply as we feel for the Niger expedition, no one lets us know any particulars,

or sends us any document respecting it. Last evening the
report we heard was, that all the captains were dead ; this,
I trust, is false. We have deeply felt with our beloved brother
in this close exercise of faith and patience, but we poor short-
sighted mortals cannot see the end of it ; the whys and
wherefores, we cannot as yet comprehend. We trust it may
please our Heavenly Father to permit Captain Trotter to return ;
but after all, we must leave it to Him, who does all things
well. With respect to my Mansion House visit, it appeared
laid upon me to go, therefore I went ; also at the most
earnest wish of the Lord Mayor and Lady Mayoress. I was
wonderfully strengthened, bodily and mentally, and believe I
was in my right place there, though an odd one for me. I
sat between Prince Albert and Sir Robert Peel at dinner, and
a most interesting time we had ; our conversation on very
numerous important subjects. The Prince, Ministers, Bishops,
Citizens, Church, Quakers, &c. &c., all surrounding one table,
and such a feeling of harmony over us all. It was a very
remarkable occasion ; I hardly ever had such kindness and
respect shown me ; it was really humbling and affecting to me,
and yet sweet, to see such various persons, who I had worked
with for years past, showing such genuine kindness and esteem,
so far beyond my most unworthy deserts.

I am,

Your tenderly, loving and sympathizing sister,

ELIZABETH FRY.

23rd, *First-day.*—I find that the newspaper report of the
dinner at the Mansion House has excited some anxiety at my
being there, from the toasts, the music, &c., &c. ; it is thought I
set a bad example by it, and that it may induce others to go to
such dinners ; and that my being present appeared like approv-
ing the toasts. I quite wish to be open to hear all sides and to
be instructed, and if I have erred in going, to do so no more,
should such an occasion occur again. At the same time, I felt
so much quietness and peace when there and afterwards, and
until I heard the sentiments of others ; that I fear being now too
much cast down or tried by these remarks. I desire to keep near

to Him who can alone help me and defend His own cause, that no harm should be brought upon it through me. I desire and pray to be kept in unity with those who love the Lord Jesus, and particularly with the people with whom I am in religious connexion. May I be guided at this time through what I feel a difficult place, by my Lord Himself, through the fulness of His love, mercy, and pity.

The King of Prussia's arrival in England, to stand in person as sponsor to the infant Prince of Wales, was an event of much interest to Mrs. Fry ; she could not be insensible to the kindness he had shown her, and the gracious reception afforded her in his dominions. She admired the magnanimity with which he maintained the right on all subjects that approved themselves to his conscience. She greatly wished to see His Majesty again, but it was not for her to make any overture ; it was therefore with much pleasure, that she received an intimation of the King's desire to meet her at the Mansion House.

First Month 29th.—To-morrow, the King of Prussia has appointed me to meet him to luncheon at the Mansion House. I have rather felt its being the Sabbath ; but as all is to be conducted in a quiet, suitable, and most orderly manner, consistent with the day, I am quite easy to go. May my most holy, merciful Lord, be near to me as my Helper, my Keeper, and my Counsellor. My dearest husband and K—— are to go with me. Oh ! may my way be made plain before me as to what to do, what to leave undone ; when to speak, and when to be silent.

30th, *First-day.*—I felt low and far from well when I set off this morning for London ; but, through the tender mercy of my God, soon after sitting down in Meeting, I partook of much peace. I was humbled before my Lord in the remembrance of days that are past, when I used to attend that meeting (Gracechurch Street), almost heart-broken from sorrow upon sorrow ; and I remembered how my Lord sustained me, and made my way in the deep waters. He also raised me up, and then He forsook me not.

I was enabled very earnestly to pray to my God for help, direction and preservation.

After this solemn and refreshing Meeting, we went to the Mansion House. We waited some time in the drawing-room before the King arrived from St. Paul's Cathedral. I have seldom seen any person more faithfully kind and friendly, than he is. The Duke of Cambridge was also there, and many others who accompanied the King. We had much deeply interesting conversation on various important subjects of mutual interest. We spoke of the christening. I dwelt on its pomp as undesirable, &c.; then upon Episcopacy and its dangers; on prisons; on the marriage of the Princess Mary of Prussia; on the Sabbath. I entreated the Lord Mayor to have no toasts, to which he acceded, and the King approved; but it was no light or easy matter. I rejoice to believe my efforts were right. I told the King my objection to any thing of the kind being allowed by the Lord Mayor on that day; indeed, I expressed my disapprobation of them altogether. I may at the end of this weighty day return thanks to my most gracious Lord and Master, who has granted me His help and the sweet feeling of His love.

At the Mansion House, the King of Prussia arranged to meet Mrs. Fry, the following morning at Newgate, and afterwards to take luncheon at Upton Lane.

Second Month 1st, *Third-day.*—Yesterday was a day never to be forgotten whilst memory lasts. We set off about eleven o'clock, my sister Gurney and myself, to meet the King of Prussia at Newgate. I proceeded with the Lady Mayoress to Newgate, where we were met by many gentlemen. My dear brother and sister Gurney, and Susannah Corder, being with me, was a great comfort. We waited so long for the King that I feared he would not come; however, at last he arrived, and the Lady Mayoress and I, accompanied by the Sheriffs, went to meet the King at the door of the prison. He appeared much pleased to meet our little party; and after taking a little refreshment, he gave me his arm, and we proceeded into the prison and up to one of the long wards, where every thing was prepared ; the poor women round the table, about sixty of them, many of our Ladies' Committee, and some others ; also numbers of gentlemen following the King, Sheriffs, &c. I felt deeply, but quiet in spirit—fear of man much removed. After we were seated, the King on my right hand, the Lady Mayoress on my left, I expressed my desire that the attention of none, particularly the poor prisoners, might be diverted from attending to our reading by the company there however interesting, but that we should remember that the King of Kings and Lord of Lords was present, in whose fear we should abide, and seek to profit by what we heard. I then read the 12th chapter of Romans. I dwelt on the mercies of God being the strong inducement to serve Him, and no longer to be conformed to this world. Then I finished the chapter, afterwards impressing our all being members of one body, poor and rich, high and low, all one in Christ, and members one of another. I then related the case of a poor prisoner, who appeared truly converted, and who became such a holy example ; then I enlarged on love and forgiving one another, showing how Christians must love their enemies, &c., &c. After a solemn pause, to my deep humiliation and in the cross, I believed it my duty to kneel down before this most curious, interesting and mixed company, for I felt my God must be served the same every where, and amongst all people, whatever reproach it brought me into. I first prayed for the conversion of prisoners and sinners generally, that a blessing might rest on the labours of those in authority, as well as the more humble labourers for their conversion ; next I prayed for the King of Prussia, his Queen, his kingdom, that it might be more and more as the city set on the hill that could not be hid, that true religion in its purity, simplicity and power might more and more break forth, and that every cloud that obscured it might be removed ; then for us all, that we might be of the number of the redeemed, and eventually unite with them in heaven, in a never-ending song of praise. All this prayer was truly offered in the name and for the sake of the dear Saviour, that it might be heard and answered. I only mention the subject, but by no means the words. The King then again gave me his arm, and we walked down together :

there were difficulties raised about his going to Upton, but he
chose to persevere. I went with the Lady Mayoress and the
Sheriffs ; and the King with his own people. We arrived first ;
I had to hasten to take off my cloak, and then went down to
meet him at his carriage-door, with my husband, and seven of our
sons and sons-in-law. I then walked with him into the drawing-room, where all was in beautiful order—neat, and adorned
with flowers : I presented to the King our eight daughters and
daughters-in-law, (R—— E—— C—— only away) our seven sons
and eldest grandson, my brother and sister Buxton, Sir Henry
and Lady Pelly, and my sister, Elizabeth Fry—my brother and
sister Gurney he had known before—and afterwards presented
twenty-five of our grandchildren. We had a solemn silence
before our meal, which was handsome and fit for a King, yet not
extravagant—every thing most complete and nice. I sat by the
King, who appeared to enjoy his dinner, perfectly at his ease
and very happy with us. We went into the drawing-room, after
another solemn silence, and a few words which I uttered in
prayer for the King and Queen. We found a deputation of
Friends with an address to read to him—this was done ; the
King appeared to feel it much. We then had to part.

The King expressed his desire that blessings might continue
to rest on our house.

Two very diverse interests shortly followed : the departure of
a grandson for the China seas, in H.M.S. Agincourt, and preparations for a sale for the benefit of the Funds of the British
Ladies' Society. The Lord Mayor had offered the use of the
Egyptian Hall for the purpose, and Lady Pirie had volunteered
to make every possible arrangement to lessen the fatigue of Mrs.
Fry, and render it easy and agreeable to her coadjutors and
friends.

Upton, Third Month 15th.—My son and daughter C——,
and several of their children are staying here ; little Gurney
C—— just going into the navy. It really oppresses me in
spirit, I so perfectly object to war on Christian principles ; it is

so awful in its devastating effects; naturally, morally and spiritually.

Fourth Month 17*th.*—I feel the prospect seriously of our dear grandchild's going to sea; he leaves us to-morrow! It is no light matter. May our God, through His tender mercy, bring good out of this apparent evil. I have exceedingly regretted his going, but I am now more reconciled.

This week we have a very large sale at the Mansion House for the British Society. Although, on the whole, I approve these Sales, there are many difficulties attached to them. I earnestly desire and pray, that through the tender mercy of my God, no harm may come of it; but, in whatever we do, the cause of truth and righteousness may be exalted.

Oh Lord hear! Oh Lord help! Oh Lord protect and forgive, for Thine own Name's sake; and I pray, gracious Lord, that Thou wouldest be very near to me this day and this week, and help me, in deep humility, godly sincerity, and faithfulness, to do Thy will. And be near, I pray Thee, to all my children and friends, as their Helper and Keeper, and to my dear little grandson in this his most serious going out. I ask Thy protecting care over him, and if it be Thy will, make him feel the dangers, temptations, and difficulties of the line he has chosen, that he may never be one to promote war, but rather peace upon earth.

24*th, First-day.*—We commended our dear little grandson in faith to the keeping of his God, this day week in the evening, ourselves, my brother Gurney and some of his family, his father, mother, and brothers. I read first a solemn portion in the Proverbs, most applicable to him and his state. I spoke to him and prayed for him. .He left us the next morning for Devonport with his father.

On Third, Fourth and Fifth-day, we were fully occupied, principally by the Sale. It was very largely attended; quantities of things given and sent to us; extraordinary kindness shown to us by numbers, and the Lord Mayor and Lady Mayoress treating us with almost unbounded hospitality and kindness. One day they gave dinner and luncheon to three hundred persons, and I should think nearly as many another day or days. We sold

things to the amount of about thirteen hundred pounds, still
many things were left on hand ; when I consider the great
trouble, the enormous expense, the time taken up, the obligation we put ourselves under to so many persons, and the fatigue
of body, I think I never can patronise another Sale. However,
in mercy, I was carried through without much suffering. I
think I was rather humbled than exalted by the great kindness I received ; but my Lord only knows my real estate, and
to Him alone can I go to have my heart kept humble, watchful
and faithful. These public events bring me into care about
myself, and a fear lest like Ephraim, I should be mixed amongst
the people, and lose my strength.

About this time she addressed to her eldest son the following
letter, on his becoming a magistrate :—

MY DEAREST J——,
Ever since I heard of the prospect of thy being a magistrate,
I have had it on my mind to write to thee ; but, alas ! such is
the press of my engagements, that in my tender state I cannot
do what I would. I now, however, take up my pen to tell thee
a little of my mind. I think the office of magistrate a very
weighty one, and often, I fear, too lightly entered, and its very
important and serious duties too carelessly attended to ; and this
I attribute to a want of a due feeling of the real difficulty of
performing any duty ; particularly one where much true wisdom is required in doing justice between man and man, unless
governed and directed by that wisdom that cometh from above,
which is pure, then peaceable, gentle, easy to be entreated,
full of mercy and good fruits, without partiality and without
hypocrisy. I believe it is thy desire to be governed by this
wisdom, and to do justice, and love mercy ; but remember this
requires a very watchful and subjected spirit, and those who have
to sit in judgment on others must often sit in judgment on
themselves : this fits the mind for sympathizing with the wanderers, and adopting every right measure for their reformation
and improvement. I think it is of the utmost importance to
enter the duties attached to a magistrate in a very prayerful

spirit, seeking the help and direction of the Spirit of God, and that the understanding may be enlightened to comprehend His will. I am perfectly sensible that a justice of the peace must keep to the laws of his country in his decisions, and further, that he should be *well acquainted with these laws;* but I also know much rests with him, as to leaning on the side of *mercy,* and not of *severity;* and I know from my experience with so very many magistrates, how much they do in the prisons, &c., &c. to *instigate* or *increase* suffering; and also how much they may do for the improvement, and real advantage of criminals. Much is in their power; they may do *much* harm or much good: too many are influenced by selfishness, party spirit, or partiality, both in individual cases and where public good is concerned; but the simple, upright, faithful, just and merciful magistrates, are too rare, and they are much wanted. Mayst thou, my dearest John, be of this number; but remember it can only be by grace, and being thyself directed and governed by the Holy Spirit of God.

I advise thy reading Judge Hale's life—I know a judge and a justice are different things; but the same wise, truly impartial spirit, should govern both. I wish to remind thee, that in petty offences, much is left to the magistrate's own judgment, and the utmost care is needful that crime is not increased by punishment, and the offenders become hardened, instead of being brought to penitence. I fear for young people. Our prisons in Essex generally only harden; therefore, try any other means with boys or girls: get them to Refuges, or try to have such measures adopted as may lead them to repentance and amendment of their ways. My very dear love to thy wife, and all thy children; and with deep and earnest desires that through the grace of God thou mayst perform all thy duties, domestic and public, to His glory, thy own peace, and the good of mankind.

I am,
Thy very affectionate mother,
ELIZABETH FRY.

I forgot to say that a late Act of Parliament gives very great liberty in not sending young offenders to prison, but much rests with the judge or the magistrate, as to what is to be done with them; this Act was I think about two years ago. Many of the

late Acts of Parliament respecting persons need much studying,
accompanied with the reports from the different Inspectors, these
give such an excellent knowledge of the subject. I believe I could
send thee most of them. The prisons in Essex are considered to
need much improvement. I hope before very long to visit you at
Warley Lodge, and to enter upon many particulars with thee.

How delightful the weather is, quite summer like ; I think your
country must be very beautiful.

Upton, Fifth Month 8th.—On Third-day, the Lady Mayoress
and I paid interesting and satisfactory visits to the Queen
Dowager, the Duchess of Kent and the Duchess of Gloucester.
I went with my heart lifted up for help and strength and direction, that the visits might prove useful, that I might drop the
word in season, and that I might myself be kept humble, watchful, and faithful to my Lord. I have fears for myself in visiting
palaces rather than prisons, and going after the rich rather than
the poor, lest my eyes should become blinded, or I should fall
away in any thing from the simple, pure standard of truth and
righteousness. We first called on the Duchess of Kent, and had
interesting conversation about our dear young Queen, Prince
Albert, and their little ones. We spoke of the Sale—my foreign
journey—the King of the Belgians, and other matters. I desired, wherever I could, to throw in a hint of a spiritual kind,
and was enabled to do it. I gave the Duchess some papers, with
a note to Prince Albert, requesting him to lay the suffering
state of the Waldenses from their fresh persecutions, before the
Queen. We next visited the Queen Dowager, and met her sister,
and the Duchess of Saxe Weimar, and her children. We had a
delightful time : much lively and edifying conversation upon
the state of religion in Europe, particularly amongst the higher
classes, and the great advancement of late years in the conduct
and conversation of the great of this world.

" How blind are we to ourselves, so that neither nations,
churches nor individuals, see in themselves the symptoms of
decay visible to all around ! the pride which leads to break the
law of God, leads to this self-flattery." I have felt much
warning and instruction in these words, they lead to the prayer,

O Lord, open Thou mine eyes, lest I sleep the sleep of death ! and lest the light that is in me become darkness !

Mrs. Fry's health continuing in an infirm and suffering state, although better than during the winter, some change appeared necessary, and absence from the continual tide of London engagements, which reached her at Upton Lane.   Her brother-in-law .Mr. Hoare, offered the loan of his house at Cromer, a commodious and agreeable residence on the top of the cliff, commanding fine sea views.   The little village of Cromer and its beautiful church in the foreground, and at the back, the Light-house hills ; their easy ascent and smooth short turf, dry in even the wettest weather, affording a delightful resort for one whose failing powers could no longer encounter exertion.   Cromer, too, was associated with the days of happy childhood.   She greatly enjoyed this time, and was cheered by the singular kindness and affection of many whom she had long loved, and others with whom she then for the first time became sociably acquainted.   Her sister, Mrs. Catherine Gurney, was with them at the Cliff House ; she saw much of the beloved residents at Northrepps Hall.   Northrepps Cottage, Sherringham, and Cromer Hall, were also points of light on the landscape ; two months thus passed pleasantly and rapidly away.

(On the journey), Seventh Month.—I have been poorly part of every night, or early in the morning, since I left Upton, so as to feel discouraged and flat at being so far from home ; but I desire to trust entirely.   I have sought to have my steppings directed by Him, who knows what is best for us.   I have not felt a will in these arrangements, and I desire to leave all to Him who orders all things well.   I at times feel, particularly at night, so sunk, that I am ready to apprehend my natural powers are really failing.   I occasionally ask in prayer for passing revival from my states of suffering, which prayers are often remarkably granted ; but I am not disposed really to ask for prolonged life,

because I fear lest, like Hezekiah, I should live to transgress
before the Lord. I have probably an undue fear of an imbecile
or childish state, and becoming a burden to others ; at the same
time the idea of life being continued to me is pleasant, and the
fear of death and the grave to my nature great; not that I fear for
the everlasting state, although this confidence arises from no
trust in any thing in myself, but faith in the mercy of God in
Christ, who tasted death for every man, and a full belief that
the tender mercy of my God is over all His works ; and, unworthy as I am, that through His mercy, He will not cast me
out of His presence, (which I delight in), nor shut up His tender
mercies from me.

Cromer, 6th.—Here I am, in what was my dearest sister
Hoare's little room, looking on the sea, but poorly after my
journey, feeling the air almost too cold for me ; but I am
favoured to be quiet and trustful in spirit, and desire to leave
all things to Him, who only knows what is best for me. My
sister Catharine being with us, and my brother Joseph and his
Eliza and dear Anna near to us, is very pleasant, and our
dear brother and sister Buxton and Richenda being still at
Northrepps.

Every week was marked by slow but sure increase in strength.
But her amendment was retarded by anxiety on account of a
daughter, then very ill in the Isle of Wight. To this daughter,
who was under much trial, she wrote—

I am not very well to-day, but have not by any means lost the
ground I had gained, though your trials appear to have brought
me some steps back. If, in the ordering of Providence, things
should be brighter, I think I should rally again ; but I desire to
have my will given up to the will of Him who knows what is
best for us all, and earnestly desire to be very thankful that
our trials are not of a deeper dye; and being as far as I know
brought on us by Infinite Wisdom, I do not feel them like
those produced by the exquisite suffering of sin.

I am, thy loving, sympathizing, and yet hopeful mother.

E. F.

She was also distressed by her eldest grandson entering the army, having a strong objection to war, and grieved that any belonging to her should directly or indirectly promote it.

First-day, Eighth Month 14*th.*—I have deeply and sorrowfully felt our grandson Frank C—— determining to go into the army. I truly have tried to prevent it, but must now leave it all to my Lord, who can, if He see meet, bring good out of that which I feel to be evil.

Mrs. Fry, with her brother Joseph John Gurney, who, with Mrs. Gurney and his daughter, had been staying at Cromer, endeavoured to establish a reading-room and library for the fishermen, to draw them from the public-house and its attendant evils. Some good was effected, but circumstances precluded permanent benefit. The affection many amongst them evinced to her was, however, extraordinary; as one of her German friends had expressed it, her very name was a "word of beauty" amongst them.

Eighth Month 14*th, First-day.*—I have felt the weight of undertaking to establish a library and room for the fishermen, and something of a friendly society, as in my tender state the grasshopper becomes a burden. I was encouraged however in the night by these words, " Stedfast, immoveable, always abounding in the work of the Lord." In weakness and in strength, we must, as ability is granted, abound in the work of the Lord. May our labour not be in vain in Him ! I have had very comforting accounts from Denmark—our representations attended to respecting the prisons, and likely to have much good done in them ; also from Prussia ; surely our Lord has greatly blessed some of our poor efforts for the good of our fellow mortals.

In Denmark, the King had given his warm sanction to the measures proposed by the Royal Danish Chancery for adding new buildings to the Police Prison, for the purpose of affording more

space and the opportunity of classification, for employment to be
provided and the cells heated in winter. Endeavours also were
to be made to place the female prisoners under the care of
women. In the House of Correction at Christianhaven this was
to be attempted immediately, and continued, if found to answer.
Bibles, New Testaments, Psalms, and other religious books were
to be fully supplied to all prisoners, also works of general information and instruction. Moreover, that the opportunity was
to be given them for attending public worship—a chaplain was
appointed expressly for the House of Correction. On the same
occasion, His Majesty received a petition from Pasteur Raffard
and several others for permission to form a Prison Society, and
was graciously pleased to resolve with regard to it as follows:—

" We have heard with the greatest satisfaction of the desire of
benevolent individuals to unite together to form a Prison Committee, whose object should be the moral improvement of the
prisoners, and their employment, and return to society on obtaining their freedom.

" Therefore, we gladly give an opportunity to the members of
this Committee, by means of visits and the distribution of religious
and other fitting books, to exercise a good influence on the prisoners. But it must be remembered that these visits, and the
distribution of books, must not take place without speaking
beforehand to the Chaplain and Director of the prison ; they must
be told which of the members of the Committee are going to
undertake the visiting. To them it must also be left to decide
which of the prisoners are to receive the benefit of these visits.
They must also fix the time and place when and where these
visits are to take place.

" To visit the prisoners in the House of Detention is not
allowed by the rules ; but at any rate, these visits must be entirely
dependent on the inquiring judges. The defects in the internal
arrangement of the Stock House, will also cause difficulties in the
way of visiting this prison ; but the useful activity of the Society
may best be practised in the House of Labour Punishment and

Correction, where particularly female prisoners may be visited by those ladies of the Committee, who, submitting to the annexed conditions, will turn their attention and care to this suffering and depraved part of mankind.

" It is our will that those authorities who have the chief super-intendence of the prisoners, should weigh with attention any proposition for a change in the treatment of the prisoners, or in the arrangement of the prison, considered as desirable by the Society.

" Finally, we acknowledge the usefulness of the Society's object to endeavour to procure situations and work for the liberated prisoners, in order to secure them a maintenance, and to prevent their return to their former courses ; and to this end would con-sider it desirable that the Society should act in concert with the police, and the Poor-Law Commission."

From Berlin Dr. Julius, who was then there, wrote to her that the construction of the four new penitentiaries was to be begun immediately: one at Berlin ; one at Münster, in Westphalia ; one at Ratibor, in Silesia ; and another at Königsberg. " Two of the penitentiaries to be exactly like the Model Prison in London, according to the express will of His Majesty. In the two other penitentiaries, three of the wings to be on the plan of separate confinement by day and night ; but in the fourth wing to be only nightly separation, and by day the convicts to be kept at work in small classes of picked men, as much as possible in silence."

The Countess Reden gave her a most gratifying account of the successful labours of the devoted chaplain at Jauer ; adding, " he has established a sort of refuge or asylum for those who leave the prison, and have no home where to return, and need obser-vation and religious instruction longer. An excellent, simple man, preparing for a missionary station, resolved to begin at Jauer for this purpose, and has taken into his lodging, five of the prisoners. It is a beginning, and from the very small income of this man and the chaplain all that could be expected."

From Düsseldorf she heard, through Miss Goltstein, of the continued exertions of the Ladies' Committee for visiting female prisoners; also, that from the great prison at Werden all the female prisoners were to be removed to Cologne, to a separate prison. Miss Goltstein also mentioned, that at Ratingen, a borough not far from Düsseldorf, an Asylum had been established "for young girls dismissed, and showing repentance, where, under the guidance of an excellent monitor, they obtain instruction in every work required of a good servant. This establishment is in such good repute, that as soon as they are able to go into service the opportunity is never wanting for it. We hear many instances of their behaving well, and leading a good life. The best proof of the good effects of our Asylum is, that in the two years of its existence, none dismissed from thence have been committed again."

The scenes which had occurred in the "Surrey" and "Navarino" female convict ships, and in the "Rajah" the preceding year, increased the conviction long felt by Mrs. Fry and her coadjutors, of the necessity which existed for the presence of female officers to receive the convicts on board, and remain in charge of them from the time of their embarkation until they reached the land of exile.

Under this impression, no sooner were the Ladies of the Convict Ship Committee informed that the "Garland Grove" was chartered for the conveyance of 205 female prisoners to Van Diemen's Land, than they exerted themselves to find suitable persons to accompany them as matrons; having first applied to Sir James Graham, then principal Secretary of State for the Home Department, for his sanction and aid in effecting this object.

The following note addressed to Mrs. Fry, who was at this

time at Cromer, much out of health, will shew the readiness and kindness with which Sir James listened to her request and that of her colleagues.

Whitehall, *August 9th,* 1812.

" Madam,

" I am directed by Sir James Graham to assure you, that he will, to the utmost of his power, procure every accommodation for the two ladies (matrons) proceeding with convicts in the " Garland Grove."

" The favourable consideration of the Board of Admiralty will be requested to the subject this day.

" The heavy pressure of business attending the close of the Session, prevents Sir James addressing you himself.

" I have the honour to be, Madam,
" Your most obedient servant,
" D. O'Brien, Private Secretary."

Some difficulty occurred, after this kind permission on the part of Government had been granted, in procuring a matron in the room of one of two who had been fixed upon by the Ladies' Committee, and who afterwards declined the proposal made to her.

Mrs. Fry's anxiety on this subject was evinced in the notes written by her to her friends in London. She longed (to use her own expression) for health and power to come and aid them.

The conclusion of one of these notes is so characteristic, that it is inserted.

I truly feel for you all, my beloved friends, who have now to bear the burden and heat of the day. May grace be granted you, and help from above, that you may be strengthened for your important work ; and may your way be made plain before you ; and may our Heavenly Father undertake for us in this weighty matter, and lead us to the right parties to send abroad, who may be a blessing to those they go amongst, and be kept and blessed

themselves ! I long to hear from thee, or one of you, again, and
hope I may one day be enabled again to take a labouring oar.
Farewell, in much true love and sympathy, to thyself and all thy
fellow-labourers.

I am,

Very affectionately, thy friend,

ELIZABETH FRY.

This letter is dated Cromer, Eighth Month 20th, 1842.

Two very suitable persons were subsequently recommended by
the ladies, and appointed by Government to the arduous and
important office of matrons in the " Garland Grove." Before
their embarkation the following admirable letter was written
by Mrs. Fry to Miss Fraser :—

Cromer, *Eighth Month 27th*, 1842.

MY BELOVED FRIEND,

Thy note received to-day has been a real comfort to me ;
the post brought some sorrows, and thy note brought weight in
the other scale ; but I have sat at home weeping, as I did not
feel much inclined to meet a delightful party of brothers, sisters,
&c., at my brother Buxton's, but rather to sit alone, and look to
my own vineyard, and my own very deep interests in my family
and my beloved friends, and for the causes that are near my
heart. I humbly thank our Heavenly Father, who has regarded
our very unworthy prayers, and raised up those that we trust
may be suitable in the convict-ship, and helpful in the colony ;
may grace and wisdom from above be poured forth upon them ;
may they remember that the servants of the Lord must prove
their faith more by *conduct* than word or profession ; they must
avoid anything like religious *cant*, if I may so express myself,
and in an upright, holy, self-denying and watchful deportment,
be preachers of righteousness, and prove who it is that they
believe in, serve, and obey. I am often inexpressibly bound and
brought low in spirit when I look at the standard and holy
example of our blessed Lord, and then behold my own short-
coming. I long for a closer walk with God, for myself, and all

that I love ; and that, through the help of the Holy Spirit, we should more constantly prove our love to Him who died for us, and hath loved us with an everlasting love. Pray impress on these matrons the extreme importance of their prudent and circumspect conduct, as it respects the gentlemen on board ; and towards the women, the need of sound discretion, and the meekness, of wisdom ; and amongst all, to be wise as serpents, harmless as doves, and to be pitiful and courteous. I quite feel my indulgent life, and am very ready to work when my Lord may enable me. I do not desire to save myself unless duty calls me to do it ; indeed, dear friend, I have always felt it an honour I have been unworthy of, to do anything for my Lord, and to be made an instrument of good to my fellow-creatures. I have been thankful for thy letters, because they have encouraged me to hope that you are not discouraged, but that the Spirit of our God is poured forth upon my beloved friends, to help them in this weighty and important work, and to make them willing to labour in this service, and for the good of their poor fellow-mortals. My dear love to all our sisters in this service ; and I am truly, in gospel bonds,

Thy attached friend,
ELIZABETH FRY.

The appointment of these matrons was justly regarded by Mrs. Fry, and her fellow-labourers, as a step of the utmost importance. It mitigates most materially the evils attendant upon the transportation of females. Objections had been urged to the measure in former years, but now it was clearly admitted that none were so fit to have charge of these unhappy women, as persons of their own sex, if such could be found who, influenced by right motives, and possessing the requisite qualifications, were willing to encounter the privations and perils of a long voyage in such society.

Northrepps Hall, Ninth Month 18*th.*—I exceedingly value the company of so many of my most tenderly beloved brothers and sisters, and other near and dear relations, so many nephews and nieces, and others also. How I wish that I upheld amongst these tenderly-beloved ones a more holy example. I do not often apprehend it my place to speak much of spiritual things; but I most truly desire constantly to uphold the Christian standard in an humble and watchful walk before the Lord, and before my fellow-mortals.

25th, First-day.—I have not enough dwelt upon the extraordinary kindness of our dear brother and sister Buxton and their children to us at this time, truly humbling to me, a poor unworthy worm of the dust, also my dear brother Hoare, and all that family—such a sweet renewal of love amongst us. How blessed and how sweet is love, and how delightful to believe that it has in measure the Heavenly stamp upon it. Our dearest sister Catharine left Cromer yesterday,—quite a loss to us ; her kindness has been great indeed.

Cromer, Tenth Month 23rd.—Perhaps the last journal I may ever write in this place, as to-morrow we mean to depart for Lynn. Yesterday, I was very much affected and touched by something that occurred ; it was almost overwhelming. We paid our farewell visit to Northrepps. My brother Hoare and his family went also ; and at our beloved Fowell and Hannah's were Andrew and Priscilla Johnston, Edward, and Catharine, and Richenda Buxton. After dinner, Gurney Hoare brought me a beautiful piece of plate, a silver inkstand, and my husband a Testament, of fine paper and print, most beautifully bound. They gave these presents in the kindest way, expressing love and gratitude to us, and saying that dearest Anna Gurney and those absent of their families united in the present. I felt before receiving it, that I had been unduly loaded with gifts and kindness. My spirit was humbled, and really bowed within me under a very deep feeling of unworthiness at these proofs of love. My Lord only knows my sense of it ; a poor, weak, unprofitable servant as I am, that He should thus put it into the hearts of His servants to show so much love and pity to me in my poor, low, weak and unworthy estate before Him. Gracious Lord ! Thou knowest how little I can do for all these beloved ones. I pray Thee reward them with spiritual and temporal blessings, and if it be Thy will, let the sickly in body be more strengthened and restored, the sickly in soul healed, that all may be more filled and satisfied with the unsearchable riches of Christ.

On her way home, she stayed at Lynn for a few days, her last visit! Never was she more bright or lovely in spirit. She had a wise, kind word for all—children, servants, dependents. All loved her, all felt that her message was not from herself, nor of man's invention ; but that in her Master's name she invited others to "love and to good works." How she condescended to all ; listening to the minutest details of their cares and pleasures. How ready in devising means for helping others, not merely in the great, but the little things of life ; for who so prompt in expedients ? in the sick room ? in the nursery with an unmanageable child, or a froward servant ? She returned home the end of October, but great pains and anxieties awaited her there !

CHAPTER XXIV.

A heavy family affliction awaited Mrs. Fry's return home—the illness and death of her lovely little grandaughter, Harriet Streatfeild, between seven and eight years old. She was much with her children during their sorrowful nursing, and a close participator in their grief.

To an absent daughter she wrote thus from the house of mourning :—

My dearest R——,

Although I know that thou art written to fully, I add a line of most tender love ; and to express my earnest desire, that as our Heavenly treasures are increased, we may all more diligently seek the city which hath foundations, whose maker and builder is God. Grace appears all-sufficient here.

Thy most loving mother,

E. F.

Her bereaved daughter having decided upon attending the funeral of her child, Mrs. Fry resolved to accompany her. It was a bright clear winter's day ; besides her parents, nearly twenty of their children and grandchildren followed to the silent tomb, the first with the exception of their own little Elizabeth, of their forty-six descendants, who had been taken at an age of understanding. The solemn procession arrived at East Ham Church, when with no spectators but the weeping villagers, the Vicar the Rev. William Streatfield, commenced that most impressive service, which from this time was to be so frequently heard in the family circle. Mrs. Fry went in the carriage with her daughter, and stood by her at the grave : when the service was ended, an impressive pause ensued; then, as the mourners prepared to move away, might be heard the tone of her gentle voice, " a solemn breathing sound" as she addressed her weeping daughter, —." It is the Lord, let Him do what seemeth Him good."

A family party gathered in the evening: after the fifth chapter of the 2nd of Corinthians had been read, Elizabeth Fry addressed a heart-searching exhortation to her "children, grandchildren, and all the dearly beloved ones present," to be ready " when the next summons should come—thanksgiving that the lamb taken was a believing child, one rather peculiarly impressed with the fact of redemption, and forgiveness of sins through Christ ; and in practice, an obedient gentle spirited creature, and according to the measure of so young a child, unusually full of good works and alms deeds ;" for she gave much to the poor, whose tales of woe (whether true or false, she did not stop to inquire) always touched her ; and her *good mark* money, which she saved till it amounted to a pound, she had given to the Ceylon Mission. Thus, even in so young a child, did the good tree bring forth little blossoms of good fruit ! gone to mature and fructify in Heaven ! through Christ who died for her, and in whom she truly believed." Many other things were spoken by her. Then she prayed for all the three generations present, a soul-touching prayer, committing all to God.

Upton Lane, First Month 1st, 1843.—Another year is closed

and passed never to return. It appears to me that mine is rather a rapid descent into the valley of old age.

Second Month 6th.—I am just now much devoted to my children and all my family, and attend very little to public service of any kind. May my God grant, that I may not hide my talents as in a napkin; and on the other hand that I may not step into services uncalled for at my hands. May my feeble labours at home be blessed. Gracious Lord, heal, help, and strengthen Thy poor servant for Thine own service, public .or private.

Third Month 19th.—It has been a week of various interests. On Second-day we met Lord Ashley at dinner at Manor House (my dear son William's), to consider the subject of China and the Opium Trade. Lord Ashley is a very interesting man, devoted to promoting the good of mankind, and suppressing evil —quite a Wilberforce I think.

Fourth Month 2nd, First-day.—I entered the last week very low in my condition, bodily and mentally; so much so, that some of my family could hardly be reconciled to my attending the Quarterly Meeting. In the select Quarterly Meeting of Ministers and Elders, the subject of unity was much brought forward; several spoke to it, and I had to express rather strongly my belief is that there is a great work going forward in the earth, and Satan desired to mar it by separating the Lord's servants. I warned Friends upon this point, because there are diversities of gifts, differences of operation and administration; they should not sit in judgment one on another, or condemn one another, or suppose they are not of the same spirit, and one in the same Lord and the same God.

With somewhat of restored health, Elizabeth Fry believed it her duty once more to visit the Continent. Her attraction was peculiarly to Paris. Matters of importance that she earnestly desired to have completed awaited her attention, and there appeared an opening beyond any thing she had known before, for usefulness in that great capital. There were Christian and benevolent persons whom she desired to see again "in the flesh," and build them up, if enabled, in faith and hope. She had retained her certificate, granted her by Friends for her last journey. Her brother, Joseph John Gurney, also believed it his duty to visit Paris, as part of a more extended journey. Mrs. Gurney accompanied him, and Josiah Forster consented to join their party. In addition to these three participators and supporters in the various religious and philanthropic objects which might open before them, one of her daughters went as her mother's especial companion, to watch over and care for her health.

They landed at Boulogne. The voyage had been so trying to Mrs. Fry, from a heavy rolling sea and the weather being cold and unfavourable, that her fellow-travellers doubted the practicability of her pursuing her journey. By setting off late, and resting an hour or two in the middle of the day, she seemed revived, when at the end of two days they arrived at Amiens. Here the Sunday was passed. In the evening they were permitted to worship in the simple mode of Friends, in the room used by the Protestants as their chapel, where a venerable pastor, eighty years of age, laboured among a small flock in the midst of a large Roman Catholic population. Many of these were present; their hearts appeared touched and animated by the ministry on this occasion, which tended to console the discouraged, and strengthen the feeble-minded.

At Clermont-en-Oise, the ladies were permitted to inspect the Great Central Prison for women, calculated to contain twelve hundred, although nine hundred only were in confinement when they were there. It is under the charge of a Supérieure and twenty-two nuns, no men being allowed to enter. The Supérieure was an intelligent, powerful minded woman, greatly afraid of the abuses to which the solitary system is liable, and the silent system also, when carried to extremes. The prisoners work in large cheerful rooms, a hundred together, under the closest inspection of the nuns, who relieve the monotony by not unfrequently uniting in singing hymns. But a splendid prison extremely well managed, is not so rare a scene as that which concluded the visit. On first arriving, Mrs. Fry had expressed a great wish to see all the nuns, but the Supérieure considered it impossible, as they never leave the women ; however, just before quitting the prison, Mrs. Fry was conducted into an apartment around which sat, some on chairs, some on extremely low seats, some apparently on the floor, the twenty-two nuns in their grey dresses, and the lay sisters in black ; placed in the middle were Mrs. Fry and her sister, Mrs. Joseph John Gurney, the Supérieure between them, holding Mrs. Fry by the hand, whose daughter was requested by the Supérieure to interpret for them. It was no light or easy task to convey exactly her mother's address, on the deep importance of maintaining, not alone good discipline amongst the prisoners, but endeavouring to lead them in living faith to Christ, as the only Mediator between God and man, and through whom alone they could be cleansed from the guilt and power of sin. At His name every head bowed. She then went on to tell of Newgate, and the effects of the Gospel there ; many tears were shed at this recital. She concluded by a lively exhortation to these devoted nuns, whom she could " salute as sisters in Christ," to go forward in their work, but in no way to rest upon it, as in itself meritorious. Here the Supérieure interposed, " Oh non, mais il y a un peu de mérite, l'homme a de mérite en ce qu'il fait :" an old nun, who probably understood English, rejoined, " Ma mère, Madame thinks that if the love of God does not sufficiently animate the heart to do it without feeling it a merit, or desiring reward, it falls short." " Ah c'est bien ! comme elle est bonne !" replied the Supérieure. Mrs. Fry concluded by a short blessing and prayer in French. It was a curious scene, and a solemn feeling pervaded the whole.

Mrs. Fry had strong hopes of effecting much during her stay

at Paris, another spirit prevailed there.   M. Guizot in fact head
of the Cabinet, though the Duke of Dalmatia was President of
the Council, having proved himself ready to support any measure
for the moral benefit of the people, and their advance in sound
knowledge and civilization.   In 1833, when Minister of Public
Instruction, he had shown his genius for education and lively
interest in the good of his countrymen, by the ordinance which,
prepared by himself, and promulgated as law, raised in an exceedingly short space of time, in nine thousand Communes, the
village school-room, for the instruction of the village poor.

Mrs. Fry believed that she should find in him the enlightened
philanthropist, and the prudent yet fearless politician ; one who
taught in the school of the French Revolution, had marked and
comprehended its horrors, without being blind to the benefits it
had conferred upon his country and mankind, in sweeping away
the accumulated tyranny and bigotry of centuries ; one who,
whilst he shrank from changes for the sake of novelty, was as
capable in devising expedients for the remedy of real evils, as
he was resolute in carrying them into execution.   Unblemished
in personal character, exemplary in private life, and professing
the Reformed faith in religion, Mrs. Fry looked to him as
eminently calculated to receive and respond to her own opinions
and experiences.

Paris, (Hôtel Meurice,) Fourth Month 22nd.—We are
favoured to be very comfortably settled here, and I may most
thankfully say, feel in our right place, after a time of unusual
conflict to my own mind.

I was little fit to enter Paris ; the day was hot, and the rooms
at the hotel oppressive ; the noise of the street so great, that I
feared, in my poor state, I could not support it, and was frightened
about myself and felt as if it were altogether too much for me,
but I revived towards evening ; was favoured with a peaceful night,
and awoke much refreshed and comforted.   Our beloved friend

the Countess P——— has been a real helper to me, quite a spiritual comforter; so encouraging as to the time of our visit. She expresses her belief of our being surely guided by a spirit within, safely leading us to places at the right time. Others really dear to me show much faithful love, and they appear delighted to have us with them. On Fifth-day, we attended the little Meeting of Friends in the Faubourg du Roule. The next day, some of our serious friends came to us in the evening. And the following, we spent a very agreeable evening at the Malets', where there was, to my feelings a sweet sense of love and peace over us, with the numerous members of that interesting family.

I may thankfully say, I now feel greatly healed and helped and encouraged, although it appears but little I have done for my Lord in any way; but I must wait His time and His putting forth, and not enter anything in my own way and time.

Lord be pleased to grant, through Thy tender mercy in Christ my Saviour, that our visit to this place may be really profitable to ourselves, and to those we are come amongst, and that it may promote love and charity amongst Christians generally; help to remove dependence on the arm of man, and to have it placed on Thy arm of power, and stimulate many more diligently to seek Thy kingdom and Thy righteousness—that some worldly-minded and wanderers may be led to return, repent and live—that some that are dead may be made alive again—and that those that are lost may be found in Thy fold of peace and safety. Grant also, gracious Lord! that the great blessing of preservation may be with my tenderly beloved family at home.

On the 25th, Mrs. Fry waited, by appointment, on the Duchess of Orleans, at the Tuilleries; but finding some difficulty in fully conveying her meaning, her daughter was sent for to interpret. In a letter to her sisters, she describes herself ushered into an immense drawing-room, the size, and heavy crimson and gold magnificence of which exceeded any room she had ever seen. On a sofa, about half way up the room against the wall was seated her mother; by her side a young lady, in deep mourning, over whose white and black cap hung a large long crape scarf or veil that reached the ground on either side: her figure tall and elegant, her face and features small and delicate, her eyes blue, and her complexion very fair,—a lovely blush came and went as she spoke. From her dress and appearance no one could for a moment doubt, but that it was the widow of the heir of France. Opposite to her on a chair was an elderly lady the grand Duchess of Mecklenburgh, her step-mother, who had brought her up from childhood. These three were the only occupants of that vast saloon: its walls were hung with crimson velvet, embroidered in heavy gold columns, with vine leaves twisted round, and all things magnificent in proportion. The conversation at first was upon the Duchess of Orleans' affliction; they had each a Bible in their hand. Mrs. Fry read to them a few verses, and commented on them, on affliction and its peaceable fruits, afterwards. They then spoke of the children of the House of Orleans, and the importance of their education and early foundation in real Christian faith; the grand Duchess of Mecklenburgh, an eminently devoted, pious woman, deeply responded to these sentiments. It was an hour and a half before this interesting conversation came to a close.

The following Sunday, after attending their own little Meeting, a large public one was held in the Methodist chapel. Mr. Gurney spoke well in French, Mrs. Fry through an excellent interpreter.

The evening of the next day, they gathered round them a very singular party, about thirty persons of colour, chiefly from Hayti, the Isle of France, and Guadaloupe: they were principally students of law or medicine; one a painter, who had some good pictures in the exhibition. Several of them spoke excellent French, and were intelligent-looking young men. Mr. Gurney was desirous of obtaining from them any information he could on the state of the different West Indian Islands.

The evening concluded with reading in the Bible. Mrs. Fry addressed her auditory on the words of St. Peter, " I perceive that

God is no respecter of persons ;"—Acts x. 34—going on to that glorious passage in the Revelations, which tells of the company that cannot be numbered, gathered out of every nation, kindred, tongue, and people.

Speaking of the close of the day, she says: " I laid me down and slept in peace."

Wednesday was a dinner at Count Pelet de la Lozère's. Thursday, at M. Guizot's : seated by their celebrated host, this dinner was felt by Mrs. Fry to be an occasion of great responsibility. She was encouraged by his courteous attention, unreservedly to speak to him on the subjects which had so long been near to her heart. It was no common ordeal for woman, weak even in her strength, to encounter reasoning powers and capabilities such as his : their motives of action arising probably from far different sources, but curiously meeting at the same point ; her's from deep-rooted benevolence, directed by piety in its most · spiritual form ; his from reflection, observation, and statesman-like policy, guided by philanthropy, based on philosophy and established conviction—yet in the aggregate the results the same : an intense desire to benefit and exalt human nature, and arrest the progress of moral and social evil, and an equal interest in ascertaining the most likely methods of effecting the desired end. They spoke of crime in its origin, its consequences, and the measures to be adopted for its prevention ; of the treatment of criminals ; of education and of Scriptural instruction. Here Mrs. Fry unhesitatingly urged the diffusion of Scriptural truth, and the universal circulation of the Scriptures, as the one means capable alone of controlling the power of sin, and shedding light upon the darkness of superstition and infidelity.

The following evening, Mrs. Fry and her brother received at their hotel a large party of Greeks ; amongst others, their Ambassador, M. Coletti. The Duke de Broglie was kind enough to interpret for Mrs. Fry. Before the party separated, Mr. Gurney read the account of St. Paul's visit to Athens; his comments on this portion of Holy Writ were luminous, powerful, and appropriate.

When in Paris in 1839, Mrs. Fry had become interested in a large party of Greeks who met at her hotel one evening. On the present occasion that interest was confirmed. The want of books in Greece, even those of elementary instruction was fully discussed, and it was decided to form some regular plan to supply this want. That this might be done effectually, a second evening was appointed for the purpose. There were assembled on this occasion some very superior men, among others M. de Comnène, who though not " born in the purple," was one of a family recognized, as lineally descended from the Emperors of Constantinople. A committee of Greeks, French and English, was formed to draw up rules, and endeavour to raise subscriptions, though not till after much animated discussion; the young Greek students in Paris undertaking to translate some works of elementary instruction. A spelling book with pictures was to be the first thing attempted, a desideratum not existing in that country. There was reason to expect that, through influence with the Government at Athens, these books would be dispersed into every Commune for the use of the schools and poor. Mrs. Fry had before been interested on the subject of female education in Greece, and in this important movement for supplying that country with elemental literature, she believed that the women also would eventually partake in the benefit.

Paris, Fifth Month 7th, First-day.—Second-day last was a very great festival called the Fête du Roi, when it was striking to observe such great crowds of people so orderly and well conducted. There is something in the French very attractive to me, —their lively yet sober habits—their politeness to one another— indeed they are to me peculiarly agreeable. During the day we had various calls of duty, and an evening of rather quiet recreation with a family who spent it with us.   From our windows we saw the most beautiful fireworks, which was pleasant ; as perfect order prevailed, I rejoiced that the poor should partake of such innocent refreshment and recreation, for there appeared no drunkenness or dissipation.   I wish we had more innocent recreations for our poor at home, to keep them out of the public-houses.

Fifth-day evening the 1st.—We had a most weighty and serious time.   We met at our friend Mark Wilks' about a hundred persons, perhaps forty of them pasteurs and missionaries. They had a religious service of their own—first singing a hymn, then reading the Holy Scriptures, afterwards prayer ; which when concluded, Mark Wilks said any brother or sister present was at liberty to speak.   I ventured in fear to open my mouth ; an interpreter at hand.   First, on the state of Protestant Europe, the religious persecutions in it, and dependence on forms.   I also expressed my desire that they might stand fast in the liberty wherewith Christ had made them free, and not be again entangled with any yoke of bondage ; my hope that they might arise and shine, manifesting that their light was come, and that the glory of the Lord had risen upon them ; and further said that I believed this would be the case.   I then addressed the pasteurs only, desiring that the Spirit of God might be poured forth upon them, that sinners might be converted, mourners comforted, and the weak strengthened.   I felt humbled afterwards, ready to hide my head from the sight of man ; yet I returned home, laid me down and slept, for the Lord sustained me.   But He only knows the deep exercise of my spirit at such times.

On Sixth-day, we paid a long visit to the St. Lazare Prison, with both Catholic and Protestant ladies, spoke to the women at different times, as did my sister, through much difficulty in being heard, or properly interpreted for ; yet the truth did appear to reach many hearts, and I believe this visit was not in vain in the Lord.

Several very large parties succeeded each other, in which religious communications were blended with social intercourse.

Mrs. Fry again saw the Duchess of Orleans ; with the grand

Duchess of Mecklenburgh, she was permitted several interviews, in which the intercourse between these eminently Christian ladies assumed a deeply religious character.

It being the period of the annual religious meetings, many pasteurs were assembled in Paris: about thirty of them were invited by Mr. Gurney to breakfast, at the Hôtel Meurice.

Paris, 14*th.*—On Second-day, about thirty pasteurs to break-fast, from different parts of France, a very interesting set of men. First we had a Scripture reading; Joseph and myself had much to express to them at the time; a most weighty concern it was. My brother prayed, and one of the pasteurs spoke. We then breakfasted, and had really a delightful meal. I remembered that our Lord condescended to attend feasts, and this was a feast offered to His servants, of which we partook in love and peace. The pasteurs afterwards gave us an account of the religious state of the people around them; a good work certainly appears going on amidst many obstructions. We then spoke to them. I particularly recommended religious unity with all who love the Lord, and kindness to the Methodists as a valuable body of Christians.

One evening M. Guizot dined with Mrs. Fry's party. The topics before discussed were then resumed:—the state of Protestants in France, La liberté de culte, and Negro Slavery. Mrs. Fry entreated M. Guizot's attention to the state of the Sandwich Islands. She had received from Kamehameha III. the King, a letter a few months before, entreating her good offices to second his endeavours to prohibit the importation and use of spirituous liquors in his kingdom, the baneful and demoralizing effects of which he stated to be lamentable.

Much had been done for the improvement of prisons since Mrs. Fry was last at Paris. The importance of the subject had been fully recognised, and a bill brought before the Chamber of Deputies.

The following extract from the opening speech of the Minister of the Interior, shows by what means he contemplated conciliating the requirements of humanity with the interests of the community at large.

" Our object," says the Minister, " is not entirely to sequestrate the prisoner, or to confine him to absolute solitude ; such is not the object of our bill, and this is what makes it differ from the American system.

" We want to exclude convicts from the society of their fellow-prisoners, to keep them free from bad examples, and wicked associations ; but we want at the same time to multiply around them moral and honest connexions.   Besides their being visited by the Director of the Jail, they will be in frequent communication with the teacher and the medical attendant.   The chaplain, or the ministers of the several denominations acknowledged by the State, will have easy access to the cells at the hours appointed by the prison regulations.   It is to be the more efficacious, as the infection of bad example and contaminating influence will be removed.   Some of the provisions of the bill will mitigate the principle of solitary confinement, in a manner which has been suggested by the commission of 1840, and should not pass unnoticed by the Chamber.   Convicts sentenced to more than twelve years hard labour, or to perpetual hard labour, after having undergone twelve years of their punishment, or when they shall have attained the age of seventy, will be no longer separated from the others, excepting during the night.   Prisoners sentenced to " réclusion" or undergoing a correctional punishment, when seventy years of age, will not be subject to individual confinement."

The bill laid down as a principle that the " Bagnes" were to be ultimately replaced by houses of hard labour ; that houses of " réclusion" were to be erected, to take in all convicts sentenced to " réclusion" now detained in central houses.   It introduced considerable improvement into the management of houses of imprisonment, especially those supported by Departments.   In conformity with the principles of the system adopted, the bill had

also for its object, to bring under the direct authority of the
Minister of the Interior, as a centre, all the prisons in the kingdom.   M. de Tocqueville was a strong advocate of the separate
system, although he desired to see some modification in the
manner of its execution.   Mr. Carnot, also a member of the
commission for the improvement of prisons, entertained rather
different opinions, and was less favourable to the entire separation of prisoners.

With this dawn of promise for the future, and so much improvement already effected, it was sad to think of the St. Lazare
prison and its twelve hundred inmates, still in a state of wretchedness and neglect.

Paris, Fifth Month 21st, First-day.—My birthday, sixty-
three !   My God hath not forgotten to be gracious, nor hath He
shut up His tender mercies from me.

The last week has been an interesting one.   We were first
sent for by the King.   My brother, sister, and I paid rather a remarkable visit to him, the Queen and the Princess Adelaide.
To my surprise and pleasure yesterday, there arrived from the
Queen a most beautiful Bible with fine engravings, without
note or comment, given me as a mark of her satisfaction in our
visit.

Boulogne, 28th.—Through the condescending mercy of our
Heavenly Father we are safely and peacefully arrived here, after
a quiet journey with my dearest K——.   We were near meeting with a very serious accident, but through mercy, we escaped
without injury.   Our leaving Paris was no common occasion.
The morning before, several of our beloved friends were with us ;
they literally loaded us with presents ; indeed, it appeared as if
they did not know how to show their love to us enough.   Before
we parted from each other we had a most solemn time in prayer,
little knowing whether we should see each other's faces more.   I
hardly knew how to accept all their generous kindness.   What
can we say, but that their hearts being thus turned to us must
be " the Lord's doing, and is marvellous in our eyes."

The previous evening many of our dear Friends, English and French, came to take leave of us; we read together the 121st Psalm. In the morning I visited a Roman Catholic Refuge and finished well with the Greeks in the afternoon.

On Third-day we visited the great military prison at St. Germain, accompanied by a French general, an English colonel, our excellent friend Count Pelet, and Moreau-Christophe. We were received very kindly by the Colonel Governor of the Prison, and his wife, and took our dejeuné with them.

In the evening we went to a large Meeting in one of the Faubourgs with the French Methodists in humble life. How curious the changes in my daily life!—what a picture they would make!—In the morning surrounded by the high military and the soldier prisoners—in the evening in a Methodist meeting-house, with the people and their pasteurs, and afterwards by poor little French children, hearing them read.

Another day I was at a large Prison Committee of Protestant ladies. I think they have been greatly prospered in their work of Christian love, in which they have persevered ever since my first visit to Paris; there have been many instances of great improvement in the prisoners under their care. After prayer for them I left them.

The afternoon of the Sabbath I paid a distressing visit to the St. Lazare Prison; such a scene of disorder and deep evil I have seldom witnessed—gambling, romping, screaming. With much difficulty we collected four Protestant prisoners, and read with them. I spoke to those poor disorderly women, who appeared attentive, and showed some feeling. I have represented, to many in authority the sad evils of this prison, and have pleaded with them for reform, for religious care, and for Scriptural instruction.

In the evening, the dear Countess Pelet was with us, and we had a large assembly mostly of English, it was thought ninety or a hundred. I was tired and poorly, my flesh and my heart ready to fail, but the Lord strengthened me, and I felt really helped by a power quite above myself. With this company I had a most satisfactory parting time, and a sweet feeling of love and unity with these servants of the Lord.

A quiet resting day was spent at Passy with her old and valued friends the Delessert family, with whom she had some solemn religious communications on this, the last day she spent amongst them.

On returning home, she was able to attend one or two sittings of the Yearly Meeting in London, and for a short time to encounter the current of life better than she had done before her journey.

Sixth Month 25th.—A week of considerable occupation. Second-day, the British Society committee, an interesting meeting with those beloved ladies; so much oneness in heart and purpose, a delightful evidence of the sweetness of Christian unity, and how those who differ in secondary points may agree in the most essential ones, and be one in Christ. We have cause for thankfulness in the excellent arrangements made by Lord Stanley for our poor prisoners in Van Diemen's Land; he appears so carefully to have attended to the representations we made respecting the evils existing there, and to have proposed good measures to remedy them.

The attention of Mrs. Fry and her friends in the Prison Committee, had been awakened anew to the condition of the female prisoners in Van Diemen's Land, the only colony to which they then were sent. She had received letters from Lady Franklin, and Miss Hayter (the late matron in "The Rajah"), depicting in lively colours the various evils to which these banished ones were exposed. The assignment of men had nearly ceased, but female convicts were still disposed of in that way to which the term "domestic slavery" had been so successfully applied, that the whole system, so far as male prisoners were concerned, was at an end.

But the assignment of women continued. When a convict ship arrived from England, as many or more persons than there were prisoners on board, were immediate candidates for their services. These candidates were not bound to shew any qualification of their fitness to be the employers of convicts. Publicans or ticket-of-leave holders were not permitted to take them into their employ; but with these exceptions, they might immediately on landing from the ship be located in the families of the colonists. Those supposed to be the best, were assigned to the best masters and mistresses, while the refuse fell to the lot of the lower ranks of society; the word "best" being applied to the upper classes. As a great proportion of the tradesmen are emancipated convicts, a fair estimate of the chances of improvement (so to speak) of the prisoner servants may easily be formed.

" The Cascade Factory is a receiving house for the women on their first arrival, (if not assigned from the ship), or on their transition from one place to another; and also a house of correction for faults committed in domestic service, but with no pretension to be a place of reformatory discipline, and seldom failing to turn out the women worse than they entered it. Religious instruction there was none, except that occasionally on the Sabbath the Superintendent of the prison read prayers, and sometimes divine service was performed by a chaplain, who had also an extensive parish to attend to.

" The officers of the establishment consisted at that time of only five persons: a porter, the superintendent and matron, and two assistants. The number of prisoners in the Factory, when first visited by Miss Hayter, was five hundred and fifty. It followed, of course, that nothing like prison-discipline could be enforced, or even attempted. In short, so congenial to the taste of its inmates was this place of custody, (it would be unfair to call it a place of punishment), that they returned to it again and again when they wished to change their place of servitude; and they were known to commit offences on purpose to be sent into it preparatory to their re-assignment elsewhere."

This brief account, drawn from the letters already referred

to, may be summed up with a passage extracted from one of
them :—

"Yet after visiting the Factory, and hearing every body speak
of its unhappy inmates, I could not but feel that they were far
more to be pitied then blamed. No one has ever attempted any
measures to ameliorate their degraded condition. I felt that had
they had the opportunity of religious instruction, some, at least,
might be rescued. I wish I could express to you all I feel and
think upon the subject; and how completely I am overwhelmed
with the awful sin of allowing so many wretched beings to perish
for lack of instruction. Even in the hospital of the Factory, the
unhappy creatures are as much neglected in spiritual things as if
they were in a heathen land; there are no Bibles, and no Christians to tell them of a Saviour's dying love."

On the receipt of these letters, Mrs. Fry lost no time in communicating their contents to Lord Stanley the Secretary of State
for the Colonial Department, accompanying the large extracts
which she sent to his Lordship, with a detailed account of the
plans adopted by Sir Ralph and Lady Darling at the Factory
at Paramatta, which was, on their arrival in New South
Wales, in almost every respect in the same state as that at
Hobart Town.

It was necessary there to alter the building, so as to admit of
a perfect separation into classes. Employment was supplied by
the Ladies' Committee; daily religious services were performed,
schools brought into operation, and by degrees the whole establishment conducted, as far as was found practicable, in the
manner recommended in Mrs. Fry's work on visiting prisons,
and according to the Rules of the British Ladies' Society.

The state of the prisoners of Van Diemen's Land was already
occupying the attention of Government, and measures were taken,
which have since much changed the circumstances in which
female prisoners are placed when transported. An account of

the alterations which have been made, would occupy more room than can be devoted to the subject ; but it may briefly be stated that a man-of-war, fitted up as a temporary prison, was shortly after this period sent out to Van Diemen's Land, and moored in the Derwent, the river on the banks of which, Hobart Town is built. A large staff of officers, male and female, was sent out, and Dr. and Mrs. Bowden were placed at the head of the establishment. In this ship (the "Anson"), all females transported from the United Kingdom are received on their arrival in the colony. They remain under systematic instruction for six months, and are then placed in the service of the colonists. An opportunity of testing their characters is thus afforded. If they are well disposed, they are recommended to situations where they are not exposed to temptations, too strong, for their newly-formed resolutions of amendment to resist. But the factories are as yet the only receptacles for prisoners who leave their situations, whether on account of incompetency to the fulfilment of their duties, or in order to be punished for offences committed in servitude. A new prison is in progress of erection, and it may be hoped that when completed it will be placed under such regulations, as to remove some, if not all, the evils which still exist.

On the 21st, Elizabeth Fry attended the Quarterly Meeting at Hertford, accompanied by her brother Samuel Gurney and one of his daughters ; it was the last time she left home on a mission of this character, expressly for religious service.

The following evening a large party of the Delegates from different parts of the world assembled in London, to attend the Anti-Slavery and Peace Society Meetings, and came to Upton Lane ; the evening was closed by Scripture reading and prayer.

JOURNAL RESUMED.

Last First-day was not one to be forgotten ; much of the morning without clouds. My dear brother and sister Buxton

were at Meeting.   I felt it my duty to encourage the weary, and
enlarged upon our foolishness, yet how the Lord is made unto
His people wisdom, righteousness, sanctification, and redemption.   There were some who appeared much impressed.   Through
the whole of that day and into the next, renewed peace rested
on my spirit.

I feel that I am pressed rather beyond my present power of
mind or body, and I really forget things : my desire is lively and
strong to serve all, one omission has been a real pain, and led me
to endeavour afresh to bring myself and my deeds to the light, that
they may be reproved, or be made manifest, that they are wrought
in God.

In July, Mrs. Fry showed increasing symptoms of illness,
partly the results of over fatigue and stress upon her body and
mind, and partly as she always considered from a chill, when
sitting one evening in the garden at Upton Lane.   In this
increased state of indisposition she went to Sandgate, chiefly
for the sake of her sister-in-law, Elizabeth Fry, whose declining health induced her husband and herself to wish to be
near her, much being due to his own and only sister.   The
only house that could be obtained was on the lower road to
Folkestone ; this part forms a complete undercliff, and from
its southern aspect is extremely hot, which was obviously unfavourable for Mrs. Fry.

Sandgate, Seventh Month 29th.—We arrived here yesterday.
I have been permitted to pass through rather an unusual time of
late, I think ——— (alluding to a painful circumstance), hurt
me, bodily and mentally, and discouraged me.   Our house was
rather too full for me, and I got too anxious (my easily besetting
sin), about some nearest to me.   I was uncommonly pressed by
other people, and then business of various kinds, and from a fine
state of health, such as I have not enjoyed for a long time, and
the most excellent refreshing nights, I have lately frequently
been awake nearly all night, and from some cause become in so

irritable a state of constitution as to be for hours in the day really distressing. It particularly depresses, and rather flurries the spirits, and this with an extraordinary press of engagements has rather overwhelmed me. I have very earnestly prayed for help and patience, night and day, and it has been hard to come at a resting place, bodily or mentally. I find myself here in a lovely place by the sea, the air delightful, and the house pleasant. Thus the Lord provides for me in this my tried estate. If it please my Holy Helper, may He soon see meet to heal me.

First-day afternoon.—No one of the family at home but myself; how very unusual a circumstance. I have at times passed through a good deal of conflict and humiliation in this indisposition, and it is a real exercise of faith to me, the way in which I am tried by my illness. I suppose it arises from my extremely susceptible nerves, that are so affected when the body is out of order, as to cast quite a veil over the mind. I am apt to query whether I am not deceiving myself, in supposing I am the servant of the Lord, so ill to endure suffering, and to be so anxious to get rid of it; but it has been my earnest prayer that I might truly say, " Not as I will, but as Thou wilt." Lord! help me. I pray that I may be enabled to cast all my burthen and all my care upon Thee, that I may rest in the full assurance of faith in Thy love, pity, mercy and grace. I pray Thee help me, that my soul may be less disquieted within me, and that I may more trustfully and hopefully go on heavenward. Increase my faith in Thy faithfulness gracious Lord, whilst I believe that those who are once in grace are not always in grace; yet help me ever to feel that faithful art Thou, O Lord! who hast called us out of darkness into Thy marvellous light, and Thou only canst do it; therefore be pleased to hearken to the prayer of Thy poor servant, increase her faith, and be Thyself, for Thine own name sake, not only the author, but the finisher of it. Amen.

First-day.—Again alone, or nearly so; the rest gone to Meeting. I have passed a humbling week, still poorly by day and night. I think a place so remarkably void of objects does not suit my active mind, but it is well to be brought where I may rest on my oars; for there is a danger of depending on active occupation for comfort, and even for a certain degree of diversion. I feel this when at the sea, at night in my wakeful hours; generally in the day I have something to occupy me; but this place has been unusually dull to me, though I have the sweet company of several of our own dear family. Dear Edward and Catherine Buxton, and their children, my sister Elizabeth Fry, and her companion, have been here, and their company has been acceptable; but I think the lowness has been very much from my bodily indisposition. I think I mend a little, but it is very slowly. But truly do I pray night and day for mercy and help. I feel so peculiarly in need of it, seldom more so; however, perhaps when we feel most in danger we may be more safe, than when we apprehend ourselves in a place of safety. Gracious Lord, keep Thy poor servant by Thine own power and Spirit, who cannot keep herself even for a moment!

Sandgate, Ninth Month 4th.—Oh Lord! in Thine own time deliver me from my fears, enable me patiently to bear this chastisement, until Thou seest it has accomplished that which Thou sentest it for, and deliver me out of it, and cause, in Thine own time, that I may return Thee thanks on the banks of deliverance.

It was at Sandgate, that she received the account of the death of her lovely niece Harriet C——. Nine weeks before, a beautiful and blooming bride, she had been united to the object of her especial choice; one of whose principles and character, Mrs. Fry entertained a high estimate, and whose affectionate attentions to herself ceased not, till the last sad duties had been paid to her memory. In the state in which she then was, these tidings were very grievous to her; and very sorrowfully she writes respecting the event.

In how many ways the Lord teaches us; surely the present is no common lesson.

Three days later she says:—We live with you in spirit; (and after naming the most bereaved, adds,) and all most dear to the beloved departed. It is sweet to remember that help is laid on

One that is mighty, who, blessed be His holy name, is ever near to His dependent servants. I feel, as if I could write to one or other of you more than once in the day, I have such a drawing towards you. How curious, that the only place in the world I have longed to be in, since my indisposition, has been West Norfolk. Had I not had others to consider, and only followed my own inclination, I believe, that I should have been amongst you through this deep trial.

After several distressing weeks, Mrs. Fry was moved to Tonbride Wells, closely and faithfully nursed by her two youngest daughters.

Tonbridge Wells, 10th.—We are favoured to be settled here in a comfortable house, where many accommodations abound, which, in my delicate state, I find a real help. I have been favoured to partake of sweet resting sleep ; thanks to my Heavenly Father for His great mercy.

Third-day.—My case has been rather increasingly distressing, from an almost total loss of appetite, and at times great lowness. Many fears creep in for my natural health, more particularly, as it respects the nervous system. Hitherto my Lord has said to the waves that would overwhelm me, " so far shalt thou go and no further." And, merciful Lord, if it be Thy holy will, continue to keep them from overwhelming Thy poor unworthy servant, in this time of weakness and of frequent distress. Let not the waterfloods prevail. When my spirit is overwhelmed within me, enable me to look to the Rock that is higher than I, as a " refuge from the storm, a shadow from the heat, when the blast of the terrible one is as a storm against the wall."

24th.—I desire in this my sorrow and suffering, to cast myself and my whole care on my Lord. I know that I am poor, miserable, blind and naked, and I look to my Lord for every thing. The kindness of all around me is great, indeed wonderful to me, and their pleasure in being with me comforting, for I feel as if I must be burdensome to them. Most gracious Lord, if it be Thy will, let not this be the case, but bless this trying, humbling illness to them, as well as to myself; and may it please

Thee to grant me grace, minute by minute, to hold fast my confidence, stedfast unto the end, that continuing faithful unto death, I may through Thy merits receive a crown of life!

She returned to Upton the end of September, and very reluctantly renounced the hope of spending part of the autumn in Norfolk. Her eldest daughter, who had been awaiting her there, returned home on the 2nd of October, joining her aunt Lady Buxton on the road. She found her mother very ill, more so, she thought, than she had ever seen her. She was laid very low, her illness had its fluctuations; but she did not come down stairs after October the 5th. She however often told those around her, in her great bodily suffering—that the everlasting arms were always underneath her—that the under current was peace and' comfort, though the surface was so much tempest-tossed.

In a letter, dictated October 2nd, she thus expresses herself.

I have been very much struck in this illness, with the manner in which my children have been raised up as my helpers, and when I look back upon the deep and unutterable travail of spirit I have had on their behalf; and now that it has pleased the Lord that His hand should, in some respects be heavy upon me, how it has pleased Him to enable them to minister to my support and help, I think it should be to all of you who are parents, an encouragement to do your best, and commit the rest to God. I think this is more especially to be felt as respects our sons, that our first aim must be (in asking for a blessing on our endeavours) that we bring them up for the kingdom, and little can we calculate, how the Lord may bless and deliver them, and make them a blessing to ourselves.

Lady Buxton remained near her for some time, visiting her continually, and frequently uniting in reading and religious intercourse with her and her daughter L——, who was then, and continued to be for several succeeding months, peculiarly devoted to her as her personal nurse. On one occasion, after having read

the 7th chapter of St. John, she remarked how injurious the
spirit of priestcraft had ever been to the progress of true Christianity in all ages and under all forms.   She went on to express
her longing desire, that the day of grace might come, when. all
nations would be filled with the knowledge of the Lord.   In
reference to this, the first twelve and two last verses of the 47th
chapter of Ezekiel were read, so beautifully descriptive of the
gospel rising and spreading as waters, and covering the earth to
fructify and bless.

On hearing the 8th chapter of St. John, she commented upon
the freedom of the gospel, remarking that she had known much
of it, but that her prayer had been to obtain liberty, not laxity.
She also said, she had felt a portion at times of that peace which
passeth understanding, but, that this life was a state of warfare
and would be so even to the end.

Upton, Tenth Month 10*th.*—My God hath not forgotten to be
gracious, or shut up His tender mercies from me ; it appears to
me that all of nature is to be brought low, for all that is of the
Lord only, can stand the day of humiliation.   I may thankfully
say, I am quiet and sustained in spirit, but do not often know
peace to flow as a river, as at some former times ; still help is
constantly near from the sanctuary, though I abide under a sense
of deep unworthiness before the Lord ; but what can I do but
wait in faith, until He be pleased fully to clothe me with the
garments of His righteousness and His salvation.   I feel I can
do nothing for myself.

The only daughter who had not been with her, since immediately after her return from France, came to her at this time ; she
found her in a singular state, one of great natural depression, but
unshaken in faith.   The complaint being so much upon the
nerves, produced sensations of irrepressible distress and discom-
fort.   Yet never under any circumstances could the chord of
religion be touched, but it immediately vibrated.

One afternoon, when one or two members of her family were reading with her, she was unable to attend to a very interesting religious biography, saying, it was "too touching to her—too affecting." She added, after a pause, " How I feel for the poor when very ill, in a state like my own, for instance, when ' good' ladies go to see them." "Religious truths so strongly brought forward, often injudiciously." She went on speaking on this subject, and then dwelt on "the exquisite tenderness of the Saviour's ministrations ;" of " His tone and manner to sinners !"

Soon afterwards she resumed, in the most impressive manner, saying, that " religious truth was opened to her, and supplied to her inwardly, not by man's ministration, but administered according to her need ;" adding, " if I may so say, it is my life."

She constantly spoke of not being called to active service now, and that she had no desire as to recovery ; on the contrary, she was " able quite to leave it." Frequently she repeated to those about her, " I feel the foundation underneath me sure."

One evening she opened her heart on her deep and earnest desires for the good of her children. Of her " great sufferings" —" greater than any one knows"—that if they were to last, no one could wish for her life ; but soon added, " there is one thing I would willingly live for—the good of my husband and children, and my fellow-creatures."

On the night of October the 25th, she poured out a wonderful stream of rejoicing after she was in bed, a perfect flood of faith and hope: quoting many passages of Scripture, to prove that faith must work by love ; and that faith, if true, must produce works. She said, " with the text, ' He that keepeth my sayings shall never see death,' take this one also, ' He that believeth on me shall never die.' " She afterwards expressed in a tone of the deepest feeling her " perfect confidence, her full assurance, that neither life, nor death, nor angels, nor principalities, nor powers, nor things present, nor things to come, nor height, nor

depth, nor any other creature, should be able to separate her from
the love of God which is in Christ Jesus our Lord;" adding,
" my whole trust is in Him, my entire confidence."—" I *know* in
whom I have believed, and can commit all to Him, who has loved
me and given Himself for me, whether for life or death, sickness
or health, time or eternity."

In the course of the same day, she said very emphatically,
" My dear R—— I can say one thing: since my heart was
touched at seventeen years old, I believe I never have awakened
from sleep, in sickness or in health, by day or by night, without
my first waking thought being, how best I might serve my Lord."

Mrs. Fry had greatly wished to attend the marriage of her
niece Anna G—— ; but as the time approached, all hopes of
accomplishing this passed away. With the promise of a family
Bible, (her favourite wedding present), she sent this note
(dictated) :—

MY DEAREST ANNA,

I was very glad to receive thy note. I hope the Bible will
be ready in a few days ; the one I had ready for thee, I sent to
Lady ——, hoping that it would induce Lord —— and her to
have family reading. It is a great and unexpected disappointment to me, to see no probability of being able to attend thy
wedding; but " it is not to him that walketh, to direct his
steps:" the humiliation of my suffering may be better for me
than going to the house of rejoicing, and if so permitted, we
cannot doubt it. At all events, I think thou art sure that few
more earnestly desire thy peace and prosperity than I do, in
spirituals and in temporals ;—that thyself, and thy companion
in life, may be enabled to serve the living God faithfully, through
the power of His Holy Spirit ; and that through the faithfulness of
the Saviour's love, His richest grace and peace may be with you,
in heights and in depths, in sickness and in health, in riches and
poverty, in life and in death. My very dear love to my sister
Catherine, thy father and mother, and the rest of your circle ;

also to thy dear intended husband. Thy much-attached and well-wishing aunt,

ELIZABETH FRY.

At this time, her regular attendants were her daughters ; her youngest, L——, with her husband and children, remaining for many months at Upton Lane, to assist her eldest sister in devotion to their mother ; the other daughters and daughters-in-law resident in the neighbourhood, taking their regular days to spend in the sick-room.

Her eldest son also, leaving his family at Geneva, paid her a particularly acceptable visit, remaining for several days with her.

On Sunday, November the 6th, her son William remained from church to be with her, and her daughter L——. After reading a chapter in Job, and the 3rd of St. John, she prayed in a very striking manner, that after all the sorrows and fluctuations of time were ended, "We might behold His face in glory, that whilst here we might not deceive ourselves, but be true and decided followers of Him, who in His own good time would arise with healing on His wings to deliver us from all our pain."

The following day, a very beautiful note being read to her, from one who preceded her to the heavenly mansions, a few days after writing it—in which, with reference to her, the three first verses of the 41st Psalm were quoted. She lay quiet for a short time, and then calling one of her daughters to her bedside said, " May they not be deceived !" " One thing is certain, I have desired and sought to serve the Lord."

11th.—When suffering from intense thirst, and drinking Seltzer water with some wine in it, which much refreshed her, she observed " what a beautiful provision of nature and blessing of God, is water—natural waters to heal the body, and everlasting waters to heal the soul"—adding, " when awake and distressed with thirst, a few nights previously, this thought of the natural and spiritual waters springing up, made the night almost pleasant."

13th.—Her nephew, the Rev. Edward Hoare, came to see her. He sat down by her sofa and said to her, " My dear aunt, what a consolation to know you to be of the church of God, which He hath purchased with His own blood." After a little pause she said with great humility, " But we must avoid false confidence." He replied, that there could be no false confidence, when our hope is fixed on Christ alone. She said with emphasis, " There, indeed, is no false confidence;" and added, that in this illness she had entirely felt without carefulness; so able to commit every person and every thing, and leave them in His hands; that she felt no service now called for from her, only to endure, as seeing Him who is invisible.

Her nephew reminded her, how St. Paul had to endure the thorn in his flesh, and how encouraging it was to remember that he had prayed three times for its removal, which prayers were not answered by removing the thorn, but by giving grace to bear it, quoting the Scripture, " My grace is sufficient for thee." He then moved to go away, but she detained him, saying, " Dear Edward, if thou hast anything on thy heart for me, do not fear to express it." His answer was, " Yes, dear aunt, I have a few words of prayer much on my heart for you." It was, however, rather an earnest giving of thanks for the assured hope he entertained concerning her. When he ceased, she added, as she laid on her sofa, an intercession, " For this beloved nephew and his work of the ministry, and that in these difficult times he may have wisdom and judgment to act, and power to stand fast in the liberty wherewith Christ had made him free, and not be entangled in any yoke of bondage."

To her Children in Norfolk.

Upton Lane, 20*th.*

My Dearest F—— and R——,

Often, in the night especially, I feel the pain of the difficulty of communicating with those I love at a distance ; I therefore thought I must express a few words to you myself, to tell you how deeply I feel all your kindness. Thy gifts and loans, dear R——, are truly useful, and so often bring thee pleasantly to my remembrance. At present, I think we are well off for help ; I may thankfully say that I am well cared for in every way, and my opinion is, that this care which has now been extended to me for so many weeks has not been in vain in the Lord. Although yet in a state of serious illness, I feel in some degree raised in myself, of course amid great fluctuations. I may thankfully acknowledge, I not unfrequently partake of hours of rest and peace, through the tender mercy of Him, who is touched with a feeling of our infirmities, and is our ever-loving Advocate. Times of sore conflict are now and then permitted, but I have been sooner delivered out of them, than I was. As to outward help (with regard to medicine), I believe little can be done, but as it respects sympathy and care, much ; but as I abound in these latter, in such a remarkable degree, I trust, if it be the will of my Heavenly Father, they may tend to raise up, if not that they may be blessed to my soul. My particular love to dear Frank in Edinburgh, Addison and Gurney, when you write. All your dear children dwell much in my heart, with earnest desires for their present and everlasting welfare. I remain, with dear love to the little boys, and much to my brother ——,

Your tenderly attached mother,

Elizabeth Fry.

But the degree of amendment described, slight as it was, did not continue.

On Sunday, November 26th, one of her sons, a daughter, and her little grandson Walter F——, being by her bedside, she prayed

nearly as follows, after the 18th chapter of St. Matthew had been
read to her :—

Gracious Lord, grant that the promise to those, where two or
three are gathered together in Thy name, may be fulfilled in our
experience ; and that Thou wilt look upon our whole circle, as well
as the little group now present.　Heal as far as is consistent with
Thy will, and grant patience and submission to whatever Thou
mayst order.　Lord, enable us to cut off the right hand and pluck
out the right eye, if they are likely to lead us into temptation.
For ourselves, and those especially who are nearest to the little
one whose spirit passed to Thee yesterday, enable us to give
thanks, that he is among those innocent ones, whose angels
redeemed by the mercy of Christ Jesus, are for ever in Thy
presence ; and for all who are in affliction, we would ask Thy
support.

This alluded to a lovely infant of her nephew and niece
Buxton ; they had been her near neighbours, and much with her
at Sandgate.　The loss of this child, to which she had attached
herself, afflicted her very much.

In one of the remaining entries in her journal she thus
expresses herself :—

Upton, Twelfth Month 7th.—Lord ! undertake Thyself for me ;
Thy arm of power can alone heal, help and deliver ; and in Thee
do I trust, and hope, though at times deeply tried and cast down
before Thee ; yet O Lord ! Thou art my hope, and be therefore
entreated of Thy poor sorrowful and often afflicted servant, and
arise for my help.　Leave not my poor soul destitute, but through
the fulness of Thine own power, mercy and love, keep me alive
unto Thyself, unto the end ! that nothing may separate me from
Thy love, that I may endure unto the end ; and when the end
comes, that I may be altogether Thine, and dwell with Thee, if
it be but the lowest place within the gate, where I may behold
Thy glory and Thy holiness ; and for ever rest in Thee.

I do earnestly entreat Thee, that to the very last I may never

deny Thee, or in any way have my life or conversation lucon-
sistent with my love to Thee, and most earnest desire to live to
Thy glory ; for I have loved Thee, O Lord, and desired to serve
Thee without reserve. Be entreated, that through Thy faithfulness, and the power of Thy own Spirit, I may serve Thee
unto the end. Amen !

On the 28th, she said to her son J——h, " I see the gates of
mercy open, and rays of light are shining from them."

A few memoranda from the journal of her son William, are
here introduced, not merely as illustrative of her state, but as
descriptive of his communication with the tenderly beloved mother,
whom he was to precede by so short a period to that land, where
parting is unknown.

" ' The evening of the 29th, was one of the greatest suffering
and distress, such as I never remember to have witnessed. But,
through all, her faith was triumphant, and her confidence unshaken. I endeavoured to remember a few of her expressions,
and have succeeded in calling to mind the following :—

" I believe this is not death, but it is as passing through the
valley of the shadow of death, and perhaps with more suffering,
from more sensitiveness ; but the ' rock is here ;' ' the distress is
awful, but He has been with me.'

" ' I feel that He is with me, and will be with me, even to
the end. David says why hast Thou forsaken me ? I do not
feel that I am forsaken. In my judgment I believe this is not
death, but it is as death. It is nigh unto death.' Her agony
appeared almost unbearable ; but she frequently expressed fears
of being impatient. ' May none of you, be called to pass through
such a furnace ; but still my sufferings have been mitigated
through mercy and grace ! fulness of grace ! Now my dear
William, be stedfast, immoveable, always abounding in the work
of the Lord ; and then thy labour shall not be in vain in the
Lord. O ! the blessedness of having desired to be on the Lord's
side ! (not that I have any merit of my own). I cannot express,
even in my greatest trials and tribulations, the blessedness of Ilis

service. My life has been a remarkable one ; much have I had to go through, more than mortal knows, or ever can know ; my sorrows at times have been bitter ; but my consolations sweet ! In my lowest estates, through grace, my love to my Master has never failed, nor to my family, nor to my fellow-mortals. This illness may be for death, or it may not, according to His will ; but He will never forsake me, even should He be pleased to take me this night."

February 1st.—Her son William, her brother Samuel Gurney, and two of her daughters, being around her bed, she prayed in a low voice, and at broken intervals, to the following purport :—

For help for this poor afflicted servant in her deep tribulations, that in passing through the floods they should not overflow her, and through the fire she should not be burned ; that these trials in the hands of the great Refiner might tend to more perfect purification and refinement, and preparation for His service, whether in time or in eternity ; but she wholly left this to His will. That if raised up, she desired it might only be to more entire devotedness to His service, and as an instrument to spread the knowledge of Christ and His truth amongst her fellow-mortals ; and that mercy might be granted in body, soul, and spirit, to her husband, children, brothers, and sisters, and all beloved by her, even by Him whom she had steadily loved and desired to serve from childhood, though, through sore temptation and tribulation.

The evening of the same day, holding her husband's hand in one of her's, and her son-in-law, R—— P——'s, in the other, she burst forth into a most remarkable and triumphant expression of her faith ; her certainty of the truths of Revelation : " I know my foundation to be sure : I feel the rock *always* under-neath me."

The following morning, on her son William's reading an expression of love and sympathy from her eldest grandson, who was at Edinburgh with his regiment, she said, "my very dear love to him; tell him to be stedfast, immoveable, always abounding in the work of the Lord, for in *whatever circumstances*, it will not be in vain in the Lord."

Her only absent daughter was at this time, again summoned from Norfolk. Her mother had suffered some days before with most painful neuralgic symptoms, but just then there was a degree of respite; the change, however, since she had seen her before was sorrowful indeed to witness, and could but lead to the most alarming apprehensions. She spoke of her own recovery as a thing hidden from herself, and concerning which she had no desire. One day it was said to her, "that many a Christian had slept in this world and to their own surprise awakened in glory;" she exclaimed directly, with most striking emphasis, "Oh! what a sweet thought." She spoke occasionally of her "timid nature;" of her "natural fear of death;" but on Monday night, the 19th, when very low in body and spirit, she said emphatically, "should I never see the light of another morning, remember I am safe!"

Her dependence on her Saviour, and utter rejection of every merit of her own, was entire. On one occasion, she breathed forth, when under deep illness and distress, "I am nothing, I have nothing; I am poor, miserable, naked, helpless. I can do nothing, but my Saviour is every thing, all-sufficient—my light, my life, my joy, my eternal hope of glory."

One night, her husband sitting by the fire, she said, "I have never felt before so sunk and faint as I have to-day; never so like one whose 'feet draw nigh unto the gates of death;'" he not distinctly hearing her words, she asked some one to repeat them to him. She appeared not to desire to know what was before her, continually saying, "I wish to leave it in better hands."

To one of the "nursing sisters" who were attending her, she

thus expressed herself, "I am of the same mind as Paul, I can say, 'to me to live is Christ, but to die is gain.' What a grand thought it is! everlasting to everlasting, without trouble and without pain: to meet there, and together be for ever with Christ."

Her gratitude to all about her was unbounded, continually saying, "How I am cared for! I am fed surely on the finest of the wheat." This, particularly alluded to the innumerable little gifts and tokens of love, that she received in every form that could be devised to tempt her appetite, and induce her to take more nourishment. "Love! all love; my heart is filled with love to every one," was amongst her frequent expressions. Her delight was great in the attendance of her husband and children: "they minister to my wants; my children's attendance upon me is perfect."

Towards the end of February her sufferings became most afflicting: how unutterably awful then appeared the curse of sin and death, when a servant so devoted was thus permitted to endure. Night after night a sorrowing band was mustered for the conflict. Fervently was prayer offered in her behalf, far and near it rose for her help; but though it pleased her God and Saviour eminently to abide with her in the furnace, yet the time was not come for Him who watches over His people, as a refiner and purifier of silver, to conclude the process and to quench the flames.

She was comforted, as were her attendants, by occasional visits from members of her own religious persuasion, and other Christian friends. Prayer was offered from time to time in her chamber. The visits of her sister, Lady Buxton, were a true solace to her, she clung to her with inexpressible tenderness. She was also very dependent on the services of her faithful attendant Christiana G——. On one occasion she was heard to say, "Dear C., how little I thought when thou wast a little

girl, what a comfort thou wouldest become to me ! how many are
my mitigations !" She often repeated these lines :—

> " Come what, come may,
> Time and the hour run, through the roughest day."

She had 'letters frequently of much value ; some addressed
to herself, others to her family. One from her brother Joseph
John Gurney to one of her daughters was very consoling to
her :—

" Earlham, Second Month.

"MY BELOVED NIECE,

" Thy truly interesting and affecting letters are both received
this morning. Had the first come yesterday, we should, of
course have answered it, as we are all here together, thy uncle
and aunt Buxton, thy uncle and aunt Cunningham, my dearest
wife and I. It is a favour that the letters of yesterday's date
are more comfortable, as it regards our tenderly beloved sister's
sufferings, and the bright gleams of a spiritual nature which
have been permitted to penetrate your gloom, are hailed by us all
with humble thankfulness (I trust) to the Author of all our
sure mercies. I need scarcely tell thee how heartily and nearly
we all sympathize with her and with you. Prayer on her account has flowed from more than one mouth amongst us this
morning,—may I not say the prayer of faith and sweet assurance
—that He who sees meet thus to bring into the furnace, is, and
ever will be, near to her, for her support, consolation, and final
deliverance. I have been afraid of writing to her, lest it should
not be proper for her to receive letters ; but our tenderest love
is with her, and in the midst of the deep tribulation of having
her brought so low, we would wish her to know that we feel a
precious serenity of mind in thinking of her, and in mentally
visiting her bed of sickness and sore affliction. There is a holy
hand stretched forth, which is holding up her head, far above all
the boisterous waves ; and we think we can, in some measure,
not only submit to being baptized with her, with this baptism of

pain and sorrow, but rise with her in faith, and hope, and love, above the billows. It appears to us that the faithfulness of Christ, and the eternal stability of His truth, are manifested in no common degree on this most trying occasion. On that faithfulness and stability we must all endeavour quietly to repose, in the full belief that every passing day will bring its own support and alleviations, as well as its own appointed measure of conflict; what a blessing it is that none of these things move us, and that the things which cannot be shaken, are not only still in full force, but are more than ever developed to our view.

As March advanced, there was perceptible improvement, less severity of pain, and rather more appetite ; she was moved now and then into another room, in a wheeled chair, and she began strongly to wish to be taken to Bath for the benefit of the waters. St. Paul tells us of body, soul and spirit, in 1 Thessalonians v. 23 ; and again in Hebrews iv. 12 ; he tells us of soul and spirit ; her state was a curious illustration of this—the body suffering and infirm—the natural powers of mind enfeebled—but the immortal and renewed spirit rising superior to it all, and shining but the brighter for the surrounding darkness.

To a son and daughter, who had left her two days before.

Upton Lane, *Fourth Month 1st.*

My dearest F——k and R——l,

I felt so poorly in body, and low in spirits, there was very little I could say when we parted ; but I thought I must tell you without delay, how peculiarly acceptable your visit has been. Though parted, I hope you will hold me in remembrance, in this my low estate. It has been very precious to find the best of bonds strengthening with our years, which I humbly trust we may acknowledge to be the case, that being united in Christ, and bound together under his banner, we may all fight the good fight of faith, until we obtain the victory through our Lord and Saviour Jesus Christ: and join that company which cannot be numbered, gathered out of every nation, kindred, tongue, and people, who have washed their robes, and made them white in the blood of the Lamb, and are for ever at rest. But then we must press towards the mark, faithfully, diligently and watchfully, until we obtain the prize of our high calling in Christ Jesus. I must tell you, that when you left me, dear L—— came to me almost immediately, which was acceptable and very seasonable, and William soon after brought a Christian Missionary to see me, and we had a sweet time in prayer, which refreshed my spirit.

I am your tenderly attached mother,

ELIZABETH FRY.

After many weeks of difficulty and doubt, the decision was come to, and her husband accomplished her removal to Bath. Sir Fowell and Lady Buxton were already there; and, though he, like Mrs. Fry, was bowed under infirmity, yet the closeness of the union, natural and spiritual, which existed amongst them, rendered their being near one another an important solace to them all. Various members of their families successively joined them; among others, her son William, and his little Emma. How merciful is that arrangement in God's government of the world, which denies to His frail, feeble creatures, the knowledge of the future! Much of sorrow and infirmity had they to endure, but they could not foresee how soon the brightest and the best were to be laid low; the most pleasant pictures marred.

She gained strength at Bath, and was unquestionably in better health on her return home. But she was closely touched by the rapid decline of her sister Elizabeth Fry. They had been affectionately united for a long course of years. They had travelled together as ministers, among Friends, they had, year after year sat side by side in the meeting-house at Plaistow, and now in her low and weakened condition, the severing of this tie was to her very painful.

Her sister died on the 2ud of July; rejoicing that the hour of her deliverance had arrived, to lay down her frail tabernacle, and appear in the presence of her God and Saviour.

There was an extraordinary weight upon Mrs. Fry's spirit, she dwelt much and often on the invisible world, her sleep partook of these impressions. Did not coming events cast their shadows before? And was not she thus, in some measure prepared for the woes that were to follow? Her little grandson Gurney Reynolds was an especial object of interest to her; he was frequently with her, delighting in her gentle tenderness, and the pursuits she provided for him, so well suited to his feeble health. He left her not more unwell than usual. Tidings came of his being worse, and three days afterwards that he had breathed away his patient, lamb-like spirit, as he laid upon the sofa in his mother's room. This was the 18th of July.

On the morning of his funeral she wrote to his parents,—

MY DEAREST F——R AND C——A,

I deeply feel my separation from you this day; I long to be present with you to minister to your consolation. You have my earnest prayers that the best help may be with you, sustaining, healing, comforting you; enabling you to behold your beloved child at rest in Jesus, consequently that death has lost its sting, and the grave its victory. In the midst of this sore trial, may grace, mercy and peace continue to be with you, and in His own time, may the Lord grant you " beauty for ashes, the oil of joy for mourning, and the garment of praise for the spirit of heaviness."

Your tenderly attached and sympathizing mother,
ELIZABETH FRY.

A change of scene and air seemed so important for her, that her son William's success in obtaining a very suitable house at Walmer, was a real matter of gratulation; but there was another office of love for that beloved one to perform by his mother, singularly suited to the bond of love and sympathy which had so long united them, and eminently fitted to be his last.

She had long and earnestly desired again to attend the Meeting for worship, at Plaistow. It was proposed from Sunday to

Sunday, but the difficult process of dressing was never accomplished till long after eleven o'clock, the hour when the Meeting assembled. An attempt was made on the 28th of July, but totally failed. Her disappointment was extreme, and the hold it took of her spirits so grievous, that it was resolved to make the effort at any cost the following Sunday. Her son William undertook to carry out her wishes: drawn by himself and a younger son in her wheeled chair, she was taken up the Meeting, a few minutes after the Friends had assembled, followed by her husband, her children, and attendants. Her son William seated himself closely by her side, and the rest near her. The silence that prevailed was singularly solemn. After some time, in a clear voice she addressed the meeting. The prominent topic of her discourse was "the death of the righteous;" she expressed the deepest thankfulness, alluding to her sister Elizabeth Fry, for the mercies vouchsafed to "one who having laboured long amongst them, has been called from time to eternity." She quoted that text, "Blessed are the dead who die in the Lord, for they cease from their labours, and their works do follow them." She dwelt on the purposes of affliction, on the utter weakness and infirmity of the flesh; she tenderly exhorted the young, "the little children amongst us," referring to the death of little Gurney R——. She urged the need of devotedness of heart and steadiness of purpose; she raised a song of praise for the eternal hope offered to the Christian, and concluded with those words in Isaiah,—"Thine eyes shall see the King in His beauty, they shall behold the land that is very far off." Prayer was soon afterwards offered by her in much the same strain. He, joined her in that solemn act, who never was to worship with her again, till, before the throne and the Lamb, they should unite in that ineffable song of praise, which stays not night nor day for ever.

Her removal to Walmer was accomplished without much difficulty, from thence she wrote :—

I walk in a low valley, still I believe I may say the everlasting arm is underneath, and the Lord is near to me. I pass
through deep waters, but I trust, as my Lord is near to me, they
will not overflow me.   I need all your prayers in my low estate ;
I think that the death of my sister, and dear little Gurney, have
been almost too much for me.

Thus was this servant of God permitted to go sorrowing upon
her way.   But the storm had not blown over ; again the thunder
clouds rolled up.   On the 15th of August, the lovely little
Juliana, the second daughter of her son William, one of the
sweetest blossoms that ever gladdened parents' hearts, was cut
off after thirty hours, inexplicable illness.   One day, however, but
too fully sufficed to solve the doubt, three of the servants at
Manor House being attacked by scarlet fever.   But all preceding sorrows seemed light in comparison, when the beloved and
honoured head of that happy home, was himself laid low by the
tremendous malady.   He had written on the death of his aunt
shortly before : " Yesterday, we followed the remains of our
dear aunt to the grave.' We have the comfort of feeling assured,
that she has entered into the joy of her Lord.   May such
be the case with us all !—but if we would ' die the death of
the righteous,' as the righteous we must do our day's work in the
day."

All stood aghast at these fresh tidings, and with breathless sus-
pense awaited the accounts from hour to hour, and day to day.

" He surely will not be taken—so fearful an overthrow, so
terrible a blow cannot be coming," thus spoke hope and natural
affection ; but there was a response from the inmost heart of those
who had watched his life and conversation, his growth in religion,
the simple earnestness of his piety—Is not his Master calling
for him ?

The children were removed to Plashet Cottage, vacant from
the death of Mrs. Elizabeth Fry.   As one and another showed
symptoms of fever, they were carried back to Manor House.

The servants continued to sicken successively, and were conveyed to a ward prepared for them at Guy's Hospital. The help of the nursing sisters became invaluable, two or three being in constant attendance. For about a week, strong hopes were entertained that the most precious life would be spared to his family but the fiat was gone forth, and the summons given. On the day of the funeral of his little Juliana, he had asked to have his door open, that he might see the coffin as it was borne by, when, to the nursing sister by his side, he exclaimed, "I shall go to her but she shall not return to me."

The fever ran its course, the excitement attending it came and went, but there was no recovering, all seemed to depend upon his powers of taking nourishment. He was calm, even cheerful; there appeared to be little, if any suffering; he perfectly knew his danger; he said that he "should like to recover, if it were right, but he was quite willing to leave it in God's hand." When remarked to him, how great the mercy that sustaining patience had been granted him, he held up his hand with a great effort, and most emphatically replied, "God never has forsaken me, no not for a moment, and He never will." As his last day commenced upon earth, his window wide open by the bed-side, and the sweet morning air blowing freshly in, he spoke of the fair view to be seen from it, and listened with interest as the scene was described to him, the grey tints passing from the garden and terrace, and leaving them in light and sunshine. He spoke of his place, of his family, of his many blessings. Some little effort exhausting him, a stimulant was given; as he recovered, with a bright smile he exclaimed, "God is so good;" and they were his last words. Never was a dying-bed more favoured—more wonderful the evidence that "God was with him of a truth:" a most solemn calm prevailed; beautiful was the smile which lingered on his dying features. Unseen realities were felt and understood then; it had been heard before, but now was known, and appropriated, "Blessed are the dead who die in the Lord."

" Can our mother hear this and live?" was the natural exclamation of her children. Thus wrote one of her sisters :— " We are perfectly thunderstruck! What a wonderful dispensation of sorrow and loss! The loss of him in life so entire; the fever so alarming! How will your precious afflicted mother bear it? I fear she will not live under such calamity; but let no one dare to murmur." No one need have feared her enduring the blow, for He who sent it bestowed His Holy Spirit with it. The Christian's faith proved stronger than the mother's anguish. She wept abundantly, almost unceasingly; but she dwelt constantly on the unseen world, seeking for passages in the Bible which spoke of the happy state of the righteous. She was enabled to rejoice in that rest, upon which her beloved ones had entered, and in a wonderful manner to realize the blessedness of their lot.

Her natural affections and interests were, moreover, occupied for his widow and children, all his little ones having the fever.

The medical men insisted on the necessity of every one quitting the house. The little children were carried back to Plashet Cottage, where the others had become ill, and with the exception of three servants in one corner of the basement story, the house was deserted. There are minutes which burn themselves into the brain, from which there is no recovering to be the same again. It was such an one, to the two, who standing on the steps, had seen all depart, and remained themselves but to give one last look and follow. They traversed the empty apartments where the light struggled to force its way through the closed shutters. They turned the key and stood in the chamber of death; and as they went away, they remembered that not one fortnight before, the " voice of joy and mirth" had been within that dwelling." Two days later, the family carriages assembled under the trees, near the Lodge gate. The day was glorious; the house in the distance all in light. The heavy sound of wheels was heard; the black-plumed hearse passed, to be followed by the different carriages;

and the procession wended its way to Little Ilford church. A flood of light fell on the old grey tower, and the rich masses of foliage of the noble trees around it. Never was the funeral service more deeply needed, or its force and its beauty more entirely to be felt. Here he had come from week to week to worship with his family; here he had joined with child-like humility in the services, and knelt in meek reverence to partake of the Sacraments of his Church. Here he was again come, for his beloved remains to be deposited, "in sure and certain hope of a joyful resurrection."

Mrs. Fry was earnest to hear every thing, and to have all particulars given her. The illness of her grandchildren occupied much of her thoughts; the accounts from them continued to fluctuate; but on Monday the 2nd of September, Emma, the eldest, was worse. She had been intensely anxious about her father—her inquiries continual; and after his death and her own illness begun, he was still the object of her thoughts. She was a child of strong feelings, and very sensitive nature. At first, some endeavours were made to divert her, but they wholly failed, and it was the truth and all the truth which alone had power to soothe her; she responded to the glorious hope set before her, and partook in the assured confidence of his eternal happiness.

Early on Tuesday morning, she followed him to that Saviour whom her young heart had loved, and desired to obey, just one week after his departure, and eighteen days from the death of her sister. One grave contains all that is mortal of the father and his daughters. " They were pleasant in their lives, and in their death they were not divided." The tidings were conveyed to Walmer the same day by some of her children; others of them had been with their mother from the time she went there.

Her eldest son was with his family in Switzerland, when he received accounts of the alarming illness of his brother; they travelled rapidly home, but before they could reach England, had letters announcing his death.   On landing at Dover, they turned aside to Walmer, and joined the large family party already assembled there.

The following Sunday was a memorable one; the two last chapters of the Revelations were read, and then some memoranda concerning the beloved departed and their closing hours upon earth.   The service was concluded by solemn thrilling prayer, offered by their mother for those who remained, and for herself in her " low estate:"—for such as had fought the good fight, kept the faith, and obtained the victory, thanksgiving and praise!

Her own journal tells her feelings:—

Walmer, Eighth Month 29th.—Sorrow upon sorrow!   Since I last wrote, we have lost by death, first, my beloved sister, Elizabeth Fry; second, Gurney Reynolds, our sweet, good grandson; third, Juliana Fry, my dearest William and Julia's second daughter; and fourth, above all, our most beloved son, William Storrs Fry, who appeared to catch the infection of his little girl, and died on Third-day of scarlet fever, the 27th of this month.   A loss inexpressible—such a son, husband, friend, and brother! but I trust that he is for ever at rest in Jesus, through the fulness of His love and grace.   The trial is almost inexpressible.   Oh! may the Lord sustain us in this time of deep distress.   Oh! dear Lord, keep thy unworthy and poor sick servant in this time of unutterable trial; keep me sound in faith, and clear in mind, and be very near to us all—the poor widow and children in this time of deepest distress, and grant that this awful dispensation may be blessed to our souls.   Amen. This tenderly beloved child attended me to Meeting the last First-day I was at home, and sat by me on the women's side. Oh! gracious Lord, bless and sanctify to us all, this afflicting trial, and cause it to work for our everlasting good; and be very near to the poor dear widow and fatherless; and may we all be drawn nearer to Thee, and Thy kingdom of rest and peace, where there will be no more sin, sickness, death, and sorrow.

EARLHAM HALL.

CHAPTER XXV.

"Sorrow upon sorrow" was the language of her wounded spirit. In an unusual manner was this devoted servant permitted to partake of the Master's cup, and through much tribulation to enter the Kingdom. Nor was it only in the greatness, but the character of her afflictions, that so deep a lesson is to be read. Possessing extraordinary natural powers, with extraordinary gifts in grace, she obtained a marvellous influence over the spirits of others, to control the will and win the affections. She

could not but know her power, and be conscious of the love she
inspired, and the strength she imparted. She was proportionably
to be emptied of self, and furnish a striking exemplification of
the truth of the scriptural assertion, that "no flesh shall glory
in His presence." It was permitted that she should endure, till
those who had felt that life would be a dull blank without her,
dare no longer desire her tarriance. The habit of dependence
was to be altogether broken, and she who had been as a tower of
strength, was to require and depend upon all that human tenderness could invent, and cherishing love bestow, for her daily
and hourly comfort. She yielded to the wishes of those about
her, to continue a short time longer at Walmer.

The regulation of her mind, and her established self-discipline,
was at that period very instructive; her health infirm, her
natural spirits broken, she persevered as much as possible in
regular habits and certain hours for different occupations; in no
degree refusing to be comforted, willing to be diverted, driving
out in the carriage, or on fine days drawn in the beautiful little
pony chair that her son J——h had given her, whilst some of
the party walked by her side. But after a little while she
became irresistibly desirous of returning to Upton, principally
that she might see her bereaved daughter, before the birth of
her expected little one.

The return home was sorrowful indeed; all outwardly the
same—but the void—the want so great of a member of the
circle, who, whilst he was the tried friend and faithful counsellor,
was wont to bring with him an atmosphere of cheerfulness and
love. His habit was to go by Upton Lane on his road to
London. His mother and her attendants would watch for the
glad tone of his voice, as he hastened in, for his little morning
visit. It is long before the heart realises, that a pleasure daily
repeated at a given time, and for a lengthened period, can
never recur.

Another beloved son, W. C—— S——, had taken the fever, one of her "married children," as she designated those, not by birth belonging to her. The day of the return from Walmer, all hope of his recovery was abandoned.

It is possible that her intense anxiety, whilst the life of one so dear hung suspended on a thread, and then the gradual deliverance from it, tended to withdraw her thoughts from the afflictions which had preceded it. Her mind was also occupied by her bereaved daughter-in-law.

Upton, Tenth Month 13*th.*—We returned from Walmer on the 17th of the Ninth Month. We first went to my dear brother Gurney's at Ham House, where I was received with every kindness. Our beloved daughter J—— was here when we came home, and stayed a few days afterwards. She was then removed to her sister's E—— R——s, where she (I may thankfully say,) has since been confined. She has a sweet little girl, and is doing well. So we see that the "Lord gives and the Lord takes away ; blessed be his holy name."

A few days later, to her sister Mrs. Samuel Gurney who had been from home, she wrote,—

Upton, *Tenth Month* 21*st.*

MY DEAREST ELIZABETH,

I must thank thee before thy return home for thy sweet letter, but as we hope soon to meet, I will not say much. I also received one from our dear sister Eliza, which I hope to answer in a day or two.

I cannot give a very bright account of us, as I feel very poorly, very low and flat, and that we have many causes of deep sorrow —the effect of William's loss is hardly to be told. But I desire always to feel that our God is able to supply our needs, through the riches of His grace, in Christ Jesus our Lord.

I long to visit Earlham, but fear that the season is too far advanced.

May you all feel for, and remember us, in our very low estate ;

and hoping soon to see your party home, I am, with dear and tender love to all of you, including John and his sweet wife,

Thy much attached sister,

ELIZABETH FRY.

On the 1st of the Eleventh Month she addressed her last written communication to the Committee of the Ladies' British Society.

MY MUCH-LOVED FRIENDS,

Amidst many sorrows, that have been permitted for me to pass through, and bodily suffering, I still feel a deep and lively interest in the cause of poor prisoners ; and earnest is my prayer that the God of all grace may be very near to help you, to be stedfast in the important Christian work of seeking to win the poor wanderers to return, repent and live ; that they may know Christ to be their Saviour, Redeemer, and hope of glory. May the Holy Spirit of God direct your steps, strengthen your hearts, and enable you and me to glorify our Holy Head, in doing and suffering even unto the end ; and when the end comes, through a Saviour's love and merits, may we be received into glory and everlasting rest and peace.

In christian love and fellowship,

I am affectionately your friend,

ELIZABETH FRY.

As might be reasonably expected, Mrs. Fry's health suffered from all her sorrows, and there were threatenings of the return of some of her most painful symptoms ; but they were in mercy averted. She went for a few days to Kensington, to be with her son and daughter—mourners like herself for a beloved child ; this little change suited her, and on her return she was rather cheered by a visit from her brother, Joseph John Gurney, and her sister-in-law.

But a new sorrow awaited her. On the 1st of December, Catherine H——n, the daughter of her late beloved sister Louisa Hoare, died—a few days after her infant son. Though young in years, she was not young in religion: devoted in heart and life, she was apparently ripe for glory, when God took her.

Eleventh Month 2nd.—The accounts of to-day are deeply affecting—to have the grave once more (and so soon,) opened amongst us. What can we say but that it is the Lord, for the flesh is very weak, and these things are hard to our nature. I have felt the pain of this fresh sorrow, but desire that all most closely concerned may find Him very near to them, who "healeth the broken in heart and bindeth up their wounds." My love and sympathy to all most nearly interested. We have our poor dear J—— and her children here, and very touching it is to be with them. I am I think just now very poorly, and much cast down, but I remember the scriptural words, "cast down but not destroyed."

This "fresh sorrow" involved much personal loss and grief to one of her daughters, which occasioned her writing to her two days later.

A few lines of most tender love to thee and thine. My spirit is so much broken within me, and bowed down, that I cannot write much. As the body so much affects the mind, I feel the more sunk under our trials from my state of illness, still the Lord sustains me in mercy and in love. I need all your prayers in this time of deep affliction, and you need mine. May our Lord sanctify our deep afflictions to us, that they may work for us here, the peaceable fruits of righteousness, and hereafter a far more exceeding and eternal weight of glory.

The increasing illness of her brother-in-law, Sir T. Fowell Buxton, occupied much of her thoughts, and excited her tenderest feelings.

To her Niece Priscilla J——.

December, 1844.

My dearest Priscilla,

Thanks for thy kindness in writing to me at this time of deep sorrow; but strange to say, before thy note came, I had been

so much with you in spirit, that I was ready to believe thy
dearest father was sinking. I have felt such unity with him
spiritually. My text for him in my low state this morning, was,
" The sun shall be no more thy light by day ; neither for brightness shall the moon give light unto thee : but the Lord shall be
unto thee an everlasting light, and thy God thy glory !'' I believe
this will be his most blessed experience, whenever our Lord takes
him to Himself. I write with difficulty and in haste, but my
heart is so very full towards you, that I must express myself. My
dear love to every one of your tenderly beloved party, particularly thy mother. I feel as it respects thy dearest father, whether
a member of the Church militant or the Church triumphant, all
is well—and we may through all our tribulations return God
thanks, who giveth us the victory, through Jesus Christ our
Lord ! Most near and tender love to you all.

I am,
Thy much attached aunt,
E. F.

To the same, on the last day of the year.

Upton, Twelfth Month 31st.

My dearest Priscilla,

Thy mother's and thy letters have been truly consoling. I
dwell much with you in spirit, and I feel near sympathy and
unity with your beloved invalid, and with you all. How weighty
to come to the close of this year, wherein so much has passed !
The Lord has given, and the Lord has taken away, but through
all we may say, blessed be the name of the Lord ! I desire
your prayers, for my estate is a very low one, for myself, for my
husband and children, as we have all been brought very very
low before the Lord. May our afflictions be sanctified to us,
not leading us to the world for consolation, but more fully to cast
ourselves on Him who died for us, and hath loved us with an
everlasting love. I write sadly, as it is difficult to do it, my
hands are so much affected by my general state of health. With
thy dearest father I have felt in life no common religious bond.
How sweet, how blessed to feel, that we have one Lord, one faith,
one baptism.

Though of a different character, another trial awaited her. Her son-in-law W—— C—— S——, had not rallied from the effects of the fever, and he was now ordered without further delay to Madeira.   To part from him, and especially from her daughter, · was very grievous to her : two of their children remained near their grandmother, the others with their parents took their departure on the 16th of January.   She committed them in earnest supplication to Him, " who holdeth the winds in his fists" and with whom are the issues of life ; and so they parted, never to meet again on earth.

As the winter wore away there was some revival ; her widowed daughter, with her broken band, returned to Manor House ; she resumed some of her former pursuits, she wrote more letters, took more part in the daily interests of life.   For the sake of her grandchildren, in whom she was anxious to encourage a taste for such objects, she endeavoured to re-arrange her collections of shells, minerals, corals, and other natural curiosities.

She was generally carried down stairs in a chair about noon, and wheeled from room to room ; she was dressed as usual, sometimes joining her family at table, and was able to look occasionally at a book.   She now generally attended Meeting once in the Sabbath, her ministry often very beautiful, and not at all partaking of the sort of infirmity which clouded all earthly matters. She enjoyed occasional visits from her friends, and conversed upon various topics.

She was much interested in the engagement of her nephew Fowell B——, and her niece Rachel G——.   She knew from former experience, the pain that her brother and sister had to encounter in the marriage of their daughter, leading her from Friends ; and yet for them, as for herself, she desired to take the highest ground of Christian liberty.   She was present at their wedding breakfast ; she gave them her blessing, and offered prayer on their behalf.

In February, she paid her first visit to Manor House since all was so changed there. She greatly shrunk from the pain of this visit in prospect, but in fact bore it far beyond expectation. The children won her attention ; their delight at seeing her gave her pleasure, and, to a certain extent, her thoughts were occupied. The touch of infirmity which had attended her illness, certainly had its effect, as to the manner in which she felt her afflictions. She was more easily diverted by little things, and for the moment became interested in them ; but those reasoning powers were enfeebled, which would have enabled her to grasp the causes of her grief, to encounter its circumstances of pain, and arrange them in her own mind. Sorrow is an enemy that can never be escaped by flight or evasion—it must be grappled with to be subdued.

The 19th of February, her brother, friend and early coadjutor Sir Powell Buxton quitted this world,

> " To be a glorious guest,
> Where the wicked cease from troubling,
> And the weary are at rest."

These successive departures could not but have their effect, not only in weaning from earthly things, but in making it of small import, whether a little sooner, or a little later, summoned to join the band that was mustering so strongly on the other side Jordan. In the mind of this way-worn traveller it was very perceptible. She dwelt more in spirit with those who were gone. Unseen realities increasingly opened upon her view. Many so near and dear had been gathered round the throne, that her heart and soul continually ascended thitherward.

There was one thing which rested upon her mind,—an intense desire again to visit Norfolk, and stay once more at Earlham. With great difficulty it was accomplished, her husband and daughter taking her there. She remained at Earlham many weeks; often able to partake of enjoyment, and highly valuing the communion with her brother Joseph John Gurney, his wife, and her beloved sister Catharine. There were also familiar faces, whom it gladdened her heart to see, and friends of every grade who came to visit her, and were all welcomed. Occasionally, her sufferings overcame her and weighed her down; and when her young relative, John B——, sank and died, she was afflicted for his family, and her own wounds bled afresh: the close communication between Keswick and Earlham rendering it impossible to shield her from the daily alternations of hope and fear.

She went frequently to Meeting at Norwich. She was drawn up the Meeting, seated in her wheeled chair, and thence ministered with extraordinary life and power to those present; her memory in using Scripture in no degree failing her, or her power in applying it.

What a history had her's been, since the time of the scarlet riding habit—since she sat and wept under the ministry of William Savery. Her ardent aspirations had been strangely granted; she had passed a long life of blessing to others, but by a path of singular sorrow to herself. She had been eyes to the blind, and feet to the lame: when the ear heard her then it blessed her. She had trodden regal halls to plead for the afflicted and the destitute; she had not withheld unpalatable truth when the language of warning was called for at her lips. She had penetrated, nothing daunted, the gloom of the felon's dungeon, nor had she shrunk from the touch of the unclothed maniac; she had nourished and brought up children, and they had risen up to call her blessed; and now, helpless and suffering in body, enfeebled in memory, all that could be shaken tottering to its base—she came again, to take a last look at the home and the haunts of her childhood.

She went for ten days to North Repps; the atmosphere of that

place was very genial to her.   Her sister and she were fellow-
mourners, close participators in the greatness of their sorrows,
and the vastness of their consolation.   They held sweet counsel
together ; they dwelt on the blessedness of their departed ones ;
and together sought and found comfort in the Book of Life.

Whilst there, upon one occasion, Elizabeth Fry spoke of her
prayers as constant for those she most closely loved.   Being asked
how this could be, with other occupations and hindrances ; she
replied, " It is always in my heart ;" adding, " even in sleep I
think the heart is ever lifted up," (putting it as no uncommon
experience) ; " it is, if I may venture to say it, living in communion with Christ,"—" in Him."—"What ! should I be without
Him ?"—" Where should I stand ?"   She continued, " I never
have known despondency ; whatever may have been my depths of
suffering in mind or body, still, the confidence has never left me
that all was and would be well, if not in time, in eternity—that
the end would be peace."   " I never lose the feeling of this, and
am always on the rock—that conviction never leaves me."   " I
have been so comforted by the sense of the glory and happiness of
those taken, that it has proved a preparation for the sorrows."

Whilst at North Repps, hearing of the dangerous illness of her
little grandson, Oswald C——, she wrote to his parents :—

I have indeed drunk the bitter cup with you : perhaps I . may
say in my low estate I am too much disposed to drink it to the
dregs ; but I desire to look upwards to Him, who not only can
heal and raise up, if it be good for the beloved child and those
nearest, but can also, through the fulness of His love, mercy, and
merits, fit this sweet lamb of the flock for a place in His kingdom,
if it be the will of God that the work should be cut short in
righteousness.   Our Lord's words are very sweet respecting these
little ones : " Suffer little children to come unto me, and forbid
them not, for of such is the kingdom of heaven."   I understand
by this, that we must not be too anxious for their lives ; but I
know it is hard, very hard, to human nature, to have no will in

it. My prayer is for the darling little one, that whatever awaits him, he may be the Lord's child and servant; and if it be His holy will, that he may here fill a place in the militant church of Christ, to the glory of God, the good of mankind, and the peace of his own soul; and then join those who " rest from their labours and whose works do follow them," and who " for ever rejoice in the presence of our Lord and our God !" but I desire to leave all to Him, who knows what is best for us and for him.

I am your tender, loving, and sympathizing mother.

The last letter she ever addressed to her husband was from North Repps, dated Fourth Month 10th, 1845 :—

My dearest Husband,

I am anxious to express to thee a little of my near love, and to tell thee how often I visit thee in spirit, and how very strong are my desires for thy present and thy everlasting welfare. I feel for thee in my long illness, which so much disqualifies me from being all I desire to thee. I desire that thou mayst turn to the Lord for help and consolation under all thy trials, and that, whilst not depending on the passing pleasures and enjoyments of this world, thou mayst at the same time be enabled to enjoy our many remaining blessings. I also desire this for myself in my afflicted state, (for I do consider such a state of health a heavy affliction), independent of all other trials. I very earnestly desire for myself, that the deep tribulation I have had to pass through for so long a time may not lead into temptation, but be sanctified to the further refinement of my soul, and preparation for eternal rest, joy, and glory. May we, during our stay in time, be more and more sweetly united in the unity of the Spirit, and in the bond of peace.

We have much to be thankful for in H——'s prospect ; I must write to him ; I long to see him.

We have been deeply anxious about dear little Oswald, and I long to return to Lynn to see him and his father and mother, yet rather fear the exertion may be too much for me ; still, I should feel more easy and happy to have seen them ; but I wish for thy opinion on the subject.   *   *   *   *

After she left Earlham, she came for a few days to Runcton,

as it was thought better than her going to Lynn. Her children met
her and stayed with her there. She had not been at Runcton since
death had last entered that pleasant dwelling : she had greatly
loved the mother and the daughter who had successively gladdened
and adorned it ; she had deeply mourned their loss, and in her
weakened state of spirits, sorrowful associations mingled with
the enjoyment she experienced, in being again with her brother
and his children. She liked their cordial glowing welcome, and
the affectionate attentions of that young party. It was pleasant,
to see them occupied alternately in performing for her the little
offices of love. The old servants vied in attention to her, whilst
those who were married away, or lived in the village, pressed to
see her, and obtain a word of counsel or kindness. Before
she left Norfolk, she heard of the intended marriage of her
son. Nothing could be more agreeable to her, than the prospect
of this event ; towards this, her last-born child, her motherly
care had been peculiarly extended. She very much liked her
future daughter-in-law, and her being a member of the Society
of Friends afforded her no small gratification. It was indeed a
boon for all who loved her, to feel that she returned home under
a ray of sunshine, and that the brightness of this event to her
feelings, was permitted a little to enlighten the last few months
of her home-life. Whilst the various arrangements and preparations connected with it, occupied, without wearying her mind, and
her attention was in some degree withdrawn from dwelling upon
her sorrows and deprivations. In her eldest grandaughter, the
first-born of her eldest son, and bearing her own name, she had
during this spring a helpful cheerful companion, who, with the
elasticity of youth (which is so pleasant to the infirm and
declining), cheered, whilst she cared for her grandmother. She
had also many visitors, who came to her in their abundant kindness ; for the hearts of all who had ever loved her, were drawn
out towards her in tender compassion.

The Duchess of Sutherland and her daughters, the Chevalier Bunsen and his family, and many others, besides her own relatives and connexions, and the excellent of the earth of various denominations, would drive down to Upton Lane, and sit awhile by her side, to mark that "love," which George Herbert designates "a present for a mighty King."

The latter part of May, accompanied by her grandaughter Elizabeth Fry, she attended two sittings of the women's Yearly Meeting of Friends in London; the women being wholly separate from the men in all matters of business. A person not a Friend, would scarcely credit the order and regularity with which women Friends carry on a system of discipline, extending in fact through all the ramifications of the Society. The desired information is elicited by a list of queries, which are answered by the Monthly or Particular Meetings, with reference to the individuals composing the Meeting. The Quarterly Meetings answer the same queries to the Yearly Meeting, with reference to the Monthly Meetings composing the Quarterly Meeting; and thus a condensed view of the state of Society is brought before the Yearly Meeting.—The information to be obtained relates to the regular attendance of Friends at their meetings for worship and discipline—their frequent reading of the Bible and religious books—their punctuality in money matters, and in the fulfilment of engagements—the sober temperate and orderly conduct of themselves and their families—their not frequenting places of amusement, nor joining in vain sports, and their adherence to the simple garb and language of Friends. A summary of these answers having been prepared, was to be laid before the Meeting on the day of Mrs. Fry's first attendance. A sitting of the women's Yearly Meeting must be seen to be imagined. It is a singular and striking sight, and may vie with any of the deliberative assemblies in which men are convened throughout the world, in gravity, in absence of display, and in steady attention

to the business before it.   Many hundred women, arrayed, with
but slight variation, in the same peculiar attire, seated in a large
lofty apartment, preserving entire silence, their countenances
bespeaking unusual good sense and power of attention, listening
to, and weighing the matter laid before them.   Those who, from
being " ministers" or " elders" of the Society, take a more prominent part, rising, one at a time, to give information or offer an
opinion ; but the person of least account in the Meeting equally
at liberty to address the assembly, and equally sure of being
heard with kind and courteous attention.   Elizabeth Fry had
for many years, been regular in her attendance upon these
Meetings, and had taken a lively interest in their proceedings.
After an illness so critical, and still in a state of such great
infirmity, to see her again among them, was scarcely less gratifying to many of the Friends there, than it was interesting to
herself.   On this occasion she spoke of the Saviour's declaration,
" I am the true vine,"—" ye are the branches,"—" as the branch
cannot bear fruit of itself, except it abide in the vine, no more
can ye, except ye abide in me."   She alluded, in the course of her
observations, to the day that is " fast approaching to every one ;"
but urged the blessed truth on her hearers, that those " who loved,
served, and obeyed Him, who alone is worthy of all glory and
praise, would find death deprived of its sting, and the grave of its
victory."   The second Meeting she attended, was one when a
Friend named Edwin Tregelles, gave a relation of his missionary
labours in the West Indies.   This recital drew from her, some
account of her own travels on the continent.   She afterwards
enlarged upon the various instruments, by which God accomplishes
His own work in the world.—She referred to the simile of the
different living stones, which compose the temple of God.—She
addressed those of every age who heard her, especially such as
might be compared to the hidden stones of the building.—She
encouraged them to go forward fearlessly in the path of right-

eousness and good works ; for though they might not be so much
seen and known, as the more polished stones in the ornamental
parts of the structure—though perhaps not so fitted to shine, or
to occupy a conspicuous situation—yet were their places each
equally ordered, equally important, and equally under the direction and all-seeing eye of the Divine Architect. She expressed
her doubts, as to whether she should again be permitted to meet
her beloved Friends in that place.—She offered prayer, her rich
full voice filling the house ; and concluded with that sublime
passage, " Great and marvellous are thy works, Lord God Almighty, just and true are thy ways thou King of saints."

On the 3rd of June, Mrs. Fry was present at the Annual
Meeting of the Ladies' British Society. To spare her fatigue,
the Committee kindly arranged, to hold it in the Friends'
Meeting-house at Plaistow, instead of the one at Westminster,
which hitherto had been the place chosen.

At the Committee of the Society, held on the 3rd of the
November following, there was drawn up by its members, a
touching memorial of the feelings they entertained towards her.

In it they speak of this Meeting :—

" Contrary to usual custom, the place of Meeting fixed on was
not in London, but at Plaistow in Essex ; and the large number
of friends who gathered round her upon that occasion, proved
how gladly they came to her, when she could no longer with ease
be conveyed to them. The enfeebled state of her bodily frame
seemed to have left the powers of her mind unshackled, and she
took, though in a sitting posture, almost her usual part in repeatedly addressing the Meeting. She urged, with increased
pathos and affection, the objects of philanthropy and Christian
benevolence with which her life had been identified. After the
Meeting, and at her own desire, several members of the Committee, and other friends, assembled at her house. They were
welcomed by her with the greatest benignity and kindness, and
in her intercourse with them, strong were the indications of the

heavenly teaching, through which her subdued and sanctified spirit had been called to pass. Her affectionate salutation in parting unconsciously closed, in regard to most of them, the intercourse which they delighted to hold with her, but which can no more be renewed on this side of the eternal world."

When Mrs. Fry attended for the last time the Meeting of the British Ladies' Society, she had the happiness of knowing that Newgate, Bridewell, the Millbank Prison, the Giltspur Street Compter, White Cross Street Prison, Tothill Fields Prison, and Cold Bath Fields Prison, were all in a state of comparative order.; some exceedingly well arranged, and the female convicts in all more or less visited and cared for by ladies—varying according to their circumstances and requirings. The prisons generally throughout England much improved, and in the greater number, ladies encouraged to visit the female convicts.

Let the state of prisons and female prisoners be recalled as it existed thirty years before—not, that to Elizabeth Fry this vast improvement is attributed—much has resulted from the spirit of the day, and the tone that has pervaded and increasingly pervades the upper ranks of society. She was but a type of her times, an illustration of the benevolent and enlarged philanthropy, which is diffusing its influence throughout all classes.

Though unquestionably, she accomplished much ; and above all had the joy of knowing, that the principles she had so long asserted were universally recognized—that the object of penal legislation is not revenge, but the prevention of crime ; in the first place, by affording opportunity of reform to the criminal, and in the second, by warning others from the consequences of its commission. But there was one thing she was not permitted to see accomplished,—a refuge for every erring and repentant sinner of her own sex ; the opportunity of reformation for all who desired to reform. There are those, who have striven to connect the memory and the name of Elizabeth Fry, with such a shelter for the outcasts of our great metropolis ; the arrangements are not yet matured, nor has the call for funds, to carry the measure into effect, been hitherto responded to, in a manner at all commensurate with the greatness or the importance of the undertaking ; but the need of such an asylum is too obvious, and the evils which it would remedy too sorrowful, to doubt of its final accomplishment.

On the 26th of June her youngest son was married. She described the Meeting as "a very solemn one, something like a token for good ;" and spoke of the connexion as a "ray of light upon a dark picture."

There was through all the real brightness of the occasion a deep feeling of the past ; when dear J——'s children joined us in the afternoon, then the miss of dearest William was keenly to be felt.   C—— and H——too so very far off, that there was much to cloud over the scene, as well as my poor state of health, making it more difficult to estimate my many present blessings, as I ought and desire to do.

As the summer advanced, sea air was considered desirable for her, and after some difficulty her husband obtained a house at Ramsgate, exactly suited to her necessities.   She went for a week to see it, and to make her own arrangements, accompanied by her husband and her daughter R—— R——.   The day before leaving home, she wrote to her brother and sister Gurney.

MY DEAREST SAMUEL AND ELIZABETH,

I have rather longed to bid you farewell before accompanying my husband to Ramsgate for a few days.   My heart is much with you and our dear brother Joseph also, just now.   I particularly feel for you in your conflicts, as well as your joys.   Humiliations we must expect to pass through, if we are to drink of the cup our Lord drank of, and be baptised with the baptism that He was baptised with ; therefore we must not fear, but when our spirits are overwhelmed within us, we must look to the "rock that is higher than wê, as a shelter from the storm, a shadow from the heat, when the blast of the terrible ones is as a storm against the wall."

From Ramsgate, was written the last letter, her eldest daughter ever received from her mother.

Ramsgate, Seventh Month 5th.

——————,

I much desire to be at our own Meeting on First-day with dearest H—— and L——, and hope it may please a kind Providence to enable me to do so.

I have felt very poorly here in the morning, more so than usual, which has been rather discouraging. I much like the house as far as I have seen it, but I have not been up stairs. I have felt unusually low, and am sensible of my poor condition, as it is most feelingly brought home to me in almost every fresh effort. I desire in heart to say, "Not as I will, but as Thou wilt." I think none of my friends need fear (as I believe they used to do), my being exalted by the good opinion of my fellow-mortals. I think my state is "cast down but not destroyed." May my Lord, whom I have loved and sought to serve, keep me alive unto Himself, and may He clothe me with His armour that I may "stand in the evil day and after having done all, stand."

*   *   *   *   *   *

I am, in most tender love, thy much attached mother,
E. F.

The return of her son and his young bride, to Upton Lane, she wished to make as cheerful as under existing circumstances was possible; and in celebration of the event, a large family party was arranged for the garden. She asked the company of her brother and sister from Ham House, in the following note.

My dearest Samuel and Elizabeth,

In true love, I advise your joining our simple evening party, which I humbly trust will be conducted on Christian grounds. The fact is, in my low estate I felt much indisposed for a large dinner; I then wished for our dear little children to have some innocent pleasure, and also to show some mark of the deep interest we feel in the bride and bridegroom here, and in the bride and bridegroom elect. We wish to do it in the most simple manner. Remember our most blessed Master attended the wedding feast.

Your most loving sister,
E. F.

She received her guests in a room opening into the flower garden, and thence was wheeled to the end of the terrace; a very large family circle surrounded her, many connexions and others of her friends. It was a beautiful scene,—the last social family meeting at which she presided; and although infirm and broken in health, she looked and seemed herself.

In an easy chair, under the large marquee, she entered into animated discourse on various and important topics with the group around her: the Chevalier Bunsen, M. Merle D'Aubigny, Sir Henry Pelly, Josiah Forster, her brother Samuel Gurney, and others of her friends. An event of great interest shortly followed: the marriage of her faithful niece, Elizabeth G——, to Ernest B———. This connexion was one which her aunt liked, inasmuch as she valued the individual and highly esteemed his excellent and gifted parents, though not unmingled with regret that the children of her brother and sister, as so many of her own had done, should leave the Society of Friends by marriage, and thus separate themselves from that body of Christians, to which their parents were so warmly attached. The wedding took place on the 5th of August. She joined the party afterwards at Ham House. It was an occasion of singular interest; Christian love, unity and good feeling prevailing over "diversities of administration," yet all owning "the same Lord."

The week following, she was moved to the house on Mount Albion at Ramsgate, which had been prepared for her. A spacious bed-chamber adjoining the drawing-room, with pleasant views of the sea, in which she delighted, added to her hourly comfort and enjoyment. She found objects there well suited to her tastes. She distributed tracts when she drove into the country, or went upon the Pier in a Bath chair. Seafaring men have a certain openness of character which renders them more easy of access than others. They would gladly receive her little offerings, and listen to her remarks. She was also anxious to ascertain the state of the Coast Guard Libraries—whether they required renewing, and were properly used.

The party were scarcely established at Ramsgate, when the family of her beloved son William came to them, and remained for some weeks. She delighted in them all; but little Willie Fry was something to her, almost beyond anything left in the world. He read the Bible to her every morning on her awakening. She strove to impress upon his young mind the value and beauty of the Christian life; she endeavoured to cultivate in him a taste for natural objects; she encouraged drawing and similar pursuits. Partly his name — partly his character, so much resembling his father's in early boyhood—excited her tenderest love.

Her prayer for her daughter and her children, the evening before their departure, was beautiful, comprehensive, and touching; and so she commended them, whom she was to see no more in the flesh, to Him, who has promised to be a " Husband to the widow, and a Father to the fatherless." Her eldest son, and her daughter R—— R——, with their families, were near her in the town; and the daily intercourse with them, was also a source of much comfort and pleasure to her.

On the 27th of August, in a hand almost illegible, she thus
wrote in her journal:—

Ramsgate, Eighth Month 27th.—It still pleases my Heavenly
Father that afflictions should abound to me in this tabernacle,
as I groan, being burthened. Lord, through the fulness of Thy
love and pity, and unmerited mercy, be pleased to arise for my
help. Bind up my broken heart, heal my wounded spirit, and yet
enable Thy servant, through the power of Thy own Spirit, in
everything to return Thee thanks, and not to faint in the day of
trouble, but in humility and godly fear to show forth Thy praise.
Keep me Thine own, through Thy power to do this, and pity and
help Thy poor servant who trusteth in Thee. Be very near to
our dear son and daughter, and their children in Madeira. Be
with them, and all near to us, wherever scattered, and grant that
Thy peace and Thy blessing may rest upon us all. Amen
and Amen.

On the 16th of the following month, she again, and for the
last time, recorded her feelings there, but written in a firmer
hand, and with apparently more power.

Ramsgate, Ninth Month 16th.—My dearest son D——
H—— F—— was married to dear L—— S—— last Sixth
Month 26th. We had a very solemn Meeting ; peace appeared to
rest upon us at the Meeting, and at her father's house afterwards.
My humble trust is, that the blessing of the Most High God is in
this connexion. They spent some very satisfactory time with us
before we left home. May grace, mercy and peace rest upon
them, and neither the fatness of the earth, nor the dew of heaven,
be withheld from them, through the fulness of the love, mercy
and pity of our God, in Christ Jesus our Lord.

Our dearest niece Elizabeth was also married the latter end of
the Seventh Month to my dear young friend Ernest B——.
May the blessing of the Most High God also rest upon them
naturally and spiritually. I pray the same for them as for
H—— and L——.

Here the journal ceases ; the above being the last entry.

Her sister Lady Buxton, and her daughter Richenda, went to her on the 17th of September.   There was much opportunity for intercourse, after her waking in the morning, and especially during her lengthened toilet ; her sister generally read the Bible with her at these times.   She found her mind clear and powerful in spiritual things, enlarging upon them with comprehension of their import ; her heart entirely in the things of God, choosing Him and his service solely, seeking first the kingdom of God, with deep earnest constant desires (beyond words to express) for her husband and children, grandchildren, brothers and sisters, nephews and nieces, and all who were dear to her.   She was wonderfully alive to all good things going on in the world, receiving with thankfulness any instance of this, without partiality or distinction.   After her sister went, her youngest son and his bride stayed a few days with them.   Different members of the family came also to see her.   Her son J——h and his wife left her a grandchild when they went away.

The 14th of September, with a large party of her children, she attended the small Meeting at Drapers, about four miles from Ramsgate.   On this occasion she preached a most powerful and remarkable sermon on the nearness of death, and the necessity of immediate preparation and repentance ; for she believed to some of that small congregation it was the eleventh hour of the day.

Her ministrations were much of the same character the two following Sundays.   Her brother and sister Gurney stayed near her for some days, and some ladies from Zwolle did the same ; she also valued the near neighbourhood of her kind friends, Sir John and Lady Pirie.

On the 29th, the large family party dispersed.   The meeting of the preceding day had been one of great solemnity, and though little imagined at the time, well fitted to be a parting occasion with so many dear to her.   The next day she was left with only her

husband and eldest daughter ; but the nursing was too arduous
for them to bear alone, and it was a great relief to them when her
daughter and her family arrived from Norfolk.   At the Pier
gate, awaiting them in the carriage, they found their mother.
Her daughter had not seen her, since her visit to Runcton, six
months before : a great change was perceptible.   There was
a look of heaviness and weight ; she rarely smiled, but on the
other hand, far less often looked distressed ; she walked rather
better, her appetite was improved, and her nights not so disturbed ; but there was a new symptom—occasionally severe pain
in the head.   It had first appeared ten days before, and had
often been acute, but then was better.

   The next Sunday she went as usual to Meeting.   On her return,
she asked some of the party, who from circumstances had been
precluded from accompanying her, and had attended their own
place of worship, if they had had " a comfortable church ;" her
general question when she met any of her children under similar
circumstances.   Then without waiting to be asked, she said, that
they had had " a very remarkable Meeting, such a peculiarly
solemn time ;" that she had been so impressed by the " need of
working whilst it was day, to be ready for the Master's summons
come when He might."   Here the subject dropped, but she
reverted to it more than once during the day.   Those who were
present described the occasion, as a very peculiar one.   She had
urged the question, " Are we all now ready? If the Master should
this day call us, is the work completely finished ? Have we any
thing left to do ?"   Solemnly, almost awfully reiterating the
question, " Are we prepared ?"

   Her habits at this time were apparently those of former times.
She was a good deal occupied by writing.   She arranged and
sorted Bibles, Testaments and tracts.   She had applied to the
Bible Society for a grant of foreign Bibles and Testaments,
which was liberally acceded to, and in the distribution of which,

among the foreign sailors in the harbour, she took great delight. She expected intelligence on subjects that interested her, and was more disposed to carry on objects continuously. She liked having her grandchildren with her ; one of them read her a Psalm invariably, before she rose, and whilst dressing, a younger one was in her room, sorting shells under her direction, or looking at the many prints and picture-books, which she had collected for their use.

On Tuesday, when driving out, her lively interest for the good of others appeared if possible greater than ever. Her natural character, acquired habit, and Christian duty, alike combined to strengthen this, but the judgment and power to direct it had in measure passed away.

On Wednesday she was grievously distressed by her little grandson Oswald encountering a fearful-accident, one knee slipping through the area bars of a window. It was at least ten minutes before help could be obtained to extricate him. The child's cries, and her knowledge of the fact, though at the time borne apparently well, occasioned a severe return of pain in the head at night, and she was very unwell the next morning, though through the day she had appeared but little the worse for it, and was perfectly self-possessed and judicious in giving directions. The same morning, her friend Mary Fell paid her husband and herself a religious visit, she derived much comfort from it, as she had done from the society of this long known and valued Friend for some weeks preceding.

Generally, whilst she dressed, one of her daughters sat with their mother. On one occasion, the Bible was opened at the text, " Beloved, think it not strange concerning the fiery trial which is to try you, as though some strange thing happened unto you." She entered with lively interest into the subject, and mentioned other passages of somewhat similar import, which were sought for and read. The participation of the disciple in the sufferings of his Lord, was dwelt upon. She expressed herself with peculiar power, in a manner startling to the hearer. She had, through all her conflicts, seemed to cling to something, like the hope, almost expectation, that the western sky would be bright, that her sun would not set behind clouds ; but now there was no allusion to any idea of the kind. The high privilege of suffering as a member of Christ, was the point she the most dwelt upon. The world, even in its beauty and pleasantness, even the renewed regenerated aspect which it bears to the Christian, appeared to have lost nearly all attraction. She had long done the will of God, to her active mind comparatively an easy duty, she had now completely learned the far harder lesson of being willing to endure it.

There was another wonderful change. Her powerful understanding and great capacity had given her the habit of control— she was accustomed to power. During her long illness, this continued more or less to show itself, and it was not always easy to distinguish, how far her opinions about her own treatment and capabilities were well founded or not. This feature of her character had disappeared. The will seemed wholly broken, the inclination to resist, or even strongly to desire any thing, passed away ; and she was content to leave little things and great to the direction of others. It was inexpressibly affecting to see her look of meek submission, to hear her plaintive answer, " Just as you like," to those about her.

One morning of acute suffering, the remark was made to her, How marvellous it was that she never seemed impatient to depart, believing, as there was good ground to do, that she had been fitted for the great change. Her inherent fear of death had probably prevented this, for there was something in her mind, which, whilst she desired " the kingdom," caused her to shrink from the encounter with the great enemy—the last grapple before

the victory can be won.   But this too was altered; she expressed her entire "willingness to stay the Lord's time;" that
whilst "there was any work for her to do, she wished to live,"
but beyond that, expressed not the smallest desire for life.   She
added, that she had come to an entire belief, that any remaining
dread would be taken away from her, when the time came, or that
in "tender mercy to her timid nature," she should be permitted
to pass unconsciously through the dark valley.

On Thursday, she wrote to her youngest daughter :—

Ramsgate, Tenth Month 9th.

MY DEAREST L——,

I think that a visit from thee and thy dear husband would be
highly acceptable to us; but much as I should like to see the
dear boys, I fear that the house is now too full to take in more
than we should have with R——d and thyself.

I feel so shaken and so broken down, that I wish to see as
much of my beloved children as I can; my love is very strong,
and my flesh is very weak, I think increasingly so.   I wish dear
Christiana G—— to know how much I miss her.   Pray tell G——
and S—— also how much I should like to see them; indeed, my
heart is drawn very near to you all, and deep are my desires
for your present, and above all, your everlasting welfare.

*   *   *   *   *   *

I am, with dear love to R——d and the boys, and love to all
the dear Plashet family, our dear J—— and the children, thy
tenderly attached mother,

ELIZABETH FRY.

On Friday morning, though very languid and feeling uncomfortable, she addressed this note to a lady, an old attached friend,
with some texts for a young person, who desired to possess her
autograph.

Ramsgate, 11th.

MY DEAR FRIEND,

I have copied thee, these valuable texts, that prove salvation is
open to all, through a Saviour's love and merits, who believe in

Him, who no longer live unto themselves, but unto Him who died for them and rose again.   May we all be of this blessed number. I should much like a nice long letter from thee.   With true desires for thy present and everlasting welfare,

I remain,

Thy affectionate friend,

ELIZABETH FRY.

"We trust in the living God, who is the Saviour of all men, specially of those that believe," 1 Tim. iv. 10.   "And I, if I be lifted up from the earth, will draw all men unto me," John xii. 32. "Therefore as by the offence of one, judgment came upon all men to condemnation ; even so by the righteousness of one, the free gift came upon all men unto justification of life," Romans v. 18.

After finishing this note, she brought out some sheets of Scripture selections, which she had prepared with a view to eventually publishing another Text-Book on the same plan as her former one.   She turned over the leaves of her small travelling Bible, without spectacles, to look for others ; she had also written the note in a firm, clear hand, with no glasses.   On this being observed to her, she replied, "Oh yes, my eye-sight is so much better ;" which was corroborated by her own maid, for many years her devoted attendant.   This was not a symptom to pass lightly by.

Later in the morning, whilst she drove out, she was strangely oppressed—scarcely noticed the lovely views of the sea which she generally so much enjoyed ; but the most unusual thing was, that when her grandchildren were eager to give some tracts, she scarcely noticed their request till repeated two or three times. On passing some open country, where a ruddy farmer's boy was keeping cows, he told the children that he was there all day, that he had nothing to do, and should very much like to have "some reading."   Their grandmother took no notice, nor until her tract-bag was put into her hand did she attempt to choose any for him ; then she did it with a slow distracted air, as if her thoughts were far away.   That evening she was heavy and oppressed, and complained of suffering from the light.

These many circumstances, each trifling in itself, brought and weighed together, gave such cause for uneasiness, that her husband and children resolved the next day to send to Broadstairs, to learn if Dr. Paris were still there, for they had heard of his being at that place a short time before, and call in his assistance ; but he was gone.

On Saturday morning she awakened, suffering severely in her head.   One of her grandchildren went to her at half-past seven o'clock : he read the 27th Psalm, which she asked for.   Half an hour later, another went to her.   She in no way referred to his brother having been there before, but again asked for the 27th Psalm.   Her dressing was very slowly accomplished ; she leaned her head upon her hand, and spoke very little.   A text or two out of " Great and precious promises," that excellent selection for the sick chamber, seemed all that she could receive.   She had not asked for a child whilst she was dressing, the only morning she had omitted to do so, nor did she remark their absence.   She had invited the children of Lady Arthur Lennox, to take their dinner at her luncheon.   It was proposed that their coming should be deferred to another day, as she was so uncomfortable, but this she would not allow : when they came she was scarcely able to notice them, and sat looking very ill, leaning her head upon her hand. Afterwards Lady Arthur Lennox, and her sister Mrs. Langford Brook came for the children ; she received them in the drawing-room and conversed a little, but they thought her unwell, and made a very short visit.   They had been frequently with her before, they had paid her much kind attention, and their society had been very pleasant to her.

About five o'clock, whilst her husband and daughters were consulting as to the best method in which medical help might be obtained, her bell rung. She was in her own room, according to her usual custom in the afternoon, lying on the sofa, whilst an attendant read to her. She had nearly fallen, in moving from the sofa to her chair by the fire, and help was wanted, to accomplish it. After being placed in her chair, she leaned to one side, as if unable to hold herself upright. Her own maid, who was accustomed to her, was alarmed and uneasy, but the little dressing before dinner was completed without difficulty, and she was wheeled into the drawing-room, where it was proposed that she should dine, being nearer to her room than the dining-room. After her dinner, on attempting to move to the sofa, she twice sunk to the ground, though entirely assisted by two persons. With extreme difficulty she was removed to her bed, where she lay with a calm, almost a torpid expression of countenance. She was quite willing to see a medical man, and answered his questions correctly. The attendance of one so kind and skilful was a great help and comfort, but her worn out constitution forbade stringent remedies, so that little was attempted either by him or the physician, who twice saw her in the course of the following day. As no fresh symptoms appeared, and she was herself very anxious for it, it was arranged that she should settle as usual for the night. Even at that period, the real seat of the complaint appeared doubtful. Diseases of the nerves are so various in character, that they often, when quite unaccompanied by danger, bear the semblance of fatal maladies. A few texts were repeated to her, and her daughters left her to her husband's care, who throughout her lengthened illness attended her by night ; but scarcely had they reached their rooms, when her bell rung loudly. Throughout the night, though occasionally for an instant confused, the mind was there. Some passages of Scripture were read to her, which she appeared to comprehend, and she entirely responded to any observation made to her. This was favourable, but other symptoms were not so—she lay so heavily, and the limbs appeared so wholly powerless. The morning broke at last, but it brought no comfort. About six o'clock, she said to her maid, " Oh ! Mary, dear Mary, I am very ill !" " I know it dearest ma'am, I know it." " Pray for me—It is a strift, but I am safe." She continued to speak but indistinctly, at intervals, and frequently dosed, as she had done through the night. About nine o'clock, one of her daughters sitting on the bed-side, had open in her hand that passage in Isaiah, " I the Lord thy God will hold thy right hand, saying unto thee, fear not thou worm Jacob, and ye men of Israel, I will help thee saith the Lord, and thy Redeemer, the Holy One of Israel." Just then, her mother roused a little, and in a slow distinct voice uttered these words, " Oh ! my dear Lord, help and keep thy servant !" These were the last words she spake upon earth she never attempted to articulate again. A response was given, by reading to her the above most applicable passage ; one bright glance of intelligence passed over her features, a look of recognition at the well-known sound, but it was gone as rapidly, and never returned. From this time, entire uncon- sciousness appeared to take possession of her—no sound disturbed her—no light affected her—the voice of affection was unheeded—a veil was between her and the world about her, to be raised no more.

As the morning of Sunday advanced, all hope became extin- guished. A messenger was dispatched, to summon those of her absent children, who might be able to come to look upon her once again in life. Whilst they who were with her, made ready for the conflict, to go down with her as into the valley of the shadow of death ; for they whose lot it has been to watch the dying-bed, must be conscious, that there is generally a given moment of anguish, when the tremendous conviction pierces the heart, that the "inevitable hour" is come.

The difficulty of breathing, with convulsive spasm, increased ; at first occasionally, but after midnight it became almost con-

tinuous. From three o'clock there was no pause, but such
absolute unconsciousness to every impression, as satisfied those
around her, that the anguish was for them—not for her. Yet, as
they marked the struggle, the irresistible prayer of their hearts
became, " How long, Oh Lord !—how long !"

Suddenly, about twenty minutes before four, there was a change
in the breathing ; it was but a moment. The silver cord was
loosed—a few sighs at intervals—and no sound was there.
Unutterably blessed was the holy calm—the perfect stillness of
the chamber of death. She saw " the King in His beauty, and
the land that is very far off."

The night had been dark and lowering, but the morning broke
gloriously, the sun rose from the ocean, commanded by her
chamber windows, and as a globe of living fire,

> " Flamed in the forehead of the morning sky."

The emblem was too beautiful to be rejected—one of the types
and shadowings furnished by the material world, to illustrate
and adorn the Christian's hope.

Before evening, the greater number of her children were assembled at Ramsgate. There was much kindness and attention
shown by the inhabitants. Sir Moses Montefiore was deputed to
call upon the family, to propose that the hearse bearing her remains should, when taken from Mount Albion, be followed through
the town by such gentlemen of the place as inclined to do so,
with the shutters closed, and other marks of respect. Arrangements made in Essex prevented the proposal being accepted ; but
it was none the less gratifying, as a token of the estimation, in
which, though so lately come amongst them, the departed had
been held. The different members of her family successively
quitted Ramsgate, till none remained but her eldest son and one of
his brothers-in-law, who stayed to share with him the sad office of
following the hearse to Upton. They travelled through the night.

Monday at noon was fixed for her funeral. In the grey of the early morning, the loved, the revered, was brought for the last time, for a few short hours to her home of many years. Vast numbers of persons attended the funeral. The procession passed between the grounds of Plashet House, her once happy home, and those of Plashet Cottage. In the Friends' Burying-ground at Barking, her grave was prepared, close by that of her little child, whom she had loved and lost, and tenderly mourned so many years before. There is no appointed funeral service amongst Friends. A deep silence prevailed throughout the multitudes gathered there. Her brother Joseph John Gurney was the first to address the assembly, and by him solemn prayer was offered. A Meeting was held afterwards ; but her immediate family were thankful to withdraw, and seek the shelter and recollections of Upton Lane.

CONCLUSION.—There may be some, who expect a sketch to be here given of the character of Elizabeth Fry—but a little reflection will show, that in the present case to attempt doing so would be presumptuous. Neither is it necessary. Her actions and conduct in life have been narrated. Her letters to her family and friends, pourtray her domestic feelings and her powers of loving. Her communications to others, supply the knowledge of her opinions upon the subjects, to which she gave her attention. In her journal may be found the outpourings of her heart, the communings between God and her own soul.

But there is a voice from the Dead—and the living are called to proclaim, before their work is concluded, and the memory of the departed committed to the stream of time—something, of her earnest desires for the well-being of her fellow-creatures, especially for that of her own sex. She was willing to spend and be spent, in her Master's service. She considered herself, called to a peculiar course. She was very young when she first saw a prison ; she had an extraordinary desire to visit one, and at last her father yielded to her wishes, and took her to see a bridewell—when and where is not exactly known ; but not long before her death, she narrated the circumstances to a friend, and how powerful an impression it had made upon her mind. It must be a question whether this visit was occasioned by, or led to the peculiar bent of her after career ; that it tended to strengthen it is indubitable, and that it was one link in the chain of Providential circumstances, which produced in the end, such signal results. But she would have shrunk, from urging the same course upon others. She feared her daughters, and young women generally, undertaking questionable or difficult or public offices ; but she believed, that where one erred from over activity in duty, many more omitted that, which it behoved them to perform. " Woman's Mission" has become almost a word of the day. Elizabeth Fry was persuaded that every woman has her individual vocation, and in following

it, that she would fulfil her mission. She laid great stress on
the outward circumstances of life ; how and where providentially
placed—the opportunities afforded—the powers given. She considered domestic duties the first and greatest earthly claims in
the life of woman ; although in accordance with the tenets of
the Society to which she belonged, she believed in some instances,
her own amongst others, that under the immediate direction of
the Spirit of God, individuals were called to leave for a time their
home and families, and devote themselves to the work of the
ministry. She did not consider this call to be general, or to
apply to persons under an administration different to her own.
But it was her conviction, that there is a sphere of usefulness
open to all. She appreciated to the full the usual charities of
gentlewomen ; their visits to the sick and aged poor, and their
attention to the cottage children, but she grieved to think how
few complete the work of mercy, by following the widow or dis-
abled, when driven by necessity to the workhouse ; or caring for
the workhouse school, that resort of the orphaned and forsaken,
less attractive, perhaps, than the school of the village, but even
more requiring oversight and attention.

A fearful accident, or hereditary disease, consigns the mother
of a family or some frail child to the hospital. In how many
cases does she lie there from day to day, watching the rays of the
morning sun reflected on the wall opposite, tracing them as they
move onwards through the day, and disappear as it advances ;
and this perhaps for weeks and months, without hearing the voice
of kindness and sympathy from her own sex, save from the
matron, or the hired nurses of the establishment. What might
not, and when bestowed, what does not, woman's tenderness effect
here ?

She heard of thousands and ten thousands of homeless
and abandoned children, wandering or perishing in our streets.
She knew that attempts were made to rescue them, and that

unflinching men and women laboured and toiled, to infuse some portion of moral health into that mass of living corruption ; but she mourned that so few assisted in this work of mercy, compared to the many who utterly neglect the call. She saw a vast number of her own sex, degraded and guilty, many a fair young creature, once the light of her parents' dwelling, fallen and polluted,—many who had filled useful situations in business or domestic service, sunk and debased. The downward road open wide before them, but no hand stretched forth to lift them—the first step up the rugged path of repentance, or assist in their hard struggle against sin. She encountered in the prisons every grade and variety of crime. Woman bold and daring and reckless—revelling in her iniquity, and hardened in vice—her only remaining joy to seduce others, and make them still the more the children of Hell than herself.——The thoughtless culprit, not lost to good and holy feeling, nor dead to impression from with‑ out.—And lastly, the beginner—she who from her deep poverty had been driven to theft, or drawn by others into temptation. Elizabeth Fry marked all these, and despaired of none amongst them. Here again, in her estimation, a crying need existed for influence, for instruction, reproof, and encouragement. But it was not to all, she would have allotted *this* task, though she could never be persuaded, but, that in every instance, women well qualified for the office might be found, to care for these outcasts of the people.

These were the things that she saw, and bitterly deplored. She believed that a mighty power rested with her own sex to check and to control this torrent of evil ; a moral force, that the educated and the virtuous might bring to bear upon the ignorant and vicious. She desired, to have every home duty accomplished, every household affection met ; but reason and Scripture taught her, that each individual has something to bestow, either of time or talent, or wealth, which spent in the

service of others, would return in blessing on herself and her own
family.   In the little parlour behind the shop, in the suburban
villa, in the perfumed boudoir and the gilded hall, she saw powers
unoccupied, and time unemployed.   She lived to illustrate all that
she enforced.   She wore away her life, in striving for the good
of her fellow-sinners.   Does she now regret these labours? or
find any service to have been "in vain in the Lord?"   When our
great Redeemer declared, that in feeding the hungry, and giving
the thirsty drink, receiving the stranger, clothing the naked,
and visiting the sick, it was done unto Him; He added, " I
was in *prison* and ye came unto me."   She was one who felt the
force of this commendation, and she took it in its largest sense;
not as applicable to those alone, who " suffer for conscience sake,"
but to the guilty and the wretched—in the spirit of Him, who
came to seek and to save that which is lost.   Through weariness
and painfulness, she laboured to fulfil it.   And now, that her
conflicts upon earth are ended, and her work done, may it not be
confidently believed, that for her, and such as her, are those
words of marvellous joy—" Come ye blessed of my Father, inherit the kingdom prepared for you, from the foundation of the
world."

RICHARD BARRETT, PRINTER, MARK LANE, LONDON.

CHARLES GILPIN'S
LIST OF NEW WORKS.

Preparing for Publication, in Demy 8vo.

By HENRIETTA J. FRY, author of the Hymns of the Reformation, &c.

Illustrated with Eight Engravings.

" PORTRAITS in MINIATURE," or Sketches of Character in verse. This little volume holds many a name dear to the best interests of Society, like those of Elizabeth Fry, J. J. Gurney, W. Wilberforce, Hannah More, Bishop Heber, &c.; and it is thought that such a transcript of those who have as it were trodden the paths of life by our side, may serve to quicken amongst us, the fragrance of their Christian graces, and like living Epistles written on our hearts speak to our spirits the language " Come up hither."

1.

A POPULAR LIFE of GEORGE FOX, the FIRST of the QUAKERS ; compiled from his journal and other authentic sources, and interspersed with remarks on the imperfect reformation of the Anglican Church, and the consequent spread of Dissent. By JOSIAH MARSH.

The work abounds with remarkable incidents, which pourtray a vivid picture of the excited feelings that predominated during those eventful periods of our history—the Commonwealth and the Restoration. 8vo. cloth. Price 6s. 6d.

2.

LIFE of WILLIAM ALLEN, with Selections from his Correspondence. 3 vols., 8vo., cloth. Price 24s.
" The loveliest and holiest of Friends."—*Dr. Campbell.*

3.

A MEMOIR of MARIA FOX, late of Tottenham ; consisting chiefly of Extracts from her Diary and Letters. 8vo., cloth. Price 8s.

** Friends are desired to secure copies of this work, as it is nearly out of print.

4.

THE WHOLE WORKS of JOSEPH JOHN GURNEY, in 7 vols., 8vo., cloth, price £2. 12s. 6d. ; or 7 vols. bound in 6, calf, blind tooled marbled edges, £3. 17s.

5.

WAGSTAFF'S HISTORY of the SOCIETY of FRIENDS ; compiled from its standard records, and other authentic sources. 8vo., cloth, price 12s.

6.

MEMORIALS of DECEASED MEMBERS of the SOCIETY of FRIENDS. Compiled from various authentic sources. By SUSANNAH CORDER. Price 7s.

7.

A MEMOIR of JAMES PARNELL, with Ex-

tracts from his Writings, by HENRY CALLAWAY. 18mo., cloth. Price
1s. 6d.

8.

A SELECTION from the WRITINGS of JOHN

SYDNEY TAYLOR, A.M., Barrister-at-Law. 8vo., cloth. Price 12s.
" On this rock we stand—on the adamantine basis of Christian principle we would build the whole fabric of legislation which regards the
public morals."—(p. 213).
" The volume before us is a noble testimony to the worth of the
deceased writer.—*Yorkshireman.*

9.

MEMOIR of the LIFE of RICHARD PHILLIPS.

" He being dead yet speaketh."
8vo., cloth. Price 7s. 6d.

10.

JOURNAL of the LIFE, TRAVELS, and RELI-

GIOUS LABOURS of WILLIAM SAVERY. Price 3s. 6d.

11.

JOURNAL of the LIFE and TRAVELS of

JOB SCOTT. Price 3s. 6d.

12.

SOME ACCOUNT of the LIVES and RELI-

GIOUS LABOURS of SAMUEL NEALE and MARY NEALE (formerly Mary Peisley). Both of Ireland. Foolscap 8vo., cloth. Price
4s. 6d.

13.

LIFE and TRAVELS of JOHN PEMBERTON.

A Minister of the Gospel of Jesus Christ. 12mo., cloth, lettered.
Price 3s. 6d.

14.

A MEMOIR of MARY ANN GILPIN, of Bristol;

consisting chiefly of Extracts from her Diary and Letters.
" Yea, doubtless, and I count all things but loss, for the excellency of
the knowledge of Christ Jesus my Lord."—Phil. iii. 8.
" For me to live is Christ, and to die is gain."—Phil. i. 21.
Third Edition. 12mo., cloth lettered. Price 2s. 6d.

15.

THE LIFE, TRAVELS, and CHRISTIAN EX-

PERIENCE of SAMUEL BOWNAS. New Edition. Price 3s. 6d.

16.

AN ENCYCLOPÆDIA OF FACTS, ANEC-

DOTES, ARGUMENTS, and ILLUSTRATIONS, from History, Philosophy, and Christianity, in support of the principles of Permanent
and Universal Peace. Ay EDWIN PAXTON HOOD, Author of " Fragments
of Thought and Composition," &c., &c., &c. 18mo , sewed. Price 1s. 6d.

17.

A MEMOIR of ISAAC RICHARDSON, of
NEWCASTLE-UPON-TYNE; who departed this Life at Ventnor, Isle of Wight, Fifth Month 3rd, 1840.

" Be ye followers of them, who through faith and patience inherit the promises."—Heb. v. 12.

Second Edition, 12mo. cloth. Price 10d.

18.

DYMOND'S ESSAYS, on the PRINCIPLES of
MORALITY, and on the PRIVATE and POLITICAL RIGHTS and OBLIGATIONS of MANKIND. Royal 8vo., paper cover, 3s. 6d. Neat embossed cloth, 4s. 6d.

The high standard of morality to which these Essays aim at directing the attention of mankind, justly entitle them to the extensive circulation which they have obtained in three previous editions; and the present cheap and popular form in which they now appear, having reached a sale of nearly Seven Thousand in twelve months, is an unequivocal proof of public approbation.

19.

THE PEASANTRY of ENGLAND; an Appeal
on behalf of the Working Classes, in which the causes which have led to their present impoverished and degraded condition, and the means by which it may best be permanently improved are clearly pointed out. By G. M. PERRY. 12mo., cloth, 4s.

20.

THE HISTORY and ANATOMY of the NAVI-
GATION LAWS. By JOHN LEWIS RICARDO, Esq., M.P. 8vo., cloth. Price 7s. 6d.

" A most masterly work,—a perfect text-book of information and argument."—*Chronicle.*

21.

THE PEACE READING BOOK; being a series
of Selections from the Sacred Scriptures, the Early Christian Fathers, and Historians, Philosophers, and Poets,—the wise and thoughtful of all ages; condemnatory of the principles and practice of war, inculcating those of true Christianity. Edited by H. G. ADAMS. 12mo., cloth, Price 2s.

22.

HYMNS of the REFORMATION. By LUTHER
and Others, from the German; to which is added his Life from the original Latin of Melancthon, by the Author of the " Pastor's Legacy." 18mo., neatly bound in silk. 3s. 6d.

23.

THE PASTOR'S LEGACY, or DEVOTIONAL
FRAGMENTS. From the German of Lavater. By HENRIETTA J. FRY. 18mo., neatly bound in silk, 2s. 6d.

" This is an exquisite little gem."—*Christian Examiner.*

*** An edition may be obtained with the German appended to the work, done up in the same manner, for 3s.

THE WELLS of SCRIPTURE. illustrated in

EVA-

:arn how
id them,
)ssessor ;
that the
Notting-

ian, and
tion."—

RITT,

(The LEARNED BLACKSMITH).

This is the *only complete edition of the above work.* It is published under the immediate supervision of the talented Author, and is the only Edition in the sale of which he has any pecuniary interest.

"These are Sparks indeed of singular brillancy."—*British Friend.*

"They deserve to be stereotyped, and to form part of the standard literature of the age."—*Kentish Independent.*

12mo., sewed. Price 1s.

Lightning Source UK Ltd.
Milton Keynes UK
UKHW021245070119
335137UK00013B/488/P